*To Magda Stefanelli and Fabrizio Mai,
extravagant priests of the equestrian cult,
my first masters*

*A Magda Stefanelli e Fabrizio Mai,
stravaganti sacerdoti del culto equestre,
miei primi maestri*

Italian edition: *Le opere della cavalleria: La tradizione italiana dell'arte equestre durante il Rinascimento e nei secoli successivi*

Copyright © 2013 Cavour Libri

This edition: *The Italian Tradition of Equestrian Art: A survey of the treatises on horsemanship from the renaissance and the centuries following*

ISBN: 9780933316386
Copyright © 2014 by Xenophon Press LLC

Translated by the author

Edited by Richard F. Williams, Frances Williams M.D.

All rights reserved. No part of this work may be reproduced or transmitted in any form or by any means, electronic or mechanical, including photocopying, or by any information storage or retrieval system except by a written permission from the publisher.

Published by Xenophon Press LLC

7518 Bayside Road, Franktown, Virginia 23354-2106, U.S.A.

e-book ISBN   9780933316430
PRINT BOOK
ISBN-10   0933316380
ISBN-13   9780933316386

Cover design by Naia Poyer
Cover Image: Gozzoli, Benozzo (1420-1497): Procession of the Magi: Wall with Lorenzo
Firenze, Palazzo medici-Ricciardi. © 2013 – Foto Scala Archive, Firenze.
Licensed by Ministero Beni e Attività Culturali

THE ITALIAN TRADITION
OF
EQUESTRIAN ART

*A SURVEY OF THE TREATISES
ON HORSEMANSHIP FROM
THE RENAISSANCE AND THE
CENTURIES FOLLOWING*

by GIOVANNI BATTISTA TOMASSINI

With Forewords
by Arthur Kottas-Heldenberg
and
João Pedro Rodrigues

Translated by the Author
Edited by Richard F. Williams

© Xenophon Press 2014

Xenophon Press Library

Xenophon Press continues to bring new works to print in the English language whether they be new works, such as this, or translations of older works. Xenophon Press is dedicated to the preservation of classical equestrian literature. Here is a sampling of the current offering from Xenophon Press available at www.XenophonPress.com

30 Years with Master Nuno Oliveira, Michel Henriquet 2011
A Rider's Survival from Tyranny, Charles de Kunffy 2012
Another Horsemanship, Jean-Claude Racinet, 1994
Art of the Lusitano, Yglesias de Oliveira, 2012
Baucher and His School, General Decarpentry 2011
Dressage in the French Tradition, Dom Diogo de Bragança 2011
École de Cavalerie Part II (School of Horsemanship), François Robichon de la Guérinière 1992
Equine Osteopathy: What the Horses Have Told Me, Dominique Giniaux 2014
François Baucher: The Man and His Method, Baucher and Nelson, 2013
Gymnastic Exercises for Horses Volume II, Eleanor Russell 2013
Healing Hands, Dominique Giniaux, DVM 1998
H.Dv.12. German Cavalry Training Manual, Stefanie Reinhold, 2014
Horse Training: Outdoor and High School, Étienne Beudant 2015
Legacy of Master Nuno Oliveira, Stephanie Millham 2013
Methodical Dressage of the Riding Horse, and *Dressage of the Outdoor Horse*, Faverot de Kerbrech 2010
Racinet Explains Baucher, Jean-Claude Racinet 1997
System of the Art of Riding, Louis Seeger 2015
The Art and Science of Riding in Lightness, Robert Stodulka DVM, 2014
The Art of Traditional Dressage, Volume I : The Seat and Aids, DVD, de Kunffy 2013
The Écuyères of the Nineteenth Century in the Circus, Hilda Nelson 2001
The Ethics and Passions of Dressage Expanded Edition, de Kunffy 203
The Gymnasium of the Horse, Gustav Steinbrecht 2011
The Handbook of Jumping Essentials, François Lemaire de Ruffieu 1997
The Maneige Royal, Antoine de Pluvinel 2010
The Portuguese School of Equestrian Art, de Oliveira and da Costa, 2012
The Spanish Riding School in Vienna and Piaffe and Passage, Decarpentry 2013
Total Horsemanship, Jean-Claude Racinet 1999
What the Horses have Told me, Equine Osteopathy, Dominique Giniaux, DVM 1996, 2014
Wisdom of Master Nuno Oliveira, Antoine de Coux 2012

Available at **www.XenophonPress.com**

contact: XenophonPress@gmail.com

Table of Contents

Introduction to the English Edition	7
About this Book	8
About the Author	8
Foreword by Arthur Kottas-Heldenberg	9
Foreword by João Pedro Rodrigues	13
Acknowledgments	15
Introduction	17
I The Birth of Educated Equitation	21
The equestrian art in pre-Renaissance age	23
The Aragonese influence	26
Evolution of combat techniques	29
From tournaments to new equestrian performances	30
The horse and politics	31
The horses of the Gonzaga	35
Horse riding and the birth of the modern courtier	38
The most beautiful and valiant knight of the century Galeazzo Sanseverino	43
The transmission of the equestrian knowledge	47
II The first treatises dedicated to the horse	49
Giordano Ruffo of Calabria	50
The *De equo animante* by Leon Battista Alberti	54
Antonello Scilla: the Horse discipline	56
The equestrian treatise by Dom Duarte, King of Portugal	58
III Naples, capital of Renaissance's equitation	61
Equitation in Naples	62
The horse in Naples at the time of Viceroy	67
The Neapolitan coursers	70
The horses of Pandone Palace in Venafro	74
Decadence of the Neapolitan breed	76
IV *The Rules of Riding* by Federigo Grisone	79
His life	80
The Rules of Riding	84
The origins of High School riding	86
The nature of the horse according to Grisone	90
The training of the horse	92
The technique of the rider	95
Grisone's bad reputation	98
V Cesare Fiaschi: The harmony of riding well	103
Equestrian traditions in Ferrara	103
Cesare Fiaschi and his treatise	105
Equitation and music	109

The canon of the new school equitation	114
The art of bridling	116
A higher ideal	118
The school airs and jumps	123
Shoeing	125

VI Claudio Corte: The Horseman as a social figure — **137**

Claudio Corte	137
A horseman and an intellectual	141
The comparison with the tradition	142
The colors of the coats and the theory of humors	145
Technical innovations	148
The horses for the palio (racehorses)	153
The horseman, brother of the Courtier	155

VII The other Renaissance treatises — **161**

Giovan Battista and Pirro Antonio Ferraro	161
Pasquale Caracciolo	174
Marco de Pavari	180
Ottaviano Siliceo	184
Alessandro Massari Malatesta	185

VIII Giovan Battista Pignatelli and the riding academies — **191**

An uncertain biography	193
Pignatelli's legacy	201
"*L'arte veterale*"	204
The mystery of the Academy of Naples	207
The knightly academies in Italy	210
Academy or riding school?	213

IX Cantering through four centuries of history — **215**

The Delia academy in Padua	218
D'Aquino, Santapaulina and the seventeenth-century treatises	221
Survey of eighteenth century Europe	229
The Italian Treatises of the eighteenth century	233
Between two epochs: Federico Mazzucchelli	241
A century of challenges	245
The long Italian transition	250
Caprilli and the "natural system"	253

Conclusion	**259**
APPENDICES	**263**
Web resources about equestrian treatises	263
Bibliography on the treatises on horsemanship	**265**
Italian treatises on horsemanship	265
Treatises on horsemanship by foreign authors	269
Bibliography	**273**
Table of Illustrations	**284**

Introduction to the English Edition

Classical horsemanship has captured the imagination and passion of riders for centuries, even millennia. Where did it all begin? Many will argue the origins and will cite an earlier, and still earlier foundation, but true horsemen share the love of the horse and a keen interest in pursuing how best to bond with their equine partners. Classical riding lives on in the daily activities of its current-day practitioners. Today's dressage is not Italian, French, German, American or any other nation's legacy. History teaches us that knowledge and wisdom moves from teacher to student through the centuries.

Giovanni Battista Tomassini shows the significant epochs, beginning in the Italian Renaissance, when a confluence of cultural traditions and patrimony elevated the art of riding allowing equestrian knowledge to develop for centuries until it was dispersed widely over Europe.

What does this mean to today's rider? Intelligent horsemen throughout history have always sought out equestrian expertise irrespective of national or language boundaries. Riding masters with talent, insight, drive and opportunity have embellished the art through careful discovery using the scientific method. Many practice and few revolutionize—incrementally adding to the science of horsemanship. Although there may be few, this does not mean that we are without the possibility of finessing this art.

Mr. Tomassini has taken great care to help us put our modern riding into its rightful historical context. The roots of classical horsemanship in Renaissance Italy had been previously muddied and filled with half-truths retold, repeated and distorted—with much forgotten.

Tomassini assumes nothing, researches every fact, each source, and cites these in a readable, yet scholarly style. I found myself reading the manuscript compulsively while drawn into its lively tales as if they'd happened just yesterday. His work brings alive the musty old texts that had been largely inaccessible to most riders even though they hold great wisdom and secrets from the past.

This English edition is made possible through a collaborative editing process between the author and generous, skillful and tireless proof reading of Stephanie Millham. We are exceptionally grateful for this team effort. The mission of Xenophon Press is to reveal the lessons of past experts by bringing their works to light in the English language. We simultaneously celebrate and give voice to current experts who help us understand the art better; whether they be trainers, riders, or historians. We hope you enjoy this fantastic journey through Italy, the Renaissance and beyond as it sheds light on your riding today.

Richard F. Williams
Publisher/Xenophon Press

About this book

At the mid point of the sixteenth century, a Neapolitan gentleman, Federico Grisone, published, for the first time, a printed book about the art of training the horse "for the use of war" and on the secrets to "emend his defects." The work was a huge and immediate success and was soon emulated by other authors. The new literary genre of equestrian treatises was thus born and its tradition, with ups and downs, became alive and remains vital up to this day. It is no coincidence that this first work was printed in Italy because, between the fifteenth and sixteenth century, it was in that country that a new culture of the court, in which horse riding had a key role, was developed. During this time, Italian riding masters were sought out by the members of European courts. The scions of the European aristocracy ventured to Italy to perfect their skill in the art of riding with renowned masters.

Following the thread of equestrian treatises, this book traces the history of Italian and European equitation, recounting the rich cultural implications, the evolution of the techniques, and the many connections with the great events of European history. It is a story full of characters surrounded by an aura of legendary skill, of disputes between opposing schools, and of memorable deeds. It is a story that goes from the sixteenth century up to the early twentieth century, when again an Italian, Federico Caprilli, revolutionized the riding world, creating the jumping technique still in use today.

About the Author

Giovanni Battista Tomassini works as a journalist in the field of politics for RAI, the Italian public television. Since the beginning of his career, he put research in the field of literature and history alongside his work as a journalist. In addition to articles and essays in several journals, he has published books: *Il racconto nel racconto* (Rome, 1991), *I treni delle meraviglie* (Verona, 2001 and Rome, 2002) and edited the translation and the Italian edition of *The Voyage dans les steppes d'Astrakhan et du Caucase* by Jan Potocki (Milan 1996 and 1998). He is also author of the blog www.worksofchivalry.com dedicated to the equestrian culture and in particular to the tradition of the Italian Renaissance treatises.

Foreword

When Giovanni Battista Tomassini told me of his project of bringing the achievements of the Italian Masters to a new audience, I was immediately interested and so, I am delighted to contribute this foreword.

In my forty years with the Spanish Riding School of Vienna, starting as an eleve and progressing to become First Chief Rider, the value of tradition in our training of horses was very clear. This is not to say that convention is followed for its own sake, but because over the centuries, good practice has been passed down from Riding Master to pupil by word of mouth and equally important, through the written word. If we do not have a proven system by which to train our horses, it becomes a matter of chance whether our method works and since we are dealing with a highly sensitive creature, we should not play roulette with his well-being, nor with our own safety when dealing with him.

As to the author's credentials, the modest Giovanni Battista Tomassini has over thirty years riding experience, in addition to being the author of a number of published works. He brings passion to this subject and more crucially, a journalistic rigor to his research. He has returned to the original words of his subjects wherever possible rather than relying on secondary sources and therefore has avoided repeating the half-truths and misinterpretations of others. For modern equestrians, it is so important to have an understanding of where and how the Classical art of riding developed. To date, this information has not been easy to find, but here is a volume that is readable, yet scholarly and accessible, amply referenced and illustrated.

Of course, there have been many books written about training horses by people who have contributed to our fund of knowledge. There have also been many historical works which have touched upon our subject. Rarely have the two been so expertly blended together as they are in this book. The author does not treat the development of dressage in isolation, but skilfully places it within its' social, political, economic and military context.

In the past, some experts have said that modern dressage was "invented" during the Renaissance, but this book demonstrates that it was a case of evolution, not revolution. The author shows that there was already a tradition of cultured riding that was nurtured under the patronage of the rulers of the Italian States for a variety of reasons.

Riding in tournaments had long been a pastime for Princes keen to show off their skill at arms and increase their prestige, but a number of serious accidents, notably the death of Henry II of France following a jousting accident, gradually saw a move towards less dangerous equestrian activities and promoted interest in more sophisticated riding.

Noblemen had long been the main sector of society who had the wealth to keep horses and the time to learn how to ride well and this book charts the gradual transition from the medieval warrior-knight to modern horseman-courtier. During the renaissance, the nobility from many countries sent their sons to Italy to be educated. Riding gracefully became one of the expected accomplishments of a young aristocrat, along with fencing, music, an understanding of mathematics and courtly behavior. As Mr. Tomassini writes, "equestrian art was a discipline in close contact with the political arena, but also crucial in defining the identity of the European aristocracy." A nobleman who was inevitably expected to exercise authority in life, also had to be able to direct his horse with ease. This was considered the mark of a cultured individual who would also be comfortable commanding troops or those people living on his estates.

In the political and military arena, the competing kingdoms and city states of Italy became the battleground for the warring Hapsburg and Valois dynasties. Between 1494 and 1559, a series of wars saw troops from all over Europe travel to and fro, as they campaigned in Italy. Some of the commanders were more learned than those in the past and took an interest in the new riding methods, especially as good riding was considered to be essential for the military man, hence extending the influence of the Italian Masters abroad. We should also acknowledge the impact of the printing press, still relatively new at the end of the fifteenth century. The availability of printed books greatly contributed to spreading the ideas that were surfacing in Italy at the time and which brought the words of the riding masters to a much wider audience.

In diplomacy, the shifting alliances and political maneuverings of the period ensured that the well-bred horse was a prized status symbol and a useful diplomatic tool as a gift to placate a rival or to foster influence in the power politics of the day.

As a result of these favorable circumstances coming together, the sophisticated ideas and methods of the Italian renaissance Masters flourished and their teachings were spread widely due to the travels to and from Italy by the two social classes most interested in horses; namely the military and young noblemen.

Of the main characters, Federico Grisone is often regarded as the founding father of modern equitation as he recognized the importance of trot work for developing the physique of the horse and because in 1550, he published what may be considered the first dressage book, which was rapidly translated into French, German, Spanish and English. Although his reputation has suffered subsequently due to his condoning harsh punishments for a disobedient horse, his influence cannot be overlooked.

In 1556, Cesare Faschi became the second Italian master to publish his own book. He spoke of the importance of rhythm and of a steady tempo, two of the fundamental requirements in training. Besides equating music with equestrian art, he also advocated treating the horse kindly and for the rider to always proceed on the basis of reason, not whim or superstition. Another famous master of the time, Pignatelli, is credited with seeing the value of using circles in gymnastic work and their value in making a horse supple and straight. Pluvinel studied under him and later went on to establish an academy in France. In turn, his teachings influenced de la Guérinière.

These three Italian Masters and others are all discussed in depth, detailing their work and the influence they exerted on the development of our modern day dressage sport. Subsequently, this book continues through the years to the twentieth century.

Having just completed my second book, *Dressage Solutions* with collaborator, Andrew Fitzpatrick, I feel well-placed to attest to the value of knowing where our sport has come from and why. We do not exist in a vacuum but hold the legacy of the Masters of the past in our hands. We should learn from them and keep the best of their knowledge alive through our own daily training; and with apologies to the poet, Goethe: He who cannot draw on the past, is living from hand to mouth.

Arthur Kottas-Heldenberg
First Chief Rider of the Spanish Riding School (Retired)
January 2014. Vienna
Author of
Kottas On Dressage, 2010
Dressage Solutions: A Rider's Guide, 2013

Foreword

I recall an episode which I witnessed thirty years ago, between Pedro Yglesias de Oliveira, a rider of the Portuguese School of Equestrian Art and Dr. Guilherme Borba, then, Director and Chief Rider of the School, my teacher and a person of profound equestrian culture. When Pedro announced his intention to write a book about horseback riding, a very surprised Guilherme Borba replied ironically: "Dear Pedro, please forget it because everything has already been written." In reading this book, The Italian Tradition of Equestrian Art, I am glad that my friend, Giovanni Battista Tomassini did not follow the same advice. Even though his book is not about "how to ride" but instead about the history of equestrian art, it is an excellent research work on the many Italian equestrian treatises of the Renaissance and of the centuries that followed.

I met Mr. Tomassini for the first time during a clinic I gave in Rome in the spring of 2013, which he attended as a student. During lunch, we talked of equitation in Portugal and Italy. I soon recognized his enthusiasm and competence on this topic. This book should be considered an important point of reference for those who love this Art. The author proposes a very accurate synthesis and provides the reader with a clear and well-structured overview of the equestrian school which has influenced the Academic Art of riding most during the Renaissance and in subsequent periods.

For centuries, Portugal kept equestrian traditions alive which are now rare in the world. These include: combat riding (bullfighting), equitation for the work in the fields and hunting and Old School equitation, which combines the *a la gineta* and *a la brida* styles, coloring them with influences of the French school. It is precisely this type of equitation that we practice in our School including the work in hand, the use of the pillars to collect horse and all types of school jumps, as they were practiced in our ancient "Picaria Real"—the Equestrian Academy of the Portuguese Court. This Academy had its period of greatest splendor during the eighteenth and nineteenth centuries, and was restored in 1979 with the name: The Portuguese School of Equestrian Art. From the outset and still today, the Lusitano horses from the Alter Stud, founded in 1748 by King D. João V are used exclusively.

Here, I will only briefly mention the Portuguese treatises which are linked to the contents of this book. Hoping to stimulate the reader's curiosity to further exploration!

In our country, there are strong equestrian roots of the so-called *a la gineta* equitation, which was brought to us by the Berber tribes of North Africa, following the Muslim conquest of the Iberian Peninsula, and has been practiced for centuries. *A la gineta* was a combat equitation, characterized by high mobility, in which were used horses with exceptional spirit, flexibility and the gift for collection (*rassembler*). This type of riding still finds expression in the art of bullfighting on horseback and is the same kind of riding that was brought to Naples by the Spaniards at the beginning of the sixteenth century.

In Dom Duarte's work, *Livro da Ensinança de Bem Cavalgar Toda a Sela* (1434) [*The Royal Book of Horsemanship, Jousting & Knightly Combat*, Chivalry Bookshelf, 2006] which can be considered as the first equestrian treatise of the classic era, we already find a reference to Sicilian horses, fine and hot-blooded, which were very much appreciated in the Middle Ages. It is in the seventeenth century treatises by Pedro Galego (1629), Pinto Pacheco (1670) and António Galvão de Andrade (1678) that there is a transition from the riding style of *a la gineta* to that of *a la brida*. In these works, in addition to the topics of war, bullfighting and equestrian games, are discussed the airs above the ground, a series of exercises typical of the *a la brida* style . De Andrade demonstrates a tendency towards a merger of the two types of riding. The first was more instinctive and less stylized, the second, already with a great Italian and French influence, and with a certain artistic dimension, as evidenced by the many allusions to Federico Grisone in the book by Galvão de Andrade.

However, it is in the eighteenth century, with Manoel Carlos de Andrade's equestrian treatise, *Luz da Liberal e Nobre Arte de Cavallaria* (1790), our equestrian "Bible", that a greater prominence is given to the Neapolitan horse. The author recommends cross-breeding Neapolitan stallions with Portuguese mares, to produce horses suitable for dressage and for the army. The same author describes a series of exercises in preparation of the low airs and of the airs above the ground clearly inspired by the first treatises of his era, written by the Italian masters and then by Pluvinel, La Broue, Newcastle and La Guérinière. All this matter is very well analyzed in Carlos Henriques Pereira's book *Naissance et Renaissance de l'Equitation Portugaise*, cited by Mr. Tomassini in this book.

As a rider of one of the only four remaining Academies of Equestrian Art in the world and as a breeder of Lusitano horses, I want to thank Giovanni Battista Tomassini for giving me the privilege of writing this foreword. I consider this work to be of utmost importance to the contribution of understanding the Equestrian Art as a dynamic socio-cultural phenomenon vital to the civilization of mankind.

João Pedro Rodrigues
Mestre Picador Chefe
Portuguese School of Equestrian Art
Palácio Nacional de Queluz, Lisbon, January 28, 2014

Acknowledgments

First of all my gratitude goes to Cecilia Buonocore and Francesco Ferroni who gave a decisive impetus, with their sympathy and passion, to the carrying out of a project too long meditated.

I wouldn't have written this book without the active cooperation of the Library of the Italian Senate, in particular without the expertise, sensitivity and courtesy of Renata Giannella (Parliamentary Councillor of the Senate), and the accurate and friendly operational support provided to my researches by Daniela Middioni (Parliamentary Secretary of the Senate).

I then owe a sincere thank you to Giuliana Forti, of the National Gallery of Ancient Art of Palazzo Barberini in Rome, for her interest in my work and for her decisive help in the iconographic researches.

This work was also a nice pretext to meet again an old friend and find out that his generosity and curiosity have not changed over the years. I thank Giorgio Patrizi—Italianist and literary critic of rare competence, Professor of Italian Literature at the University of Molise—for his precious advice and for the availability and the interest with which he has followed this research.

My thoughts also go to my teacher Riccardo Scrivano, former professor of Italian Literature at the Universities of Padua, Rome and Rome Tor Vergata, who many years ago was the first to tell me about the equestrian similes used by Castiglione in The Book of the Courtier, *providing me a first track to be followed in this work.*

With their generosity and friendship Sue and Barry Chiverton gave an important contribution to the making of this book and to its publication in the United States. Just as precious was the encouragement and friendship of Patrizia Carrano. His sensitivity as a writer and his love for horses provided moments of unparalleled inspiration.

I am grateful to my friend and Italian editor, Alberto Collacchi, for his interest and support. But, above all, I want to express my sincere appreciation for the intellectual curiosity and professionalism of my American publisher, Richard F. Williams, of Xenophon Press, who was the first to really believe in this project with his desire to make the publication of this book a reality.

To Ilaria and Federico, who accompanied, supported and encouraged me in this work, my dedication and joy for the light with which they fill my life.

G.B. Tomassini

Introduction

At the exact half point of the sixteenth century, a Neapolitan gentleman delivered to one of the most famous printers of his city a book destined to become an immediate and uncommon success. In the following decades, Federico Grisone's *Gli ordini di cavalcare* was in fact reprinted several times and translated into the major European languages, reaching a great many of the courts of continental Europe. During the two centuries following its publication, almost every noble's library contained a copy of this book. It was the first printed treatise about the training of the warhorse. Even more significant was that based on its success and example, it was followed by a series of similar works. At first, these were written mainly by Italian authors; later, important books by foreigners followed. Although Grisone had not invented - as some still claim - the genre of the equestrian treatise, which had antecedents even in the classical era, his work, because of the extensive reach achieved through printing, took on the value of founding a new tradition of works dedicated to the horse and its riding that had a great impact on European culture. Even though the role of the horse in society is now radically changed, this tradition is still vital today.

Only very recently, shrewd scholars recognized in the widespread dissemination of equestrian treatises from the sixteenth century one of the signs of the deep cultural changes that occurred in Europe during the Renaissance. Despite being in a period of foreign domination and of great political and military weakness, Italy was the absolute protagonist for many cultural transformations including those in equestrian art. It was mainly in Italy that, between the fifteenth and sixteenth century, a new culture of the Court developed, completely redefining the identity and role of the ruling classes. Given the crucial importance that the horse had at that time, not only in the military field but also in social prestige of the aristocracy, equitation was an essential part of this new culture.

Thus far, the study of this tradition, especially with regard to the Italian context, has been neglected by professional historians and was confined primarily to enthusiasts and equestrian professionals. These works have a double interest: a) for their historical impact, and b) for their technical significance. The delay of the study of this issue has several causes, which have been well highlighted by the French historian, Daniel Roche.

"The first is of historiographical nature: there is an historical literature on the horse, that of equestrian professionals and that of historians, but they ignore each other. The first study history without knowing the tools, methodology and issues of social and cultural history, while the latter are not very interested in equestrian culture because they do not consider it part of the problems of the modern age, due to their ignorance of the current status of the horse and of their forgetfulness of its past importance[1]."

Historians rarely have the expertise to appreciate the technical value of the equestrian works hence, the failure to establish correct classifications. Furthermore, enthusiasts rarely have methodological tools to ensure the proper analysis and historical placement, and they are often influenced by the partisanship and clichés of their national traditions.

In this text, the research is based on rigorous methodical criteria and highlights the great technical, historical and cultural interest of this heritage in order to benefit the practice of equitation today. I will illuminate famous equestrian figures of the Italian Renaissance and their works with reliable biographical and histocial data. Grisone, Fiaschi, and Pignatelli may be well-known by some outsite the narrow circle of experts; however, their personal stories are mostly unknown even to specialists. Generally, only the names of these authors and sparse facts about their lives in the form of hints, in their books and in those of their followers, have been passed down to us. Not surprisingly, legends flourished and have formed enormous historical mistakes. Working from original documents, I have tried to exclude all data not supported by reliable sources, adding newly verified facts always citing the source. Similarly, the works have been analyzed starting from the texts and exposing the essential features of the equitation that was practiced at the time, comparing it with the current way of riding. Whenever possible, I tried to investigate the intersection of equestrian history with cultural and political history, providing the essential information on the many characters and events.

Thousands of years of coexistence of man and horse have established in this relationship a rich stratification of history, culture, feelings, ambitions, conflicts and dreams. Characterizing the peculiarity of this connection is the fact that the horse cannot be reduced to a mere instrument of the rider, as is the sword for the fencer or the violin for the musician. The horse is a living being, simultaneously docile and wild. He expresses strength, agility and elegance only if the one who mounts him can obtain his cooperation and bring out his generous nature. For this reason, during the centuries in which the horse accompanied humanity along the path of civilization, many have persevered how to improve their agreement with this impetuous and sensitive animal, shy, yet capable of incredible courage. In the past, this virtue was needed more than it is today specifically for the use of the horse in the military field. The difference between a good and a bad performance could have meant the difference between life and death.

Since the dawn of civilization, the need to succeed on the battlefield has prompted the development of training methods, which aimed to achieve

---

1) Roche, 2007, p. 460.

the obedience of the horse and improve his functionality to human needs. These methods tried to establish a communication with the animal, to obtain his submission, or more properly to gain his complicity, and to enhance his speed, endurance and dexterity: a difficult problem given the diversity of communication codes between the two partners. By the mid-sixteenth century the Italian horseman Claudio Corte isolated a key difficulty of training horses due to the impossibility of teaching them through spoken words. For this reason, the great French artist-rider, Bartabas said that to train a horse one must first establish a common language.

> "We faced an animal that doesn't speak and with whom we need to build a common vocabulary to begin to babble. Afterwards we need a shared grammar, and then together we must build sentences (i.e. the "school airs"), building a bond that passes - as we're sitting on the horse - through a physical relationship[2]."

The equestrian art can be considered the search and use of a code of communication between man and horse. The development of this non-verbal code has always highlighted, in addition to the need of theoretical systematization, the problem of transmission to others. From ancient times this process of elaboration and transmission led to the drafting of treatises, such as that of Simon of Athens (fifth century BC) and Xenophon (third century BC). However, until the Middle Ages, the writing of books on this subject was rather episodic; the direct communication between master and disciple prevailed as the primary method of passing the knowledge along.

The culture of the Italian Renaissance represented a true turning point in the tradition of equestrian knowledge, laying the foundations of theoretical reflection on equitation, whose implications would reverberate to current practice of this discipline. For this reason, the study of the authors of the "golden age" of Italian equitation will reveal an essential aspect of the ancient regime society, and will contribute to the revitalization of a tradition of expertise in the equestrian art that Italy seems to have recently lost, for a variety of reasons. This decline is even more serious considering that the Italian excellence in equitation continued, with ups and downs, since the Renaissance for centuries, intersecting with the great figures and the great events of European history and culture. After the splendor of the sixteenth century, the Italian equitation suffered competition from those of France and Germany, which were greatly encouraged by their respective monarchies for reasons of cultural prestige. Nevertheless, Italy did not cease to produce works of great interest. It then returned to absolute primacy in the early twentieth century, when Federico

---

2) Bartabas, 2010, pp.30–31. [When not otherwise specified, in the bibliography, translations are by the Author.]

Caprilli, an officer of the Military School of Pinerolo, developed his "natural system," revolutionized the way of riding a horse and invented a style of equitation still practiced the world over. After analyzing thoroughly the works of the Renaissance masters, I provide an overview of the Italian equestrian literature up to the time of Caprilli, contextualizing its development with respect to the evolution that the genre of the equestrian treatises and horse riding suffered in the major European countries, in the centuries from the seventeenth to the twentieth. The result is a picture further enriched by historical information which demonstrates the importance of the horse and equitation in our culture.

I
The Birth of Educated Equitation

In the sixteenth century, the Italian riders were famous for their skill and were sought out by the members of European courts. Similarly, the horses bred in the Italian peninsula enjoyed a high reputation and rivaled the celebrated Iberians for supremacy in the stables of princes and kings. The scions of the European aristocracy ventured to Italy - a journey which, at the time, was long, expensive, and often dangerous - to learn the equestrian art from the Italian masters, who ran schools which, in addition to generally teaching riding, vetrinary care, fencing and the use of weapons, also frequently taught mathematics, dance and music.

According to historians, this period coincided with a deep transformation of the equestrian practices, which resulted in the birth of a new equitation, initiated by the Italian masters. The prominence of the Italian school in the birth of modern equitation is well documented and recognized by both ancient and modern authors. Obvious evidence of the influence it exerted in Europe may be found in equestrian terminology, which is largely of Italian origin[3]. For example, the term *passage*—which is still in current use at the international level and designates an elevated and rhythmic trot, with an accentuated period of suspension - derives from the Italian "*passeggio*." This etymology is supported in what is perhaps the most famous and appreciated equestrian treatise of all time, *Ecole de Cavalerie* by François Robichon de La Guérinière [Xenophon Press, 1992], who writes:

> "The *Passage*, which was once called *Pasège*, from the Italian word, *Spasseggio*, means "walk" [meaning to take a walk][4]."

---

3) See Angioni, 2006. Despite the virtual unanimity of opinion on this subject, it's interesting to note that there are some interpretations that are veined of that kind of "equestrian chauvinism" that often affects the historians of equitation. In his memoirs, General L'Hotte (1825–1904), while recognizing the Italian origin of equestrian terms, says - but does not substantiate his claim with any evidence or document - that:
"in ancient times, when the Gallic cavalry shone around its splendor and eclipsed the other cavalry, in Rome, all the equestrian terms were Gaulish. It was different when, after the renaissance of letters, arts and sciences, the equestrian art in Italy assumed a new form. The Italian schools spread their light across Europe and, at that time, some words borrowed from Italian took, in turn, gained citizenship in our equitation and also in our fencing" (L'Hotte, 1905, p. 271).
4) LA GUÉRINIÈRE, 1733, p. 79 [for reference convenience, the equestrian treatises are collected in a separate bibliography including all the works referred to by author's last name in all uppercase].[*Ecole de Cavalerie Part II*, Xenophon Press, 1992]

A little further on, talking about the term "*volte*," instead he says:

> "The term, *volte* is an Italian expression, which means circle, round or circular track. It should be noted that what is meant in Italy by *volte* is the circle that a Horse describes going simply on a single track, and what we mean by *volte*, they call *Raddoppio* (doubling). But in France, *volte* means to go on two tracks, to one side, with the horse forming two concentric circles, or concentric squares with rounded corners[5]."

Similarly, although they are now established internationally in their French translation, the names of the so-called "school jumps" are of Italian origin and they're widely described by the Italian authors of Rennaissance treatises: *pesade*, *mézair*, *courbette*, *croupade*, *cabriole*, come down directly from "*posata*," "*mezz'aria*," "*corvetta*," "*groppata*" e "*capriola*"[6] respectively. The prevalence of Italian equestrian terms is even more evident in the first equestrian treatise by a French author: *Le Cavalerice François*[7] by Salomon de La Broue. Educated in Naples at the school of Giovanni Battista Pignatelli[8], in the second half of the sixteenth century, La Broue placed before the exposure of his precepts a real glossary of technical terms derived from Italian.

> "Recognizing" writes La Broue "the lack of appropriate terms for this art in our French language, I resorted to Italian, both because the Riders use it more commonly, both because the Italian words have a certain air much more vigorous, are more significant, and may explain the meaning with just one word, while it would take several [words] to understand it in French. However, since these and other words of the art are not known to all French riders, I wanted to relieve them of this pain with the following interpretation[9]."

---

5) LA GUÉRINIÈRE, 1733, p. 80. In several Italian Renaissance treatises, the term "*volte*" has a fairly mobile meaning. In fact it is also used with the meaning of circle on two tracks. In some cases, it seems possible to assimilate it to what we now call "pirouette" and especially "half-pirouette" (in the case of the "*volte*" at the end of the so-called "*repolone*," which will be considered below). It occurred also the term "doubled *volte*," meaning either a two-tracks *volte*, or pirouette.

6) See Barry, 2005, pp. 22–24.

7) LA BROUE, 1610. First published in 1593 in La Rochelle, the work was later revised and expanded by the author in the 1610 edition.

8) See Chapter VIII

9) LA BROUE, 1610, Livre I, p. 10.

Then the author enumerates forty-eight terms, explaining the meaning of each. Beginning with the term *Cavalerice*, "Horseman," that

> "actually means, of course, Knight [i.e. gentleman] and expert in the art of training combat and school horses: art that the Italians call the Art of the Horseman [*Cavallerizzo* in Italian]. I would have used the word *escuyer* [horseman, but also squire] if in France it meant only good horseman, but since it can adapt to other meanings I found it more appropriate to use a foreign word, also according to the opinion of some of my friends very experienced in this art[10]."

The equestrian art in the pre-Renaissance age

Despite the prestige of the Italian riders reaching its peak in the Renaissance and the early printed treatises dedicated to horse riding appearing in Italy in the mid-sixteenth century, the equestrian art did not emerge in this period from nothing. Obviously, in a civilization where the horse was so important in the art of war and in the life of the aristocracy, riding was actually widely practiced at considerably sophisticated levels in the pre-Renaissance era. Hence, in the early printed books dedicated to the subject, equitation is presented as a highly developed and refined discipline, the result of a well-established tradition. Nicolas Thouroude[11] documents that in the late Middle Ages, there was already a playful equitation which required sophisticated training of the horse. This type of riding found its expression in the jousts and tournaments celebrating various events and that, in addition to combat, involved a court ritual and a real theatrical performance in which horses always had a leading role. The equestrian education of the young nobles was considered essential. Ramon Lullo in his *Livre de l'ordre de chevalerie*[12] (1274–1276) recommends gentlemen to assure their children instruction on how to ride horses from childhood and care of the animal should also be taught. This was a widespread habit, judging from the frequency with which kings, dukes and other nobles donated horses to their young children. For example, the future Duke of Burgundy, John the Fearless[13], in the fourteenth century, was given by his father Philip the Bold[14], a small white foal, when he was just three ye-

---

10) LA BROUE, 1610, Livre I, p. 10.

11) See Thouroude, 2007.

12) Lullo, 1994.

13) *Jean Ier de Bourgogne*, known as *Jean sans Peur* (1371–1419) was Count of Nevers, from 1384 to 1405, and Duke of Burgundy, from 1404 until his death.

14) *Philippe II de Bourgogne* named *Philippe le Hardi* (1342–1404) was Duke of

ars old. At five the foal was replaced by a small mule. Then, when he was six years old, the future duke graduated to an ambler [a horse, bred and trained to walk at the amble, appreciated for travelling distances. The world in Italian is "*ambiatore.*"] and finally the father ordered the purchase of a saddle horse for him in Paris.

The custom of initiating the scions of the aristocracy to the arts of chivalry from their earliest youth was maintained for centuries. Testified by the case of Paolo Giordano Orsini[15], Duke of Bracciano, who, in 1542, received as a gift from his mother, a black pony which cost as many as 13 golden scudi, when he was not yet two years old[16]. This first mount was followed by many others. A year later, the Cardinal Farnese in person made a gift of a horse to the young Orsini who, once grown up, possessed stables renowned for the beauty of the horses and the richness of the harnesses. This weighed heavily upon the coffers of his dukedom, affecting their balance, since he had the habit of ordering new saddles and liveries for each ceremony[17].

There are many historical testimonies, from the fifteenth century, of parades, the so-called cavalcades, jousts and several other equestrian ceremonies, particularly those relating to the period of the Aragonese domination over the kingdom of Naples[18]. At the time of Alfonso the Magnanimous[19], the capital of the kingdom attracted young noblemen, as Ercole[20] and Sigismondo

---

Touraine, from 1360 to 1363, then Duke of Burgundy from 1363 and finally, by his marriage to Margaret III, Countess of Flanders, he also became Count of Flanders, Artois and Burgundy from 1384 until his death.

15) Born in 1541, Paolo Giordano was the son of Girolamo and Francesca Sforza of Santa Fiora. In 1558, he married the daughter of the Grand Duke of Tuscany, Isabella de Medici, to whom he was bound by a marriage contract from his earliest years. He participated in the Battle of Lepanto, and was one of the most important Roman barons of his era. His history, however, is mainly linked to the black legend of his violent and impulsive temper, which would have led him to murder his wife, who died in 1578. In fact, more recent and reliable studies (see Mori, 2011) have shown that both he and his wife were victims of slander. Paolo Giordano died the 13th of November, 1585.

16) See Mori, 2011, p. 29.

17) See Mori, 2011, p. 170.

18) See Lawe, 2005.

19) Alfonso de Trastámara (1394-1458), King of Aragon and Sicily, conquered the Kingdom of Naples in 1442, taking it to the Agiovines.

20) Ercole I d'Este (1431—1505) was Duke of Ferrara from 1471 until 1505. He was educated at the Aragonese court in Naples, where he was instructed in the military strategy and in the chivalry disciplines, from 1445—1460.

d'Este[21], willing to learn the art of the Neapolitan riders. In Naples[22], horseback riding had a great importance and was practiced by all of the nobility.

Magnificent chivalry feasts took place at the Neapolitan court, frequently taking on the character of triumphal cavalcades, or of jousts, anticipating the Renaissance and Baroque carousels. The first of these feasts, in the Aragonese period, was held the 26th of February 1443 to celebrate the triumph of Alfonso, who became king of Naples, after defeating Rene d'Anjou. The procession took its cue from Market Gate, where a grand triumphal arch was erected, and ended in Castel Nuovo.

One of the most lavish feasts of the time was celebrated a few years later, in 1452, on the occasion of the visit to the city by Emperor Frederick III[23], who came to Italy to be crowned by Pope Nicholas V and to marry Eleanor of Portugal. Memory of the prominent role that horses and equestrian games played in the massive celebrations comes down to us in an anonymous chronicle entitled: *Come lo imperatore Federico entrò in Napoli ("How the Emperor Frederick entered Naples")*[24]. The equestrian games were preceded by a

> "most splendid cavalcade" of four hundred steeds "made ready and trained to everything, to every fast exercise[25]."

They were followed by another four hundred horses, berbers, turks, greeks and jennets, followed by another two hundred horses bred in Alfonso's stables,

> "...which were reared in the kingdom with the mares and their Spanish stallions with extreme beauty and controllability[26]."

A great feast in which the splendor of the horses and the skill of the riders stood out, so that the author adds:

> "Would take too long to write down everything that was used of great value and pomp and that was liberally said about the horses, big, beautiful, tall, that were never seen

---

21) Sigismondo d'Este (1433—1507) was the son of the Duke of Ferrara, Niccolò III d'Este and of Ricciarda di Saluzzo. He was educated, with his brother Ercole I d'Este, at the neapolitan court of Alfonso of Aragon.

22) See Chapter III

23) Frederick III of Habsburg (1415 - 1493). He was the last emperor to be crowned in Rome, in 1452, by Pope Nicholas V. In that occasion he married Eleaonor from Portugal (1434 - 1467), that he had already married by proxy the year before.

24) Anonymous, 1908.

25) *«fatti et ammaestrati a tutto, ad ogni presto maneggio,»* Anonymous, 1908, p. 486.

26) *« ...li quali erano allevati nel Regno con le giumente e loro stalluni di razza di Spagna con estrema bellezza e bontà.»* Anonymous, 1908, p. 486.

more, and not just in a small number, that the king gave every day to ride to all the gentlemen in Naples[27]."

The king himself and his son Ferrante participated in the joust in the Piazza dell'Immacolata,

> "where King Alfonso ran the first lance and broke it so finely with Mr. Gio. Antonio, Prince of Taranto. And also Ferrante of Aragon, son of His Majesty, participated in the tournament, and was so praised that day for the way he rode, and for the way he carried and used his lance, even though he was small he seemed built on the saddle-bow[28]."

The celebrations went on for three days and were completed by large public banquets, tournaments and balls.

The Aragonese influence

The Spaniards had a remarkable influence on the Neapolitan equestrian culture. The equestrian game attended by the king and his son, in Piazza dell'Immacolata, was a kind of joust of Iberian origin called *Jogo de la Tavolata*, in which the riders had to strike a board with a lance, or with a javelin.

> "The *Jogo de la Tavolata* as the *Juego de Cannas*—in which stylish competitors were divided into teams and fought with blunted lances—were not previously practiced in Italy and were a contribution of Alfonso, who introduced them in the Neapolitan chivalry culture[29]."

In the *Juego de Cannas* the teams were chasing each other and throwing reeds with sticky tips, which would stick to the opponent's armor, or throwing small balls of clay. The game underwent further changes. For example, in the tournament held in Florence, July 5, 1558, on the occasion of the wedding

---

27) «Saría lungo a scrivere tutto quello che fu usato di gran valore e pompa e che liberalmente fu detto di li cavalli grandi, belli, alti di statura, che mai s'erano più visti, e non in poco numero, che lo re faceva cavalcare ogni dia a tutti li gentiluomini a Napoli.» Anonymous, 1908, p. 483.

28) *"dove lo re Alfonso corse la prima lancia e roppe tanto finamente con lo Sig.r Gio. Antonio principe di Taranto. Et anco giostrò don Ferrante d'Aragona figliuolo di Sua Maestà, che tanto fu lodato in quella giornata per lo cavalcare, lo portare e mettero della lanza, e benché fusse piccolo pareva fabricato sull'arcione."* Anonymous, 1908, p. 482.

29) Lawe, 2005, p. 11.

of Lucrezia de Medici[30] to Alfonso II d'Este[31], the riders contended for crock pots full of feathers. In order not to break them and to disperse the feathers, horses and riders had to act with extreme finesse[32].

This game of reeds soon became very popular not only in Naples, and continued to be practiced throughout Italy for at least two centuries. According to Benedetto Croce[33], the game actually had Arabic origins, as testified by the habit of playing it while wearing Moorish costumes, and was at the origin of the term "carousel," then widespread in the equestrian field and still in use for particular events. The balls of clay that the riders threw at each other were called in Spanish, *alcancias*, but in Naples they were called *caruselli* (a dialectal name survived, says Croce, to indicate the round terracotta money boxes, which curiously in Spanish are called precisely *alcancias*).

> "So the game of reeds, which earlier than in other parts of Italy passed from Spain to Naples, was called 'game of the carousels.' And here's the Neapolitan and genuine origin of the name '*carosello*,' which was later given to other forms of tournaments, and went to France and there became '*caroussel*.'"[34]

The Spanish contribution was particularly significant in breeding. Following the model of his homeland, the king created the so-called "*cavallerizze*" (from the Castilian *caballerizas*), real studs, pastures, stables for stallions and mares and arenas for the training of foals. These facilities were under the direction of horsemen, subject to a Master. During the reign of Alfonso this role was covered by the same Prince Ferrante[35]. In the royal stud farms was bred the so-called "breed of kings," later known as horse of the kingdom of Naples, or Neapolitan courser[36]. They were animals of great value, often given as gifts to kings of other kingdoms. The stables were models of efficiency. A chronicler of the period underlined their safety features, including the use of separate entry and exit doorways for the stables.

---

30) Fifth daughter (1545—1561) of the Duke of Florence, then Grand Duke of Tuscany, Cosimo I de Medici and Eleanor of Toledo. In 1558 she married Alfonso II d'Este in place of her sister Mary, who had died of malaria. The marriage sealed the peace between Ercole II d'Este and Philip II of Spain who was allied with Cosimo I.

31) Son of Ercole II d'Este and Renée of France, Alfonso II d'Este (1533–1597) was the fifth Duke of Ferrara, Modena and Reggio and reigned from 1559 until his death.

32) See Mori, 2011, p. 83.

33) See Croce, 1922, pp. 193–195.

34) Croce, 1922, pp. 194–195.

35) See Lawe 2005, p. 12.

36) See Chapter III.

Horseback riding maintained an important role in the life of the Neapolitan court with the heirs of Alfonso: his son Ferrante[37] and his grandson Alfonso II[38]. Naples increased its prestige as a center of equestrian culture, with jousts and parades which enriched the celebrations of all civil and religious solemnity. The royal family often participated in the cavalcades through the streets of the city and showed particular affection for their famous coursers. The manuscript of Giuliano Passaro[39] recounts the jousts held in 1477, in Piazza della Sellaria, on the occasion of the celebrations for the wedding of Ferrante with his cousin Joanna, sister of Ferdinand the Catholic. In particular, Passaro focuses on the sumptuous trappings of horses and riders and on the steed of the Duke of Calabria, eldest son of Ferrante and his first wife Isabella of Clermont, then king of Naples, by the name of Alfonso II. The author writes that the mount of the Duke, who participated in the tournament and "broke four gilded lances very worthily," "went in the air with jumps." Clear evidence of the practice of the above-mentioned "school jumps" in the fifteenth century, fully eighty years before the publication of the first equestrian treatise by Federico Grisone. On the other hand, in *Bernadino della Ciarda unhorsed*, one of the three famous paintings by Paolo Uccello dedicated to the Battle of San Romano[40], painted between 1438 and 1440, to the right of the captain pierced by the opponent lance, can be seen a chestnut horse performing a perfect *croupade*[41] (see illustration p. 130–131).

In light of these examples, it would be an oversimplification to consider the Renaissance the starting point of the modern equestrian tradition, as many historians argue[42]. Different evidence, instead, demonstrates the spread, since at

---

37) Ferdinand of Aragon (1424–1494), the only son, even if illegitimate, of Alfonso of Aragon. He was king of Naples from 1458 to 1494. Also known as Ferrante I or Don Ferrando.

38) Alfonso II of Aragon (1448–1495). Ferrante's firstborn, was Duke of Calabria and king of Naples from 1494 to 1495.

39) Passaro, 1785. See also AA.VV. 1893.

40) In which the Florentines, led by Niccolò Maurizi da Tolentino, defeated the Sienese in 1432.

41) Here, we use the term with reference to its modern meaning, i.e. the croupade as is still performed by the riders of the Cadre Noir of Saumur: "the horse leans on the front legs, elevates the croup and delivers an energetic kick." Barry, 2005, p. 35. In ancient times, however, this term meant a jump in which "when the horse leaps into the air and in its horizontal position, gathers the hind legs under the mass, placing them to the same height as the front legs." Barry, 2005, p. 24.

42) In the case, for example, of Patrizia Arquint, a scholar who despite having the merit of studying the history of equitation with the exactitude of the philologist, considers the flowering of equestrian academies and the publication of the first printed treatises in the sixteenth century the result of a clear break, due to "a significant technical change in the decade prior to 1550." See Arquint, 2002, p. 7.

least the fifteenth century, of an already extremely refined and not merely utilitarian equitation, which includes the use of particularly advanced techniques, such as the "airs above the ground," which later characterize the so-called High School. However, during the Renaissance, the equestrian practices matured and evolved under the influence of different historical, political and even cultural factors, culminating in the publication of the first treatises specifically devoted to horseback riding.

Evolution of combat techniques

One of the first changes impacting horseback riding was the evolution of combat techniques, resulting in the increased use, in the sixteenth century, of portable firearms and the reappearance of infantry as an organized and effective force[43]. Knights could no longer simply charge with lances, suited in heavy armor. Instead, they had to advance toward infantry, stop at a certain distance, shoot, and then retreat to reload their weapon.

Therefore, they needed more agile horses, trained to execute the manoeuvre called *caracollo*[44]. The knights advanced toward the enemy at a slow pace, usually at trot, arranged in formations consisting of a dozen lines with a frontage of 20–30 men. Once the first line came within range, the knights fired with their guns, turning to one side, to eventually performing a half *volte* and fired with their second weapon. Once the first line discharged their guns, they turned to the left and withdrew to the rear of the formation to reload, while being replaced by the next line. Generally, after a certain period of shooting with firearms, the operation was concluded with a charge against the now disorganized enemy ranks in order to proceed to fight hand to hand. Mario Gennero[45] considers the time at which this transformation happened in the military tactics of the Renaissance to be during the Franco/Spanish wars, that on several occasions between 1521 and 1559, opposed Francis I[46] and Charles V[47], then later Henry II[48] and Philip II[49]. In that period, there were

---

43) See Franchet d'Espèrey, 2002.

44) The term comes from the Spanish *caracol*, "snail."

45) See Gennero, 2001, p. XVII.

46) Francis I de Valois (1494—1547), was king of France from 1515 to his death.

47) Charles V (1500—1558). Son of Philip of Habsburg, called the Handsome, and Joanna of Castile, known as the Mad. He was king of Spain (1516) and Emperor of the Holy Roman Empire. He was elected in 1519 and crowned by the archbishop of Cologne in Aachen Cathedral the following year.

48) Henry II de Valois (1519—1559), was king of France from 1547 to 1559.

49) Philip II of Habsburg (1527—1598) was king of Spain from 1556 to 1598, king of Naples and Sicily from 1554 to 1598, king of Sardinia and the eighteenth king of Portugal and the Algarve (Filipe I) from 1581 to 1598.

two different ways of making war and two types of riding faced on the battlefields. On one side were the French cavalry, heavily armed and mounted on big horses, protected by bulky harnesses, on the other side were the Spanish troops mounted on light horses, well-trained, faster and easier to handle. The Spaniards won the battle. The Spanish *arquebusiers*[50] pierced the French armor with their bullets and so forced the radical change in methods of warfare. Then the armor of chivalry gradually disappeared, just as quickly spread the use of *arquebusiers* and artillery; light cavalry and infantry took an increasing role. Though the gradual decline of medieval chivalry commenced two centuries earlier, with the annihilation of the French cavalry of Philip the Fair[51] by the Flemish infantry at the Battle of Courtrai (11 July 1302) followed by the defeats suffered by the French knights during the Hundred Years War (1339–1453), in Crécy (26 August 1346) and Agincourt (25 October 1415)[52].

From tournaments to new equestrian performances

Another factor giving a new course to European horseback riding was the gradual abandonment of tournaments. In the mid-sixteenth century, two tragedies marked the history of what for centuries was one of the most significant expressions of chivalry. On 30 June 1559, the king of France, Henry II, was wounded in the eye by the fragment of the lance of Gabriel I of Lorges, Earl of Montgomery, during the tournament in honor of the marriage of his daughter Elizabeth to Philip II of Spain. He died ten days later[53]. On the 20th of January of the following year, Prince Henry of Bourbon died, at the age of fifteen years, crushed by his horse. The general greif and consternation following these events led, especially in France, to progressively replace tournaments with less bloody games, thus promoting the development of a more sophisticated equitation, which celebrated the quality of riders without exposing them to death[54].

---

50) The arquebus or sometimes spelled harquebus, harkbus or hackbut; from the Dutch: *haakbus*, meaning "hook gun", or "hook tube", is an early muzzle-loaded firearm used in the 15th to 17th centuries. The word was originally modelled on the German: *Hakenbüchse*, this produced haquebute. Also refers to the mounted soldiers equipped with these guns.

51) Philip IV of France (1268—1314) called Philippe le Bel, was king of France from 1285 to his death.

52) On the profound changes in military tactics of the time, see Parker, 1988; Pieri, 1952; Hale 1985. On innovations in the art of war by the Spanish cavalry, Puddu, 1982. See also Cardini, 1987, pp. 451–480. An evocative interpretation of the crisis of the traditional cavalry in the beautiful novel by Antonio Scurati, *Il rumore sordo della battaglia*. Scurati, 2006.

53) See Erspamer, 1988, p. 27.

54) See Balestracci, 2001; Franchet d'Espèrey, 2002, pp. 183–84.

This process, however, was rather slow and uneven. Tournaments were still held throughout the sixteenth and the seventeenth century. Seven years after the death of Henry II, in the courtyard of the Belvedere in the Vatican was held, for example, a great tournament to celebrate the wedding of Annibale Altemps and Ortensia Borromeo[55]. In 1561, instead, the best of Roman nobility battled in a tournament held on St. Peter's Square[56].

Gradually, the fights were replaced by less bloody chivalry trials, such as the *giostre di caroselli* (jousting carousels) and *joust of the Saracen*, or at least, were increasingly conceived alternating bloodless equestrian choreography with combats. For example, this was the case with the tournament organized in Florence by Paolo Giordano Orsini, on the occasion of the marriage of Francesco de Medici to Joanna of Austria, in 1565. During the spectacle, briefly described by Vasari in his *Lives of the Artists*, as well as fighting with various weapons at the bar, "with singular pleasure of the audience and with very well trained horses, was held that pretty dance called 'the battle'[57]." As Elisabetta Mori writes, a show that "mixed theater dance with the medieval tournament, sublimating it and making it more gentle, enriching it with choreographic and spectacular elements[58]." This type of display became one of the most popular in Florence for the entire next century.

The horse and politics

Another very important factor which characterized the equestrian art in the Renaissance was the increasing role the horse and equitation played in political games between European kingdoms and principalities during the fifteenth and sixteenth centuries. A clear example is offered by the ambassadors of Mantua, who ably exploited the famous stud of the Gonzaga, known as the *race of Mantua*, to foster and develop the relationships of the major rulers of the Duchy with the main sovereigns of Europe, in particular with the king of France[59]. Early in the reign of Francis I, the correspondence of the Mantuan ambassadors testifies an intense diplomatic equestrian activity. To better understand the importance of this type of exchanges it should first be considered that, at the time, in the French court, there were kept between eight and ten thousand equines, including horses, mules and donkeys. Most of these were used for the transport of people and goods in the constant movement of the court from one palace to another, or they were used during the frequent hunting, or serving at the guard. Of course, most of these animals should not be

---

55) See Chapter VIII.

56) See Mori, 2011, p. 104.

57) Vasari, 1857, Vol. XIII, p. 190.

58) Mori, 2011, p.124.

59) See Malacarne, 1995 and Chatenet, 2002.

confused with the superb horses used by the king on the occasion of jousts and parades. The most popular among these were Neapolitan steeds, jennets from Spain, Turkish and Barbaresque horses[60].

By studying the correspondence of the time, Raffaele Tamalio and Monique Chatenet[61] have reconstructed a series of significant events that occurred in 1515, during the stay of Francis I in Milan, after the battle of Marignano that gave the King of France control over the Lombard duchy. At that juncture, to obtain the King's forgiveness for his unfaithfulness, the Marquis of Mantua, Francesco II (1466–1519), granted his son Federico[62], aged fifteen, to his custody. Knowing Francis I's passion for horses, the young Gonzaga took advantage of the prestige of his father's studs to make his way to the court. Thus between October and November 1515, Federico organized a series of presentations of his best horses in the presence of the king and his Italian *Grand Ecuyer* [Master of the horse], Galeazzo Sanseverino[63]. The horses were ridden by Francesco Gonzaga's horseman, Giovanni Ratti[64], and by Federico himself, who offered his best specimens to the sovereign. After congratulating the young gentleman for his qualities as a rider, the king accepted his gifts promising to return with a beautiful stallion to improve the breed of Mantua, as Louis XII[65] already had done in the past. With great foresight, Federico did not fail to please Sanseverino and when he came to visit him at home to evaluate the specimens offered to the king, and gave him his very own, prized, Turchetto, knowing that the *Grand Ecuyer* wanted him and considering—in the words of a diplomat, referring to the Mantuan court—that his intercession with the king would be very useful.

Monique Chatenet highlights that the Gonzagas were not the only ones to use their best steeds as a diplomatic tool. On the 20th of November 1515, the Duke of Ferrara offered to the king of France a magnificent Mantuan gray stallion, with a peculiar name, "Falbo no te intendo"[66] (that the Duke of Ferrara had previously purchased from Federico Gonzaga). It became one of the favorite steeds of Francis I, who called him "Virgil." According to

---

60) Namely what we now call Arabian and Berber horses

61) See Tamalio, 1994 and Chatenet, 2002.

62) Federico was already granted to the custody of Pope Julius II for three years (from July 1510 until February 1513), as a hostage. The Pope, in fact, interceded with the Republic of Venice to liberate his father, Francesco II, who was made prisoner during the war against the League of Cambrai (1508–1509). Given the frequent turnaround of the Mantuan captain, this way the Pope wanted to grant his fidelity.

63) See forward in this chapter.

64) Who a year before was sent by Francesco II to offer some horses to the English court.

65) Louis XII (1462–1515), was king of France from 1498 until his death, in 1515.

66) The name means literally: "Sorrel, I don't understand you"

Giancarlo Mazzoleni[67], also Baldassare Castiglione, the author of the *Book of the Courtier*, who was ambassador of various Italian courts, actively participated in the exchange of equestrian gifts. In this regard, the author cites (albeit with more than a few inconsistencies) the journey that Castiglione made to England in 1506, to receive on behalf of the Duke of Urbino, Guidobaldo da Montefeltro[68], the Order of the Garter from Henry VII[69]. On this occasion, according to Mazzoleni, Castiglione was the bearer of many gifts for the king[70]. Among these was also a beautiful bay horse, who fell ill before his departure for England, and was then replaced by a mare. Taking a reconstruction already established by Federico Tesio, Mazzoleni asserts that from that broodmare came one of the blood lines of the English thoroughbred.[71]

Similar exchanges of equestrian gifts followed throughout the Renaissance and continued in the following centuries. The Spanish scholar, Hernando Sánchez recalls how Charles Frederick, Crown Prince of the Duchy of Cleves[72], during his visit to Rome, in 1575, "was gifted of horses and other refreshments by the viceroy of Naples, Antonio de Perrenot Granvella[73]. In other cases, the guests were to offer a gift of valuable specimens. For example, when in 1543 the King of Tunis, Muley Hassan visited Naples, brought as a gift to the Vice-

---

67) Mazzoleni, 2002.

68) Guidobaldo da Montefeltro (1472—1508) was the third Duke of Urbino.

69) Henry Tudor (1447—1547) was king of England from 1509 until his death, in 1547.

70) Mazzoleni (who does not explain how or why) argues, however, that the gifts were from the Marquis of Mantua, Francesco II Gonzaga. They would be two: a bay horse and a painting by Raphael. The picture is, obviously, *St. George and the dragon* now in the National Gallery of Art in Washington, which, however, is widely recognized as a gift of the Duke of Urbino, in gratitude for the award of the Order of the Garter, as testified by the fact that the artist depicted a garter prominently on the calf of the rider, with the inscription "Honi," which is the first word of the order's saying ("*Honni soit qui mal y pense,*" i.e. "Evil be to him who evil thinks"). On the other hand, we know that "from 1504 Castiglione is at the service of the Dukes of Urbino, having as a comrade his cousin Cesare Gonzaga." Mutini, 1979.

71) About the possible Italian ancestors of the English Thoroughbred, see Tesio, 1947 and Malacarne, 1995.

72) Son of William of Jülich-Cleves-Berg and Maria of Austria, daughter of the Emperor Ferdinand I. Born in 1555, he came to Rome for the Jubilee of 1575 and was received with great honor by Pope Gregory XIII, who hoped to use his help in the conversion of the Protestant German princes. A few days later, however, he became ill and died of smallpox. He is buried in the Roman Church of Santa Maria dell'Anima.

73) Born in 1517, of French origin, was appointed cardinal by Pope Pius IV in 1561. He was bishop of Arras, Archbishop of Malines, advisor to Charles V, ambassador in Rome and Viceroy of the Kingdom of Naples (1571–1575) on behalf of Philip II. He died in 1586.

roy Pedro de Toledo a hundred horses, which a chronicle of the time defines "beautiful and very richly trimmed[74]."

Another remarkable case is that of Luigi Carafa, second prince of Stigliano[75], heir to a huge feudal estate, which he contributed to enrich further during his lifetime. His wonderful stud farm was famous and had over one hundred horses. It is said that the prince took all of them with him when he went to Bologna for the coronation of Charles V in 1530. On that occasion he behaved

> "with such splendor ... that he overcame in chivalrousness all the gentlemen ... who came in large numbers, from all nations ...[76]."

He magnanamously donated some of the horses to the Emperor and distributed the others amongst the gentlemen present. This generosity was usual to him, so that he

> "retained the obligation of almost all of the princes of Italy and those outside Italy and that of the cardinals, continuously donating to them horses of high price and good training[77]."

Perhaps due to his generosity, the Emperor awarded him the dignity of a grandee of Spain. Alessandro Massari Malatesta—author of a treatise in the late sixteenth century dedicated to his nephew, also called Luigi[78]—shows that this tradition of equestrian gifts passed down also to his descendant, who every year

> "made a gift of his most excellent horses to the Emperor, and to the Catholic king, and to the greater part of the Princes of Christianity, and especially of Italy[79]."

---

74) See Hernando Sánchez, 1998, pp. 292–93, n. 13.

75) He was born in 1511, eldest son of the Prince of Stigliano Antonio and of Beatrice of Capua of the Counts of Altavilla. He first married Clarice Orsini whose mother, Felicia Della Rovere, was the illegitimate daughter of Pope Julius II and then married Lucrezia del Tufo of the Marquis of Lavello. He died July 17, 1576.

76) *"con tanto splendore... che supero particolarmente di cavalleria quanti signori... che in gran numero concorsero, di tutte le nationi..."* Aldimari, 1691, II, p. 381.

77) *"teneva obbligati tutti i principi quasi dell'Italia e fuori e i cardinali col donare loro cavalli continuamente, di prezzo e di maestria."* Aldimari, 1691, p. 383.

78) See Chapter VII.

79) *"far dono de suoi eccellentissimi cavalli all'Imperatore, e al Re Cattolico, e alla più gran parte de' Prencipi di Christianità, e in particolare d'Italia."* MASSARI MALATESTA, 1599, p. 23v.

In the sixteenth century, between the European courts there was a great circulation of prestigious horses, many of Italian origin. For example, in addition to the aforementioned steeds of the Mantuan race, the French royal stables also possessed numerous specimens of Neapolitan horses, as reported in the correspondence by Antonio de Beatis, secretary of Cardinal Luigi d'Aragona[80], nephew of the king of Naples. In 1517, during the visit to France of the cardinal, he could see that the royal stables of the castle of Blois[81] were full of Italian horses, under the care of Roberto Sanseverino, son of Galeazzo, who was in the service of Ludovico il Moro and then, the king of France. De Beatis noted in particular a dapple gray of Neapolitan origin. This was a *"jumper"* offered as a gift to the king of France, who considered him one of his favorites. Note that in the diplomatic correspondence of the Italian kingdoms of the time, the Neapolitans ambassadors do not refer to the Mantuan horses; likewise the Mantuan do not mention the Neapolitans, testifying the high competition among Italian studs in the diplomatic game.

The horses of the Gonzaga

The most explicit consecration of the role of the horse for the Renaissance aristocracy is located in the magnificent Palazzo Te in Mantua. Here Federico Gonzaga, then Duke, commissioned Giulio Romano—the artist that conceived and created this magnificent residence, devoted to leisure and parties—to portray his favorite steeds in the room reserved for banquets and dances. They survive today in an elegant architectural backdrop of *trompe l'o-eil* (see pictures on pp. 129, 136). The horses are represented lifesize in profile. The name of four specimens is still readable: *Morel Favorito, Glorioso, Battaglia* and *Dario*[82]. A curious episode in the youth of Federico, dating back to the previously mentioned period of his stay in Milan, anticipates, in some sense, the triumph of the Gonzaga horses, immortalized by the paintbrushes of Giulio Romano and of the artists of his workshop, and illustrates well how the love of horses by the aristocracy of the time involved a close intimacy of the nobles with their favorite animals, even at banquets. In November 1515, the fifteen-year-old Mantuan scion invited Galeazzo Sanseverino and the Duke of Ferrara to assist in a new presentation of his best specimens, in the building where he lived in Milan. After the lunch, the horses were led one by one into the same room where the guests had eaten, so that they could be admired. The court jester, Presteffano, amused those present making his

---

80) See Chastel, 1995.

81) Royal residence in which the wife of Francis I, Claude of France (1499–1524), intended to transfer the court, from the castle of Amboise.

82) See Belluzzi, 1998, pp. 365–371.

entrance in peasant clothes, riding backwards singing songs, accompanying himself on his theorbo[83].

Given the inclination of Federico to the equestrian art, it is conceivable that, in the years of his maturity, he read with some apprehension the correspondence sent to him by Leonardo Arrivabene, tutor of his third son Lodovico (1539–1595). The young man, who was compelled to go to France at the age of ten to take possession of the property left to him as an inheritance by his maternal grandmother, Anna d'Alençon[84], spent a long time at the court. In a letter of 1552, Arrivabene emphasizes the necessity for Lodovico to learn well the equestrian art if he wants to be distinguished, given that there is nothing more widely appreciated by the French nobility. Unfortunately, although descended from a family of famous riders and breeders, the young man, at the time, showed little aptitude ("*non ha grandissimo principio*"), and for this his tutor considered it urgent to entrust him to the care of an experienced teacher like Tommaso Cardi, horseman to the king at the royal stud of Saint-Léger:

> "In four days, with the consent of Milord d'Orfé, I will lead my illustrious Lord to Saint Legier, a place that is only ten miles from here, where the horses are under the care of Tommaso, so that for eight days he will teach him to improve his ability in riding, because, to be honest, His Lordship does not show great aptitude, and it would be a shame not to make him exercise, because in France there is nothing more appreciated and loved by His Majesty and there is no doubt that only courage and arms will make His Lordship rise in the consideration of this court. Because among the nobility of this region there is nothing more practiced and most prized of these two [85]."

In this brief account of Arrivabene, it is clear that valor in arms and mastery in the art of riding were at that time an inseparable pair of qualities that identified the principal virtues of an aristocrat. During the Renaissance, the horse was considered a distinctive feature of its rider's personality, so much that in the funerals of important people the coffin was followed by the

---

83) See Chatenet, 2002.

84) Widow of William IX Palaeologus, Marquis of Monferrato.

85) "*Fra quattro giorni condurò pero con conseso de Monsr de Orfé lo Illmo S^{or} mio a Santo Legier, loco a qui discosto dieci miglia dove sta li cavalli ero Thomaso affine che per otto giorni lo vada alquanto comodando a cavallo perch'in vero Sua S^{ia} non ha grandissimo principio, e saria peccato non farlo essercitare tanto più che in Francia non vi è cosa più aprezzata, né da Sua M^{tà} più amata, né vi è ponto da dubitare che sol il valore, et le arme, causarono che Sua S^{ia} salirà grande in questa corte perché tra la nobleza di questa regione non vi è cosa più essercitata né più estimata di queste doi.*" Archivio di Stato di Mantova, Archivio Gonzaga 644 (3 luglio 1552, Saint-Germain, Leonardo Arrivabene). Quoted in Chatenet, 2002, p. 49.

Libro Terzo.

Merco della razza de'Corsieri del Duca di Mantoua. La razza è stata famosissima per tutto il Mondo per la lor bellezza, grandezza, e per rispetto delle guerre era andata a male. Hoggi si rimette in piedi con grandissima cura.

Merco della razza de'Caualli Giannetti del Duca di Mantoua, e riescono leggiadri, e belli passeggiatori.

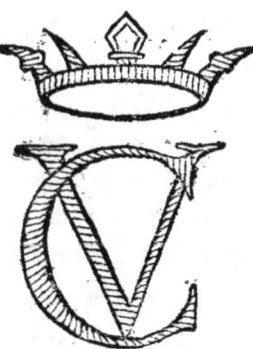

Merco della razza de'Caualli Gubinij del Duca di Mantoua, riescono buonissimi.

Merco della razza de'Caualli Barbari del Duca di Mantoua. Riescono veloci, e braui.

The brands of the race of the Dukes of Mantua, from Francesco Liberati, *La Perfettione del cavallo*, Roma, per Michele Hercole, 1639.

deceased's favorite steed, led out by hand and covered with a caparison with the insignia of his master. On the other hand, it has been noted that

> "riding provides a model for those who command and those who obey. Demonstration of strength, and also of ability, especially because the means to achieve the obedience are discrete, or even nearly invisible. The horse then obeys, but must also embody both the strength and science of his rider[86]."

Therefore, the equestrian art was a discipline in close contact with the political arena, but also crucial in defining the identity of European aristocracy.

Horse riding and the birth of the modern courtier

Between the fifteenth and the seventeenth centuries in Europe occurred the slow metamorphosis of the knight-warrior still of medieval style into the modern horseman-courtier[87]. The complexity of this process involved political, economic, social and, as stated above, military factors. In this transformation, the ruling class of nobles reacted by profoundly rethinking their cultural and symbolic identity[88]. From the identity of the *bellator*, the knight whose sole occupation was the profession of arms, they progressively transitioned to the more nuanced gentleman that integrated the military profession with the "supreme ornament" of active competence in the field of literature, arts and music and thus became "the protagonist of a new form of life in civil conversation, for useful, and for honor[89]." Although Italy was enslaved to the domination of foreign powers during this period, the role of Italian culture in the development of these new prospects is particularly relevant. As written by Amedeo Quondam:

> "is the 'best form' devised by the Italians, defeated and humiliated in their military and political virtue, to establish itself as the experience dynamically productive of European modernity, in its models and in its practices."[90]

---

86) Grange, 2002, pp. 320–321.

87) About this matter see Domenichelli, 2002, especially pp. 15–38; see also Roche, 2007 e 2007a; Quondam, 2003, especially pp. 77–114; Quondam, 2010; Bianchi, 2010.

88) Tucker, 2007; see also Raber & Tucker, 2005.

89) Quondam, 2003, p. 86.

90) Quondam, 2003, p. VIII, see also pp. 88–89.

Among the latter riding is crucial, as the ability to ride was considered a constitutive feature of the noble's identity[91]. Since classical times, only the most wealthy and powerful elite of the nobility could afford to own and keep horses intended for riding and for war. Similarly, only a few had the money, the relationships and the time to learn the art of riding[92]. So that the term "*cavaliere*" ("rider") became identified with that of "noble," as noted by Pasquale Caracciolo in his treatise *La gloria del cavallo* (1566, *The Glory of the Horse*):

> "No doubt that the name *cavaliere* ['knight,' but also 'rider'] came initially from the military life, because it did not properly mean nothing but 'mounted soldier' [...] But then, as derived from the first meaning, you can already see the ancient habit of calling *cavalieri* ['knights,' or 'riders'] those that, being born of noble blood dedicate themselves to the exercises of chivalry and lead a splendid and magnificent life.[93]"

The importance attached to equitation in the identification of the constitutive features of the new aristocratic appears clearly in what Quondam calls "the European archetype-text of the modern gentleman's new form of life,"[94] that is to say Baldassare Castiglione's the *Book of the Courtier*. Which, defining the characteristics of the modern aristocrat, insist on the fact that above all, he must carry on the profession of arms:

> "But, regarding some details, I am of the opinion that the principal and true profession of the Courtier ought to be that of arms; which I would have him follow actively above all else, and be known among others as bold and strong, and loyal to whomever he serves." (Book 1, 17)[95]

---

91) As early as the thirteenth century, Giordano Ruffo (see below Chapter II) stated in his treatise on the art of treating horses that "no animal is nobler than the horse, because through him, princes, great men of influence and wealth, and knights are distinct from ordinary people" («*nullum animal sit equo nobilius, eo quod per ipsum principes, magnates et milites a minori bus separantur*»), and adds that "no one can be properly recognized as a gentleman among individuals if not through him" ("*nullum animal sit equo nobilius, eo quod per ipsum principes, magnates et milites a minori bus separantur*"). Ruffo, 1999, p. 2.

92) Cfr. Tucker, 2007.

93) "*Egli senza dubbio dalla milizia incominciò primieramente questo nome di cavaliere, perché altro propriamente non dinotava che "soldato a cavallo" [...] Ma poi, quasi tratto da quel primiero significato, si vede anticamente l'usanza aver portato che cavalieri diciamo quelli i quali nati di sangue nobile e signorile attendono agli essercizi cavallereschi con vita splendida e magnifica.*" Caracciolo's work was first published in Venice in 1566. See Chapter VII. CARACCIOLO, 1566, pp. 42–43.

94) Quondam, 2003, p. 87.

95) "*Ma per venire a qualche particularità, estimo che la principale e vera profession del*

He must, therefore, be physically fit and trained to warlike exercises and to riding, disciplines in which he must show force, but also lightness and fluency:

> "And so, I would have him well built and shapely of limb, and would have him show strength and lightness and suppleness, and know all bodily exercises that befit a man of war: whereas I think the first should be to handle every sort of weapon well on foot and on horse, to understand the advantages of each, and especially to be familiar with those weapons that are ordinarily used among gentlemen (Book I, 20)[96]"

The ability to use weapons is inseparable from the skill in riding. A gentleman must excel in every kind of equestrian exercise[97] and show the particular skill of the Italian riders in handling even difficult horses and in participating in the lance games (*hastiludium*) and in jousts, and he must match the skill of the French in tournaments and the Spaniards in the games of reeds and in bullfights (that at the time were also held in Italy, especially in the regions under Spanish rule). But this is not enough, because the rider must execute his exercises with grace and good judgment: the two new qualities that characterize the ways of the modern gentleman and at the same time would foreshadow the stylization of Equestrian Art, culminating in the birth of what we now call the High School.

> "I would hope that our Courtier is a perfect horseman in every kind of saddle, and in addition to understanding horses and knowledge of riding, I would have him work diligently to elevate himself a little above others in everything, so that he may be well-recognized for his excellence. And as we read of Alcibiades[98], that he surpassed all the nations with whom he lived, each in their particular province, so I would have our Courtier exceed all others, in each of their best professions. And since it is the special

---

cortegiano debba esser quella dell'arme; la qual sopra tutto voglio che egli faccia vivamente e sia conosciuto tra gli altri per ardito e sforzato e fidele a chi serve." Castiglione, 1528, p. 25.

96) "*E perciò voglio che egli sia di bona disposizione e de' membri ben formato, e mostri forza e leggerezza e discioltura, e sappia de tutti gli esercizi di persona, che ad uom di guerra s'appartengono; e di questo penso il primo dever essere maneggiar ben ogni sorte d'arme a piedi ed a cavallo e conoscere i vantaggi che in esse sono, e massimamente aver notizia di quell'arme che s'usano ordinariamente tra' gentilomini.* Castiglione, 1528, p. 29.

97) Between the equestrian exercises vital for the education of the gentleman, Castiglione also includes vaulting, as "although it be fatiguing and difficult, makes a man very light and dexterous more than any other thing" (Book I, 22). Castiglione, 1528, p. 31.

98) Athenian statesman and general in the Peloponnesian War: brilliant, courageous, and unstable, he defected to the Spartans in 415, but returned and led the Athenian victories at Abydos (411) and Cyzicus (410).

pride of the Italians to ride well with the bridle [*a la brida*], to school wild horses with consummate skill, and to play at tilting and jousting—in these things let him be among the best of the Italians. In tournaments and in the arts of defence and attack, let him shine among the best in France. In lance throwing, bull-fighting and in casting spears and darts, let him excel among the Spaniards. But above everything, he should temper all his movements with a certain good judgment and grace, if he wishes to merit that universal favor which is so greatly prized (Book I, 21)[99]."

Grace, the supreme virtue of the courtier, is the ability to veil the difficulties and the fatigue of the more daring deeds, the most complex works, as well as of the more challenging physical exercises.

"But having often wondered whence this inborn grace springs, aside from those men who have it naturally, I find one universal rule concerning it, which seems to me worth more in this matter than any other in all things human that are done or said: to avoid affectation to the utmost as if it were a very sharp and dangerous rock; and to possibly use a new word, to practise in everything a certain nonchalance [the word in Italian is *sprezzatura*] that shall conceal design and show that what is done and said is done without effort and almost without thinking (Book I, 26)[100]."

"Grace—as well, explains Giorgio Patrizi—stands as a quality of appearing, of dissimulating, of showing "nature" or rather "naturalness" where there is artifice. If affectation is the excess of art and excess of imitation, *sprezzatura*

---

99) « *Però voglio che 'l nostro cortegiano sia perfetto cavalier d'ogni sella, ed oltre allo aver cognizion di cavalli e di ciò che al cavalcare s'appartiene, ponga ogni studio e diligenzia di passar in ogni cosa un poco più avanti che gli altri, di modo che sempre tra tutti sia per eccellente conosciuto. E come si legge d'Alcibiade che superò tutte le nazioni presso alle quali egli visse e ciascuna in quello che più era suo proprio, così questo nostro avanzi gli altri, e ciascuno in quello di che più fa professione. E perché degli Italiani è peculiar laude il cavalcare bene a la brida, il maneggiar con ragione massimamente cavalli aspri, il correr lance e 'l giostrare, sia in questo de' migliori Italiani; nel torneare, tener un passo, combattere una sbarra, sia bono tra i miglior Franzesi; nel giocare a canne, correr tori, lanzar aste e dardi, sia tra i Spagnoli eccellente. Ma sopra tutto accompagni ogni suo movimento con un certo bon giudicio e grazia, se vole meritar quell'universal favore che tanto s'apprezza.* » Castiglione, 1528, pp. 30–31.

100) « *Ma avendo io già più volte pensato meco onde nasca questa grazia, lasciando quelli che dalle stelle l'hanno, trovo una regula universalissima, la qual mi par valer circa questo in tutte le cose umane che si facciano o dicano più che alcuna altra, e ciò è fuggir quanto più si può, e come un asperissimo e pericoloso scoglio, la affettazione; e, per dir forse una nova parola, usar in ogni cosa una certa sprezzatura, che nasconda l'arte e dimostri ciò che si fa e dice venir fatto senza fatica e quasi senza pensarvi.* » Castiglione, 1528, p. 35.

is the dissimulation of art"[101]. It is significant that Castiglione, an expert horse breeder, as testified by the correspondence with his mother from the court of Rome,[102] uses an equestrian example to explain the "most universal rule" with which a noble must conform in order to become a modern gentleman:

> "You see how ungraceful a rider is who strives to sit bolt upright in the saddle in the manner we call 'Venetian' as compared with another who seems not to be thinking about it, and sits his horse as free and steady as if he were on foot (Book I, 27)[103]."

The comparison used by Castiglione not only clarifies the discriminating factor that identifies a gentleman, but also expresses the canon of classical riding that has been handed down almost unchanged from the Renaissance to today[104]. According to this criterion, excellence can only be achieved when even the most difficult exercise is carried out by the rider with absolute confidence, that is to say disguising the effort and the aids with which he directs his mount, which appears to perform the exercises in the most natural way, almost by himself. From this point on, equitation becomes an ever more refined pursuit of indescribable communication with the animal, that has the purpose of reproducing on command the most elegant and energetic natural aptitudes of the horse, hiding the hindrance produced by the weight of the rider. Fully consistent with classical aesthetics that informed the Renaissance, riding is sublimated in the supreme paradox: using the maximum artifice to attain maximum naturalness. Thus, the equestrian art is considered the privileged domain of the "*sprezzatura*" and becomes the essential discipline for the education of the gentleman. Through equitation, nobles learn the art of command, but also of

---

101) Patrizi, 1984, p. 866.

102) See Mazzoleni, 2002, p. 40 and Quondam, 2003, p. 195.

103) "*Vedete come un cavalier sia di mala grazia, quando si sforza d'andare così stirato in su la sella e, come noi sogliam dire, alla veneziana, a comparazion d'un altro, che paia che non vi pensi e stia a cavallo così disciolto e sicuro come se fosse a piedi.*" Castiglione, 1528, p. 37.

104) By way of example, we cite below some excerpts of some of the greatest equestrian writers of the eighteenth, nineteenth and twentieth centuries, which show the persistence of the Renaissance canon in the equestrian art. "*Grace* is such a beautiful ornament for a Rider and at the same time such an important encouragement to science that all those who want to become Horsemen must, before anything else, take the time necessary to acquire this quality. By grace, I mean an air of ease and freedom [...] and that the movements of the Rider are so subtle that they serve rather to embellish his seat, than to help the horse," LA GUÉRINIÈRE, 1733, p. 82–83; "Nothing in the rider must show the effort or emphasize his commands [...]. In some way, the rider must forget himself, to become one with his horse," L'HOTTE, 1906, p. 172; "Without grace there is no refined equitation and without finesse it's impossible to think about art. Hardness and strength are the prerogative of mediocre people, who do not ever want to be true.," OLIVEIRA, 1991, p. 309.

self-control, as they must learn to lead the animal and at the same time to refine their sensibility and their technical skill to hide from the eyes of the observers the means by which their control is exerted. Consequently, the equestrian art changes and is coded to progressively enhance his "artistic" qualities. The old ordeals of chivalry, jousts and tournaments, are too violent and too risky to be compatible with the new code of grace and "*sprezzatura*"[105] and are replaced by spectacles, such as the triumphal cavalcades, the carousels and the equestrian ballets[106]. In addition to utilitarian equitation, mainly directed towards the art of war, then a more refined way to ride a horse develops. It is characterized by exercises designed to show the skill of the rider and the perfect submission of the animal, which in time will be structured in a code (the so-called "school airs") to constitute the elements of real equestrian choreography.

You may be born noble, but you have to become a gentleman. The model established by the humanists prescribes a course of training that integrates the profession of arms with the supreme ornament of the knowledge of letters and of arts. Riding is also a crucial part of this educational process, which found its fulfillment in the birth of the equestrian academies: the institutions where, in addition to the art of riding, the humanities, music, mathematics and drawing were taught[107]. This educational paradigm stands out in Europe and becomes the common feature of all the aristocracy on the continent. The young scions began to travel in order to become disciples of the best teachers, especially to Italy, where they were attracted by the reputation of riders, artists and writers. Thus arrived the *grand tour*—the educational journey that, for at least four centuries, represented a fundamental aspect of the educational process of the European aristocracy—and the desire to learn the art of riding in its most sophisticated form is one of the reasons that mandated it as an obligation for the young nobles.

The most beautiful and valiant knight of the century: Galeazzo Sanseverino

Castiglione emphasizes the importance of learning the equestrian art from good teachers and cites the figure of Galeazzo Sanseverino that we have already met in Milan, next to the king of France, Francis I.

> "Although it is almost a proverb that grace is not to be learned, I say that whoever would acquire grace in bodily exercises (assuming first that he is not naturally incapable),

---

105) See Balestracci, 2001.

106) See Tucker, 2007; Baldassarri, 1985, Gareffi, 1982.

107) See Chapter VIII.

ought to begin early and learn the rudiments from the best masters. [...] And of the men we know at the present day, consider how well and gracefully my lord Galeazzo Sanseverino, Grand Equerry of France, performs all bodily exercises; and because in addition to the natural aptitude he possesses, he has taken utmost pains to study with good masters, and always to have about him, men who excel and to select from each the best of what they know (Book I, 25)[108]"

The figure of Sanseverino is one of the most eminent among those of the many Italian riders in the sixteenth century in service in the European courts. Descendant of a family of Neapolitan origin, son of Roberto, one of the most important *condottiere* of the Duchy of Milan, Galeazzo came as a young man in the service of Ludovico il Moro, who gave him in marriage his eldest illegitimate daughter, Bianca, in January 1496, giving in dowry the fiefdom of Voghera. Following the Battle of Novara in 1500, he was imprisoned by the French, but after a few months, thanks to a ransom paid by his brothers, was freed. Then he was the guest of Emperor Maximilian[109], in Insbruck for two years. Thanks to the intervention of his brother, Federico, who was an influential cardinal, he went to France in the service of Louis XII. He became Knight of the Order of St. Michael and Grand Equerry of King Francis I. With the French army he took part in all the battles in Italy, from Agnadello to Pavia, where he died on the 24th of February 1525. Monique Chatenet[110] recalls his great riding skill in an episode that dates back to the marriage of the Duke of Urbino, Lorenzo II de Medici[111], held in Amboise, the 5th of May 1518. On that occasion, at the end of the joust celebrating the marriage, Sanseverino mounted a Mantuan horse in the presence of the king and his court, with which he performed two magnificent series of jumps, proving despite his age a force that aroused the wonder of all of those present. Paolo Cortesi (1465–1510) in his *De cardinalatu*[112] states that he had the habit of mounting without

---

108) "*Benché è sia quasi in proverbio che la grazia non s'impari, dico che chi ha da esser aggraziato negli esercizi corporali, presuponendo prima che da natura non sia inabile, dee cominciar per tempo ed imparar i princípi da ottimi maestri [...]. E delli omini che noi oggidì conoscemo, considerate come bene ed aggraziatamente fa il signor Galleazzo Sanseverino, gran scudiero di Francia tutti gli esercizi del corpo; e questo perché, oltre alla natural disposizione ch'egli tiene della persona, ha posto ogni studio d'imparare da bon maestri ed aver sempre presso di sé omini eccellenti e da ognun pigliar il meglio di ciò che sapevano.*" Castiglione, 1528, p. 34.

109) Maximilian I of Habsburg (1459—1519) was Emperor of the Holy Roman Empire from 1493 until his death.

110) Chatenet, 2002, p. 56–57.

111) Lorenzo (1493—1519) was duke of Urbino from 1516 to 1519.

112) Cortesi, 1510, libro II, capitolo VI.

stirrups, "in the Spanish way"[113]. Pietro Del Monte[114] in his *Exercitiorum atque artis militaris collectanea*[115] describes him as a skilled *voltigeur* on horseback, and inventor of several of more than thirty "vaults" (that is to say vaulting exercises), which the author describes in his work[116]. The magnificent horses cared for by Sanseverino, at the time when he was serving Ludovico il Moro, were used by Leonardo da Vinci as models for the preparatory drawings of the equestrian monument of Francesco Sforza[117]. Leonardo himself designed the apparatus of the great tournament that was held in the house of Sanseverino, in Milan, in honor of the wedding of Ludovico il Moro and Beatrice d'Este, celebrated in January 1491[118]. Sanseverino was, along with Giovanni Ratti, Federico Gonzaga's master of equitation.

---

113) It should be noted that the habit of mounting without stirrups to perform school jumps (or airs above the ground) is still in use in the four European schools of Vienna, Saumur, Jerez de la Frontera and Lisbon.

114) Another historical figure quoted by Castiglione in the *Book of the Courtier*, indicating him as master of the same Sanseverino (Book I, chap. 25) in the use of weapons. Descendant of a cadet branch of the Marquis of Bourbon del Monte Santa Maria, he was remembered for his deeds also by Guicciardini and Bembo. Born around 1450, he died at the Battle of Agnadello in 1509, sided in the ranks of the Venetian army, led by Bartolomeo d'Alviano, that opposed that of his friend and student Sanseverino, who was fighting for Louis XII.

115) See Del Monte, 1509.

116) The excerpts of Del Monte's work about vaulting are published and translated into French in Fontaine, 2002.

117) Cfr. Huyghe, 1988 e Bernardoni, 2007. In 1482 Ludovico il Moro commissioned to Leonardo da Vinci an equestrian monument of his father, Francesco, who was duke from 1452 to 1466 and founder of the House of Sforza. The statue, which would be a horse in the act of rearing, was to be the largest ever built. Leonardo studied in depth the best specimens that were in the ducal stables, carrying out numerous preparatory drawings. Among his notes are comments like, "Morel Fiorentino is big and has a nice neck and a very beautiful head," or "Ronzone, white, has nice hind legs and is located in Porta Comasina." The work proceeded very slowly, raising the apprehension of Ludovico. The project was changed, because the realization of the rampant horse posed too many problems of balance and was replaced by a walking horse. However, the proportions were increased, and they became huge, at least four times the natural ones. In 1491, Leonardo prepared a model made of clay, which was exhibited in 1493. At that point, however, there were more than 100 tons of bronze needed for the casting, but all the metal was used for cannons to defend the Duchy of Este from the French troops of Louis XII. Leonardo abandoned the project and left Milan. When in 1499 the French, led by Giacomo Trivulzio, conquered Milan, the model that was kept in the Castello Sforzesco was destroyed by the soldiers, who used it as a target for firing with their muskets and their crossbows.

118) See Leonardo da Vinci, 1998, pp. 131–134.

Pirro Antonio Ferraro, *Cavallo Frenato,* Napoli, Pace, 1602. The growing importance of riding in the formation of Renaissance gentleman put emphasis on the transmission of the equestrian knowledge, highlighting the fundamental relationship between master and disciple.

The transmission of equestrian knowledge

The growing importance riding assumed in the education of Renaissance gentlemen emphasized transmission of equestrian knowledge, which was becoming structured in a code of exercises designed to exalt the qualities of the rider, in particular his "*sprezzatura.*" It was [and remains] an extremely difficult challenge, due to the fact that the essence of riding involves the relation with another living being, and therefore could not be simply reduced to technique. In fact, it requires the rider to be athletic, knowledgeable about the exercises necessary for war and spectacular performances, and to have knowledge of the animal, mastery of the means to submit the horse to the will of the rider and experience in the methods of how to train him. This resulted in the need for a thorough systematization of equestrian art for educational purposes and for a method to effectively disperse this knowledge. This evolution led to what is perhaps the most important paradigm shift in modern equitation, namely the publication of the first treatises devoted entirely to the art of riding horses[119]. Although these books, which gained an immediate success throughout Europe[120], could not replace the fundamental relationship between master and disciple[121] they contributed to a deep transformation of equitation into a cultivated occupation, susceptible to speculative elaboration that could elevate it from the status of a mere practical discipline. As Patrice Franchet d'Esperey acutely observes, it is writing that makes possible the birth, since the Renaissance, of an educated (*savant*) equitation, which for centuries to come would develop into a discipline that has the traits of an esoteric practice, in which the physical exercise and the relationship with the animal lead to the rarefied territory of the spiritual quest.

For the reasons we have seen above, it is therefore no coincidence that the first equestrian treatise, *Gli ordini di cavalcare*, was printed in Naples, by the printing office of Giovan Paolo Suganappo in 1550. Since then, the name of its author, Federico Grisone, Neapolitan gentleman, is remembered as the "father of Equestrian Art."[122]

---

119) On the other hand, the printed publication of the first equestrian treatises is placed in the larger current of the treatises about behavior, which is inaugurated by Castiglione's book: "a work unique, isolated in an unrepeatable architectural complexity; but, at the same time, a proliferating work, with a very large descent." Patrizi, 1984, p. 855. Patrizi defines the equestrian treatises as a "paradoxical technical translation of the courtly discourse." Patrizi, 1984, p. 887.

120) Studying the disposition by will of the time, Leandro Perini demonstrated that the books dedicated to horses and riding were, in addition to Castiglione's *Courtier* and to Alciato's *Duello* (*Duel*, 1541), among the most popular in the libraries of noble, or however wealthy families, of Prato, Florence and of other Tuscan cities. See Perini, 1983.

121) On this point see the fundamental study by Patrice Franchet d'Esperey: 2007.

122) Podhajsky, 1965, p. 18.

II
The first treatises dedicated to the horse

The oldest written text dedicated to the care of the horse is one by Kikkuli, squire of the king of the Hittites Suppiluliuma, dating to a period between 1375 and 1335 BC. It was found engraved on five clay tablets in cuneiform, among thousands unearthed during the excavations conducted by Hugo Winckler in the site Boghaz-köy, in Central Anatolia in 1906[123]. The text is a type of manual on the care and training of chariot horses of the Hittite army. At that time, cavalry was still relatively unknown to the civilizations that flourished around the Mediterranean. The text describes a detailed training program, lasting 184 days. For each of these days was prescribed the rations of feed, the number of waterings, the workouts and the periods of rest.

About a thousand years later the Greek, Xenophon (who lived approximately between 430 and 335 BC) wrote the first equestrian treatise that survives in its entirety. This is *The Art of Horsemanship* (*Péri Hippikés*)[124], a work still amazing for the subtlety with which it portrays the relationship between horse and rider, consecrating it as a real touchstone for the equestrian treatises that followed. The author's interest concentrated on the warhorse, with some references to parades. Five chapters are devoted to equitation itself. Others relate to the purchase of the horse, the training of foals (that Xenophon treats rather quickly, suggesting to entrust it to a professional), the care of the animal and the instructions for the groom. The last chapter describes the armament of the rider. Xenophon is also the author of another text of similar subject, the *Hipparchikos*, dedicated to the duties of the commander of the cavalry, but it has more the character of a manual of military technique and of a guide for those wishing to pursue a political career. The command of the cavalry in Athens was in fact attributed to two generals who were elected annually by the city assembly (*ecclesia*) and who held a position of great political and military prestige. These two works have been handed down by a score of manuscripts, dating from a period from the thirteenth to the sixteenth century. In Italy, the Greek text was first printed in Florence by Filippo Giunta, in 1516. The first to translate it into Italian was Evangelista Ortense, attendant to the Duke of Mantua. The work was published, in

---

123) Monteilhet, 1979 e Neyland, 2008. About the horse in ancient times see Sestili, 2012.

124) Senofonte, 2007. See also Sistili, 2006 e AA.VV., 2008.

Venice, under the title *Il modo di cavalcare* (*The way to ride*), by the editor Franco Ziletti in 1580[125] and dedicated to Vincenzo Gonzaga[126].

There are various other works of the classical age about the horse, its breeding and its diseases, but none specifically dedicated to riding as was that of Xenophon. Among the works devoted to the beginnings of veterinary medicine, we can mention those of the so-called Greek Hippiatres, which had a relatively wide circulation in the Middle Ages, those of Hierocles (Bartolomeo da Messina translated into Latin his *De curatione equorum* in the mid-thirteenth century), Eroteus (whose works belong to the corpus of texts of the pseudo-Hippocrates translated from Arabic by Moisé from Palermo in the thirteenth century) and Apsyrtus (whose work was partly translated into the nineth book of Claudio Emerote's *Mulomedicina* in the first century AD). The *Digesta Artis mulomedicinalis* (or *Mulomedicina*) of Vegetius (fifth century AD) also had a great influence.

In medieval times, the theme of the care and breeding of the horse is often treated in texts of encyclopedic character. For example, the *Geopónica*, overall a work about agronomy, was compiled in Constantinople under the Emperor Constantine VII Porphyrogenitus (X century), whose sixteenth book is about how to breed, attend, treat and feed the horse, the donkey and the camel. Other examples include *Liber de animalibus* by Albert the Great (1206–1280), *De rerum proprietatibus* by Bartholomew de Glanville, English (XIII c.), and the *Ruralium Commodorum libri XII* (1304) by Pietro de' Crescenzi.

Giordano Ruffo of Calabria

Of particular importance is the treatise of Giordano Ruffo of Calabria, *Miles in Marestalla*[127] in the court of Frederick II. Born around 1200, in Gerace or Monteleone di Calabria, he wrote a work transmitted through a manuscript tradition under various titles: *Mariscalcia equorum*, *Liber de curis equorum*, *Cyrurgia equorum*[128]. The text was definitely written in Latin, although there are different versions in other languages: Tuscan, Sicilian,

---

125) The translation of Ortense was reprinted in AA.VV., 2008, edited by Patrizia Arquint and Mario Gennero.

126) Vincenzo I Gonzaga (1562—1612), son of Guglielmo, Duke of Mantua and Monferrato and Eleanor of Austria. He succeeded his father in 1587.

127) According to Riccardo Gualdo, the charge corresponds to the role of an officer of the second order. "The *marestalla*, which included stables and studs, is the core of the *aratie*, real farms for equine production." Gualdo, 2005.

128) Ruffo, 1999 e 2002.

Catalan, Provençal, French and also in German[129]. A Hebrew version is also known, testifying to its widespread diffusion. The work is divided into six parts. The first four books are about breeding, feeding, reproduction, hygiene, taming and training, bits and shoeing (in this case, Ruffo takes the tradition of the Arab, *hippiatres* who first treated these subjects in a direct way) and the physical structure of the horse. The last two are devoted to describing diseases, which are divided into natural (Book V), and accidental (Book VI). The latter devoted the bulk of the text: fifty-nine chapters, goes through various diseases and their treatment.

The chapters devoted to taming and training are pretty basic, but they give an idea of the equestrian practices of the time and contain precepts that will be found again in later works (some of which are still in use today). Ruffo recommends keeping the horse tethered in the stable, to prevent him from hurting his limbs, and to prepare a deep bedding of straw up to his knees. There are also dietetic suggestions, to keep the horse neither too thin nor too fat. It is also suggested to water him with turbid water, because it was considered more "nutritious" (*"ideoque efficientur equorum corporibus nutribiliores refectiores ad plenum"*). The author advises against riding in the evening, because in the cooler hours of the night, it was more difficult to make the sweat dry completely before the animal was brought back to the stable. Similarly he warns not to ride in the hottest months of summer and in the coldest of winter. Shoeing must be done with light steel horseshoes, but he recommends not to shoe the horse when he is too young, to avoid damaging his hooves.

At the beginning of the training, Ruffo recommends to use the lightest bit as possible (*"frenum debile et levius"*), making sure to smear it with honey or some other sweet syrup, to make it more pleasant to the horse. Once harnessed, the horse must be led by hand by a groom until he has learned to follow him obediently. Only then he can be mounted, without saddle or spurs, and accustomed to turn to the left and to the right. After about a month he can be mounted with the saddle and trained gradually to trot on tilled soil, so that he learns to raise his feet well. It is also recommended to train him to

---

129) Among the various versions we mention, as a curiosity, even that of the Renaissance polygraph Michelangelo Biondo (1500–1565 approx.) The work appeared in 1549 in the printing that Biondo himself started in Venice, entitled *Della domatione del poledro, del suo amaistramento, della conseruatione della sanita' del cavallo . ... da incerto philosopho antichamente scritta . ... nuouamente percio' venuta nelle mani del Biondo, da lui tradutta in lingua materna, et data in luce*. It is mentioned in Deblaise, 2002 and Angioni, 2006, as "the first book that came to light in Italy about the horse and his training." As the title warns, it is not an original work, but a translation into the vernacular of the text by Ruffo. As attested unequivocally in the Census of the Italian editions of the sixteenth century (Edit 16) by the Central Institute for the Union Catalogue of Italian Libraries (CNCE 23882).

turn, especially to the right because—it is said—horses naturally tend to turn easier to the left ("*quod equus est naturaliter pronior a sinistris*"). Once trained to trot, the horse can be ridden at the canter, but kept in a collected gait ("*in minore et breviore saltu*") and for short distances, to avoid tiring him. He also recommends both at the trot and at the canter, to keep the contact with the bit, to progressively bend the horse's neck, in order to control him better and to let him see the ground where he places his feet. To accustom him to the noise and to the crowd, Ruffo suggests to ride him often in the city, especially in noisy places (for example, where there are blacksmiths' forges), taking care not to punish him if he's initially scared and unwilling, in order to prevent him from later associating noise and movement with punishments, but on the contrary, to gently encourage him ("*blandendo ducatur*").

Nonetheless, there are also suggestions that today make us shudder. According to Ruffo, when the horse has attained his full adult teeth, his four canine teeth (*scaglioni*) must be pulled out, because they're considered adverse to the mouthpiece ("*a pluribus nuncupantur freni morsui continui adversantes*"). According to the author, the operation would also have the advantage of preventing the horse from becoming excessively fat and, if he is wild, to appease his ardent character. The bit recommended for colts is the one that in later periods would be called the "cannon," consisting of two transversal bars and one in width "*ad duas barras extransverso et una per longum composita est*"). The author then also mentions stronger bits, with twisted or grooved mouthpieces, or with a small shovel that acts on the palate, but he advises not to use them because he considers them too strong and, for this reason, he does not dwell on them. He also underlines that once the right mouthpiece is found for the sensibility of the animal, it must not be changed with others of different shape, not to ruin his mouth. The horse must be trained to stop and to respect the bit, before beginning work at a faster pace. The canter must be practiced on progressively longer distances, but without abuse, and to avoid letting the horse get too tired and becoming restistant. Similarly, he must be urged frequently to avoid that he becomes lazy.

Ruffo's text had a wide diffusion and had a considerable influence on the chapters devoted to the cures of the horse by Pietro de' Crescenzi and on the subsequent treaties about the art of farriery[130] by Lorenzo Rusio (about 1340)[131] and by the Florentine Dino Dini (1352–1359), up to the *Anatomia del cavallo infermita et suoi rimedii* ((*Anatomy of the horse, his infirmities and remedies*, 1598), the work by Carlo Ruini, the Renaissance precursor of veterinary medicine.

---

130) It's important to notice that, at the time, the farrier was not only the horseshoer, but also the veterinarian.

131) Born in 1288 and died in 1347. He practiced farriery in Rome after 1320. He dedicated his treatise to his patron Cardinal Napoleone Orsini.

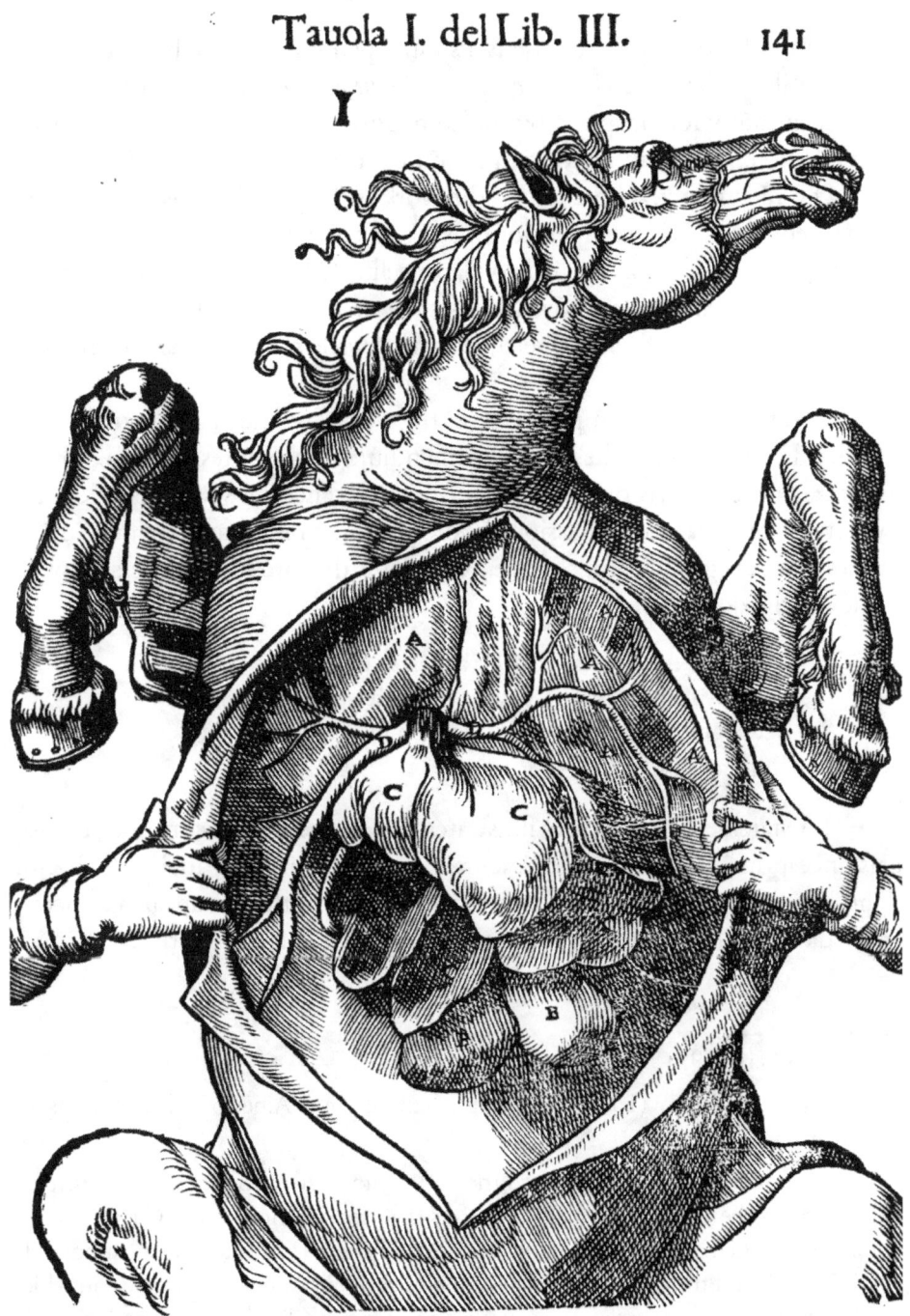

The tradition of the medieval treatises on farriery makes a qualitative leap with the work of the Bolognese Carlo Ruini dedicated to *Anatomy of the Horse* (*L'Anatomia del cavallo*, 1598), which anticipates modern veterinary medicine.

De equo animante by Leon Battista Alberti

An echo of Ruffo's treatise is also in a pamphlet of the humanist Leon Battista Alberti (1404–1472), *De equo animante*[132], a sort of erudite exercise that the author wrote inspired by the competition, launched in 1443, for the creation in Ferrara of an equestrian monument in honor of Niccolò III d'Este[133], who died two years earlier[134]. The work is dedicated to his son and successor, Leonello[135]. The competition was attended by two Florentine sculptors: Antonio di Cristoforo and Niccolò Baroncelli. Although the Council of the Twelve Wise of the city approved the sketch of the first of the two, Leonello decided to rely on his friend Alberti, "*as judge and expert,*" the task of choosing between the two projects.

From an equestrian perspective, the work does not have particular interest and consists of a rather short compendium of the notes expressed by the medieval encyclopedias on farriery, with reminiscences of several classical and Byzantine authors. The discussion devoted to the taming and training of the warhorse is very generic and concise. Relevant is the intention expressed by the author in the dedication:

> "As for the others, I wish that in reading my work, they keep in mind that I have not written for the farriers or the grooms, but for a prince, who is in addition, very erudite."[136]

A statement that clearly illustrates that in the new decorum of the Renaissance prince, equitation represents a cultural shift that included, by full right, the equestrian art in the evolutionary process of the European aristocracy at the dawn of the modern age. Amedeo Quondam writes effectively:

---

132) See Alberti, 1991.

133) Marquis of Ferrara (1383—1441), the natural son of Alberto V d'Este and Isotta Albaresani.

134) The monument was inaugurated the 26th of June 1461. The statue was destroyed at the time of the Jacobin riot of 1796, after the proclamation of the Cispadana Republic and melted together with that of Borso d'Este (1454), to make cannons. In 1864 the arch and the columns that were their basement were rediscovered, on which in 1926 were placed the two copies made by Giacomo Zilocchi, which today can be found on the facade of the Palazzo Comunale of Ferrara.

135) Leonello d'Este (1407—1450), was the second of the three illegitimate children that Nicolò III d'Este had from Stella de Tolomei. He was Marquis of Ferrara from 1441.

136) «*Quanto agli altri, vorrei che nel leggermi tengano presente che io non ho scritto per i maniscalchi o per gli stallieri ma per un principe, e per giunta eruditissimo.*» Alberti, 1991, p. 96.

"this is the decisive argument shift in the foundation of the modern hippological discourse: from the skill of the profession devoted to the horse, to the most sophisticated competence of its necessary referent [the prince]: by culture, not by nature. From this moment on, the horse enters the system [in semiology art is considered a "system of signs"] of art and virtue[137]."

Although up until the XV century, works devoted to farriery and horse breeding were relatively plentiful, we do not find texts specifically dedicated to equitation, with the exception of Xenophon's treatise. This apparent imbalance is probably due to the fact that riding was considered a practice difficult to reduce to a doctrine transmitted through writing. This conception wasn't due to the fact that it was practiced by illiterates, as it was the prerogative of kings, princes and of the elite of aristocracy. In fact, as we will see in more detail in the following chapters, the authors of treatises on the subject, in particular Grisone and Fiaschi, were well aware of the difficulty of condensing the complex nuances of the equestrian art into the necessarily schematic precepts of a manual. What changed this approach and stimulated the production of works dedicated to horse riding was not so much a change in riding techniques, but the maturation of the classicistic[138] educational project for the new figure of a gentleman. The interest of an intellectual like Alberti in the horse, even if frankly with a disappointing outcome and with the clear intent to please his powerful protector, shows how this evolutionary process was slowly coming to an end between the fifteenth and sixteenth centuries. And this was not an isolated case. Another refined intellectual of that age, Enea Silvio Piccolomini, who would become Pope under the name of Pius II[139], during his stay in Vienna, July 4, 1444, addressed to Wilhelm von Stein a letter/treatise entitled *De natura et cura equorum*, which resumed materials and quotations from Albert the Great, Virgil, Isidore and others[140].

On the other hand, even if there weren't printed works on equitation before the publication of Grisone's treatise in 1550, we know that horsemen often passed on their "secrets" to the narrow circle of their disciples in manuscript form. The horse and the care of the stables are also frequently the subject of correspondence between princes and sovereigns. For example, Ferdinand of

---

137) Quondam, 2003, p. 191.

138) Classicism is the tendency typical of the humanistic and Renaissance period, at the turn of the fifteenth and sixteenth century, to refer to models derived from the ancient Greeks and Romans, both in the arts, both in the field of politics and moral. The term has come to designate this specific side of Italian Renaissance culture.

139) Enea Silvio Piccolomini (1405—1464) became Pope in 1458.

140) See Coco-Gualdo, 2008.

Aragon wrote in various letters, equestrian topics, showing a particular sensibility for the animal, and a clear understanding of the principles expressed by Giordano Ruffo of Calabria on bits and the taming of the foal.[141]

Antonello Scilla: the Horse discipline (*Diciplina de'cavalli*)

It is precisely to Ferdinand of Aragon that a certain Antonello Scilla, "master of the stable" from Sciacca, dedicated a text about the "discipline of horses," now preserved in the National Library of Naples[142]. The work, which we couldn't consult directly, is summarily described in two repertoires of the nineteenth century that list the books of the library of the kings of Aragon in Naples. It is included in a paper codex from the end of the fifteenth or the beginning of the sixteenth century, in which are merged together three other incomplete treatises about farriery, one of which is attributed to a certain Gilberto of Gifuni. The philologist Alfonso Miola[143] writes that only one flyleaf of the original leather binding remains and that on that sheet of paper, that serves as frontispiece is written in uppercase "M. Giordano Russo di Calavria." The content, however, is completely different. In the following page, written in red Roman lowercase, there is the following title:

> "Jesus, To the Sacred Royal Majesty of the Wise Prince Don Ferrando of Aragon invincible Italic and always august king. Preface by Antonello scilla, Sicilian native of the ancient city of Siacha: stable master and slave in the service of the aforementioned great Lord: in the book about the discipline of horses and about what kind of bits should be used to moderate and control each of them: he starts happily[144]."

---

141) Mazzoleni, 2002. Se also Lawe, 2005.

142) Biblioteca Nazionale Centrale di Napoli. De Scilla, No.VIII. D.69. ff. 2r–3r. cfr. Lawe, 2005.

143) Miola, 1878, pp. 392–394; Mazzatinti, 1897, pp. LXXXIX–XC e 166.

144) «*Iesu. + Alla Sacra regale Maesta del sapientissimo Principe Don Ferrando Aragonio Invictissimo Re Italico et sempre augusto, Prohemio de Antonello scilla Siculo della veterrima citta de Siacha oriundo: mastro de stalla et creato et minimo mancipio del prefato et optimo Signore: in lo libro della disciplina delli cavalli, et con quali freni se habiano ciascuno a moderare et regere: incomincia felicemente.*»

Follows an introduction that begins:

> "Oh very gracious king, as that great Veronese Pliny neatly describes and tells in the eighth book of his Natural History, the horse is the closest and more adherent animal to the human mind. As with heroic and wonderful examples it is said in the aforementioned book...[145]"

The text ends at page 3r with these words:

> "With every effort I have undertaken to draw and describe any reason and any form of bit for a foal or trained horse, suitable for joust and suitable for every combat and military act that His Majesty may have, while recognizing that in me there is no such intelligence, etc..."

Unworthy servant and slave
Antonello Scilla Sicilian, Master of the stables[146]

Some blank pages follow, then there are the pen and ink drawings of fifty bits. After another couple of blank pages, the manuscript includes three incomplete texts dedicated to farriery[147]. Rather than a true treatise about riding, the text of Scilla is therefore more properly a repertoire of mouthpieces. It is a genre quite common until the end of the sixteenth century. Generally these repertoires of bits supplemented treatises on farriery, as *La Pratica di Maestro Bonifazio dei morbi naturali e accidentali dei cavalli* (Master Boniface's Practice of Natural And Accidental Diseases of Horses, fifteenth century) and the *Trattato dele fateze e cognitione de cavalli, cioè dele boche e d'imbrigliature* (Treatise of Features and Knowledge of the Horse, that is to say about Mouths and Bridles)[148] by Donato from

---

145) « *Secondo descrive et con ordine e narra quel gran Veronese Plinio secondo nel libro octavo della naturale historia, clementissimo Re: trovo el cavallo essere più de tutti l'altri animali al senso humano adherente et propinquante. Come per heroici et mirandi exempli in dicto libro se innotesce e pande..*»

146). "..*me sono con ogni mio conato excogitato adinvenire pingere et figurare ogni ragione e forma de freni per qualunque politro et cavallo facto, apto a giostra et a ogni pugna et acto militare acadesse havere V. M.^{ta} confessando in me non essere tale ingegno, etc. / De V. S. R. M.^{ta} / Indigno creato et schiavo / Antonello scilla Siculo: / Mastro de stalla de quella.*»

147) The first (page50r) is entitled *Per fare consideracione bona de le infirmita de li cavalli*, it is followed (page 56v) by the *Extracto da alcuni Remedii esperimentati per la M.^{ta} del S. re Ferrando primo quali sua M.^{ta} faceva tenere in guardaroba per una singularissima experiensia* and (paper 72V) by the *Remedi experimentati per mastro gilberto de gefuni, maniscalco optimo del signor Re* (which remains incomplete at page 81r).

148) See Bonifacio, 1988; Anonimous, 1983; Coco – Gualdo, 2008; Arquint, 2002 and Arquint, 2004.

Milan, master of the stables of the Duke of Ferrara, Borso d'Este[149]. As we will see in more detail in the following chapters, the art of "bridling properly," that is to say the competence to identify the correct mouthpiece for the different characteristics of each horse, was seen in the fifteenth and sixteenth centuries, as the first virtue of a good horseman. It is possible that, as in many later works, the text of Scilla could have been supplemented by further descriptions (in passages that may have been subsequently lost) of the exemplified bits, which illustrated their characteristics according to the requirements and peculiarities of the different horses.

The equestrian treatise by Dom Duarte, King of Portugal

The first treatise about horse riding that has survived after that of Xenophon is Portuguese. This is the *Livro da ensinança de bem cavalgar toda sela* (The Royal Book of Horsemanship, Jousting & Knightly Combat, Chivalry Bookshelf, 2006)[150]. The author is Edward King of Portugal, known as Dom Duarte (1391–1438), the Philosopher or the Eloquent. He was the eleventh king of Portugal and Algarve and second Lord of Ceuta. He became king on the 14th of August 1433, when his father, Joao I, died of the plague. In addition to equitation, he wrote a treatise entitled *O Leal Conselheiro* (The Faithful Adviser), which laid out a series of behavior rules and models. He also wrote poems. As did his father, mother and grandmother, he died of the plague on the 13th of September 1438.

His book on horse riding has come to us through a manuscript, written around 1434, acquired by the Royal Library of Paris, under Colbert, subsequently copied in 1830 and first published in Paris in 1842. The work, however, hasn't been studied much and only recently began to be mentioned in works on the history of equitation. Yet, as claimed by the Portuguese scholar, Carlos Henriques Pereira, writing it Dom Duarte

> "wrote the first page in history of psychology applied to equestrian sports and probably of sport's pedagogy in general[151]."

The book is intended for horsemen (*scudeiros*) charged with introducing young riders (*mocos*) to the equestrian art.

> "The first concern of the author is how to convey skill or art (*manha*) to future generations; the training of the horse is a minor topic in his work. His philosophy can be

---

149) Borso d'Este (1413—1471), was the illegitimate son of Niccolò III d'Este, Marquis of Ferrara, Duke of Modena and Reggio. He succeeded his brother Leonello d'Este in 1450.

150) Pereira, 2003.

151) Pereira, 2002, p. 141.

summed up in one sentence: The young rider cannot reach the upper spheres of the equestrian art without "spiritualizing" his apprenticeship. Dom Duarte, who had studied the problem of emotionality on horseback, focuses on the psychology of the rider. Since riding demands perfect harmony between horse and rider, a rider who does not know his own emotions cannot reach the upper spheres of the Equestrian Art[152]."

Dom Duarte proposes several solutions to the inexperienced rider to overcome his fear. Above all, he makes an apology of reason that is, along with knowledge, will and exercise the effective means to overcome apprehension. He also lists other less noble means: ignorance, anger, conceit, or the fact of enjoying a particular position of benefit. Then he adds that some people are touched by the divine gift that protects against these types of emotions.

His book is also an indictment against the equitation practiced by the old masters, according to which, young riders should be trained in a brutal way. The horses were not selected according to the needs and abilities of the debutants, which led to many accidents. Then, strength prevailed over intelligence and rash riders who, often acting out of ignorance, rode violently were the most popular.

"On the contrary, Dom Duarte shows that ignorance, the enemy of progress, leads to mediocre equitation. The master horseman cannot ignore the sensitivity of rider and horse. To act with tact, towards both the rider and the horse is an essential principle of his pedagogy."[153]

The treatise of Dom Duarte, influenced by medieval French equitation, is one of the first treatises about the "*gineta*"[154] and is the first codification of bullfighting on horseback. It is a remarkable synthesis of the equestrian tendency of his age. As Pereira magnificently writes, Duarte "un-

---

152) Pereira, 2002, pp. 142.

153) Pereira, 2002, pp. 142.

154) At the time two main types of riding were distinguished. The one called "*a la brida*," typical of Italy and France, and the one called "*a la gineta*" mainly practiced in Spain and Portugal, but afterwards also in the Italian regions under Spanish rule. The first one was characterized by the use of very long stirrups, which required the rider to keep his legs stretched out and forward. It was typical of heavy cavalry, who charged on a straight line with the lance. In the second one the rider used short stirrups and bent knees, resulting in a more immediate contact of the lower aids. Coming from a clear Arabic influence, it fostered a better maneuverability of the horse. It was used not only for military purposes, but also in bullfighting.

derstands that riding, like all human activities, is enhanced through exchanges in all their forms. The equestrian art is not the prerogative of a country, but it is the crossing of the horse's civilizations and thus evolves through the intersection of techniques and knowledge."[155]

---

155) Pereira, 2002, pp. 142.

III
Naples, capital of Renaissance equitation

Although in the sixteenth century equitation had a great diffusion in all the Italian courts and in many cities were founded riding schools and academies to practice the chivalry disciplines[156], one city stands out particularly in the geography of Renaissance equestrian art: Naples.

The tradition of horse breeding in southern Italy dates back to Roman times[157]. It was in the fertile *Campania felix* and in the pastures of Molise and Apulia that Rome mainly supplied remounts for the cavalry. We owe to the Romans the first massive introduction of foreign blood to improve the native breeds. Foreign influences continued with the barbarian invasions, the Norman Conquest and the importation of oriental horses by the armies returning from the crusades[158]. Great impetus to the breeding of horses came from the practice of hunting, especially by falconry, particularly loved by Frederick II of Swabia[159]. His reign coincided with the period of greatest prosperity of the southern regions of Italy, with important demographic and economic consequences. In the field of horse breeding was especially significant what happened in the area of the *Capitanata*[160]. The quantity and quality of horses in northern Apulia increased at the beginning of the thirteenth century thanks to the incisive and systematic intervention of the emperor[161]. Royal farms (*massarie regie*) were created, especially in the lowlands and wetlands of northeastern Apulia, drawing mainly from the oriental equine heritage of the Arabian colonies of Sicily. Frederick intervened on the matter by establishing royal studs, the so-called *aratie*[162]. In Frederick's correspondence there are several mentions

---

156) See Chapter VIII.

157) According to Giuseppe Maresca, who however does not document this claim, the spread of horse breeding in Campania can be pre-dated back to Etruscan times. Maresca—Franchini, 2002, p. 28

158) See Maresca—Franchini, 2002 e Fraddosio, 2010.

159) Frederick II Hohenstaufen (1194—1250) was king of Sicily (from 1198), Duke of Swabia (1212–1216), king of Germany (1212 to 1220). He was elected Emperor of the Romans in 1211, crowned at Aachen in 1215 and again crowned in Rome by Pope Honorius III in 1220.

160) It is an area of northern Apulia which formed an administrative unit in the kingdom of Sicily, then in the kingdom of Naples. Roughly corresponds to present day province of Foggia.

161) See Porsia, 1986 e Gualdo, 2005.

162) See Chapter II, note 5.

of this fact, for example, in a letter of 1239 in which the emperor approved the organization of his *marestalla Sicilie* (Sicily stud farm), establishing how breeding should take place and imposing that the mares be fed with barley to ensure better milk production for the foals. With a regulation in 1241, Frederick also organizes the custody of mares, stallions and foals in pastures, allocates an amount of money for the oil both for lighting for the treatment of the horses and lists qualified personnel, comprising the *marescallus* (the farrier), the *custos equorum* (the guardian of the horses), and the *scuterius* (the groom) [163].

This tradition continued in the following centuries, and received new impetus during the Aragonese and Spanish period. Evidence of the importance attributed to the equine production, the "*razze*" (i.e. the stud farms) of Apulia and Calabria was "directly submitted to the royal administration, through a legal structure which presided over all the technical and economic aspects involved. Under the Major Horseman of the kingdom, essentially a position of honor given to a nobleman of high rank, the actual functions of which were carried out by a lieutenant, stretched a complex system of offices with its own jurisdiction. Each of the two great studs had pastures, stables and a system of guardians and experts in charge of ensuring the safety, health and treatment of animals, under the close supervision of a governor appointed by the Viceroy, with extensive judicial powers"[164]. Likewise, the Spanish viceroy of Naples renewed the royal studs that, since the Aragonese age, were placed in an unhealthy area, near the Maddalena Bridge on the River Sebeto. Under the government of Pedro de Toledo they were subject to several works of improvement. At the time, King Philip II showed particular interest in the studs of the kingdom and gave instructions to the Viceroy personally on this topic.[165]

Equitation in Naples

According to Cesare Paderni[166], the diffusion of the equestrian art in Naples can be traced back to a Byzantine influence. Around 1134, several riders from the circus of Constantinople would have left and reached the city of Campania, where they founded a sort of riding school. Paolo Angioni[167] rightly notes that Paderni does not document in any way this statement, which can also be found in the item *Riding* of the Italian Encyclopaedia

---

163) See Gualdo, 2005.
164) Hernando Sánchez, 1998, p. 285.
165) See Hernando Sánchez, 1998, pp. 284–285.
166) Riding instructor at the Cavalry School of Pinerolo, from 1867 to 1893 (see also Chapter IX). The statement is contained in the written text of his lectures for the course held in Pinerolo in 1891 and cited in Angioni, 2006 and Angioni, 2009.
167) Angioni, 2009, p. 17.

Treccani. However, adds Angioni, it is established that at the fall of Constantinople to Turkish hands in 1453, many Byzantine horsemen fled to Naples and once there, they began to teach their art.

The Spaniards certainly exerted a strong influence on the Neapolitan equestrian culture, although before them, the Angevin already showed a special attention to equine breeding. Charles of Anjou[168] ordered that the breeders should keep the most beautiful mares and the best stallions separate, so that the possesion of their excellent offspring, distinguished for their nobility and beauty, could be limited to the princes and to the grandees of the kingdom[169]. As the contribution of the Aragoneses, we have already seen[170] how horseback riding had a decisive role in the typical splendor of their court. An anonymous chronicle of the time said that Alfonso the Magnanimous had the finest army and the most elegant knights of his time, without comparison to all the knights of the rest of Italy. The same chronicle tells that his son Ferrante was so fond of his coursers that when he could not ride them he spent hours looking at them through the windows of the royal palace[171]. Ferrante's passion for horses[172] was such that in 1472 he minted a copper coin for the kingdom of Naples and Sicily, named just "*cavallo*" (horse). The king's head was portrayed on the obverse and on the reverse there was a "passing"[173] horse. The impetus given by the Aragonese to the Neapolitan equitation is then summed by Pasquale Caracciolo, in his treatise *La gloria del cavallo* (The glory of the horse, 1566):

> And although here the use of combat on Horseback with wonderful dexterity and artifice has always been flourishing, more than in any other part of the world; especially under the Serene Kings of Aragon; who, when they lived in Naples, used to take delight in good riding, renewing every day various equestrian games, thus encouraging the Nobles to do the same, giving them every support and leisure, in order to make them dedicate [themselves] to weapons and Horses[174].

---

168) Son of the king of France, Louis VIII and Blanche of Castile, was born in 1226. Conquered the kingdom of Naples in 1266, defeating in Benevento the last Swabian king, Manfred of Sicily.

169) See Maresca—Franchini, 2002, p. 29.

170) See Chapter I.

171) See Lawe, 2005.

172) In his treatise *Il cavallarizzo* (*The Horseman*), Claudio Corte defines him "very excellent and horse expert" («*Eccellentissimo, e conoscitore de' cavalli*»). CORTE, 1562, p. 27v.

173) In heraldry is so defined a horse portrayed in the act of walking, with the right front leg raised.

174) «*E benché sempre sia stato qui fiorentissimo l'uso de l'armeggiare a Cavallo con meravigliosa destrezza et artificio, più che in altra parte del Mondo; massimamente sotto i serenissimi Re d'Aragona; i quali facendo in Napoli residenza, si come eglino sovra*

The same author exalts the reputation of the many excellent Neapolitan horsemen, who—according to him—were able to train their horses up to such total obedience to the aids that they seemed capable of almost human communication with their rider.

> This illustrious homeland can therefore be glorified more than other cities, being adorned by many excellent men in this very rare and difficult art, who know how to train a horse so that it seems to understand almost with human intellect, the tone of the voice, the gestures, the rewards and the threats of the Rider and exactly obey his will. So that, in a way, it seems that in its actions it became really a man, so that it can do anything but speak.[175]

Even Federico Grisone underlines the importance attached to cavalry by the Aragonese court and the splendor of the royal farms:

> In no age, did cavalry have a greater value than in the time of King Alfonso of Aragon and of the Kings Ferrante the elder and the younger, during which, for the care that they held in it, the horses were provided with a nice diposition and a wonderful attitude...[176]

Neapolitans were famous for their passion for riding and this enthusiam spread far beyond the borders of the kingdom, so that we find its satirical echo even in Shakespeare's *The Merchant of Venice* (1596–1597). In the second scene of the first act, the maid Nerissa reminds the rich heiress Portia of the long list of her suitors. When Nerissa mentions the first as a Neapolitan prince, her mistress replies in this way:

---

modo si dilettavano del ben cavalcare, ogni dì rinovando varij giochi equestri, così inanimavano i Cavalieri a fare il somigliante, dando loro ogni favore et agio oportuno, perché attendessero all'arme et a Cavalli.» CARACCIOLO, 1566, Book II, pp. 140–141

175) «*Ben si può dunque sopra l'altre Città gloriare questa inclita patria adornata di tanti huomini in questa rara e diffìcil' arte eccellentissimi, da i quali ammaestratosi un Cavallo si vede quasi con humano intelletto intendere gli accenti, i gesti, i conforti et le minaccie del Cavaliere, et osservar a punto quanto egli vuole; e in certo modo pare nelle sue attioni divenuto propriamente huomo, sì che non gli manchi altro che la favella.»* CARACCIOLO, 1566, Book II, pp. 140.

176) The quotation is from a manuscript attributed to Grisone which up until now was unknown, entitled *Razze del Regno* (*Breeds of the kingdom*), preserved at the Biblioteca Nacional de España (see Chapter IV), fol. 73v. Thanks to Sabina De Cavi who pointed it out to me.

> NERISSA: First, there is the Neapolitan prince.

> PORTIA: Ay, that's a colt indeed, for he doth nothing but talk of his horse; and he makes it a great appropriation to his own good parts, that he can shoe himself. I am much afeared my lady, his mother played false with a smith[177].

The excessive interest in the exercises of chivalry of the Neapolitan nobility at the expense of the letters was the subject of a controversy widely documented and studied by historians[178]. We find it also mentioned in Torquato Tasso's dialogue *Il Minturno overo della bellezza*, where it is said that in Naples, "musicians and singers, or even wrestlers and fencers and horseback riding teachers" were considered more valuable than the men of letters[179].

Even Montaigne, in Chapter XLVIII of his *Essays*, dedicated to *destriers*, after noting that "in riding skill and elegance no other people surpasses us [meaning the French]" [180], he recalls, however, that during his childhood he admired in Naples the ability of a rider who, riding an unruly horse, proved to have a perfectly steady seat, while he was performing all sorts of exercises:

> During my childhood, in Naples, the prince of Sulmona[181], to show the strength of his position while he was maneuvering a reluctant horse with all sorts of riding exercises kept below his knees and under his toes some reals [coins called *reals* the word in Italian means "royal"], as if they were nailed.

The episode is already reported in Caracciolo's *La gloria del cavallo*, which may be the source that inspired Montaigne to his "memory." At the end of the second book of his treatise, listing the famous riders of the city of Naples, Caracciolo wrote:

> Don Carlo of Lanoia, Prince of Solmone,
> Who exercising admirably in every way on horseback, among other trials made two which aroused great admiration and were told to me by reliable persons: once

---

177) Shakespeare, 1992, p. 19.

178) See Hernando Sánchez, 1998, p. 293 e n. 19.

179) Tasso 1958, Vol. II, p. 918.

180) Montaigne, 1966, p. 383.

181) This is Charles de Lannoy (1538–1566), Prince of Sulmona and Ortonamare, son of Philppe de Lannoy and Isabella Colonna (1513–1570), Duchess of Traetto. He married in Naples in 1559, Constanza Doria Carretto (1543–1591). His grandfather, Charles de Lannoy (1487–1527), was viceroy of Naples, for Charles V, from 16 July 1522 to 20 October 1523.

he rode with a flat saddle and without stirrups a very wild horse, keeping between the saddle and the boot, in the place of the knees, two large silver coins, that never moved; and another time keeping them with the same firmness between the feet and the stirrups, running fast with a horse. He participated in jousting with lances of enormous size and often using saddles without cantles, to show greater strength and agility[182].

The beauty of the horses and the skill of the riders were part of the image of the city of Naples and were considered one of its main attractions. In 1569, Luigi Contarino wrote that:

> not only in Italy, Spain, Turkey, but throughout the world there isn't such a rare beauty of horses as in such a noble and wonderful city, which for the natural quality of the air causes men to take delight in these beautiful horses and in the art of riding, in which are exercised not only Mercenaries [i.e. professionals] to earn their living, but also any and all honorable gentlemen and riders for pleasure. Through the practice of riding all of these people become elevated just as were Alexander the Great, Caesar and the same Mars. And to learn this beautiful art of riding, men of all conditions come to Naples from all parts of Europe, some to become perfect masters, and many nobles instead, for their solace, delight and pleasure, as the king of Naples did in ancient times, when they lived in the city, especially the Aragonese...[183]

---

182) «*Don Carlo di Lanoia, Principe di Solmone. Il quale mirabilmente in tutti i modi essercitandosi a cavallo, tra l'altre prove ne fè due di molta ammiratione, che persone degne di fede mi han raccontate: di aver una volta maneggiato, con sella rasa, e senza staffe un cavallo asprissimo, portando tra la sella, e lo stivale nel luogo delle ginocchia due monete grosse d'argento, che mai non se ne mossero, e un'altra haver con la medesima saldezza ritenuti sotto il piede in sù la staffa, correndo un velocissimo cavallo a tutta briglia. Giostrava egli con lance di smisurata grandezza, e spesso in selle senza arcione di dietro, per dimostrare maggiore forza e agilità.*» CARACCIOLO, 1566, Libro II, pp. 143–144.

183) «*non solamente in Italia, in Spagna, in Turchia, ma in tutto il mondo non vi sia una bellezza così rara de cavalli, come in si nobil e meravigliosa Città, la qual per natural inclinatione et proprietà di aria produce gli'huomini dillettarsi di questi bellissimi cavalli et dell'arte del cavalcare, nella quale non solamente si essercitano li Mercenarii per guadagnarsi il pane, ma per diletto ogni et qualunque honorato gentilhuomo et cavallieri, li quali essercitandosi nel cavalcare riescono tanti Allessandri magni, tanti Cesari e tanti Marti, et per ben intender questa bell'arte del cavalcare, concorrono da tutte le parti di Europa in Napoli huomini di ogni conditione, alcuni per diventar perfetti maestri, et molti nobili poi per lor consolatione diletto e piacere, si come antiquamente ne fecero li Re di Napoli,*

The horse in Naples at the time of Viceroy

The habit of public cavalcades to celebrate events of major importance, which we have already seen widespread in the Aragonese period[184], was kept alive even during the Spanish viceroyalty. The Spanish historian, José Carlos Hernando Sánchez[185] recalls, for example, the magnificent cavalcade that was held in Naples in 1559, during the visit of Francis of Lorraine, Grand Prior of the Order of Malta and general of the galleys of France[186]. To the coast of the Papal States, he had accompanied his brother, the Cardinal of Guise, who went to the conclave after the death of Paul IV. Waiting for the election of a new pope, he decided to visit Naples, where he was received with full honors by the viceroy Pedro Afan de Ribera[187], duke of Alcalá who became an ally of France after the Treaty of Cateau-Cambresis. The French knights found on the dock a multitude of Spanish and Neapolitan nobles that were waiting for them and a large number of horses and carriages, sent by the viceroy to receive them. There were, says a contemporary chronicler, Spanish, Berber, Neapolitan and horses of other races, one more beautiful than the next and with caparisons [decorative covering for a horse or for the tack or harness of a horse] richly decorated in gold and silver[188]. The Grand Prior mounted a superb Spanish horse, which later on, was donated to him by the viceroy. On the way to the vice-regal palace, the French commander showed off his skills as a rider performing a series of courbettes, which aroused great admiration among those who were present.

In the following days the viceroy received the retinue of the French general, composed of about two hundred gentlemen, who had been housed in the magnificent mansions of the Neapolitan nobility. Brantôme, who tells the story, said he had never seen a city so rich and full of superb horses and splendid carriages: "whoever wanted to ride a horse rode it, whoever wanted to go in a carriage boarded it because there were twenty of the richest and most beautiful and best-equipped, drawn by the most beautiful coursers that one could see."[189]

---

mentre che in essa habitarono, et massime gli Aragonesi..."» Contarino, 1569, pp. 28–29.

184) See Chapter I.

185) See Hernando Sánchez, 1998.

186) Godson of the Duke of Guise, Francis of Lorraine died in March 1563.

187) Afán Pedro de Ribera (1509–1571), was Duke of Alcalá and viceroy of Catalonia and Naples (June 12, 1559–April 2, 1571).

188) See Brantôme, 1981, pp. 343–345.

189) Brantôme, 1981, p. 344. It should be noted that the habit of magnifying the richness and elegance of a city enhancing the quantity and the luxury of carriages that moved around its streets was a commonplace fairly widespread in the Renaissance. For example, at the beginning of the ninth story of the first book of Bandello, Isabella d'Este praises the wealth of Milan, saying: "In which city you know today are there many superb carriages gilded all of pure gold, with lots of rich carvings, drawn by four very good steeds as seen in Milan at any moment? Where there are more than sixty car-

During the Spanish period, the so-called "bull hunts," the *corridas de toros,* also increased, which at the time were fought only on horseback and required highly trained and agile animals. Especially Pedro de Toledo supported them. In fact he had a real passion for bullfights and he personally took part in them. The chronicles of the time report of many of these fights. For example, in the one by Gregorio Rosso we find a description of a bullfight fought in Piazza San Giovanni in Carbonara, in 1533:

> On June 29, in the square of Carbonara, they made a great feast of bull games. The Viceroy frequently held these kinds of feasts, because he had a passion for them, and in Spain he had a reputation as great bullfighter, but on this day June 29 he was wounded in the leg by the horn of a bull. On that day, not only did this misforturne happen, but a bull ran out of the fence and killed a young man. If he would have kept running in the streets of Naples, he would have done a lot of damage, but God willed that he slipped through the Carbonara gate exiting the city. On that day, many Neapolitan gentlemen played with the Viceroy as, with their usual skill, they immediately got trained to do this exercise [bullfighting on horseback], as well as any Spaniard[190].

On the other hand, the bullfights were quite common at the time in Italy, not only in the kingdom of Naples. For example, Benedetto Croce[191] recalls those in Siena and Florence, where, in 1584, in Piazza Santa Croce, took place a magni-

---

riages with four horses, while the two are endless, with very rich silk and gold covers and of such distinct varieties that when women go for a walk in a carriage through the quarters seems that in the city is taking place a triumphal procession" (Bandello, 2011, pp. 136–136). Similar considerations can be found in Montaigne's diary of his trip to Italy, in which his secretary refers to the amazement of his lord in front of the magnificence of the papal court: "He found the appearance of a court so big and crowded by prelates and other ecclesiastics new, and it seemed to him full of rich people, carriages and precious horses, more than every other view until then. He argued that, for many things, especially for the multitude of passersby, it reminded him of Paris more than any other place in which he ever was" (Montaigne, 2010, pp. 232–233).

190) «*Alli 29 di Giugno se fece una bellissima festa alla piazza Carbonara de giochi de Tori. Il Viceré faceva spesso di queste feste, perche era profesione sua, e in Spagna teneva nome di gran toriatore e in questo giorno delli 29 de Giugno fu ferito in una gamba dalle corna di un Toro, e non solo succedé quella disgrazia in quel giorno, ma ancora scappò un Toro dallo steccato, e ammazzò uno figliolo, e se dava a correre deritto per le strate de Napoli, averia fatto molto danno; ma Dio volse, che infilò per la porta Carbonara e uscì fuori de la Città. Giocorno con lo Viceré in quello giorno molti cavalieri Napolitani, che con la loro solita habilità se adestrarono subito à fare questo esercitio, così bene come qualsivoglia Spagnuolo.*» Rosso, 1635, p. 97.

191) See Croce, 1922, p. 192.

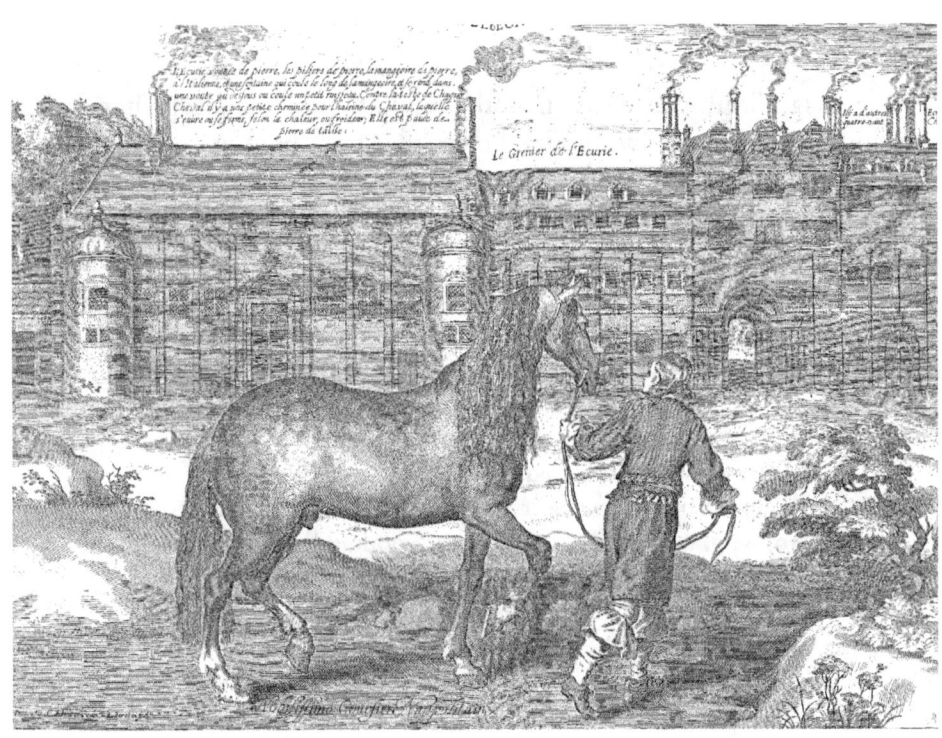

The Neapolitan horses contributed to the improvement of many different breeds (picture from William Cavendish of Newcastle, *Méthode et invention nouvelle dans l'art de dresser les chevaux,* 1658)

ficent bullfight on the occasion of the visit of Prince Vincenzo Gonzaga, heir to the throne of Mantua. Maria Bellonci, instead, tells of the passion of the Borgias for bulls and mentions the bullfight with which the Duke Valentino, Cesare Borgia[192], celebrated the New Year's Eve 1502, no less than in Saint Peter's Square in Rome[193].

---

192) Natural son of Pope Alexander VI (1492–1503), Cesare (1476–1507) was originally intended for ecclesiastical life and was nominated cardinal when he was very young. However he obtained papal dispensation and after abandoning the cardinal purple he undertook an ambitious and unscrupulous campaign to establish a kingdom in central Italy, taking possession of the territories of Romagna and of the Duchy of Urbino. The death of the pope, his father, however, marked the end of his dream of conquest. The new Pope Julius II, arch-enemy of the Borgias, took from him the domain of Romagna and had him locked up in Castel Sant'Angelo. He escaped and took refuge in the kingdom of Naples, where he was, nevertheless, imprisoned again. Once again, he managed to escape and reached the kingdom of Navarre, where he died fighting for his brother-in-law, John III d'Albret. He was known as Valentino, as he was appointed Duke of Valentinois by the French king, Louis XII.

193) Bellonci, 1939, p. 251.

The Neapolitan coursers

A significant contribution to the reputation of the Neapolitan horsemanship was also given by the fine horses that were bred in the kingdom of Naples, famous and sought after for their elegance, strength and endurance. The city on the Gulf was considered a famous horse market already at the time of Boccaccio, who recalls it at the beginning of one of the most famous stories—the fifth of the second day [The *Decameron* is divided into ten days. In each day the characters tell ten stories. So to identify a tale of the *Deacameron* one must say the day in which it is told and its position inside that day.] – of his *Decameron*, that one of Andreuccio of Perugia (II,5):

> There was once in Perugia, as I have heard tell aforetime, a young man, a horse-courser, by name Andreuccio di Pietro, who, hearing that horses were good and cheap in Naples, put five hundred gold florins in his purse and betook himself thither with other merchants, having never before been away from home. He arrived there one Sunday evening, towards vespers, and having taken counsel with his host, sallied forth next morning to the market, where he saw a great plenty of horses. Many of them pleased him and he cheapened one and another, but could not come to an accord concerning any. Meanwhile, to show that he was for buying, he now and again, like a raw unwary clown as he was, pulled out the purse of florins he had with him, in the presence of those who came and went[194].

The adventure that follows has nothing to do with horses, but illustrates the reputation of the Neapolitan specimens, whose aptitude to the "school airs" was mentioned by Miguel de Cervantes in the last of his *Novelas ejemplares* (*Exemplary Stories*, 1613), the *Novela del coloquio de los perros* (The Dogs Colloquy), where the character of Berganza says, "he taught me how to prance like a Neapolitan charger"[195]. It should be made clear that by "Neapolitan horse," we historically mean the horses bred throughout all of Southern Italy (i.e. in the current regions of Abruzzo, Campania, Molise, Apulia, Basilicata and part of Lazio).

The Neapolitan horses contributed to the improvement of many breeds, both Italian and foreign, and were exported to all other Italian states and to Spain, France, Holland, England, Denmark, Germany, Prussia, Poland, Russia and Austria-Hungary[196]. Despite the fierce competition between the Italian studs, Neapolitan mares were used, for example, by the Marquis of Mantua

---

194) Boccaccio, 1886, p. 67.
195) Cervantes, 1972, p. 225.
196) See Fraddosio, 2010.

to improve the production of his coursers. For this purpose, the Gonzaga sent their own experts to visit the stud farms of Southern Italy to buy the best horses, because in the Neapolitan breed coexisted the merits of the Turkish, the Spanish and the Berber horses which ensured great success in breeding[197]. In fact, they were extremely strong and fast with a beautiful shape, characterized by the Roman (or convex) profile, and had very elegant movements.

In the mid-sixteenth century, however, in his *Trattato dell'imbrigliare, atteggiare, & ferrare cavalli* (Treatise about bridling, training and shoeing horses, 1556) [198], Cesare Fiaschi complains about the many crossbreeds that, in his opinion, had bastardized the Neapolitan breed.

> I would like to say my opinion on the nature of the horses of the kingdom of Naples, but I cannot decide to talk about them, because I believe that today we find a few that are not bastardized, because they no more have the strength and courage they had in the past, but as they are now they should not be beaten, except some times, just to display their value, reviving them more than usual, so that they react to beatings performing some jumps[199].

One of their enthusiastic partisans is instead—perhaps also for parochial reasons—the Neapolitan Pasquale Caracciolo, who exalts their qualities:

> But if among all horses, those who are adorned with all the qualities and suitable for every kind of exercise are very rare, only the Neapolitans are worthy of such praise, because they are excellent in walking, in performing the passage, in trotting, cantering, as well as in combat, vaulting and hunting; they also are of good size and of great beauty and endurance, they are very strong and of remarkable lightness, with a clever mind and of great courage; they have a steady head, a pleasant mouth and an amazing obedience to the bridle, and finally they are so docile and so skilled that ridden by a good rider, they move to the rhythm and nearly dance.[200]

---

197) See. Malacarne, 1995.

198) See Chapter V.

199) «*De i cavalli del regno di Napoli vorrei dir il parer mio sopra la natura loro, ma non mi so risolver intieramente di parlarne; la causa è che hoggidì mi pare che se ne trova pochi che non siano bastardati, perché non hanno la forza et animo che soleano havere pe'l passato, ma tali come sono quasi per l'ordinario non si debbono sollecitare in batterli, salvo che qualche volta, per far saggio sì del valor suo come per avivargli più del loro solito, facendone poi essi segno con alcun salto nel sentirsi percuotere.*» FIASCHI, 1556, Book I, Chap. XXXIX, p. 28.

200) «*Ma se di tutti i cavalli rarissimi sono quelli, che di tutte le conditioni necessarie*

And as proof of his assertions he mentions the Emperor Charles V who, being a horse connoisseur, wanted Neapolitan horses for his personal service:

> which was clearly approved by the judgment of the great Emperor Charles V who, having excellent knowledge and practice of all types of horses and of all the arts of chivalry, always chose the Neapolitan horses for his personal service, considering them suitable for every kind of exercise and combat.[201]

The moment of maximum splendor of the Neapolitan breed was from the sixteenth to the seventeenth century. At that time, every European monarch housed the coursers of Naples in his stables. Cosimo I de Medici[202], seated on a Neapolitan horse, was portrayed in the famous equestrian statue by Giambologna, which stands in Piazza della Signoria in Florence. The work was a huge success and established itself as the iconic model of the image of the perfect monarch in the age of absolutism. As such, it inspired the equestrian statue of Henri IV in Paris (located on the Pont Neuf, then destroyed in 1792 during the French Revolution) and those statues of Philip III and Philip IV in Madrid (in Plaza Mayor and Plaza de Oriente). The Florentine work was commissioned by Cosimo's son, Ferdinando I de Medici[203] in 1587. The horse was made in 1591

---

adornati, e à tutti gli essercitij siano idonei; di tal lode i Napolitani soli veramente al più generale si trovan degni; perché al caminare, al passeggiare, al trottare, al galoppare, all'armeggiare, al volteggiare, e al cacciare hanno eccellenza, e sono di buona taglia, di molta bellezza, di gran lena, di molta forza, di mirabile leggierezza, di pronto ingegno, e di alto animo; fermi di testa, e piacevoli di bocca, con ubbidienza incredibile della briglia; e finalmente così docili, e così destri, che maneggiati da un buon Cavaliere, si muovono à misura, e quasi ballano» CARACCIOLO, 1566, Book III, p. 323.

201) «*il che dal giudicio del grandissimo Carlo V, Imperadore, chiaramente fu approvato, il quale havendo ottima conoscenza, e prattica di tutte le specie di cavalli, e di tutte l'arti Cavalleresche, sempre elesse per servigio di sua persona i cavalli Napolitani, come idonei ad ogni essercitio, e fattione*» CARACCIOLO, 1566, Book III, p. 323. However, the Renaissance writers had different opinions about the preferences of Charles V around horses and probably this was due to parochial reasons. If, in fact, according to the Neapolitan Caracciolo the emperor preferred Neapolitan horses, the Lombard Claudio Corte (Mantuan on the mother's side) asserted instead that he preferred the ones from the breed of Mantua: "The Emperor Charles V was so delighted by the horses of this breed, that he considered them worth more than all the others.» («*De' cavalli di questa razza si dilettò tanto Carlo quinto Imperatore, che gl'anteponeva in ogni valore à tutti gl'altri.*») CORTE, 1562, pp. 22v–23r.

202) Cosimo I de' Medici (1519—1574) was the second Duke of Florence and, later, the first Grand Duke of Tuscany.

203) Ferdinando I de' Medici (1549—1609) was Cardinal (1562–1587) and later Grand Duke of Tuscany (1587–1609).

in a single casting, and the monument was completed in 1594. The enormous success of this statue and of the art of its sculptor produced countless variations and copies of reduced size. After the European success of the monument, the workshop of Giambologna was endowed with real "production lines" to achieve almost identical equestrian statuettes that differed only in some small detail and in the head of the portrait of the client, that was cast separately and then assembled[204]. We know that the horse of the monument to Cosimo I was, or appeared to his contemporaries, of Neapolitan breed, from the testimony of the German Prince Ludwig Anhalt-Köthen (1579–1650) who, passing through Florence in 1598 on his trip to Switzerland, Austria, Hungary and Italy, noted:

> On the main plaza is the figure of the Grand Duke Cosimo, brilliantly cast in bronze; he is mounted on a large Neapolitan horse posing on two feet, so that you do not ever sate your eye for the beauty of the artifice[205].

Neapolitan horses gave a crucial blood supply to one of the most popular breeds of high school horses in the world, the Lipizzaner. In the second half of the sixteenth century, Archduke Charles of Styria[206], son of Emperor Ferdinand I of Austria[207] acquired a large estate from the bishop of Trieste in the area of Lipica, Slovenia today. Here, he founded, from 1580, a great breeding farm, selecting the best mares from the regions of Aquileia, Polesine and Verona, as well as from Spain, from whence came the first stallions, to which were added some specimens coming from the kingdom of Naples. Two Neapolitan stallions in particular, although two centuries later, gave a decisive contribution to the Lipizzaner breed, that still retains these origins in the names of two of its six lines of male blood: the black stallion Conversano, born in 1767, and the bay Napolitano, born in 1790, both imported from the kingdom of Naples. The first of these came from the territory of the Murgia (Apulia), where noble families such as the Counts of Conversano and the Dukes of Martina had some of the most famous "*razze private*" (private studs) in the kingdom of Naples[208]. The memory of two other beautiful stallions of Neapolitan origin, property of the Habsburgs, Cerberus and Scaramuie, remained in the portraits devoted to them by the Scottish painter Johann George Hamilton (1672–1737) who was the court painter of the Habsburgs since 1712.

---

204) See Silvestri, 2006.

205) Anhalt-Köthen, 1859, p. 114.

206) Charles II (1540—1590) was Archduke of Austria and ruled over Interior Austria from 1564 until his death.

207) Ferdinand I of Habsburg (1503—1564), Emperor of the Holy Roman Empire from 1556 to 1564, and king of Bohemia and Hungary from 1526.

208) Bedonni, 1995.

In addition to the Lipizzaner, the Neapolitan stallions and mares were used, in the Baroque age, to improve the German breeds of Hanover, Holstein, Oldenburg, Trakehner and Württemberg, the Dutch Gelderlander, the Danish Frederiksborg and the bohemian Kladruber[209].

The horses of Pandone Palace in Venafro

Not many people know that the famous triumph of Federico II Gonzaga's horse in the Palazzo Te in Mantua[210] had a significant antecedent in the kingdom of Naples, where another Italian nobleman wanted the portraits of the horses of his breeding in his palace. This was Enrico Pandone, Count of Venafro. Born in 1494, Enrico received the county from his mother Ippolita of Aragon, who ruled it after the death of her husband, Charles, during the period in which her son was still a minor. The Pandone family, originally from Capua, ruled over most of Molise, the region of which Venafro is still a part today, bordering Lazio and Campania, in the province of Isernia[211]. Their possessions extended over an area that included the whole Volturno Valley and the county of Boiano and the entire northern and western Matese.

Enrico was a restless personality and frequented the cultural circles of Naples. In 1514 he married Caterina Acquaviva d'Aragona, daughter of the Duke of Atri. Eleven years later he participated in the campaign that repelled the troops of John Stuart, Duke of Albany, ally of the French, who, during the fourth Franco-Spanish War, arrived at the gates of Rome. His valor earned him the gratitude of Charles V, who appointed him Duke of Bojano. Nevertheless, in the next conflict, Enrico sided with the French of Lautrec, who laid siege to Naples, but were repelled by the Spaniards. The betrayal cost him his life. He was beheaded in Naples, December 28, 1528, on what is now called Piazza Municipio.

Among his possessions in Molise, Pandone maintained a stud farm, which had been started by his father, Charles, as we know from the annual income of 20 ducats that he took care to fix before his death for Lucio Schiavone, the master of his stable and probably the riding teacher of his child. Of this character we have no other information and only his name lets us assume his Slavic origin, tied to the strong equestrian tradition in that part of Europe corresponding to Slavonia, the land of the "*Schiavoni.*"

In the castle of Venafro, Enrico ordered to decorate the walls of the noble ground with the portraits of his finest specimens, of which remain significant traces even after heavy tampering which happened on several occasions

---

209) Fraddosio 2010.

210) See Chapter I.

211) Cfr. Morra, 1985; Morra—Valente, 1993; Cimmino, 2009.

over the centuries, in attempts to adapt the space for many different uses. After a recent restoration, the figures of about twenty horses are now readable, ten of which are almost completely restored. Here too, as in Mantua, the animals are portrayed lifesize, in profile, with all the details of their harnesses, richly decorated and ornamented with colored straps and tassels. To enhance the realism of the representation, the anonymous artist used a mixed media technique: the "*stiacciato*" (flattened), at first creating silhouettes in stucco into very low relief on the plaster and then painting the figures with colors in fresco.

Some of the specimens have a visible brand on the thigh: a large H (the initial of Henricus) enclosed in a square, which is overlapped by another rotated 45 degrees, with a small cross at the top. In more than one case, the horses are portrayed alongside the mouthpiece which was used to mount them. The harnesses are very refined and saddles appear covered with fine cloth. Every single specimen is accompanied by an inscription that recalls: the name, breed, characteristics, age and the date of the portrait. The last is dated 30 April 1527. In many cases, also specified is the destination. Thus we learn, for example, that the bay called "*Stella*" was a jennet (*ginecto*), a Spanish horse, and that it was sent as a gift to the Neapolitan gentleman Annibale Caracciolo, in 1524. The gray (*liardo*) "*Scorbone*" is portrayed in the act of kicking and we know that he was given as a gift to another Neapolitan nobleman, Annibale Pignatelli. As we have already seen, at the time it was common practice for the noble horse-owners to give their best specimens as gifts to their patrons. This is demonstrated by another of the coursers portrayed in Pandone Palace: the gray "*San George*," which was given to the Emperor Charles V, in gratitude for the grant of the county of Boiano in October 1522.

This is the inscription that accompanies the picture:

> THE GREY ST. GEORGE, FAVORITE
> PORTRAIT IN ITS NATURAL SIZE
> WHEN WAS BETWEEN FOUR AND FIVE YEARS
> IN THE DAY 7 OF OCTOBER 1521
> SENT TO THE CAESAREAN MAJESTY
> ON THE 8TH OF THE MONTH OF OCTOBER 1522[212]

However, only six years later, Enrico Pandone would side against the emperor, paying with his life and the confiscation of all his possessions[213].

---

212) "*LO LIARDO SAN GEORGE FAVO / RITO CHE E DE QUESTA TA / GLIA RETRACTO DE NATURA / LE E DI QUATTRO IN CIN / QUE ANNI A DI VII / DE OCTOBRE / MDXXI / MANDATO ALLA MAESTA CESAREA / ... VIII DEL MESE DE / OCTOBRE MDXXII*"

213) The equestrian paintings of the Pandone castle of Venafro inspired a very nice novel by the French bibliophile, antiquarian bookseller and horse breeder Philippe Deblaise (see Deblaise, 2006), in which he shows great erudition and

Neapolitan horse from *Description du Manege Moderne dans sa perfection* (1727) by Baron d'Eisenberg

Decadence of the Neapolitan breed

The prestige of the Neapolitan breed remained intact until at least the eighteenth-century. It is well proved by the words dedicated to the "horse of Naples" by Baron d'Eisenberg[214] in his treatise *Description du Manege Moderne dans sa perfection* (1727):

> Having been six years in Naples, where I saw all the most beautiful horses of the Kingdom, I can truly say that some of them surpass all the other horses in the world for their physical appearance and movement; their Canter is the

---

competence, while bending, of course, the accuracy of some historical references to the demands of narrative fiction.

[214] Baron Frederick William of Eisenberg, of German origin, but cosmopolitan by vocation and profession. He was educated to the doctrine of the Neapolitan school through riders who worked in Germany and England, and was later in Naples, as "Gran squire" of the Count of Daun. He was then master of riding at the Habsburg court, under Francis I and Charles VI, then director and first horseman of the Academy of Pisa. In addition to the treaty in French *Description du Manege Moderne dans sa perfection*, he also published a work in Italian: *La perfezione e i difetti del cavallo* (The perfection and defects of the horse, D'EISENBERG, 1753).

most raised I've ever seen and they perform the piaffe nearly naturally, but despite these favorable inclinations they are difficult to train, as they are capricious and often vicious; and this causes the Locals to treat them harshly as soon as they enter the stables, thinking in this way to be dreaded by them and to bend them to obedience. However I found that it is possible to get more from them with gentleness and caresses, combined with firm lessons, rather than with severe punishments; because you must know that they do not reach their full strength until they are six or seven years old, after which is certain that they are of great use and give much pleasure in the Arena[215].

François Robichon de La Guérinière has, instead, a different point of view on this subject and, in his *Ecole de cavalerie* (1733) [*School of Horsemanship, Part II*, Xenophon Press 1992], accords his favor especially to the Spanish horses, relegating the Neapolitans – of which he at least recognizes the natural disposition to the *piaffer*[216] – to the use of carriage, because of their good appearance and of their elegant movements, but also because of their lack of docility.

The Neapolitans are for the most part indocile and consequently difficult to train. At first, their figure does not well dispose towards them, because usually their head is too big and their neck is too stubby, but even with these defects they do not cease to be proud of and to have nice movements. An *equipage* [a horse-drawn carriage with attendants] of Neapolitan Horses, well chosen and well trained for this purpose is very much appreciated[217].

With ups and downs, horse breeding continued in southern Italy under the Bourbons who, with Charles[218] (1716–1788), son of Philip V of Spain, founded the royal breed of Carditello and Persano. The Unification of Italy, however, marked a progressive decline until the substantial disappearance of the characteristics that made the Neapolitan horses so popular in the world.

In recent decades, there have been at least two attempts to reco-

---

215) D'EISENBERG, 1727, p. 4.,

216) See LA GUÉRINIÈRE, 1733, p. 79 The piaffe is a school air in which the horse performs a kind of raised trot on the spot. Represents one of the moments of maximum collection, in which the horse lowers the croup and engages the hind legs under the body, with the consequent raising of the front end.

217) LA GUÉRINIÈRE, 1733, p. 30.

218) Charles Sebastian of Bourbon (1716—1788) was Duke of Parma and Piacenza (1731—1735), king of Naples and Sicily (1735—1759), then king of Spain under the name of Charles III.

ver this zootechnical heritage: one conducted by Giuseppe Maresca, starting in 1969[219], and another led, in 2004, by Giuseppe Maria Fraddosio[220]. Both experiments, however—at least in the opinion of this writer—have more the value of a passionate tribute to an extinct tradition, than a real scientific basis and a real chance of success.

---

219) See Maresca – Franchini, 2002 and Franchini – Maresca, 2003.
220) Fraddosio, 2006 and Fraddosio, 2010.

IV
The Rules of Riding (*Gli Ordini di Cavalcare*) by Federico Grisone

"From the very first time, it seems that every horse obeys his simple gesture, so that the bystanders remain astonished"[221]. In his *La Gloria del cavallo* (1566), Pasquale Caracciolo describes in these words the ability of his contemporary Federico Grisone, Neapolitan gentleman, author of the *Ordini di cavalcare* (*The Rules of Riding*, 1550), the first equestrian treatise ever printed in modern times.

We do not know very much about his life[222]. Grisone was a noble Neapolitan family, from the seat of Nido (or Nilo)[223]. But the family was originally from Ravello. In his *Descrittione del Regno di Napoli* (Description of the kingdom of Naples, 1586), Scipione Mazzella reproduces their coat of arms and summarizes their history, but without mentioning the author of the *Ordini*[224]. According to Scipione Ammirato[225], the first information about the Grisone family dates back to the thirteenth century. It was evidently a prominent family, in which there were generals, soldiers of fortune, archbishops and ambassadors. Moving to Naples in the fourteenth century, the Grisone family held important appointments at the Court. This was a prestigious role that they maintained even two centuries later. Federico's uncle, Antonio, was the first chamberlain of King Frederick I[226] and his personal counselor, as well as ambassador to

---

221) «*Dalla prima volta pare che ogni cavallo gli ubbidisca a cenno, sì che i circostanti ne rimangono stupefatti.*» CARACCIOLO, 1566, p. 141.

222) The most rigorous attempt to reconstruct the main points of Grisone's biography is that of Patrizia Arquint, in Arquint, 2010. Decidedly less reliable from the documental point of view is instead that of André Monteilhet in Monteilhet 1979, pp. 146–147, essentially followed by Marion Scali, in Scali, 2009, p. 30–33.

223) The Seats were the councils of the medieval city. Established since 1200, they were made by the representatives of the magnate families. The seat of Nilo, or Nido, dates back to the thirteenth century. It was so named because of the presence of the statue of the Nile River and in memory of the merchants from Alexandria, who lived in the area. See De Cavi 2013.

224) Mazzella, 1586, p. 716.

225) Ammirato, 1580, p. 282.

226) Frederick of Aragon (1452–1504), son of Ferdinand I, succeeded his cousin Ferdinand II, and was king from 1496 to 1503.

the Pope Alexander VI. His father, Iacopo[227], was Major Valet of King Ferdinand II, Counselor of State, lord of Gaeta and of Castelpetroso. Also dear to King Federico[228], he was appointed, in 1502, Count of Avellino, but retained the office for a short time.

His life

Federico was probably born towards the end of the fifteenth century. It is known that, as an adult, at the time of the dispute between Spain and France for the possession of the kingdom of Naples, he lined up for the French party when, in 1527, Naples was besieged by the army led by Count de Lautrec. It is in fact documented that, in the repression that followed the failure of that attempt, Federico paid for his choice of field losing an income of 50 ducats, and for the same reason, the goods of his brother Michelangelo, who was constable of Gaeta, were confiscated. We know that Federico married Lucrezia of Dura, by whom he had a son, Annibale. This last one died tragically in a night, in which—as Scipione Ammirato wrote in his book *Delle famiglie nobili napoletane* (About the Neapolitan noble families, 1580) he "licentiously wandered around in Naples." He was killed by a Genoese gentleman, "more to his own defense—says the historian—than to offend him"[229].

As for Grisone's equestrian activity, we have already seen in how great esteem he was held by Pasquale Caracciolo that of him and of another rider of the time; Berardino delle Castella wrote:

> of this couple in this noble exercise it can really be said what Petrarch said of Tullio and Marone: These are the eyes of our language[230].

From Giovan Battista Ferraro—another Neapolitan horseman, author in 1560 of a treatise entitled *Razze, disciplina del cavalcare ed altre cose pertinenti ad esercitio così fatto*[231] (Races, discipline of riding and other things relevant to this

---

227) Arquint calls him Giacomo, even if the name Iacopo can also be found in Ammirato, 1580, p. 283.

228) Said Ferrandino (1469–1496), reigned from 1495 to 1496. See Candida Gonzaga, 1875, p. 185.

229) Ammirato, 1580, pp. 283–284.

230) «*della qual coppia in questo nobilissimo essercitio veramente può dirsi quel che di Tullio, e di Marone disse il Petrarca:* Questi son gli occhi della lingua nostra.» CARACCIOLO, 1566, p. 142.

231) See cap. VII.

GRISONE.

Grisone's coat of arm, from Scipione Mazzella Napolitano, *Descrittione del Regno di Napoli* (1586)

exercise)—we know that Grisone's first teacher was Giovan Girolamo Monaco[232]. According to the same author, Grisone improved his knowledge of the equestrian art with another master: Cola Pagano, son of the Major Horseman of Ferdinand I of Aragon, who was previously in the service of the king of England, then in the service of the Viceroy of Naples, Filiberto Chalons, Prince of Orange[233]. It is not clear in which period of his career Pagano had Grisone as a student. On the basis of historical data, Patrizia Arquint assumed it could have been during the period of the Viceroyalty of the Prince of Orange, between 1528 and 1530. Cola Pagano is mentioned by Grisone in the *Orders*, when he highlights the importance of the work at the trot as a basis for the training of the horse. According to Grisone, in fact, "that great horseman"[234]

> until the horse was not steady and fully trained for anything in the world he would make him run, so that, after having ridden him for four or six months or maybe a year, in no more or less than eight days he showed him the gallop[235].

---

232) FERRARO, 1560, p. 53r.

233) FERRARO, 1560, p. 51v.

234) «*quel gran cavalcatore.*» GRISONE, 1550, p. 44r.

235) «*finché il cavallo non era fermo e compitamente ammaestrato, non lo havrebbe per*

In the past, but also recently, several authors have attributed to Grisone the foundation of a riding academy in Naples, but this idea is not proven by the documents[236]. Based on the testimony of Alfonso Ruggieri—author, between the late sixteenth and early seventeenth century, of a treatise handed down in manuscript form[237]—Patrizia Arquint[238] has, however, certified that Grisone was counted among the masters who "*tenevano campagna*" (literally: "kept campaign"), that is to say they taught on their own. It is certain that Grisone was not just a clever theorist but also a rider with proven skills, even as a trainer. From Pasquale Caracciolo, we know that horses he trained were sent as gifts to personalities of the highest rank in the Spanish court. This is the case of a horse from the breeding of the Duke of Gravina:

> The Bay, Castagno, marked in the forehead, and on one foot,
> horse of great agility, trained by Sir Federigo Grisone, and
> sent by the very illustrious Viceroy to the Prince of Spain[239].

At last, the date of the death of the author of the *The Rules of Riding* is still uncertain. Caracciolo—who publishes his work in 1566—speaks of him as a still living personality, while Pirro Antonio Ferraro—whose work was published posthumously in 1602, but was probably finished before 1589[240]—mentions him as someone he knew only by reputation. It is therefore likely that his death occurred within the last decade of the sixteenth century.

To Sabina De Cavi, Italian researcher at the Universidad de Cordoba, the merit of reporting in a recent study the presence in the Osuna Fund of the Biblioteca Nacional de España in Madrid a work in manuscript attributed to Federico Grisone, entitled *Razze del Regno, raccolte in questo volume brevemente da Federigo Grisone gentilhuomo napoletano / Dove appresso dona molti belli avisi convenienti alla cognitione de i polletri et al governo et reggere di ogni cavallo* (BNE, mss. 9246, Breeds of the kingdom, collected briefly in this volume by Federigo Grisone Neapolitan gentleman / Where below gives many beautiful

---

cosa del mondo corso; talché, dapoi d'haverlo cavalcato quattro o sei mesi o forse un anno, egli in poco più o meno di otto giorni gli mostrava il correre.» GRISONE, 1550, p . . 44r.

236) The issue of the supposed Academy of Naples is treated in detail in Chapter VIII.

237) The treatise entitled *Ordine di cavalcare et amaistrare cavalli, dar loro lettione, secondo le qualità e dispositione di ciascheduno, cominciando da che son poledri*, is contained in a codex of the seventeenth century (Innsbruck, Universitäts und Landesbibliothek für Tirol, cod. 782.).

238) See Arquint, 2010, p. 56.

239) «*Baio saporito Castagno, segnalato nella fronte, et in un piede Cavallo di grandissima agilità, ammaestrato dal Signor Federigo Grisone, e mandato dall'Illustrissimo Viceré all'altezza del Principe di Spagna...*» CARACCIOLO, 1566, p. 324.

240) See Arquint, 2002, p. 6.

GLI ORDINI
DI CAVALCARE
Di Federigo Grisone,
Gentil'huomo Napoletano.

Con gratia et motu proprio di Papa Giulio Terzo: Et con priuileggio dell'Illustriss. Vece Rè di Napoli, che per Anni Dieci nõ si debbiano stampare: & stampati in altri luoghi, non si possano uendere.
Anno Domini, M. D. L.

Frontispiece of the 1550 edition

suggestions, appropriate to the cognition of the colts and the care and the possession of any horse, BNE, mss. 9246). The work, still to be studied has, so far been ignored by the major equestrian bibliographies, such as those by Hutt and Mennessier de la Lance and represents a real discovery. The text lists the major horse farms of the kingdom of Naples, at the time of the author. "In the manuscript the plates follow each other in order of importance and of social category: from the horses of the king to those of the highest offices of the state, of the nobles and of bourgeois farmers, who used their initials to form the design of their brand. The plates associate brand and name of the breeder, sometimes complementing a brief description of the characteristics of the horses"[241].

The Rules of Riding (*Gli Ordini di Cavalcare*)

The first edition of *Gli ordini di cavalcare Di Federico Grisone Gentil'huomo Napoletano* (*The Rules of Riding* by Federico Grisone, Neapolitan Gentleman), was published in Naples in 1550 by Giovan Paolo Suganappo[242]. The edition was printed in-quarto and in addition to the text contained two plans, which reproduce in a schematic way the patterns of those that Grisone considers the fundamental exercises of training (the "*torni*"), and fifty xylographic plates of bits. The printing in *italic* is well edited, with xylographic initial letters[243]. The work had an immediate success. One could consider it as a real "best seller" of its time. Suffice it to say that, between 1550 and 1623, there were twenty printed Italian editions, fifteen French translations, six English, seven German and one in Spanish[244]. We have direct evidence of this success from the historian Scipione Ammirato, who in 1580 wrote:

> During my youth, I was in Naples when Federigo published
> a book of not many leaves about the art of riding, which
> was sold like hot cakes at the price of two scudi each[245].

Above all, Grisone's work inaugurates a whole new literary genre, exactly that of the treatises dedicated to the equestrian art, which experienced a remar-

---

241) De Cavi, 2013.

242) About Suganappo's printing office see Manzi, 1973.

243) About the typographic value of the work see Deblaise, 2002.

244) Patrizia Arquint has the merit of having listed them in Arquint, 2010, pp. 65–73. Fredrick Hutt mentions even a Portuguese translation contained in a manuscript in folio and never printed: *Ordens de cavallaria*, traduzido de Italiano em Portuguez por Leonel da Costa. See Hutt, 1887, p. 7.

245) «*Io mi abbattei nella mia giovinezza in Napoli quando Federigo mandò fuori un libro di non molti fogli intorno all'arte del cavalcare, il quale fu venduto à ruba à due scudi l'uno.*» Ammirato, 1580, p. 283.

kable expansion in the sixteenth century, especially in Italy where, in the space of fifty years, were published eight books by different authors. The text of Grisone represents a significant change with respect to the major works dedicated until the XV century to the care of the horse. In fact, those were mostly about the diseases and their remedies and only incidentally provided generic information about the taming and the training of the horse, without specific technical guidance for the riders[246]. *The Rules of Riding*, instead, expressly refers to the art of training the horse "for the use of war" and to the secrets to "correct" his vices." A novelty of which the author is well aware, as in the dedication to Ippolito d'Este[247], he said he decided to write about the art of riding although it is generally a subject "in the hands of low people"[248]. If the exercise of chivalry was, in fact, the exclusive prerogative of the highest nobility, taming and training were in prevalence entrusted to horse-dealers, grooms and horse trainers. With some exceptions, since, as the same Grisone remembers, there were also horsemen of noble origin who dedicated themselves to that art, so much so that "Kings and celebrated men were called masters [of the art of taming and training the horse]"[249].

The novelty of Grisone's work was well perceived by his contemporaries and his followers who—such as Claudio Corte in his *Il Cavallarizzo*, in 1562—recognized that he opened the way to subsequent treatises:

> I consider above all Sir Federico Grisone, who first wrote, and certainly divinely, in our times about the rules of riding, because up to the present time, no one dared before him to face this undertaking: even if many used the same orders, the same way and the same exercises, and the same aids and punishments.[250]

The Rules of Riding has mainly a technical intent and for this reason Grisone favors the accuracy of the guidance more than of the style:

> And if it may seem to you that I was not as diligent as I should have been in the way of expressing myself, think that I committed myself more to get it right, than to the ornaments of the Tuscan language, paying more attention

---

246) See Chapter II.

247) Ippolito II d'Este (1509—1572), son of Duke Alfonso I d'Este and Lucrezia Borgia, nephew of Cardinal Ippolito d'Este.

248) «*in man di gente bassa.*» GRISONE, 1550, dedica.

249) «*Re e huomini celebrati [ne] furono chiamati maestri.*» GRISONE, 1550, dedica.

250) «*sopra tutti il Signor Federico Grisone io reputo felice, che prima scrisse, e certo divinamente, à tempi nostri dell'ordine del cavalcare, da che a' tempi nostri nessuno sia stato ardito prima di lui assalire cotale impresa: ancor che molti habbino operato i medesimi ordini, le istesse vie, e i medesimi maneggi; con gl'istessi aiuti e castighi.*» CORTE, 1562, p. 77.

> to things than to words, so that everyone reading learns more how to ride, than how to talk, nor that he got more passionate about reading, focusing on that, but as driven away by the roughness of the language, quickly recourses to the outcomes and usefulness of the work.[251]

The origins of High School riding

Grisone is often referred to as the founder of what, in later centuries, will be called High School riding. In fact, his book focuses on the exercises ("*maneggi*") necessary for war and only quickly mentions some presentation "airs," which afterwards will be called school jumps (especially the *courbette*[252] and the *capriole*[253]). However the concept of riding that Grisone shows in his work in fact already shed some essential elements of what would later become the classical, or academic, riding. In particular, in the *The Rule of Riding* is already formulated that "musical" conception of rhythm in riding, which will have its most explicit expression in the original and subsequent treatise by Cesare Fiaschi[254] and that is found in most of the following treatises, up to the present day. Grisone insists on the importance of "time and measure," in order to merge horse and rider in one body and one will.

> And when he jumps, or stops, no matter what, you must accompany him in time, according to the movement that he will do, as he responds in time to your thoughts, and to every request; because it is necessary that your body, with the back, goes

---

251) «*Et se vi paresse che nel modo del dire io fossi stato non così diligente, come conviene, pensate ch'o atteso più a farlo bene, che agli ornamenti della lingua Toscana, ponendo più cura alle cose, che alle parole, acciocché ogn'uno che legge s'ammaestri più di cavalcare, che di parlare, né s'invaghisca della lettura, fermandosi in quella, ma come scacciato dalla sua ruvidezza, velocemente ricorra ai frutti, e all'utilità dell'opera.*» GRISONE, 1550, pp. 1v–2r.

252) The courbette is a school jump in which the horse, lowers his hips and lifts the front legs and then executes a jump, falling back on his hind legs. The etymology of the term is uncertain. According to Claudio Corte, it comes from the fact that in this way the horse jumps like a raven ("*corvo*" in Italian) when he is on the ground ("*corvette* is said by the raven, when he is on the ground, and goes like this with little forward jumps." CORTE, 1562, Book II, p. 72), while according to others it comes from "*curvarsi*" (to bend). See Barry, 2005, p. 23.

253) School jump that is the most spectacular demonstration of the degree of the horse's submission and collection. The horse rises on the hind legs, jumps up, and when he is in the air, kicks straight back with the hindlegs with great violence (see Barry, 2005, p. 24–25). The etymology is traced back to the analogy between this jump and the jump of the goat ("*capro*" in Italian) and of the deer ("*capriolo*").

254) See Chapter V.

in the right way, and corresponds to him, with no less concordance than if it were music.[255]

To achieve this perfect harmony between two living beings, man and horse, very different but also very compatible, it is not enough to simply practice, but it is also necessary what Grisone defines as the "true and good discourse"[256] namely the correct doctrine, which is based on experience, but also on theoretical reflection and on the transmission of the equestrian knowledge. The author is well aware of the originality of this concept, so as to defend himself in advance, from the criticism of those who consider horseback riding a practice that cannot be disclosed in words:

> I have no doubt that anyone who will see that in writing I wanted to teach these rules of riding, will not leave to expressly condemn my judgment, estimating the effort vain, being engaged in something, that, according to the general habit, seems to be learned more through the work of the body, that through words. Nevertheless, knowing that one can rise to the perfection through intelligence from what he heard, or read, (although he cannot see it), desirous of common utility, it seemed to me right to publish them [*The Rules of Riding*] such as they are; unconcerned of the many people that, not considering minutely what I write, will try to blame them, criticizing them harshly, trusting instead that there will be judicious Riders who will understand them [*The Rules of Riding*] well, and, practicing for a long time, will make clear what I foreshadowed with my pen on the paper, from which I hope, indeed I am sure, that will come rare effects and admirable results.[257]

---

255) «*Et quando salta, overamente para, e a qualunque cosa, lo accompagnerete a tempo, conforme al motivo ch'egli farà, così come egli a tempo risponde al vostro pensiero, e in ogni richiesta; perché bisogna che il vostro corpo con la schiena vada giusto, e gli sia corrispondente, et ordinato, con non minor concordantia, che se fusse musica.*» GRISONE, 1550, p. 12v.

256) «*vero, e buon discorso.*» GRISONE, 1550, p. 1r..

257) «*La onde non dubito, che qualunque vedrà, ch'io habbia voluto scrivendo insegnare questi ordini di cavalcare, non lascerà di condannare espressamente il giudicio mio, stimando la fatica vana, essendo presa in cosa, che, secondo l'universal costume, par che s'impari più col travaglio del corpo, che con le parole. Nondimeno conoscendo che anche dall'ingegno per quel che si ode, o legge, può nascer la perfettione della cosa (ben che non si vegga) desideroso dell'utile comune, tali quali si sieno, mi è paruto mandargli fuora; non curando di molti, che forse non considerando minutamente quel ch'io scrivo, cercheranno riprendergli, e avidamente mordergli, confidato che non mancheranno all'incontro giuditiosi Cavalieri, che gl'intenderanno bene, e in opra con travagliarsi a tempo in essi, al fin faranno chiaro quel ch'io con penna ho adombrato in carta; dai quali spero, anzi son certo, che nasceranno effetti rari, che da quei facilmente si caverà frutto mirabile.*» GRISONE, 1550, pp. 1r–1v.

On the other hand, the same Grisone is well aware of how difficult it is to describe from a theoretical point of view those aspects of equitation that cannot be reduced to mere technique, but call into question the sensitivity of the rider, who must interpret the reactions of the animal and communicate with him through his own body:

> and in this arises the great difficulty in knowing his feelings, and take up the time, and more or less touch him as required, which cannot be said, but will become clear to you through practice[258].

In Grisone's book are then already expressed what may be considered as the real distinguishing features of classical riding, that is to say, the value of "collection,"[259] "contact" and "*mise en main.*" [260] Grisone in fact recommends riding the horse with a collected attitude of head and neck, to ensure the correct contact with the mouth, the proper muscle tone of the back and the support of the hips:

> And although some say that it will be more useful that, when riding, he [the horse] goes with a loose and free head, keeping his natural ferocity, without giving him any punishment nor any subjection; nevertheless we see clearly that thus, the Rider would be led by him [the horse]... And be silent those modern people that said the contrary, because the more the horse goes with a loose head, and with the nose out, the more he will go with an abandoned and weak back, so that not only most of the time he will do the exercise in a bad manner, lying, wide, and with no order, but more likely he will lose his strength. But where and when he will bring down his nose in the proper way, and will go to injure[261]

---

258) « *e in ciò nasce difficoltà grande in conoscere il suo sentimento, e pigliare il tempo, e più e meno toccarlo, come si richiede, il che non si può dire, ma con la pratica vi si farà chiaro.*» GRISONE, 1550, p. 40v.

259) It is the attitude of the mounted horse characterized by the elevation of the neck, the flexion of the poll and the lowering of the hips, with the consequent engagement of the hind legs under the body, which enables him to concentrate his forces and balance the weight of the rider, making him able to move easily in any direction. An attitude which, in practice, plays at art the attitude that the horse assumes in nature when he is in danger, or when he faces a rival. About the collection as a distinguishing feature of classical riding, see Loch, 1990.

260) The serene acceptance of the bit by the horse, which is manifested through the relaxation of the jaw, as evidenced by a characteristic movement of deglutition and the search for an honest but light contact with the rider's hand.

261) Meaning that the horse keeps his forehead on the vertical. Since the horse's head armor had a pointed projecting piece in the middle of the forehand to offend [and wound] the enemy in case of impact, the author probably means that the horse should

CANNONE

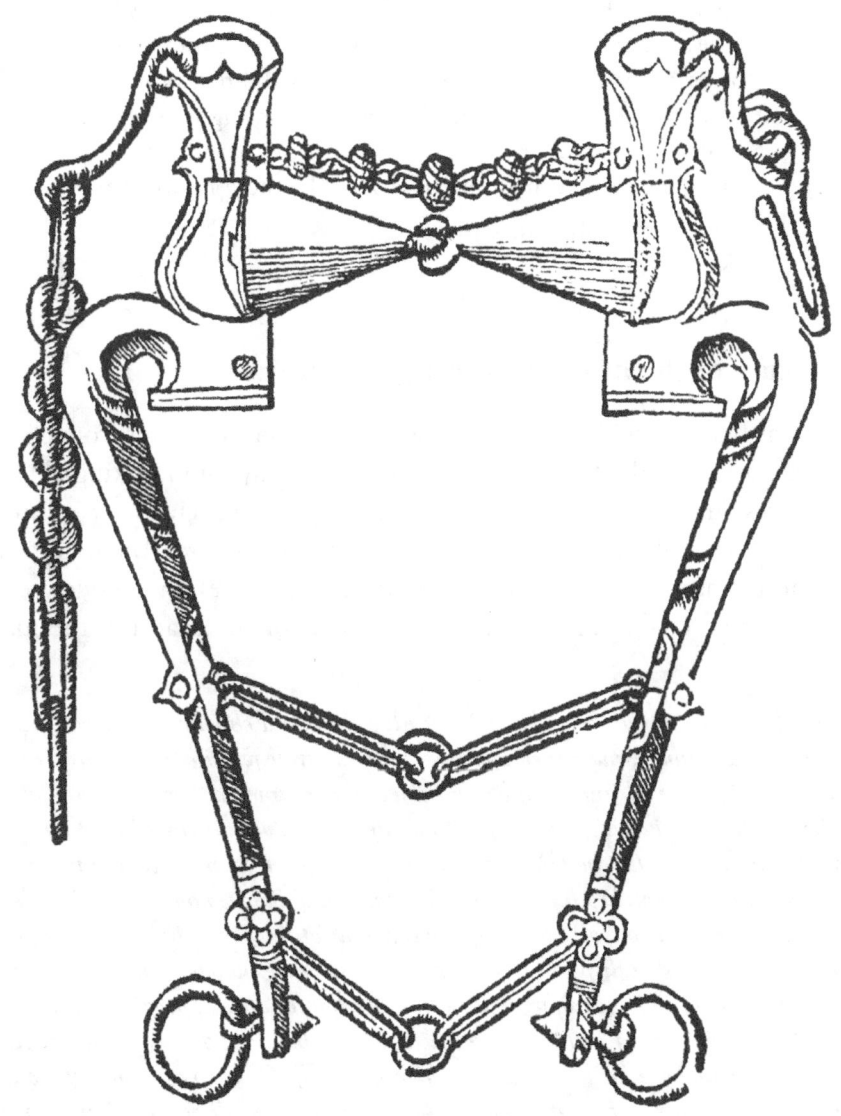

"*Cannon*" bit

maintain his forehead in the exact position to "injure" the enemy with the point on his own head armor. One can clearly see this in the picture of the "armed knight" by Pirro Antonio Ferraro on p. 179.

with his forehead, he will strengthen his back, and will keep the contact, from stride to stride, he will unite all of his power, and from this, will arise lightness, greater strength, and the greatest ease in moving [...]. When he brings the nose out, you can never stop nor completely adjust his mouth, nor his neck, nor his head, but if he keeps it [his nose] down, and goes to injure with his forehead, not only he will be stable with the mouth, but with admirable measure he will have a steady neck and head, never moving them from their place, and with a gentle support he will establish a connection between the bridle and his mouth, chewing it always so that it will look as if it were miraculously born inside it [his mouth]: and the more he works, the more he will be confirmed in his virtues[262]

The nature of the horse according to Grisone

The book is divided into four books. After some citations from classical works that celebrate the horse, "the most faithful companion of kings,"[263] Grisone focuses on the nature of this animal, stating that his character is influenced by the four natural elements: air, water, earth and fire. Then, according to a concept that was widespread at the time[264], he gives an overview of the qualities related to the different coats. The color of the coat and the marks,

---

262) «Et benché alcuni dicano, che sarà più utile che allora che si cavalca, egli vada con la testa disciolta, e libera, mantenendolo con la sua naturale ferocità, senza fargli conoscer castigo, ne suggettione alcuna; nondimeno si vede apertamente, che in questo modo il Cavaliero sarebbe da lui guidato [...]. Et tacciano que' moderni che di ciò han detto il contrario, perché il cavallo che più va con la testa disciolta, e col mostaccio di fuora, tanto maggiormente anderà con la schiena abbandonata, e lassa, tal che non solo il più delle volte farà il maneggio difettoso, colcato, e largo, e con niun'ordine, ma più facilmente perderà la lena. La ove quando egli porterà il mostaccio di sotto al suo debito luogo, e va a ferir con la fronte, d'hora in hora rafforzerà la schiena, e haverà dove appoggiarsi, e assai volte di groppo in groppo unirà tutta la possanza sua, dal che anco gli nascerà leggierezza, e maggior forza e lombo, e facilità grande in adoprarsi [...]. Quando egli porta il mostaccio di fuora, non si potrà mai fermare, et aggiustare totalmente, né di bocca, né di collo, né di testa: ma s'egli tiene di sotto, e va a ferire di fronte, non solo andrà fermo di bocca, ma con mirabile misura tenerà il collo duro, e giusta e come fabbricata la testa, non muovendola mai dal suo luogo; e con un soave appoggio apparenterà di forte la briglia con la bocca, masticandola sempre, che parerà miracolosamente vi sia nata: e quanto più gli si dà travaglio, tanto maggiormente si confermerà nella sua virtù.» GRISONE, 1550, pp. 118v–119v.

263) «fedelissimo compagno dei re.» GRISONE, 1550, p. 2r.

264) For a more detailed discussion of this belief see Chapter VI.

With the progress of the training, the horse was trained in a shallow ditch, in order to force him to follow a rigorous path. This method remained in use for a long time and was adopetd even abroad as shown in the French treatise by Pierre de La Noue, *La cavalerie françoise et italienne, ou l'art de bien dresser les chevaux...* (1620).

such as stockings, whorls, blazes, were in fact considered explicit symptoms of the horse's inclinations and characteristics of the different specimens. Grisone's favorite coat—following a current opinion at the time and not simply a personal preference—is the bay, but he also appreciated the dapple gray and the liver chestnut. In general, white hairs were considered a symptom of weakness and for this reason Grisone suggests to prefer specimens with dark limbs, or with small stockings. The author underlines that despite the fact that these considerations are drawn from experience rather than from opinion, he admits that often "these marks fail and one sees the opposite effect."[265] Furthermore he says that, even if a horse is well-marked and born under a "happy constellation," he must be well-formed and proportioned. For this reason, Grisone recommends to assess his "constitution," begin by examining him from the ground up, that is to say by the quality of his hooves and limbs. The good nature, however—he says—is not enough without the expertise of the rider and proper training:

> And do not think that even though the horse may be well organized by nature, without the human aid and the true doctrine he could work well by himself, because you have to wake up his limbs and the occult virtues that are in him through art, and with true order and good discipline he will show clearly his goodness. On the contrary when art is false it ruins and covers all his virtues, as well as when it is good it compensates for the many areas where his nature may be lacking[266].

---

265) «*questi segni falliscano, e si veda l'effetto contrario.*» GRISONE, 1550, p. 4v.

266) «*Et non pensiate che il cavallo benché sia bene organizato dalla natura, senza il soccorso humano, e la vera dottrina, possa da se stesso ben oprarsi, perché bisogna con l'arte svegliare, i membri, e le virtù occulte che in lui sono,e secondo il vero ordine, e buona disci-*

To be tamed, the horse should be at least three years old. The training is rather quick and, according to Grisone, lasts an average of four to six months. After having accustomed the animal to being mounted, it should be exercised mainly at the trot, a gait that is also considered essential to train him later to canter. The first stage is done with a padded saddle and a cavesson and then, when the horse has already been trained to the essential rudiments, it can be mounted with a normal saddle and bridle. The first bit to be used is the so-called "cannon," with straight bit shanks, that was considered the gentler. To initially make it more pleasant to the animal and to accustom him to "chew" it, Grisone suggests sprinkling it with honey and salt, according to a method already in use recommended by Giordano Ruffo of Calabria[267].

The training of the horse

The training takes place initially on a plowed field, where other horses have marked a track. In this way—the author argues—the horse is induced to follow a correct path to avoid the trouble of walking on loose soil. With the progress of the training, a shallow ditch can be used, in order to force him to follow an even more rigorous path. Grisone codifies some basic training exercises, consisting of *voltes* in both directions, alternated with a straight line at the end of which the horse should stop to execute a half-turn and return on the same straight line: these are the so-called "*torni*." In previous times—the author explains—it was not used as a systematic criterion, but the horse was accustomed to turn and to stop in the open field, or was ridden between the trees, which were used as reference points to train him to move on defined paths.

> This is the form of the "*torni*" offered by me, with some written words, by which, and also for what I said before, will be easily understood. By the way in which they are illustrated, you can see how different they are from the ancient turns, which, a few years ago, were done between the trees and in the countryside, and were done wider and with no measure of number or width, changing place and not as methodically as today.[268]

---

plina più, ò meno sarà chiara la sua bontà, Anzi l'arte, quando ella è falsa, lo ruina, e gli cuopre ogni virtù, così come quando ella è buona supplisce a molte parti, ove gli manca la natura.» GRISONE, 1550, p. 10r.

267) See Chapter II.

268) «*Questa è la forma de i torni offerti da me, con alcune parole scritte, che si per esse, e si per quello che avanti vi dissi, facilmente saranno ben intesi, et del modo che vi sono dipinti conoscerete quanto sieno differenti da i giri antichi, i quali giri, ancor pochi anni a dietro si usavano fra gli alberi, e nella campagna, e erano più larghi, e in quelli con niuna*

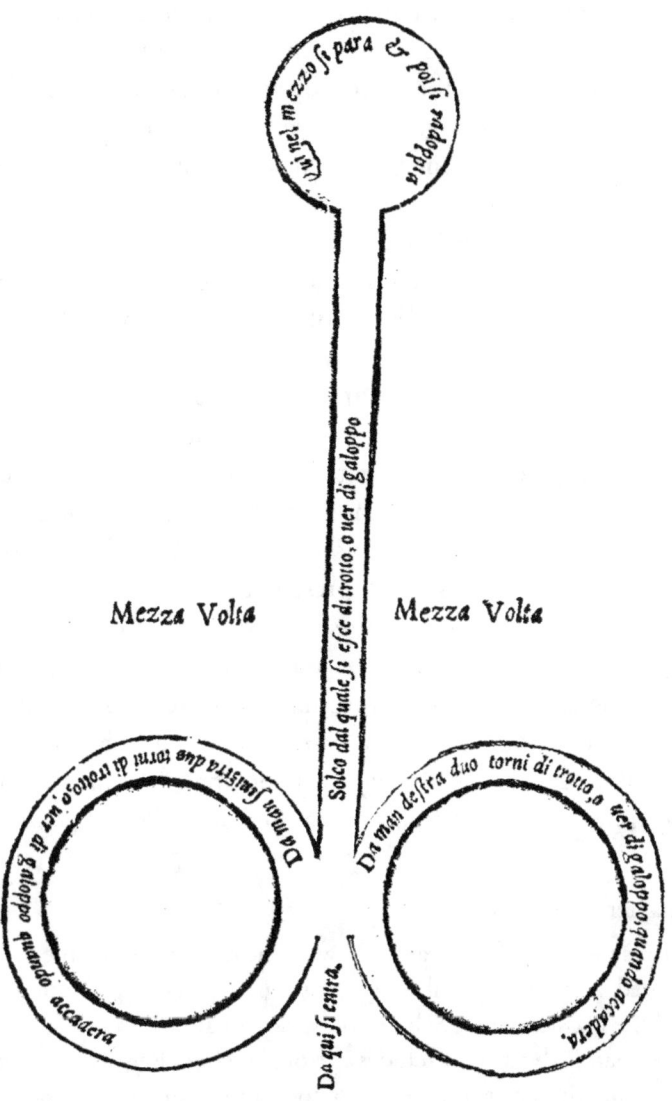

Schematic layout of the so-called "*torni*"

These exercises were used to train the horse to find its balance under the weight of the rider, in the *voltes*, in order to teach him how to make a forward charge against the enemy, stop, turn on his haunches and run again towards a new encounter. It is the so-called *passade*, namely a rectilinear charge (that the Italian authors called "*repolone*"), after which the horse had to stop and turn in the shortest possible space, with a half-pirouette, so as to immediately perform another charge. Different kinds of exercises ("*maneggi*") were distinguished de-

---

misura ne di numero ne di larghezza, cambiandosi luogo si andava, e non ordinatamente come ora si va.» GRISONE, 1550, p. 54r–54v.

pending on how the halt and the half-*volte*, or half-pirouette, were performed. To accustom the horse to face the battle on any kind of soil, Grisone also suggests disseminating stones on the path. The author insists on the importance of training the horse to stop straight, maybe even with the help of a man on the ground that puts him into frame with a stick. For the same purpose, he considers it also useful to rein-back.

In the first stage, the horse is mounted with the so-called false-reins, namely additional reins which were secured to special rings on the bit's shanks, at the ends of the mouthpiece. The bridle then functioned like a pelham bit. Soon, says Grisone, the horse must be trained to the spurs, which are considered an essential tool to aid and punish him. Then he is taught the "*pesade*" ("*posata*"), that is to say to stop by lowering his hips, bringing his hind legs under his body, and lightening the front legs up to lift them from the ground. This technique made it possible to collect the horse to the extreme, making him capable of a rapid change of direction at the end of the "*repolone*." It was also a spectacular exercise, which was also used as a presentation air. Grisone focuses, in fact, also on the correct way to present a horse in the presence of a prince, or a king, suggesting what the positions should be and the best ways to make his qualities shine. During the exhibition, the horse had to prove his skills and obedience in carrying out the various exercises ("*maneggi*"), but also his strength and elegance, performing jumps such as *croupade* ("kicking")[269], *courbettes* and *cabriole* and what we now call Spanish walk[270] (that Grisone calls "*far ciambetta*").

---

269) See Chapter I, n. 41.

270) The Spanish walk is a four beat walk, with the difference that the forelegs are raised and extended as much as possible. There is much debate if it should be considered an exercise of the classical High School, or rather an air of fantasy. The F.E.I. (International Equestrian Federation) excludes it from the exercises of academic equitation and dressage competitions, as it excludes school jumps, or the airs above the ground even if those exercises are undoubtedly part of the "classical" canon. The description that Grisone gives of this exercise is rather obscure and ambiguous, to the point that it has put many modern interpreters on a false track. The author does not dwell on the subject, considering it well known to his readers, but stresses that this movement, "is of great use to give him [the horse] ornament when he is ridden" (GRISONE, 1550, 108r). To teach it to the animal, he suggests to bring him in a ditch and to train him to execute tight *voltes*, using the same aids generally used to correct a horse that tends to turn with his haunches before his shoulders. Doing this it would be necessary to turn to the right and to the left several times, so that "at the end of the *volte* he would not be able to cross his arm [ie the foreleg] except with great difficulty and he will fear to hit his arm with the arm opposite to the direction of the *volte* [i.e. outside foreleg] so that to avoid it, with a steady neck and with his head still, he will raise it high, performing the *ciambetta*.» (GRISONE, 1550, p. 108r). The meaning of these words is rather doubtful, so much that some have interpreted this passage as a description of an exercise similar to the canter pirouette, i.e. a movement in which "the horse rises upon his

The technique of the rider

As for the technique of the Rider, Grisone gives quite detailed information on those that today are called the lower and upper aids: the action of the legs and hands. As to the first, he gives to the outside leg the role of impulsion, while the inside leg is used to "round" ("*attondare*"), that is to say to encourage lateral flexion in the *voltes*. The function of the hand is considered particularly important. It guides the horse in every movement and its action should match that of the legs, which provide the impulsion, and with those of the other aids:

> as the ship is guided by the pilot, by means of the rudder, otherwise it would be confused, so your horse will be governed according to how moves his rudder, which will be the bridle, and the reins that support it will be the helm of the rudder, which is held in the left hand, and is guided by reason, and by our discourse, and when he walks, and when he trots, and when he canters, and when he runs, and when he stops, and when he jumps, with kicks and without kicks, and when he turns in the "*repoloni*" [*passade*], and when he doubles [90 degree turn], and when he does *courbettes* and the *capriole*, it is necessary that most of the time, it is the movement of your left hand that rules [and] corresponds in time to the "oars," that is to say to your legs, namely the spurs, or joined together, or to one or to the other and to the stick, and sometimes to the voice, or tongue[271].

According to Grisone, the aids that can be given to the horse are seven: the voice, the tongue, the stick, the bridle, the calfs, the stirrups and with the spurs. The punishments are the same number and they can be imposed more

---

hindquarters with his forelegs elevated and, leading with one foreleg, navigates around a tight circle, crossing one leg over the other" (TOBEY, 2011, p. 152). Others consider the word "*ciambetta*" a variant of "*ciambella*," an Italian term which designated (to tell the truth in a following period) what we now call "*piaffer*" (BASCETTA, 1978, p. 384). In my opinion, the characteristic feature of Grisone's description, however, is the emphasis on the elevation of the foreleg. A much more detailed and explicit explanation of what the "*ciambetta*" is, in which stands out its resemblance to the Spanish walk, is in CARACCIOLO, 1566, p. 427–430.

271) «*come la nave si guida dal nocchiero, col mezo del timone, che altrimenti sarebbe confusa, così il vostro Cavallo si governerà à secondo che si muove il suo timone, che sarà la briglia e le redine che la sostengono, sarà il manico del timone, il quale si tiene dalla man sinistra, e si guida dalla ragione, e dal nostro discorso, e quando passeggia, e quando trotta, e quando galoppa, e quando corre, e quando para, e quando salta, con calci e senza calci, e quando volta ai repoloni, e quando raddoppia da fermo a fermo, e quando fa corvetti, e la capriola, bisogna che il più delle volte al moto della vostra man sinistra che tiene il governo corrispondono a tempo i remi, cioè le vostre gambe, overamente gli sproni, o giunti insieme, o l'uno, o l'altro e la bacchetta, e tal'hor la voce, overo la lingua.*» GRISONE, 1550, pp. 117v–118r.

or less with the same means (the punishment "of time" replaces the aid with the "tongue"). Grisone attaches particular importance to the punishment of the voice, which he considers the most effective way to correct the disobedience of the horse, although, as we shall see in more detail, he doesn't disdain, but rather recommends, far more brutal punishments. Similarly, an appropriate use of the voice is recommended to reward the horse once reduced to obedience:

> when he uses some malice, like moving his head, or rearing or leaning on the bridle, or proceeds in other errors, you will punish him with a horrible voice, and with a bitter cry you will furiously say, the one that you will prefer between these words: Come on! Come on! O la! O la! Ah ah traitor! Ah villain! Turn! Turn! Stop! Stop! Come here! Come here! And in similar ways; nevertheless, so that the cry is terrible, say any word you want, in order to inspire terror and correction to the Horse and continue this as long as he continues in the disorder, and you will make the voice higher or lower, depending on whether more or less [respectively] will be the seriousness of the error. But when he has already been won over, you must immediately be silent, or change your voice with a pleasanter and lower tone, reassuring him and always touching with the right hand over the arch of his neck, and sometimes scratching him on his mane, or on the withers, or softly saying this "oh, oh, oh, oh," and more or less in that you will understand if it is enough to reassure him, and at the same time you will say this with your mouth, and you will do that with your hand.[272]

---

272) «quando egli usa qualche malignità, o di muover la testa, o d'impennarsi, o si pone in su la briglia, overamente procede in altri errori, il castigo di voce sarà orrendo, e iratamente direte con un grido aspro, qualunque più vi piacerà di queste parole, or su, or su, o la, o la, ah ah traditore, ah ribaldo, torna, torna, ferma, ferma, torna qui, torna qui, et in simili modi; nondimeno pur che 'l grido sia terribile, direte quella parola che vi parerà, e al proposito a terrore, e correttion del Cavallo, e continuerete questo fin tanto che egli dura nel disordine; e farete la voce più o meno alta, secondo che più o meno sarà la gravità dell'errore. Ma quando egli sarà già vinto, dovete dapoi subito tacere, overo con un tono più piacevole e basso mutar voce, assicurandolo sempre e toccandogli con la man destra sopra la inarcatura del collo, e o in esso fra i crini, o verso il garrese alcuna volta grattargli, o con voce sommessa direte questo oh, oh, oh, oh, e più o meno secondo che conoscerete che basti per assicurarlo, e in un tempo questo direte con la bocca, e quello farete con la mano.» GRISONE, 1550, pp. 47v–48r. This famous passage of the *Rules* has earned over time more than some irony to its author, especially for those "villain" and "traitor" addressed to the recalcitrant horse. Yet, to this day, the important contribution of the voice to the training of the horse is underlined by many authors. Consider, for example, what the great French rider and former coach of the French national team, Jean d'Orgeix, wrote in his latest book: "As far as I'm concerned, I consider not only the voice part of the 'aids,' but I even consider it, especially in the early stage of the horse education, the *main aid*. It has

As we have already seen, Grisone's book is adorned with fifty plates that show different kinds of bits. Grisone dedicates a part of his work to the art of bridling—that is to say the art of choosing the appropriate bit depending on the horse —although, unlike other authors after him, he doesn't dwell in explaining in detail the characteristics and features of the different mouthpieces. In front of their variety and of the inventiveness of their forms the modern reader is rather puzzled. Because, as many have noted, these bits look very severe compared to those used today[273], so much that some consider them real instruments of torture. In fact, most of the bits presented were designed as a remedy for specific problems (horse that "drinks" the bit, which has a big or small mouth, with a thick tongue, which flip the tongue over the mouthpiece, etc..). Paradoxically, in the intentions of the Renaissance horseman the majority of the artifices used to compose the mouthpieces (pears, bells, melons, rings, etc..), that gives them such a threatening a look, served to make the bits more tolerable to horses that opposed by particular resistances[274]. In fact, it is hard to imagine that they actually reached their goal and we can assume that many of the defenses that, in the intentions of their creators, those bits should avoid were produced, or at least exacerbated, by their own use. Grisone is evidently well aware of this risk; so as to warn his readers not to deceive themselves that the horse can achieve "perfection" by continuously changing the mouthpiece (as unfortunately we still see too many inexperienced riders do nowadays):

> And because there is no doubt that to reach the foundation of all virtues it is necessary that the horse has a steady neck and head and a good mouth, I think that on this subject I am forced to let you know that you have to avoid the disorder that many people use, thinking to keep the horse's head

---

the first advantage of being easy to grasp by the horse. A sharp, guttural tone of voice clearly indicates to the horse the rider's discontent and therefore makes it clear that he had done something forbidden. For the approval it's enough a clearer sonority and if he the first few times it is accompanied by caresses and even by a small reward, the horse understands that that sound means approbation." D'Orgeix, 2007, p. 55.

273) In fact, there is much to discuss about what is actually a severe bit. The improper use of the hand can turn even the most seemingly innocuous tool into a pain for the horse, while a steady and wise hand could use a bit considered strong as a precise means of communication. "The truth—writes the General L'Hotte in his memoirs—is that the effects of any bit come mainly from the skill of the hand that uses it, we can say that the best bit is in a skilful hand." L'Hotte, 1905, p. 280. A similar statement is also found in the work of the American rider Mike Bridges, who in his fine book about the training of the horse in the style of the Californian vaqueros writes: "No bit is severe. The bridles are fast or slow, that is to say that a bit can exert its lever action faster or slower than another. It depends on how it is constructed." Bridges, 2010, p. 131.

274) See Chénière, 2002.

steady by changing many harsh and various bridles and to make him work better with more severe bits: and they don't realize that with these bits they discourage or rather exacerbate his problems; it follows that by such mistakes it will never be possible for him to reach his perfection, but with good art and true discipline, and with a pleasant bridle, on which he can gently find his contact and ensure his mouth, in trot and canter, keeping the hand gentle and steady [...] he will become accomplished in all his goodness and he will comply with the will of the Rider who mounts him[275].

The basic criterion which the author suggests is to always give priority to less "harsh" or "open" bits (Grisone calls "open," or "*svenati*," those bits that have a port that ensure freedom to the tongue of the horse), overcoming the resistances of the horse with proper training[276] and avoiding using those bits that could cause injuries to the mouth of the animal, not to "confuse him."[277] In fact, Grisone concludes, if the training is done in the appropriate way, only three bits are enough for the good rider: the "*cannone*" (cannon), the "*scaccia*" and the "*cappione*,"[278] that were relatively mild bits (at least in comparison with the others shown in the treatise).

Grisone's bad reputation

The most controversial part of Grisone's work is that relating to the punishments that the author suggests as remedies to the disobediences of the horse and that has earned a rather sinister reputation for the author of *The Rules of Riding*[279]. In reaction, the recent historiography, especially the Italian historians,

---

275) «*Et perché non è dubbio, che per haver il fondamento d'ogni virtù, bisogna che il cavallo sia fermo di arco di collo di testa, e habbia buona bocca, mi pare sopra di ciò ch'io sia costretto di farvi noto, che vogliate fuggir' il disordine che molti usano, che mutando tante aspre, e varie briglie al Cavallo, pensano con quelle fermarlo di capo, e al tener'agitarlo: e non si aveggono, che con esse si invilisce, overamente si esaspera; onde con si grave errore non sarà mai possibile, che venga nella sua perfettione, ma con la buona arte, e la vera disciplina, e con la briglia piacevole, alla qual si possa temperatamente appoggiare e assicurare di bocca e col trotto, e col galoppo, portando la man temperata e ferma [...] verrà compito in ogni bontà, et a confermarsi col volere del Cavaliero, che gli sta di sopra.*» GRISONE, 1550, p. 64v.

276) See GRISONE, 1550, p. 69r.

277) «*ponerlo in confusione.*» GRISONE, 1550, p. 74r.

278) The *cannone* was a jointed curb bit, with smooth mouthpiece; the *scaccia* was similar, but the mouthpiece was grooved. The *cappione*, or *chiappone*, was instead a port curb bit, which offered some relief to the tongue of the horse.

279) A bad reputation that, at times, it is also the result of an open denigration. It is, for example, the case of the French rider George Fizet that in an interesting recent book does not escape to this cliché expressing his repulsion for a phrase attributed

tends to minimize the brutality of Grisone's methods, rather emphasizing his role as beginner of the new literary genre of treatises on horsemanship. On the other hand, Grisone expresses a conception typical of the time, which considers the horse "created by God to serve, and to comply with the will of man"[280] and attributes his disobedience to his "malicious" and "vicious" nature, although he admits that the biggest challenge is for the "valiant Rider to make the horse understand clearly the reason why he is given the punishment, or rather the aid, not only of spurs, but of whatever kind."[281] However, even taking into account this context, we must admit that many of the "secrets" that he confides to his readers appear today, in the light of subsequent developments in equitation, unnecessarily violent, ineffective and generally counterproductive to the ideal of harmony and mutual understanding between horse and rider that the same Neapolitan master professes.

Definitely affecting our sensibility is the advice to beat the restive horse with the spurs until he bleeds[282], or the "secret" to overcome all resistance of the animal in the *voltes*: to savagely beat him until he surrenders[283]. A horse weak and "coward" should be encouraged to move forward with beatings and a "horrible voice," but also by men on the ground that throw rocks at his hocks. In some cases, the inventiveness of such abuses seems so unlikely as to appear rather a figment of imagination than a method that was really applied by someone. This is the case, for example, of the remedy that Grisone says was taught to him by the Neapolitan Vincenzo Respino. To correct a horse of the Royal riding school that was restive for many years, he tied an hedgehog to his tail, whose shrieks would terrify him to the point of finally pushing him forward[284]. Or when again to win the laziness of a horse that refuses to move forward, he suggests to tie a cat, as fierce as possible, on top of a pole and to push the cat between the hind legs, or on the horse's croup, in order to terrorize him with his claws[285]. And if a horse has the habit of lying down when fording a ditch with water in it, then

---

to Grisone: "to stop beating a horse is already a reward for him." Too bad that these words never appeared in the the treatise by the Neapolitan author and are just a malevolent figment that takes to the extreme the brutality of some passages of the *Rules...*, making for their grotesque caricature. See Fizet, 2010, p. 77.

280) «*creato da Iddio per servire, e conformarsi con la volontà dell'huomo.*» GRISONE, 1550, p. 102v.

281) «*valoroso Cavaliero di far intendere chiaramente al Cavallo la cagione, perché gli si dona il castigo, overo aiuto, non solo di sproni, ma di qualunque sorte si sia.*» GRISONE, 1550, p. 116r.

282) See GRISONE, 1550, p. 59v.

283) See GRISONE, 1550, pp. 91r–91v.

284) See GRISONE, 1550, p. 96v.

285) See GRISONE, 1550, p. 96r.

CHIAPPONE COLLE OLIVE
Coi simili Braccioli, & in cambio delle oliue potrebbon ancho esser due Meloni.

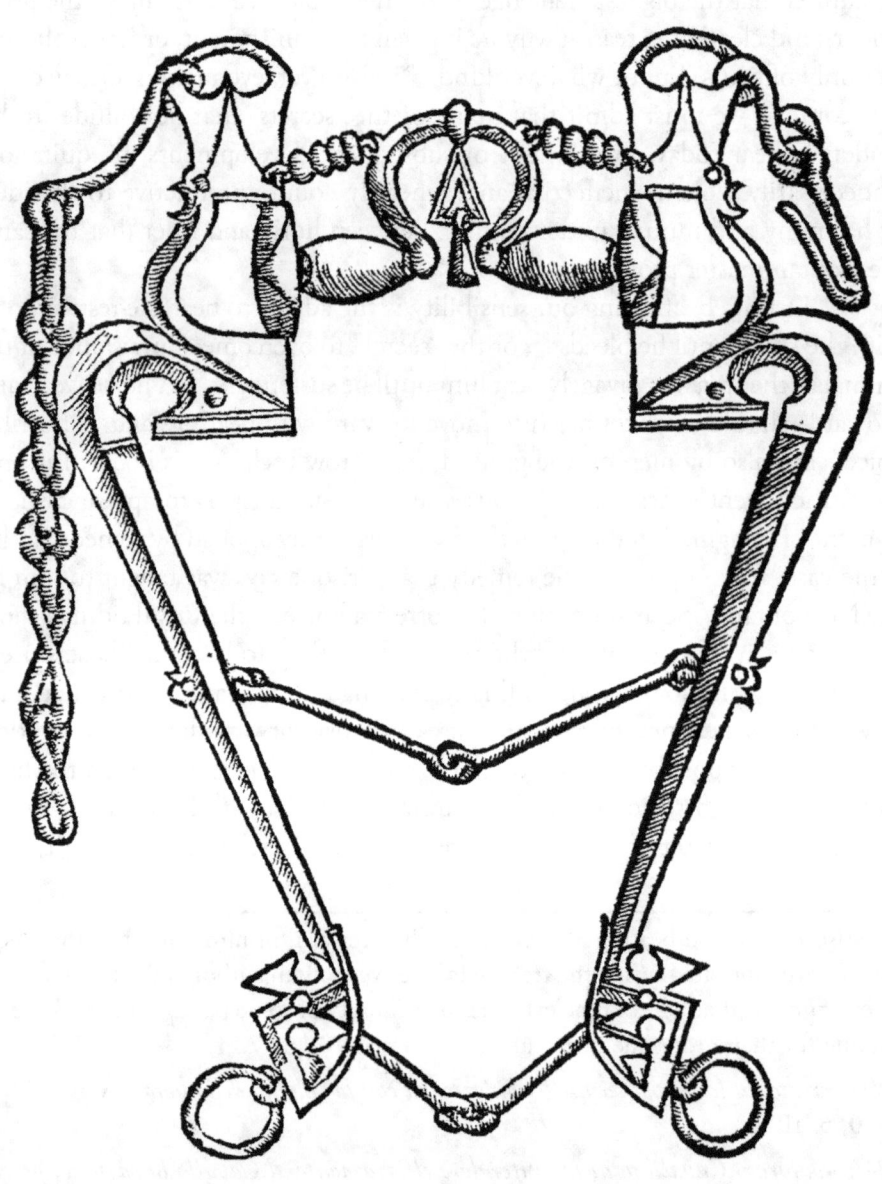

"*Chiappone*" bit

more men must jump on him and push his head under the water, shouting and beating him[286]. Alternatively, he suggested clenching the horse's testicles with a slipknot and at the slightest hint of his intention to lie down, the rider must pull the end of the rope. In short, Grisone concludes, the voice is the most effective punishment, but from beatings arise "infinite virtues." [287]

As you can see the collection of tortures is large and horrifying and surprisingly clashes with the insistence with which Grisone reaffirms in his treatise the importance of proper training. It is true that after having indicated such brutal remedies, the author argues that a good rider does not need to use them, because he's able to achieve his goals by means of his expertise:

> a Rider of good discipline will not ever use these things, because he will get the effect without them with his own virtue, and in different ways[288].

It is a mistake, he says, to use ineffective remedies that may offend the horse's health[289]. In his conception of the training, however, the punishment is more important than the prize[290], even if he insists that it should be given in the proper time and with measure and only in cases when the animal "makes some errors." The abuse of punishment only leads the animal to confusion and makes him scared. The more severe methods, in fact, are intended as a last resort.

Despite these shadows, Grisone remains as a pivotal figure in the history of equitation. The wide circulation of his treatise started a theoretical elaboration and transmission of the equestrian knowledge that still persists today. In the conclusion of his treatise, Grisone stresses the importance, "to be a proper Rider"[291], that observation and theoretical study ("continuously thinking of it"[292]) should be placed side by side with long practice. According to this Neapolitan gentleman, only a patient diligence, an insatiable curiosity and a desire for continuous learning permit to excel in an art, «which is followed by many, and such is its difficulty, that only one will be the one that in the end will come completely to his true sign»[293]. This desire of knowledge and this lesson of culture and dedication are the most important legacy of his work.

---

286) See GRISONE, 1550, p. 98r–99r.

287) See GRISONE, 1550, p. 95v.

288) «*un Cavaliero di buona disciplina non si prevalerà mai di queste cose, perché farà l'effetto senza di esse con la sua propria virtù, e in diverse maniere.*» GRISONE, 1550, p. 98r.

289) See GRISONE, 1550, p. 99v.

290) See GRISONE, 1550, p. 117v.

291) «*per essere compito Cavaliero.*» GRISONE, 1550, p. 123v.

292) «*in essa continuamente pensare.*» GRISONE, 1550, p. 123v.

293) «*la qual si segue da molti, e tanta è la sua difficoltà, che un solo sarà colui, che al fin compitamente arriverà al suo vero segno.*» GRISONE, 1550, p. 124r.

SCACCIA

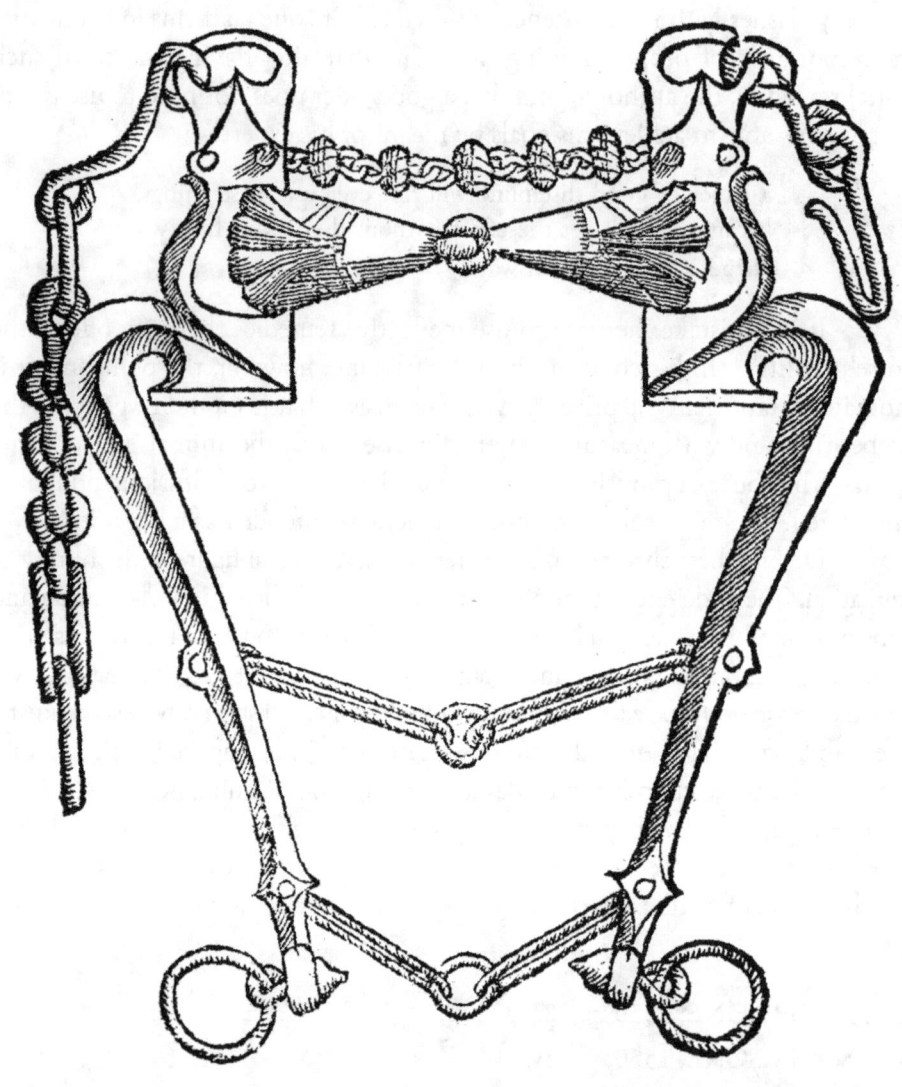

"*Scaccia*" bit

V
Cesare Fiaschi: The harmony of riding well

If the publication and the success of *The Rules of Riding* had the value of founding the new equestrian literature, the printing—six years later—of another work that gained considerable renown and spread, strengthened the prestige of Italian Renaissance equitation, and significantly contributed to the institutionalization of the new literary genre. We are talking of the *Trattato dell'imbrigliare, atteggiare, e ferrare cavalli* (Treatise on bridling, training and shoeing horses, 1556). The author, Cesare Fiaschi, was from another city with important and deep-rooted equestrian traditions: Ferrara.

Equestrian traditions in Ferrara

In the city of the Este, horses were very much appreciated and frequently involved in public events. The chronicles of the time tell us that to celebrate the victory of Azzo VII on Ezzelino III da Romano in Cassano d'Adda in 1259[294], the Ferrarese organized races of manservants and maidservants, donkeys and horses through the streets of the city, a tradition that continued for over twenty years until the establishment of the Palio in 1279. The feast was then made official in the Statutes of 1287, the first real body of laws enacted by the guilds of the city. There it was stated that the race took place twice a year: in honor of St. George, patron saint of the city, and on the day of the Assumption. The prize for the winner was a "*palio*," that is to say a cloth of fine material, while the second and third prize were a pig and a cock, respectively. During the Duchy of Ercole I[295], the Palio was joined by other races, of a more aristocratic kind, which were held in the side of the Barco estate that was closer to the city, called the Barchetto of the Duke. The Palio of St. George soon became the most coveted race in Italy. Often the Berber horses of the Lords of Ferrara, ridden by the same prince, were challenged by the specimens of other famous families. In 1466, for

---

294) In the month of March 1256 Azzo VII (1205–1264)—who sixteen years before had taken possession of Ferrara, starting the seigniory of the Este,—received by the archbishop of Ravenna the assignment of leading a "crusade" against Ezzelino III from Romano, Lord of Verona, Vicenza, Padua, Feltre and Belluno. The soldiers of Venice, Bologna, Mantua and others joined the army of Ferrara. The war lasted two years, during which Ezzelino III also managed to get hold of Brescia in 1258. But Ezzellino was finally defeated by the Guelph League of Azzo VII of Este, in the battle of Cassano d'Adda on 27 September 1259 and died soon after.

295) Born in 1431, he was Duke from 1471 until his death in 1505.

example, the king of Naples, Ferrante of Aragona sent his horses, while in 1475 the Marquis of Mantua, traditional opponent of the Este family, took part in the race with nineteen horses and won[296].

Ferrara was also famous for its sumptuous tournaments, culminating with two great feasts: the one of the carnival of 1561 and that on the occasion of the wedding of Alfonso II of Este with Queen Barbara of Austria[297] on 11 December 1565. We have a thorough description of these events handed down in the *Cavallerie della città di Ferrara*[298] (The Cavalries of the city of Ferrara), anonymous text attributed by scholars to the pen of Agostino Argenti (first decades of the sixteenth century—1576). They were real theater, in which the knightly combats were placed in an articulated drama, represented in a complex and rich scenery. The first of these tournaments was played on the 3rd of March 1561 in a magnificent theater and staged the fierce battles of the Ferrarese knights to free Colocauro, king of Panticapta, subdued by a giant and held captive in the enchanted castle of the fairy Gorgoferusa. The show took place in a theater specially constructed in the main courtyard of the Este castle, lit up by over six hundred candles:

> capable of holding ten thousand people with its very comfortable stands, in its center there was a large fence, and in prospect there was a mountain upon which was founded the castle with five towers, two of which were on the floor and three behind above the top of the mountain; and the one in the middle was much greater than the others so that it stood out over the dome of the great stairs of the palace and they [the five towers] had their turrets and domes, which shone in the top yellow and blue glass balls, which are the colors of the Duke, on which there were waving flags of the same color. Around the battlement of the towers and along the curtain walls could be seen several beautiful Trophies, some of which had the name of the knight to which belonged the weapons of those same trophies, among which neatly appeared various inscriptions appropriate to the place and the topic[299].

---

296) The Palio was disputed until the end of the seventeenth century, then gradually fell into disuse. It was restored since the Thirties of the twentieth century by Guidio Angelo Facchini, but then suffered a long interruption due to World War II. Then it started again in 1967 and it is still held today, the last Sunday of May, See Tebaldi—Vincenzi—Lolli, 1992.

297) Barbara von Habsburg, Archduchess of Austria (1539—1572), was the daughter of Emperor Ferdinand I and Anna of Bohemia and Hungary.

298) Anonimo, 1566.

299) «*capace di diece mila persone co' suoi gradi molto comodi, in mezo al quale era uno*

The scene was so articulated that the very detailed description continues for another ten pages. It is in this fairytale context that the riders made their appearance on their beautiful jennets:

> they were on horseback armed in the ancient style with morions and shields covered with mirrors of steel, which made a great reflexion and they were dressed in rich white drapes all made of gold, and with superb plumes on top[300].

The fighting, on horseback and on foot, alternated with the appearance of actors, theatrical machines and imaginary animals, with lavish use of fireworks and other stage effects, until the inevitable final triumph of the forces of good over the evil enchantments of the sorceress.

Cesare Fiaschi and his treatise

It was solely the desire to emulate the best riders he saw in a tournament in Ferrara that induced Cesare Fiaschi—as the author states at the beginning of his treatise—to look for the most experienced horsemen and men at arms, because they could "benefit me in the matters pertaining to the good knight," so that "through these means and with the constant practice I could instruct myself perfectly in this virtue"[301].

> In my homeland, Ferrara, it is customary to hold feasts, tournaments and various sorts of cavalcades in which each rider, according to his power and with every careful diligence, strives to have the very best horses available; and having to be held a magnificent and sumptuous feast for the memory of the creation of our Illustrious

---

ampio steccato, e in prospetto stava un monte sopra il quale era fondato il castello con cinque torri, due delle quali erano dinanzi in sul piano, e tre di dietro sopra la collina del monte; e quella di mezo era assai maggiore delle altre tanto che avanzava sopra la cuppola della scala grande del Palazzo e insieme havevano le loro torricelle e cuppole, nella sommità delle quali splendeano palle di vetro gialle, e turchine, che sono i colori del Duca, e vi sventolavano sopra bandiere de' medesimi colori. Attorno alla merlatura delle torri e lungo le cortine vedeansi diversi bellissimi Trofei, alcuni de' quali haveano il nome del cavaliere di chi già furono le armi di essi trofei, tra i quali ordinatamente apparivano varie inscrittioni convenienti al luogo e al suggetto.» Anonimo, 1566, p. 7v.

300) «erano a cavallo armati all'antica con morioni e con scudi coperti di specchi d'acciaio in punta, che rendevano un reflesso grandissimo e erano vestiti di ricchissimi drappi bianchi tutti messi a oro, e sopra il tutto con pennacchi soperbissimi e smontati.» Anonimo, 1566, p. 11v

301) «per questi mezi e co'l continuo essercitio in tal virtù perfettamente ammaestrarmi.» FIASCHI, 1556, Narratione alli lettori.

and most Excellent Prince, for the greater enjoyment and amusement of the gentlemen an honorable tournament was prepared in which appeared so richly armed and fairly dressed knights, riding their horses so easily and with such skill, which certainly nowhere else to be seen any better; because this filled the bystanders with wonder, I affirmed that, realizing my abilities and not being able to stand the comparison with this honorable and noble company, I was driven by the zeal for my own honor to retire from it [that company],so as not to turn red in the face in the presence of such valiant knights, and with the firm intention not to wear weapons again nor to join similar knights, until such time as I was sure to be worthy of such company[302].

Son of Girolamo and Eleonora Sacrati, Cesare Fiaschi descended from one of the most important families in Ferrara. His brother, Alessandro, had a leading role in the Este court and was ambassador to France, Spain, Rome and Germany[303]. His *Treatise about bridling, training and shoeing horses* was published in Bologna by Anselmo Giaccarelli, in 1556. The volume, in-quarto, is dedicated to King Henry II of France and, in addition to its historical importance, it has an undeniable artistic value for the quality of the printing, of the xylography initial letters and the numer-

---

302) «*Ritrovandomi io in Ferrara mia patria, ove si costumano far feste, tornei e varie sorte di cavalerie, nelle quali ciascun cavaliere secondo il poter suo e con ogni accurata diligentia si sforza d'haver di più eletti e migliori cavalli, che si trovino; e dovendosi per la memoria della creatione del nostro Illustrissimo e Eccellentissimo Prencipe fare una magnfica, e sontuosa festa, per maggior gaudio, e spasso da gentil'huomini fu preparato un honorato torneo; nel quale comparsero cavalieri tanto riccamente armati, e così leggiadramente vestiti maneggiando con tanta agevolezza, e così maestrevolmente li cavalli loro, che certamente meglio in altro luogo non si saria potuto vedere; la qual cosa si come di stupor tutti li riguardanti rimpiva, così fece, ch'io, ch'ero tra essi cavalieri raccordandomi il fine à che messo ero, e conoscendo di poter malamente stare al paragone dell'honorata, e nobil cavaleria fui spento dal zelo dell'honor mio fuor d'essa ritirarmi, per non rimanere fra si valorosi cavalieri arrossito, con ferma mente di non mai più vestire arme per pormi tra simili cavalieri, se prima io non mi conoscessi degno di tal consortio.*» FIASCHI, 1556, Narratione alli lettori.

303) Alessandro Fiaschi (1516—1585) came in 1527 at the court of the Este as page of Prince Hercules, the eldest son of Duke Alfonso I of which became later secret waiter. He was then the cupbearer, bedroom master and steward of Hercules II and then house-steward under the rule of Alfonso II. He had several diplomatic assignments; he was commissioner general of the war and had the delicate task of treating the difficult story of the wife of Duke Ercole II, Renée of France, whose propensity for reformist ideas created considerable difficulties to her husband.

TRATTATO

DELL IMBRIGLIARE. MANEG-
GIARE, ET FERRARE CAVALLI, DIVI
SO IN TRE PARTI, CON ALCVNI
discorsi sopra la natura di Caualli, con
disegni di Briglie, Maneggi, &
di Caualieri a cauallo, & de
ferri d'esso,

DI M. CESARE FIASCHI GENTIL
HVOMO FERRARESE.

IN BOLOGNA PER ANSELMO
GIACCARELLI. MDLVI.

Frontispiece

ous engraved plates. "All these features make it one of the most beautiful Italian books of the sixteenth century devoted to the horse."[304]

The text includes three treatises, each of which is opened by an initial full page xylography plate that represents a scene relating to the subject. The first introduces the section dedicated to bits and shows the workshop of a craftsman who is manufacturing a mouthpiece to fit a horse, held by a gentleman. The second depicts the interior of a riding arena and a rider on his horse in front of an audience in which stands a central figure who, according to some, would be his teacher (perhaps even the author himself), but in my opinion it is more likely a prince, surrounded by his courtiers. The custom of presenting to kings and other prominent persons (often the owners of the stables) the best horses ridden by the most skilled riders was a typical entertainment of the courts. In all the treatises of the period, it was explained how to properly make this kind of performance. Finally, the third plate represents the shoeing of a horse, inside of a forge. "It is, together with the figures of the various exercises ["*maneggi*"], the only known illustrations of men on horseback of all printed Italian works of the sixteenth century"[305]. The work also presents forty plates showing different kinds of bits, of which the last four show disassembled bits, and the very famous plans of different exercises with the musical score that keeps time. The text also contains engravings representing horseshoes and are among the first known in a printed book. In the Venetian edition of 1598 (by Vincenzo Somascho) the treatise is enhanced by a discourse on the illness of horses, again expanded in the edition of 1614 (by the same publisher), while in the Paduan edition of 1628 (printed by Pietro Paolo Tozzi), is further amended with the *Trattato di mescalzia* (Treatise about farriery) by Filippo Scacco from Tagliacozzo. These appendices are not attributable to the author who, in the introduction to the readers, regrets not having the courage to write about "the way you ought to keep in healing horses [...] if you do not find before its truth with long studies, dissections and experiences"[306].

Although not reaching the huge international success of Grisone's treatise, the work had a considerable circulation, especially thanks to the French translation of François de Prouane, published for the first time in 1564 in Paris under the title *Traicté de la manière de bien embrider, manier et ferrer les Chevaux: avec les Figures des mors de bride, tours e maniemens, e fers qui y sont propres* (Paris, chez Charles Perier, 1564), that was subsequently reprinted several times[307].

---

304) Deblaise, 2002, p. 259

305) Deblaise, 2002, p. 260.

306) «del modo che si dee tenere nel sanare cavalli [...] se non trovassi di lei prima il vero con longhi studi, notomie e isperientie.» FIASCHI, 1556, Narrattione alli lettori.

307) Both Hutt and General Menessier de la Lance list five editions, between 1564 and 1611. See Hutt, 1887, p. 7 and Menessier de la Lance, 1915–21, p. 480–482.

Equitation and music

Unique peculiarity of Fiaschi's treatise is that the explanation of some "airs" ("*maneggi*") is not only accompanied by a plan showing the layout of the exercise and the image of the horse and rider who perform it, but also by a musical score that indicates its rhythm, specifying the pitch of the voice to be taken at different stages of the work. So Fiaschi brings to the extreme that "musical" conception of horseback riding that puts the notions of time and measure as the foundation of the equestrian art. The author resorts to musical notation for the difficulty of expressing in words the rhythm of the movements of horse and rider. In particular, the score is used to specify the correct mode of the collected canter and of the different jumps (Book II, ch. XI–XVI). The solution adopted by Fiaschi highlights the difficulty of reducing the equestrian practice to a verbal description, proposing again a topic already offered up by Grisone and that would remain crucial in all equestrian treatises. Indeed, there is something in horseback riding that cannot be expressed in words and that can be possibly communicated with music, but that is ultimately assigned to the "tact" of each rider. On the other hand, despite the importance of time and measure, was a notion widely shared by riders of the Renaissance; Fiaschi is well aware of the originality and also of the difficulty of the method he chose, which requires of his readers a very high level of culture:

> And because to some rider it might seem strange that I wanted to put Music in my second treatise, judging it possibly unnecessary, in response I say that without measure and time it cannot be made good, and so I show it, and those who do not know how to do it by art will learn it through continuously riding practice[308].

So that the concern to be incomprehensible to the majority of riders, most likely lacking in musical education, dissuaded another Renaissance author, the Paduan Claudio Corte[309], from reporting the musical notation of the different airs in his treatise. Six years after the publication of Fiaschi's treatise, Corte writes in his work on *The Horseman* (1562):

> Much is to be commended Sir Cesare Fiaschi truly honored knight, who has put the above canter to music, to communicate clearly and well (as I understand it, the big

---

308) «*E perché potrebbe forsi parer strano a qualche cavaliero che io habbia voluto inserir in questo mio secondo trattato Musica, giudicando forsi essi non esser necessaria, rispondendo dico che senza misura e tempo non si può far cosa buona, e io così lo mostro; e quelli che non la sanno per arte la imparano per il continuo cavalcare.*» FIASCHI, 1556, p. 88.

309) See Chapter VI.

time) and the big measure that it requires. I would not only
place it in music, but also all the other exercises (as he did),
but knowing that most of the riders, and professor of this
art are ignorant of music, as are the majority of men, not
to confuse them, I didn't: judging that a good practice, and
time after time, and exercise will produce the effect[310].

And a sign of how widespread was the idea of a tight connection between equestrian art and music[311] can be also found in Pasquale Caracciolo, who in his *The Glory of the Horse* (1566) indicates the competence in the field of music as the first among the "sciences and the arts" that a master of horses needs to know to "come to the perfect excellence":

having said that Music is very useful, I add, that it is necessary, in order to understand the measure of time in circling and in the other airs[312].

But music for Fiaschi is something more than merely a means to try to explain the rhythm and cadence of the exercise. It is rather the art that embodies the model of harmony and discipline to which the rider must inspire himself. The author urges them, in fact, to imitate

the good Musician, who prefers to appear rather bizarre
than to play an instrument out of tune or false or not en-

---

310) «*Molto è da lodare il Signor Cesare Fiasco cavallier veramente onoratissimo, il quale ha posto il suddetto galoppo in musica, per far conoscere chiaramente e bene (secondo ch'io m'aviso, il gran tempo) e la gran misura, che se gli richiede. Io non solamente haverei posto in musica questo, ma etiandio tutti gl'altri maneggi (come ha fatt'esso) ma sapendo che la più parte de' cavalcatori, e professori di quest'arte sono ignari di musica, così anco la maggior parte de gl'huomini, non volsi per non confonderli: giudicando, che una buona pratica, e tempo, appresso col tempo, e essercitio farà effetto.*» CORTE, 1562, p. 75v.

311) This link was widely recognized by the Renaissance culture. Hernando Sánchez underlines, for example, its importance in the Neapolitan culture in the era of the Spanish viceroys. "Music and horse riding were two of the most prestigious activities in the education of young nobles, according to a local tradition encouraged by viceroys as the Duke of Alcalá—and it was reflected in an abundant literature, from the treatises written at the end of the Aragonese period up to works like the *Discorsi cavallereschi* (Knightly discourses), published in 1573 by Gaspare Toralto, noble from the seat of Nido who, in a dialogue set in the palace of the Duke of Amalfi, unfolded a compendium of the knowledge about chivalry, in which were treated all the, spiritual and physical, exercises of chivalry necessary to form the perfect knight." Hernando Sánchez, 1998, p. 280.

312) «*Tra le quali havendo detta la Musica utilissima, soggiungerò, che sia necessaria, per intendere la misura del tempo nel volteggiare, e negli altri maneggi.*» CARACCIOLO, 1566, p. 140.

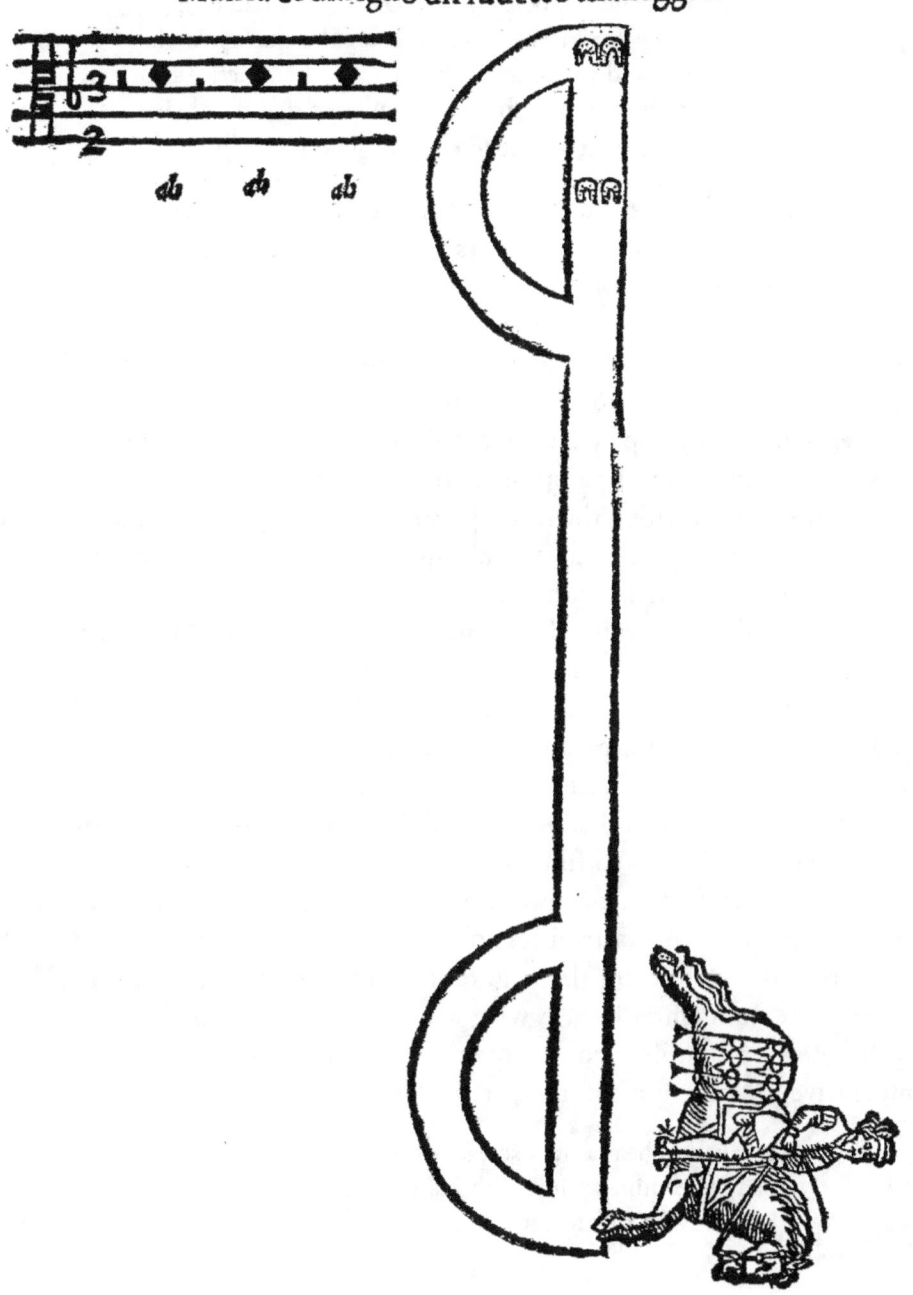

Drawing of the Capriole with its own musical score

>tirely good, nor to play Music if it is not excellent and perfect; and this happens to be excellent and rare to hear, not so much for his skill, but also for the quality of the instrument and the music: in which all who practice this exercise of chivalry will find an example, so that they make sure that they will be able to procure good horses[313].

This ideal of excellence and perfect harmony between horse and rider lays the foundation for the tradition of equestrian ballet that will have its full development in the large carousels of the seventeenth century. In the indications of Fiaschi "the pitch of the notes, the rhythm and the sonority of the vocals combine to create musical instructions for the horse, embracing the rhythm and energy of its motion."[314] For example, in the air of "one step and a jump" ("*un passo e un salto*") he uses two short and low "AH" for the preparation, a more acute "HAY" for the jump and a silence for the moment in which the horse gets back on the ground. "So the voice becomes the first instrument of training, which creates the conditions of the marriage between instrumental music and horse riding in the equestrian ballet. The oral indications enhance the magic of a horse admirably driven and allow the rider to control his mount without any visible gesture."[315] In this sense, the equitation proposed by Fiaschi accords with the Neo-Platonic philosophical ideal of the musical effect. According to this view, the horses have a special sensitivity to rhythm and measure, because they share with humans the same nostalgia for the universal harmony that the human soul dreams to find again.

As previously stated by Grisone, the voice is, for Fiaschi, a crucial aid. In fact the author attributes to it, as to music, the power to punish the unruly horse, to calm the frightened and to embolden the lazy. Nevertheless he condemns its use with a horse already trained, conforming to the ideal of complete concealment of the aids that will become a real imperative of academic equitation:

> It is bad to hear a rider scream on horseback and also very bad to see him squirm with his limbs and with his waist, because with that he must move only a little bit at a certain

---

313) «*il buon Musico che più tosto si vuol mostrare bizzarro che sonare strumento scordato o falso o non interamente buono, né ancho Musica se non ottima e perfetta; e questo aviene per farsi udir raro e eccellente, non tanto per il saper suo, ma etiamdio per la bontà dell'instrumento e Musica; il che a tutti di questo essercitio di cavaleria sara per essempio, acciò così essi procurino e attendano più che potranno ad havere a fare con buoni cavalli.*» FIASCHI, 1556, p. 94.

314) Van Orden, 2002, p. 390.

315) Van Orden, 2002, p. 390.

The air of "one step and a jump" ("un passo e un salto")

time to aid him [the horse], so that he does the rider's will, showing also, in this way, to the bystanders not to be a statue, but instead, to have elegance and good manner in staying on a horse[316].

On the other hand, in another place Fiaschi says: the grace of the rider, the composure of his gestures and the accuracy of his seat do not only have an aesthetic function, but serve to correctly address the mount, promoting his balance and facilitating his movement in the more difficult exercises:

> all those riders who will show in public must take care to keep the time with the waist and the limbs, both head and arms as legs and feet, always making every effort to appear on horseback as graceful as they can, because, besides being beautiful to watch, they will also help the horse, that will appear more graceful and better in any sort of air he will perform[317].

The canon of the new school equitation

Another distinguishing feature of Fiaschi's work is the explicit purpose of the author to codify the equestrian art, setting the rule for the proper execution of the different "airs" ("*maneggi*") to bring order in the multitude of practices. A rule whose authority would safeguard the rider who follows it from the criticisms of the many riders who at that time, rode without due accuracy. While the treatise by Grisone can be considered as a kind of real training manual for the warhorse, the one by Fiaschi is instead a canon of the different exercises, performed with a horse already perfectly trained. Fiaschi explains both exercises with an eminently military purpose (that is to say the different types of "*maneggio di repoloni,*" or *passade*), and those with a more aesthetic and virtuosic trait (as the school jumps).

---

316) «*è male udire un cavaliere gridar a cavallo e brutto veder è poi anchora dimenarsi assai con le membra e con la vita, perché solo si ha egli a movere un pochetto con quella a certo tempo per aiutarlo, acciochè da lui sia fatto il voler suo, mostrando ancho con ciò a riguardanti di non esser statua, anzi haver garbo e maniera di star a cavallo.*» FIASCHI, 1556, p. 111.

317) «*tutti quelli cavalieri che verranno di vedetta debbano procurare d'accomodarsi secondo il tempo con la vita e le membra, così capo e braccia come gambe e piedi, facendo sempre ogni opera di farsi veder più aggratiati che potranno a cavallo, perché, oltre che faran il loro bel vedere, aiuteranno anco al cavallo che in quella sorte di maneggio che farà comparirà più aggarbato e migliore.*» FIASCHI, 1556, p. 127.

> In this second part of the treatise I intend with my speech not only to set the standard for the handling of horses, but also to expose by means of designs some acts of riders on horseback and their horsetracks [indicating the position of the hooves of the horse on the ground] and the time in Music of some exercises so that no one can be blamed every time that he performs them if following these instructions. Since I have seen many [riders], both in the past and now that do not aspire to do what they entirely ought to do with the horse, I feel pressed to undertake this effort, and also because I know that currently some, for the reason of not being made aware, incur in many errors [...] but no one should disdain to accept my opinion, given that if he shall proceed as indicated in this treatise, and by means of drawings and Music, he will be honored, without fear of being considered ignorant, because with the living reasons in the hands he will shut the mouth of those who dare to contradict him[318].

Moreover, Fiaschi claims that he omitted various topics and did not dwell on others because they were already the subject of the writings of several other horsemen[319], a sign that the equestrian treatise was at the time a genre already flourishing and widespread. Evidently, the author does not refer only to his immediate predecessor, Grisone, in the publication of a printed book on the equestrian art, but also to other authors of works that probably circulated in manuscripts, now lost and perhaps yet to be rediscovered. This statement clearly demonstrates Fiaschi's awareness of the need to place his set of rules in a wider debate, in which different practices were facing each other giving birth to the ideas of modern equitation. This debate was ensured by the very widespread printing of some texts, such as that of Fiaschi's, and has contributed significantly to steer the course of the art of horsemanship.

---

318) «*Mi par in questa seconda parte del trattato non solo dar norma col dir mio del maneggio di cavalli, ma porre ancho in disegno alcuni atti di cavalieri a cavallo e ferri d'esso, e il tempo in Musica d'alcuni maneggi, acciò che non possa essere ripreso alcuno ogni volta che secondo tali raccordi li maneggerà poi. L'haver io veduto molti, sì pe'l passato come per adesso, che non mirano di far fare al cavallo interamente quel che dovrebbero, mi [h]a fatto prender questa fatica, e ancho perché so che al dì d'hoggi alcuni, per non essere avertiti, incorrono in molti errori [...], però niuno si dee sdegnare accettare il mio parere atteso, che se procederà del modo che in questo trattato si intenderà e vederasi ancho in disegno e Musica, potrà farsi honore senza tema d'essere riputato insciente, perché con le vive ragioni in mano chiuderà la bocca a quelli ch'ardissero contradirli.*» FIASCHI, 1556, pp. 87–88.

319) See FIASCHI, 1556, p. 127.

The art of bridling

The first of the three books in which the work is divided is dedicated to the art of bridling that, as we have already seen, is the art of choosing the right bit to mount each horse with. Crucial competence from which, according to Fiaschi, depends "the gaining or losing of a horse"[320] and that requires a careful evaluation of the morphology of each specimen by examining first his back, legs and feet. In fact, when these three parts are good, says Fiaschi, "it can be believed to have half, and almost the two-thirds, of the help and hope to achieve every praise and honor in bridling him,"[321] However, the readers should not be deceived by the effects of the different kinds of bit. The author warns: whoever plans to solve the physical defects of the animal by constantly changing bridles is wrong, especially when he increases its severity. The results that one gets by doing this are exactly the opposite, because the torment that is inflicted on the animal ends up making him first unruly, then numb and unrestrained. The bit must be chosen according to the overall structure of the animal and, in particular, to the anatomy of the mouth. As Grisone already explained, Fiaschi reiterates that the many bridles described in his treatise have different functions and are used to cope with the characteristics, attitudes and specific defenses of individual horses. They should not be continuously changed. Whoever does change them frequently – adds Fiaschi – demonstrates proceeding blindly due to ignorance.

> And I say this only because I dislike changing the bridle every day as is customary for many people in present times, who put some bridles in the horses' mouths, without knowing the reason. And this happens because they are ignorant of the effect produced by each bridle and of the needs of the horse, and if by chance they allege one or two good reasons, to them it sounds like much, but I say that this is like a walk in darkness.[322]

Fiaschi as well considers the gentlest bridle as the first to be used. Once the rider has chosen a bit, he must then observe its effects by making someone else ride the horse. The author also advises the reader against giving up too early the use of the cavesson, which serves to impart the

---

320) «*il guadagnare e perdere un cavallo.*» FIASCHI, 1556, Narratione alli lettori.

321) «*si può credere d'havere la metà, e quasi li due terzi dell'aiuto per se, e sperare d'havere à conseguire ogni laude, e honore nell'imbrigliarlo.*» FIASCHI, 1556, p. 1.

322) «*Et sol questo dico perche mi spiace il mutare ogni dì briglia, come al presente costumano molti, li quali mettono alcune briglie in bocca à cavalli, ne sano la cagione. Et questo avviene per essere inscienti dell'effetto, che opera la briglia, e del bisogno del cavallo, e se per sorte allegano una, ò due buone ragioni, li pare assai, ma io dico, che ciò è come un caminare alla cieca.*» FIASCHI, 1556, p. 29.

The plate which opens the first book shows the workshop of a bitmaker

basics of the training to the horse, preserving his mouth. Instead, he recommends to keep it until the horse will not take a correct posture of head and neck. At that time, three different types of cavesson were used: made of rope, of leather and of iron. The first type, considered the gentlest, was generally the first to be employed. Being more severe, those of leather and of iron were instead used in a more advanced stage of the training, depending on the need. Unlike Grisone, who prescribed their use immediately after the very first stage of training, Fiaschi is against the use of so-called "false reins." According to Fiaschi, their use hardens the horse's mouth and makes the horse completely insensitive[323].

In addition to being able to judge the physical structure of the horse, the good horseman should also know the nature of the different breeds. In fact, being born and grown in different climates, the horses have different attitudes and tendencies which affect their training. Fiaschi confirms the prejudice, widespread during the Renaissance, against the horses from northern Europe (generically referred to as Frisians), which he considers unreliable and lazy[324]; instead he appreciates the Turks, he defines the Sardinians fiery and complains about the degeneration of the Neapolitans. Above all he prefers Spanish horses, judging them sincere and willing, and therefore not worthy of being ill-treated. He prescribes instead a brutal treatment for the poor Frisians, saying that ordinarily they should be handled harshly, "beating them without respect[325]." Another decisive factor in the nature of a horse is the color of its coat and the presence of markings, such as blazes, stars, socks etc.. As we have already seen with Grisone, also according to Fiaschi the light hairs were generally considered a sign of weakness, because in them lies the phlegmatic humor.

A higher ideal

Knowing the nature of horses is not enough, since one must also know how and especially when to apply the aids, punishments and treat-

---

323) Fiaschi and Grisone do not describe the false-reins, but we find their description in later editions of the treatise by the Duke of Newcastle: "To work Horses with false Reins, is very false working, for, being tied to the Arches of the Bitt, and pulling it, that flacks the Curb: and so no Horse shall be firm and settled with it, for, that Horse that doth not suffer the Curb, shall never be a ready-horse; so it makes the Bitt like a Snaffle." (I quote from the English edition: William Cavendish (Duke of Newcastle), *A New Method of Extraordinary Invention to Dress Horses, etc.*, Dublin, James Kelburn, 1740, p. 277).

324) He defines them «*two hearted [...] and of lazy nature*» («*di due cori [...] e di natura poltroni*»). FIASCHI, 1556, p. 40.

325) «*percotendoli senza rispetto.*» FIASCHI, 1556, p. 35.

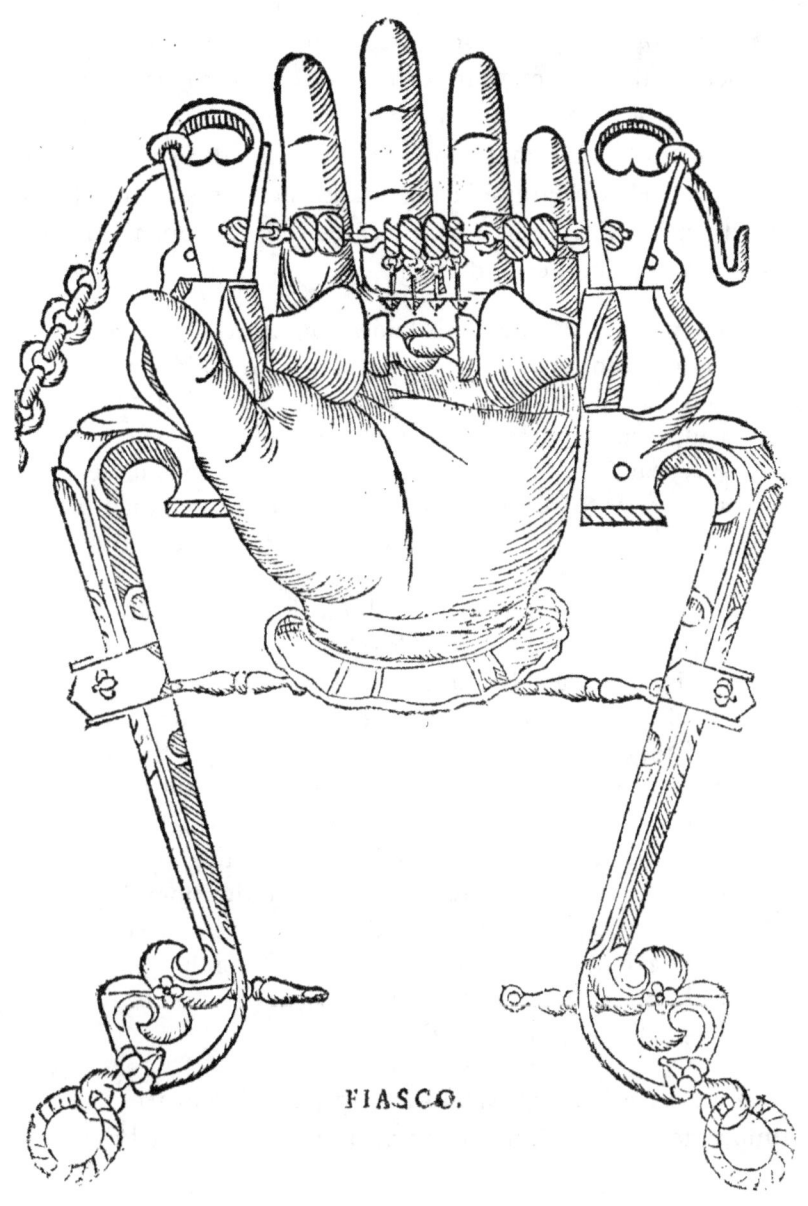

Even if Fiaschi underlines that the mouthpieces must be chosen on the basis of the mouth of each horse, he considers the canonical width of the bit that of a human fist.

ments that are necessary for each. As it was for Grisone, likewise for Fiaschi the essence of riding and of the care of the animals consists exactly of the proper timing and measure of the actions of the rider, who is supposed to act at the appropriate moment to be most effective and must adapt his behavior to the mood of the animal. However, different from Grisone, who dwelt on enumerating gruesome punishments (even if he recommends their use only in extreme cases), Fiaschi openly professes being himself against violence and anger:

> the good rider must also know how to recognize the natures and qualities of horses, and he must ride well and gracefully, with a gentle and pleasant hand, in time and with exactness, and he must be strong in the saddle, adapting himself according to the occasion and the time, so as to beat them [the horses] or to caress them, or only keep them into fear, fatiguing them more or less, in accordance with the exercise that they are doing. All the time keeping his watch on their mind and on their forces and acting in accordance with them, never fearing that there is a defect in the horse. And he must refrain from imitating those who are plagued by anger and those that do what duty and reason does not require. Neither he should follow the example of those who give so hard a toil to horses, both to win their laziness beating them a lot (which causes the opposite effect, because the more they are beaten the more they get discouraged) or because they are brave and good willing, but without much force, who doing this in the end obtain a minor effect, being unable to moderate themselves appropriately[326].

The ideal outlined by Fiaschi is very refined, and requires the maximum composure and discipline of the rider and to be carried out, it also ne-

---

326) «al buon cavaliere fa bisogno sapere ancho conoscere le nature, e qualità de cavalli, e maneggiarli bene, e aggratiatamente, con la mano suave, e piacevole, à tempo, e con giustezza, e stare in sella forte, temperandosi secondo l'occasione, e tempi, si de batterli, come di farli carezze ò di tenerli solamente in timore, affaticandoli più, e meno, secondo poi quello maneggio, che se li fa fare, havendo l'occhio di continuo all'animo, e forze loro, e secondo quelle operare, nè mai temer di vitio, che nel cavallo fusse. Et si guardi di non imitare coloro, che da colera si lasciano trasportare, e fanno quello, che'l dover non vuole, ne la ragion comporta. Ne tolga ancho essempio da quelli, che danno si aspra fatica à cavalli, ò sia per voler vincere la poltroneria d'essi con assai batterli (il che causa contrario effetto, perche quanto più li danno tanto più s'inviliscono) ò sia pure, perche li trovano coraggiosi, e d'animo gentile, ma senza molta forza, che al fin poi li vengono à meno, per non sapersi temperare come si conviene.» FIASCHI, 1556, p. 34.

The plate that opens the second book shows a rider performing in front of a person of high rank, surrounded by his courtiers.

cessitates highly trained and obedient horses, so that they can be ridden easily by anyone and not only by those who have tamed them. Even by a child. A so systematic training should become a second nature of the animal, to the point that "to the well-disciplined and taught horse it is harder to do poorly than to do well."[327] To achieve this, the rider needs dexterity and good judgment, but above all knowledge and experience, because each of his actions should be motivated by well-founded reasons. He must also avoid over-riding the horse, to preserve intact his good inclination to work, but also not to displease the public that may be assisting while he is riding. In Fiaschi's view, the equestrian art has a strong social and public dimension and must conform to that ideal of grace and *sprezzatura*, which is the rule of behavior of the perfect gentleman.

The aesthetic dimension of the equestrian art however always combines with the aim to ensure maximum mobility and agility of the horse. For this reason, even Fiaschi considers the collected position of the head and neck of the horse essential to give him a more elegant attitude, but also to assure his submission to the action of the bit and to improve his collection[328], thus enabling him to perform the most sophisticated movements. The author explains that the position of the head should be neither too open nor too closed (overbent), but with the forehead close to the vertical. To obtain this, the rider must first learn to use his hand wisely, without giving or pulling too much on the reins. Instead, with the action of the reins to "take and give" so that, four centuries later, the great Portuguese riding master, Nuno Oliveira, would consider the fundamental secret of equitation:

> ...do not keep the bridle [reins] too loose, but not very tight, but participating[329] of both, and in doing so you will obtain that he will always go forward, but just a little bit, collecting him in a way that will be nice to see[330].

---

327) «*al cavallo ben disciplinato, e insegnato è più faticoso il male, che il ben fare.*» FIASCHI, 1556, p. 95.

328) See Chapter IV, n. 259.

329) Meaning that the use of the reins should be in the middle, sometimes acting and sometimes releasing.

330) «... *non se gli lenti troppo la briglia, ne ancho si tenga molto serrato in quella, ma perticipi de l'uno e l'altro. Et cosi facendo si verrà a far che andarà sempre inanti, però pocchetto, con un aggrupar di bella vista .*» FIASCHI, 1556, p. 114.

The school airs and jumps

The second book of the treatise describes the execution of different types of school airs ("*maneggi*") and jumps. The school airs consist of all the different variations of the exercise of *passade* and, according to a classification which we have already seen in Grisone, are characterized by the *volte* performed at the end of the straight line ("*repolone*"). Therefore Fiaschi describes the air of "counter-time" (*contra tempo*)—in which the horse is first held in the direction opposite from that in which he will ultimately do the *volte* and is then turned on the straight line with a half pirouette—then that of "half time" (*mezzo tempo*) and of "full time" *(tutto tempo)*—in which the horse performs one or more *pesade*[331] at the end of the straight line and then turns on his hind legs, putting down the front legs a quarter of the way through the half-pirouette, or completes its accomplishment, the so-called "misleading *voltes*" (*volte ingannate*)—in which, at the end of the straight line, the rider pretends to turn to one side and with a quick change of direction performs the half-pirouette in the other direction.[332] There is also the one with one and a half *voltes*, in which the horse performs a full pirouette and half before heading in the opposite direction from which he came. Finally, Fiaschi explains the air called "*volte* on haunches" (*volta d'anche*), in which the horse performs a reverse pirouette on the front legs. This last kind of air is considered particularly useful for "tilts" (jousts that were held with a wooden barrier that separated the contestants), because it allowed a knight to overtake the opponent from behind, while he was still turning his mount.

As for jumps, their description starts from the "collected canter" (*galoppo raccolto*), which is the equivalent of what we now call *terre a terre*, that is to say a two beat and very collected canter, in which the horse concentrates his forces to jump and that is used as a preparation for *capriole*. The other jumps are the "the air with jumps and bounds" (*maneggio con salti e balzi*), the one "with jumps in the measure of a step and a jump ("*salti a misura di un passo e un salto*") and that "in the measure of two steps and a jump" (*a misura di due passi e un salto*), the "jump of the ram" (*salto a montone*) and finally the *cabriole*. The picture of each of these is accompanied by his respective musical score.

---

331) The *pesade* is when the horse sur-charges his weight on his hind legs, lowers his haunches and lifts his front legs from the ground.

332) This type of exercise recalls the *sorte em terrenos cambiados* of the Portuguese bullfighting, in which the rider pretends to go in one way and then suddenly changes direction at the moment of the encounter with the bull, bewildering him (this manoeuvre is also known as *ir a o corno conctrário*, that means "to go to the opposite horn" and in Spanish is called *suerte àl piton contrario*). See Fernando Somer D'Andrade, 1991, pp. 108-109.

Fiaschi, however, warns his readers against the danger of training a horse that will be used in war or in duels to the presentation airs. The risk, in fact, is that the animal could perform them spontaneously in the course of the fight, hampering the rider's ability to defend himself from the attacks of his opponent. For the same reason he is also against the widespread habit of doing the *pesade* that, in his opinion, when the horse raises his front legs too high, demonstrating little control by the rider and exposing him to the risk of being unsaddled in case of a crash during the fight. In any case, according to Fiaschi, the *pesade* must be always and only executed on command and never on the initiative of the animal. Therefore, in Fiaschi's view of horsemanship there appears a more marked distinction between an utilitarian training, aimed at military purposes, and the artistic dimension, aimed at displaying the qualities of the horse, his mutual understanding with the rider and the ability and the courage of the latter. From this point of view, Fiaschi's treatise appears more modern compared to the book by Grisone. It also shows a greater sensitivity towards the animal and hinting to exercises which are closer to the academic riding yet to come, for example, when the author suggests to finish the straight line of the *passade* with a *piaffe*[333] instead of with a *pesade*, taking care that the horse relaxes his jaw, chewing the bit:

> Instead of which [i.e. the *pesade*], not so much in this as in every other exercise, it is good to hold him [the horse], which is done on the straight [line], and make him do as most of the horses from Spain do, as one begins to hold them, go with their haunches to the ground. And while he is held, he should remain in motion, that is to say now with one, now with the other arm raised; also taking care that he chews the bridle so that it makes sound, because in doing so in addition to being beautiful to watch it will be safer, and no one will find fault with this[334].

Or when he suggests the use of counter-canter[335] on the *voltes*, to make the horse stronger and more resistant: exercise still in use today to improve collection and straightness:

---

333) See Chapter III, n. 216.

334) «*In vece della quale [cioè della posata], non tanto in questo come in ogni altro maneggio, è buone tenere, che si fa pe'l diritto, farli fare come la maggior parte dei cavalli di Spagna fanno, che come s'incominciano a ritenere vanno con l'anche quasi a terra. Et ritenuto poi stia in motto, cioè hor con l'uno, hor con l'altro braccio levato; facendo ancho di maniera, che mastichi la briglia di modo, ch'ella faccia suono; perche oltre il bel vedere così operandosi, sarà ciò più sicuro, ne d'alcuno biasimato.*» FIASCHI, 1556, p. 106.

335) When the horse canters on the outside lead, instead of the inside.

And when in this way whether they trot or canter, if it will be done on the right hand, the left shoulder and arm will have to go forward [lead], and if on the left the right shoulder and arm similarly. And this exercise is extremely profitable, not only for young horses, but also for those who are not [young], because it is of use in a lot of effects to the younger to teach them and to help them improve their endurance, while to the older to keep in their memory what they have learned and maintain their strength[336].

Shoeing

The third and final book is dedicated to the art of shoeing. It is a subject that, according to the author, was considered "low" [337] by many but that the good rider must learn in order to avoid the damages that can be done by a bad farrier. Moreover it is a matter which requires "quite a lot of light"[338] and therefore cannot be entrusted to the mere practice, but requires a deep knowledge of the different qualities of the hoofs and of the different tools and methods to correct their defects. The author then surveys them, concluding his review with the drawings of various types of horseshoes, providing an interesting overview of the different models in use at the time.

Like Grisone, even Fiaschi concludes his treatise with an exhortation to those who want to excel in the knightly virtues not only to study and read everything that has been written about them in the past, as in the present, but also to observe the other riders, to pay attention to the discussions on this issue and, especially, to cultivate the friendship of the real experts, devoting themselves to win and retain their confidence:

---

336) «*E quando a questo modo si trottaranno, overo gallopparanno, se si farà a mano destra bisogna fare, che'l braccio, e spalla sinistra vada innanzi, e se alla sinistra il destro, e spalla similmente. Et questo maneggio è sommamente profittevole, non tanto per cavalli giovani, come ancho, per quelli che non lo sono; per che giova in molti effetti a giovani per insegnare, e farli far lena, a quelli di più tempo per tenerli in memoria l'imparato, e mantenerli con lena.*» FIASCHI, 1556, p. 108.

337) This is, for example, the opinion of Claudio Corte, who in this regard writes: "Before I say more, I warn the reader that as well as many ancient authors Sir Cesare Fiaschi, Ferrarese gentleman and knight truly worthy of praise, wrote quite extensively about horse shoeing. But as I do not consider that this matter belongs to the horseman, that we are going to establish [as a social figure], but to the responsibility of the farriers, I will pass over this point." CORTE, 1562, p. 54v

338) «*alquanto lume.*» FIASCHI, 1556, p. 130.

that rider who wants to perfect and take delight in the virtue of horsemanship must first of all put all his effort toward winning the friendship of those who are very competent and scientific in it, so as to be well instructed and taught, and this applies to knowing [good] horsemen, as well as bit makers and farriers; and he must do everything to preserve their friendship[339].

In this patient intellectual and physical discipline, the true rider must try to emulate the best and most honest horsemen, ignoring the negative example of those who exercise their profession caring only for profit. Of the first he should instead emulate their dedication to the equestrian art. He says, "that even when they are sleeping they dream of it"[340].

---

339) «*quel cavaliero che perfettamente si delettarà della virtu cavaleresca, ha primieramente da usare ogni studio per acquistare la benevolenza di quelli, che di essa saranno ben scienti, per poter essere, come bisogna, bene istrutti, e ammaestrati; e si de cavalcatori, come de morsari, e maniscalchi; l'amicitia de quali egli ha da fare ogni cosa per conservare.*» FIASCHI, 1556, p. 160.

340) «*che sin dormendo si sognano d'essa.*» FIASCHI, 1556, p. 160.

Fiaschi is the first author of a treatise about riding to devote an entire book to shoeing.

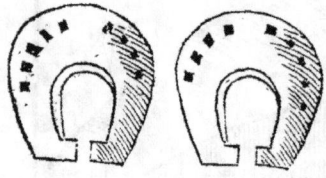

Fer. imborditi, cō le uerghe di dietro piu uicine

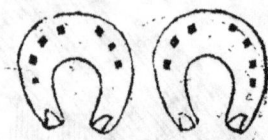

Fer. cō due ramponi.

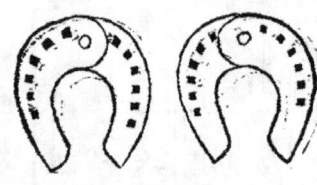

Fer. detti disferre, che sono di due pezzi, con una brocca nel mezo della punta.

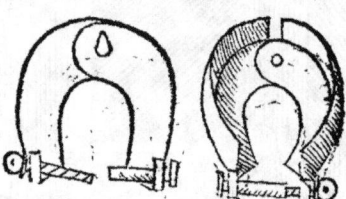

Fer. che si pongono senza chiodi.

FERRI PER PIE DI DIETRO.

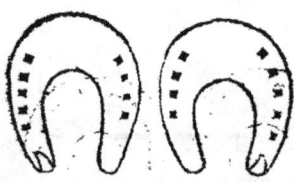

Fer. con un rampone di fuori.

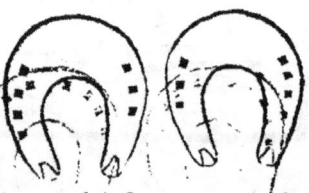

Fer. con due ramponi.

Different types of front horseshoes

The Hall of Horses of Palazzo Te in Mantua (courtesy of the Municipality of Mantua)

In Paolo Uccello's picture (front page) Niccolò Mauruzi da Tolentino unseating Bernardino della Ciarda at the Battle of San Romano (1438-1440) it is portrayed a chestnut horse performing a croupade (detail, above) Florence, Galleria degli Uffizi (© Italian Ministry of Cultural Heritage and activities and tourism). Facing page: Paolo Uccello *Niccolò Mauruzi da Tolentino unseaing Bernardino della Ciarda* at the Battle of San Romano (1438-1440)— Florence, Galleria degli Uffizi (© Italian Ministry of Cultural Heritage and activities and tourism)

The bay Stella, one of the horses portrayed on the walls of Enrico Pandone's Castle in Venafro, sent as a gift to Annibale Caracciolo in 1524. Note the richness of the magnificent saddle "*a la gineta*" (by permission of the Ministry of Cultural Heritage and Activities and Tourism – Soprintendenza per i beni storici, artistici ed etnoantropologici del Molise)

The gray Scorbone, gifted to Annibale Pignatelli in 1524, portrayed in the act of kicking. On the right, note the picture of the bit with which was ridden, that is to say a "*scaccia*" (by permission of the Ministry of Cultural Heritage and Activities and Tourism - Soprintendenza per i beni storici, artistici ed etnoantropologici del Molise)

The horse Dario, surmounted by the image of Hercules killing the Hydra on the north wall of the Hall of horses, Palazzo Te – Mantua (courtesy of the Municipality of Mantua)

VI
Claudio Corte
The Horseman as a social figure

With the publication in 1562 of *Il cavallarizzo* (The Horseman) by Claudio Corte, not only do the books on equestrian art begin to speak to each other—inaugurating a game of quotes, cross-references, emulation and arguments that lasts to this day—but they also make an important literary qualitative leap.

Claudio Corte

It is the same Corte who provides in his work most of the news about his life. Born in Pavia, probably around 1514[341], Claudio followed his family tradition. His father, Giovanmaria della Girola, from a family of minor nobility in Padua, served Ludovico il Moro[342] and Bartolomeo of Alviano[343], was horseman of Isabella of Aragon[344], then of Prospero Colonna[345], whom he fol-

---

341) In the preface of the first edition, published in 1562, the author claims in fact to be 48 years old. See CORTE, 1562, p. 2v.

342) Born the 27th of July 1452, he was the Duke of Bari since 1479, later Duke of Milan from 1480 to 1499. Defeated by the French at Novara in 1500, was taken prisoner and died in the castle of Loches, France, in 1508. See CORTE, 1562, p. 124r.

343) Mercenary commander (1455–1515), fought for the Orsini and for the Church. He was then hired by Ferdinand II of Spain. At the service of the Venetian Republic, he defeated the imperial army and obtained the lordship of Pordenone. He was defeated by the French at the Battle of Agnadello and taken prisoner. Released in 1513, he returned to fight for the French. He died during the siege of Brescia. See CORTE, 1562, p. 124r.

344) She was the Duchess of Milan, Bari and Rossano (1470—1524). Second child of Alfonso II, heir to the throne of Naples, and Ippolita Maria Sforza. In December 1488, she married in Naples Gian Galeazzo Sforza. When the couple arrived in Milan, Ludovico il Moro, uncle of Gian Galeazzo, assigned them the castle of Pavia, in order to remove his nephew from the government of the duchy. The hostility of the Moro and the adverse political conditions caused her to return into the kingdom of Naples. There she obtained the duchy of Bari, of which she took possession in 1501, living among the Apulian city and the capital of the kingdom until her death. See CORTE, 1562, pp. 5v e 124v.

345) (1452–1523): he was an ally of Charles VIII of France. During the brief period of rule of the French crown over Naples, he received the duchy of Trasetto and the County of Forlì. Despite this he then lined up to defend the kingdom of Naples against the French. So he entered in the service of the viceroy of Naples and of the

lowed in the Battle of the Bicocca. Giovanmaria was in turn a disciple and nephew of Evangelista Corte, who was also a famous horseman, to whom the author attributes the invention of a kind of martingale (called "*camarra*") and of a particular way of braiding the horses' tails[346].

   Claudio also asserts to be Mantuan on his mother's side and by his own admission, this was the reason why he held the horses of the breed of Mantua in such high esteem[347]. During his life, he served in various courts. It was, first of all, in the service of Isabella of Aragon[348]. When she died, he became page of Vespasiano Colonna[349], Duke of Trasetto and Count of Fondi. Later, during the war between Philip, King of Spain, and Paul IV (1556–1557)[350], he was horseman of Bonifacio Caetani[351], then in the service of Cardinal Alessandro Farnese[352], to whom he dedicated the first edition of *Il cavallarizzo*. It is not exactly clear in which period of time Corte was in the service of the latter. From what the author writes in the preface of the work, it could be argued that it was probably for a short period, just before the

---

346) See CORTE, 1562, pp. 5v e 101.

347) See CORTE, 1562, p. 33r.

348) See CORTE, 1562, p. 6r.

349) Following in his father's footsteps, Prospero (1480–1528) embraced a military career. He fought for the Church and then, in 1524, the emperor granted him the county of Belgioioso in Lombardy, to which he gave up the following year, having been confirmed in the Duchy of Carpi, granted to his father by the same Charles V. His second wife, Giulia Gonzaga, was one of the most famous ladies of her time. The growing tensions between the pope and the Colonna family culminated in the capture of the city by the troops led by the Cardinal Pompeo, by Ascanio and the same Vespasiano. The pope was forced to an agreement, which he subsequently did not respect, and the Colonna could then return to Rome only after obtaining the forgiveness of Clement VII in 1527. See CORTE, 1562, p. 19r.

350) It is the "salt war," so called because the conflict between the papacy and the Spanish monarchy was started by the decision of Pope Paul IV to double the duty on salt that came from the Kingdom of Naples.

351) He was born in November 1514, eldest son of Camillo, lord of Sermoneta, and Beatrice Gaetani d'Aragona. In 1530, he was sent to study in Rome, hosted by Cardinal Alessandro Farnese, who later became Pope Paul III. In 1550 he entered the service of the king of France, Henry II, as a captain in arms. In 1557, Paul IV appointed him captain general of the papal militia, while Pius IV entrusted him with the defense of the Papal State coast from pirates. See CORTE, 1562, p. 22v.

352) Also known as the "Great Cardinal" (1520–1589), he was appointed cardinal by his grandfather Paul III, at the age of fourteen. In 1535, he became Vice-Chancellor of the Church. He then came into conflict with the successor of Paul III, Julius III, and went to France (November 1552–June 1554) where he received the bishopric of Grenoble and other benefits, which convinced him to give his Roman palace to the French ambassadors to the Holy See [the Holy See is the name of the Governement of the Papal State] (palace which is still the seat of the French Embassy in Italy).

IL CAVALLARIZZO

DI M. CLAVDIO CORTE
DI PAVIA.

NEL QVAL SI TRATTA DELLA NATVRA de' Caualli, del modo di domarli, & frenarli;

ET DI TVTTO QVELLO, CHE A' CAVALLI, *& à buon Cauallarizzo s'appartiene.*

Con Priuilegio.

IN VENETIA
Appresso Giordano Ziletti all'insegna della Stella.
M D· LXII.

The first edition of *Il cavallarizzo* was published in Venice by Giordano Ziletti in 1562

stay of the Farnese in France (from November 1552 to June 1554). The same Corte says that he did not follow the Cardinal on his trip to the other side of the Alps[353].

Afterwards, perhaps because of the international fame he acquired after the publication of his treatise, Corte was invited to England by Robert Dudley, Earl of Leicester[354], who was one of the favorites of Queen Elizabeth I and her Master of the Horse. Corte's work was translated into English by Thomas Bedingfield and published in London by H. Denham, unter the title, *The Art of Riding*, in 1584. From a letter preserved in the archives of the Earl of Leicester, dated Paris, the 4th of February 1571[355], we know, however, that Corte had left England several years earlier. In the letter, the Italian asked for payment for the service he rendered at the English court. Probably Corte passed directly from England to France, where in 1573 he published a new edition of his work[356], dedicated to Charles IX[357]. In the dedication letter, the author says that he served the father of the king, Henry II, while he was fighting along the Rhine[358] and stayed in Paris for seven years, then from 1563, or 1564.

---

353) CORTE, 1562, p. 2v.

354) He was born the 7th of September 1533, youngest son of John Dudley, Duke of Northumberland, who was executed in 1553 for attempting to raise Lady Jane Grey to the throne of England. He was imprisoned with his father in the Tower of London, where he met for the first time Elizabeth Tudor, who was imprisoned by order of her older sister, Queen Mary I of England. With the accession to the throne of Elizabeth, with whom he had an affair, he was appointed Master of the Horse and then later Earl of Leicester. In 1585 he obtained the command of the campaign in Holland and he was granted the title of Governor-General of the Dutch Republic, but had to return to England after the defeat in the Battle of Zupthen. In 1588, he was appointed to the command of the British land forces against the Spanish Armada, but died shortly after, the 4th of September 1588.

355) *Dudley Papers*, Longleat House, f. 124.

356) *Il cavalerizzo di messer Claudio Corte di Pavia*, in Lyone, appresso Alessandro Marsili, 1573. About this edition we report a curiosity which illuminates Corte's work with the opinion of an authoritative expert: on the inside front cover of the copy of this treatise preserved in the Bibliothèque nationale de France (FRBNF37303898) there is a handwritten note by General L'Hotte who says: "the most complete work of the time and which contains the best exposition of the equestrian doctrines professed in Italy in the 16th century. Given by the commander Campagnac..."

357) King of France from 1560 to 1574. He was born in Saint-Germain-en-Laye the 27th of June 1550 and died in Paris the 30th of May 1574. He was son of Henry II and Catherine de' Medici.

358) "Though I moderate and held the brake to the great Henry your father (invincible, King Charles) while he was operating wonderful things on the Rhine with his army." Probably he alludes to the military campaign in 1552 in which Henry II annexed the bishoprics of Metz, Toul and Verdun to the kingdom. Although the statement seems to contradict what Corte says about the trip to France of Cardinal Farnese (See n. 12).

Horseman and an intellectual

Unlike Grisone and Fiaschi, Corte did not come from a family of high descent. What distinguishes him from its predecessors, however, is another feature that characterizes his work. Besides being a horseman he was also a refined intellectual, with a remarkable literary culture, which is reflected in the richness of his quotations, as well as in the use of sophisticated literary techniques in his treatise. Corte's book is not only a technical work, like those of his predecessors, but is also an elegant text, which denotes a broad culture and a good knowledge of Greek and Latin—that the author shows off translating into Italian verses by Virgil and other classical authors. Corte devoted a substantial part of his education to humanities, so much that he complains of having damaged his health by studying too hard and says that he partially regained it by returning to ride:

> ...having ceased to ride horses to devote myself to the studies, I spoiled my constitution; whereas when I resumed riding, I have, if not at all at least in part, recovered it[359].

This peculiarity causes him to make a kind of preventive self-defense against the criticism of those who would blame him for writing a work about the equestrian art although he has never been the horseman of a king, or of an emperor[360] and he never trained really famous horses. Such an argued and precise peroration justifies the suspicion that he had some bad conscience about this point. Also due to the fact by his own admission, that he never took part in a tournament, or in other knightly combats[361]. To the alleged objections of his detractors Corte refutes that he always served important nobles, as Cardinal Farnese, and that the good theorist doesn't need to be versed in the practice:

> Therefore even if I have not made these great buildings, nor have I made their medicine with my own hands, I have written precepts for knights and riders without having been one, and in conclusion without having done these things, they say, famous horses, I built this construction, under whose roof they will by chance gracefully lodge too, if I'm not mistaken[362].

---

359) «*per li studi havendo lasciato l'aggitar de' cavalli, m'havea guasto la complessione; dove riasumendo queste tali aggitationi, me la sono se non in tutto, in bona parte racconcia.*» CORTE, 1562, p. 128r.

360) The fact that to this objection the author did not oppose his alleged attendance of Henry II of France, suggests that what is stated in the dedicatory letter of the Lyon edition of *Il cavallarizzo* was more a boast than a historical datum. See n. 18.

361) See CORTE, 1562, p. 125v.

362) «*Posso dunque ben io senza haver fabricato questi gran palazzi, senza haver composto di man propria queste lor medicine, senza esser soldato havere scritto precetti da cavallieri,*

The work is divided into three books. The first concerns the nature of horses, how to breed them, how to select them and how to take care of them. The second is about riding and about the art of bridling. Finally, the third is dedicated (in the form of dialogues) to the figure of the horseman. Even though he professes the intention to write about everything that "belongs to the matter of horses and of a good horseman"[363], Corte explains that he intentionally does not talk about shoeing and about the treatment of diseases, considering these subjects under the purview of the "farrier and of the blacksmith"[364]. However, further in the book, he announces the intention to write a treatise specifically dedicated to "all the infirmities that can occur to a horse, with their origins and their treatment"[365]. But we have no other news of this work.

The comparison with the tradition

In his treatise Corte demonstrates the sharp awareness to follow in the wake of tradition and of a debate about the equestrian art that in those years was asserting itself not only in Italy, but throughout Europe. He seems particularly aware of the significant innovation introduced by the printed publication of books about equitation, which guaranteed to the treatises of Grisone and Fiaschi a widespread reputation never reached by the other manuscripts that circulated at the time. Corte explicitly mentions his predecessors, including also Giovan Battista Ferraro, who in 1560 published in Naples his treatise *Races, discipline of riding and other things relevant to such exercise* (*Razze, disciplina del cavalcare ed altre cose pertinenti ad esercitio così fatto*)[366]. However, if on one hand the author praises them for starting the new genre of equestrian treatises, on the other he clearly underlines the originality of his own work, pushing his reasoning up to an explicit controversy. The main target of this dispute is Federico Grisone, with which the author disagrees in several places, openly criticizing his brutal methods. Explaining, for example, the system to win a reluctant horse, Corte suggests that he must be urged by men on the ground, armed with sticks, which should immediately cease all action as soon as the animal moves forward. Therefore, he denies the efficacy of the imaginative cruelties recommended by Grisone, listing them in detail:

---

e in somma senza haver fatto questi, che lor dicano famosissimi cavalli, haver composto questa mia fabrica, sotto il cui tetto potranno per aventura agratiatamente albergare ancor loro, s'io non mi inganno.» CORTE, 1562, p. 3r.

363) «*à materia di cavalli, e a buon cavallarizzo s'apartiene.*» CORTE, 1562, p. 1r.

364) «*marescalco e del ferraro.*» CORTE, 1562, p. 1r.

365) «*tutte le infermità che possino avenire al cavallo, con le origini e cure loro.*» CORTE, 1562, p. 54r.

366) See Chapter VII.

> It seems to me that we should not give him other punishment, because continuing this and the other for a whole day [he will move forward], without laces to the testicles, no rocks, no cats, dogs nor hedgehogs attached to the tail and without holding nails in hand and with those sting his haunches and the many other tricks they want: which although may be needed, they are only needed by a horse that is completely evil and of malicious nature[367].

Corte is more indulgent with Fiaschi, even if, as we have already seen, he does not share his interest in shoeing, a subject that he considers far too low for the horseman, and with respect to the adoption of musical notation to indicate the rhythm of the exercises, he fears it to be incomprehensible to the majority of his readers. As for the classical and medieval authors, Corte points out that— with the partial exception of Xenophon – they dealt only with specific aspects, devoting their works mainly to the care and the breeding of horses. Rightly distinguishing himself from this tradition, Corte claims to have published a work that was far more extensive and documented, covering every aspect of the equestrian knowledge needed by a good horseman and recognizing to that knowledge a full cultural dignity.

> I touched on a few more stories, poems and philosophies discussing about them longer than what would be appropriate, so that everyone in this way, will know better the truth of the thing, and more entirely; in doing so not wanting to imitate the great Orators, who allude the fact of the stories, and of philosophies; not to be, or seem, rhetorical or eloquent speaker, contenting to dress up the book with not so many colors as they [the great Orators] would do, but to adorn it in such a way that it can be seen without any disgust. I am certain that if I published it so dry and naked, as many wanted, without fattening it with these things, and amplifying it with digressions and discourses, it would

---

367) «*Ne altro castigo à me pare che se gli convenga; perche con continuare tutto un giorno questo e l'altro, senza lacci à i testicoli, senza sassi, senza gatti, cagnoli e ricci attaccati alla coda, e senza tener chiodi in mano, e con quelli pungerlo nè fianchi; e tant'altre manifatture che costor vogliano: le quali se pur si richieggono, à caval perfido del tutto, e di natura maligna si richieggono.*» CORTE,1562, p. 101r. Corte argues explicitly against Grisone, even denying that the technique of the "*torni*" was invented by Cola Pagano, as stated by the Neapolitan master (See CORTE, 1562, p. 61R), and prescribing to mount with both stirrups of the same length, rather than the right shorter (See CORTE, 1562, p. 88r). He also distinguishes himself from the Neapolitan master bringing from seven to nine the basic aids that the rider can give to his mount ("of voice, of stick, of bridle, of calfs, of stirrup, of spurs, of person, of fields, and of water." CORTE, 1562, p. 76v).

not be different enough from [the works] of many other modern [authors], and it also may displease [the readers], nor I would have done what I intended to do, which beside making profit to the readers and delighting them, is to raise the subject and the true art of horsemanship, and the same horseman as much as possible.[368]

The richness of Corte's text is immediately apparent when one considers the enumeration of those which, according to the author, are the infinite profits that the horse brings to man. First, Corte claims that the horse has a twofold nature, in which coexist the traits of the domestic and of the wild animal. Exactly to get the better of this complexity, his training requires reasoning and patience in the horseman. Moreover, riding benefits the body, generates cheerful humor and banishes melancholy. The horses are also extremely useful to the states, because they provide a formidable instrument of war to the armies, which makes of cavalry the most noble of troops[369]. The horse makes a man great in battle, compensates for his physical weakness and exalts him in jousts and tournaments. Therefore, the horse is the necessary complement to any gentleman, who is estimated by others for the way he rides and maintains his mount. Finally, the author adds a remark which is still fully valid today: the horse gives the pleasure to contemplate places that without him would be difficult to reach:

> And that it is true you can see in considering that without the horse it would be difficult to enjoy that great pleasure and happiness, which the view of the countryside away from the tumult of the city and the goodness of the weather and the serenity of the sky give to men, being impossible to go there on foot without a lot of effort and discomfort, which would take away the pleasure, either in whole or in large part.[370]

---

368) «*Ho tocco ancora alcune historie, poesie, e filosofie con piu lungo parlare di quello forse, che saria stato di mestieri, accioche ciascuno sappi ancor meglio per questo la verità della cosa, e piu integralmente; non havendo in questo voluto imitare i grandi Oratori, che sol accennano il fatto delle historie, e le filosofie; per non essere, ne parere retorico, ne facondo dicitore, contentandomi di vestire il libro non con tanti colori come essi havrebbero fatto, ma in tal modo solo ornandolo, che anch'esso possi esser visto senza fastidio alcuno. Essendo certo che se così secco, e nudo com'altri havrebbero voluto, lo davo fuori e non ingrassatolo con le suddette cose, e ampliato con digressioni, e discorsi, niente da molt'altri moderni sarebbe differito, e per aventura sarebbe ancora dispiaciuto, ne io havrei fatto quello, che l'intento mio è di fare, che è oltra il far profitto alli Lettori e dilettarli, inalzar il suggetto e l'arte d'un vero cavallarizzo, e il cavallarizzo insieme piu che si puote.*» CORTE, 1562, p. 58r.

369) In this regard, Corte denies the idea that the defeat suffered by the French cavalry at the hands of Swiss infantrymen in Novara (6 June 1513) marked the crisis of chivalry. See CORTE, 1562, p. 12r and Chapter 1.

370) «*Et che sia vero si vede, che quel gran piacere, e allegrezza, che dà à gl'homini la*

According to Corte the shows with horses are the most beautiful, so that there is not a man so rough and savage as to not wonder and take delight in seeing these animals performing the school exercises. Docility, obedience, intelligence, love and memory are finally the qualities that make the horse similar to humans. In Corte's view, it is exactly from this resemblance that springs the myth of the Centaur, who had the top of his body in the form of a man, which implies an almost human intelligence dominates the uncontainable physicalness of the body of the animal.

Corte says that the horse has a warm nature "and is very fit for coitus and very inclined to love"[371] and, like man, he dreams when he is sleeping (view confirmed by modern ethological studies). His passionate description reaches an unexpectedly poetic tone when—echoing a passage by Xenophon – he says that in the spring, like charming women, the mares boast for the beauty of their manes and tails and for this reason they refuse to mate with donkeys, imposing a strategy to the horsemen who want to produce mules:

And in the manner of the women they usually boast for the mane and tail. So that for this reason they do not tolerate in any way that the donkey rises above them and covers them, but shrewd masters of the horsemen immediately cut their mane and tail, and then they bring them to drink to the spring, so that they see in it, as in a mirror, their deformity and ugliness: and since they have lost the dignity that the hairs and tail gave them:

they do not more refuse the donkey: from which with the mare is done the mule.[372]

The colors of the coats and the theory of humors

Corte also demonstrates extensive knowledge and good skills as a popularizer [someone who is able to explain scientific ideas to the public] when he describes in detail the pseudo-scientific doctrine according to which it was believed that the color of the coat would witness the nature of each individual. This view was based on the theory of the humors by Hippocrates and Galen. As we have already seen, this doctrine was shared by the previous authors (and also by those that follow, for at least two centuries), who however did not provide such

---

vista della campagna lontano dal tumulto delle città, e la bontà del tempo, e serenità del cielo, malagevolmente si potrebbe godere senza il cavallo, non potendovisi andare à piede senza molta fatica, e incommodità, la quale levarebbe il piacere, ò in tutto ò in gran parte.» CORTE, 1562, p. 13v.

371) «*ed è molto atto al coito e all'amore inclinatissimo.*» CORTE, 1562, p. 18v.

372) «*Et à guisa delle donne sogliono molto insuperbire delle chiome, e della coda. Di modo che per niente per questo rispetto patiscano che l'asino le salisca e cuopra; ma gl'accorti perorighi, e capi cavallari subito le tagliano i crini, e la coda, e poi le menano al fonte à bere; accio che in quello come in specchio, vedano la lor deformità e bruttezza: e visto che hanno perduto il decoro, che i crini, e la crinatura della coda le recavano: non ricusano di poi l'asino: dal quale con la cavalla si fa il mulo.*» CORTE, 1562, p. 39r.

a detailed explanation. This theory was the first attempt to explain the cause of diseases, replacing the previous religious and magical beliefs, and this was based on the idea of the Greek philosopher Anaximenes of Miletus (fourth century BC) that the universe was made up of four basic elements: air, fire, earth and water. From these four elements Hippocrates identfied four basic humors: blood (red humor), yellow bile, black bile, and phlegm. The blood corresponds to air also known as sanguine, yellow bile to fire (also known as anger), black bile corresponded to the earth (also known as melancholy), and phlegmatic to water. Four temperaments (sanguine, choleric, melancholic, and phlegmatic) corresponded to the four humors, and further to: four elementary qualities (cold, warm, dry, moist), four seasons (spring, summer, autumn and winter) and four seasons of life (childhood, youth, maturity and old age). According to this scheme, health would depend on the humors' balance within the body and the predominance of one of them would influence the personality of the subject, defining his temperament and physical constitution (known as "complexion").

According to Corte, the natural heat governs the digestion of the humors in the body of the animal. This process generates "sooty vapors," which are pushed upward by the force of the same heat and exert a pressure to exit from the body. The leakage occurs through the pores and "through that flesh, which they find more suitable and open to give them way"[373]. When they get in contact with the air, they "conglutinate," that is to say that they thicken, forming the hairs and the mane, which are thicker, or thinner, depending on the greater or lesser heat which has pushed them out and then take on different colors depending on the humor from which the vapor producing them was generated. Similarly, the hairs are straight or curly depending on how much dry, moist, straight or crooked are the ways by which they are released. For this reason, Corte says, the quality of the coat gives a clear indication of the nature of horses, "of their greater warmth or coldness, dryness and moisture"[374]. Thus, the color and quality of the hair derive from the four humors (blood, anger, melancholy, and phlegm) and from the corresponding qualities (warm, cold, dry, moist).

Each of these humors and qualities generate a coat color: blood produces bay, anger produces chestnut, from melancholy comes the black and from phlegm comes the grey ("*leardo*"). These qualities are almost never absolute, but they generally combine one with the other:

> And since you can not find on earth any body totally simple, or rather of simple quality, we will say that one cannot find a fire that is not warm and dry, air that is not warm and moist, water that is not moist and cold, earth that is not cold and dry. So we can also say that there is no horse, that is simply sanguine, nor only choleric, but choleric-sanguine, cho-

---

373) «*per quella carne, che trovano più atta, e aperta à darli via*». CORTE, 1562, p. 23r.
374) «*della loro più calidità ò freddezza, siccità, e humidezza.*» CORTE, 1562, p. 23r.

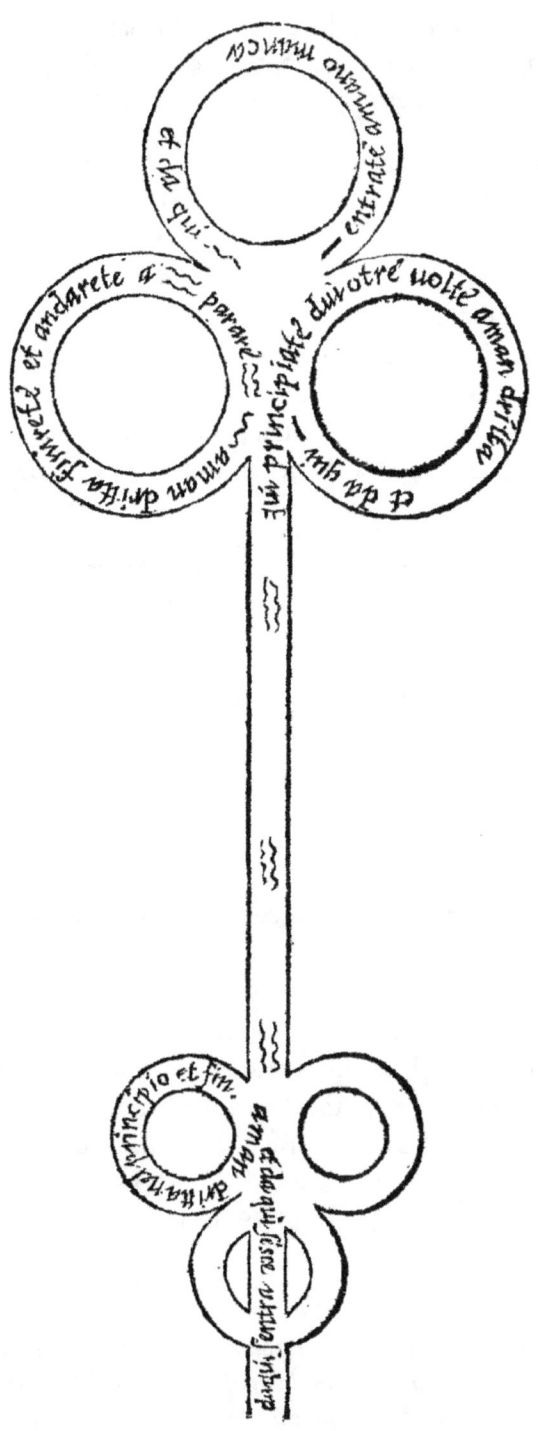

The pattern of "*rote*", which incorporates, updating it, the pattern of the "*torni*" by Grisone

leric-burned, choleric-melancholic, phlegmatic-sanguine, phlegmatic-melancholic, earthy-melancholic and icy, and melancholic-choleric...³⁷⁵

As for the coats, Corte agrees with the general opinion of the time, granting a preference to the bay, the dapple gray and the liver chestnut. Roans are also appreciated, because they combine the natures of the four main coats. He shows, however, very little consideration for the black, although he admits that there are some very good examples. Finally, he's skeptical about the meaning of socks. Having failed to find convincing explanations, he claims to refer to the authority of the ancients, according to whom the leg with the sock would be slower and weaker. On this point, however, he maintains some reservation, concluding that experience shows the irrelevance of the socks and of other signs, such as blazes and whorls.

> And to fortify my opinion, the experience, master of things, shows that the weakness and strength, speed and slowness come and depend on the climate of the whole body and on its disposition and proportion and not on small socks, as well as little force [does not depend] on little humor.³⁷⁶

Technical innovations

Compared to the treatises of its predecessors, the work of Corte introduces a certain number of technical novelties, illustrating a number of new training exercises, which are still used today (albeit with slight differences). Clearly these were not invented by Corte, but he had the merit to explain them in his treatise, consolidating their use. These innovations are aimed at the training of the warhorse and are added by Corte to the same exercises and school jumps already mentioned by Grisone and Fiaschi. Corte also mentioned a series of what we can call "airs of fantasy," or "special training," as the horse that makes a bow, that picks up objects from the ground with his mouth and hands them to his rider,

---

375) «*Et da che non si pò trovar in terra alcun corpo totalmente semplice, ò per dir meglio di semplice qualità, diremo ancora che non si troverà fuoco che non sia caldo, e secco; aere, che non sia calido, e humido, acqua che non sia humida, e fredda, terra che non sia fredda, e secca. Per il che diremo ancora, che non sia cavallo alcuno, che sia sanguigno semplice, ne colerico solo, ma si bene colerico sanguigno, colerico addusto, colerico melanconico, flemmatico sanguigno, flemmatico malenconico, malenconico terreo, e agghiacciato, e malenconico colerico...*» CORTE, 1562, p. 24r.

376) «*Et l'esperientia delle cose maestra, mostra per fortificare l'opinion mia che la debolezza, e fortezza, prestezza, e tardezza dalle temperie di tutto il corpo, e dalla dispositione, e proportione sua, non da piccole balzane, e poco forza di poco humore nasce, e depende.*» CORTE, 1562, p. 29r.

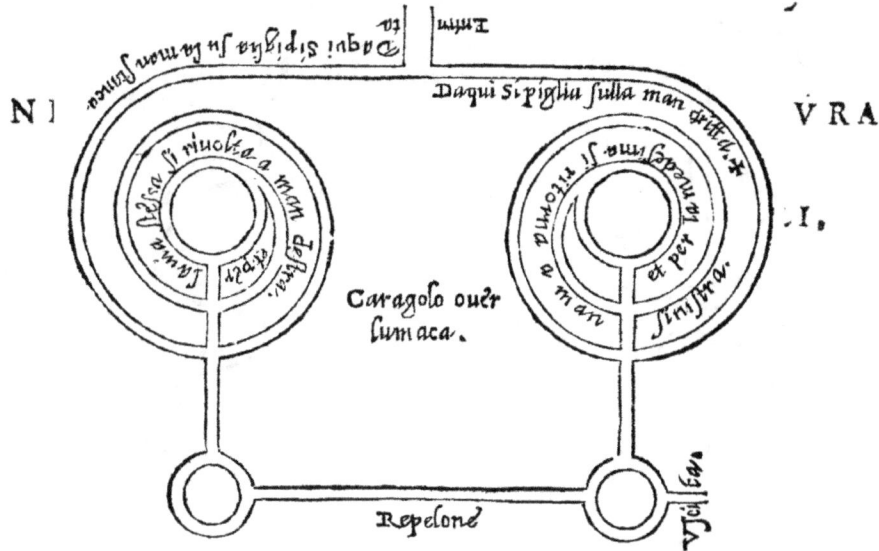

Spiral pattern or the "*caragolo*"

who allows only his master to ride him, who can be ridden without reins or curb chain, or that works without a rider.

The starting point of the training is the work on the circles, the use of which, according to Corte, dates back to ancient Greece, since they are already mentioned by Plato and Xenophon. Therefore he proposes an updated scheme of Grisone's "*torni,*" which he calls "*rote*" ("wheels"), contesting the Neapolitan author, who attributed their invention to his master Cola Pagano. Compared to Grisone's "*torni,*" Corte's "*rote*" provide that the horse is ridden on a straight line on top of which the horse should turn on three contiguous circles with a diameter of 8–12 meters, then that he come back on the same straight line, after which he turns on three smaller circles (of about 2–3 meters of diameter). The aim is to train the horse to make him more agile and elegant, to accustom him to take the right contact with the bridle and to overcome any resistance on both leads.

After confirming the horse in the work on circles, Corte suggests to start him to a new exercise, the so-called "*caragolo*"[377] i.e. the spiral[378]. In the rather complex diagram of this exercise, the spirals are two, to go along at the trot in both directions. They are connected by a "*repolone*" (i.e. a straight line, opened and closed by a *volte*). Corte considers this the most important and effective exercise, capable of producing the same benefits of the work on the "*rote*" (circles), but allowing the horse to become more agile in a shorter time. Once the horse is able to do it even at the canter, it also has a significant aesthetic value,

---

377) From the Spanish "*caracol,*" i.e. snail.

378) About the actual use of the spiral and of other training patterns already treated first by Corte, see, for example, Henriquet – Durand, 1991, pp. 81–85.

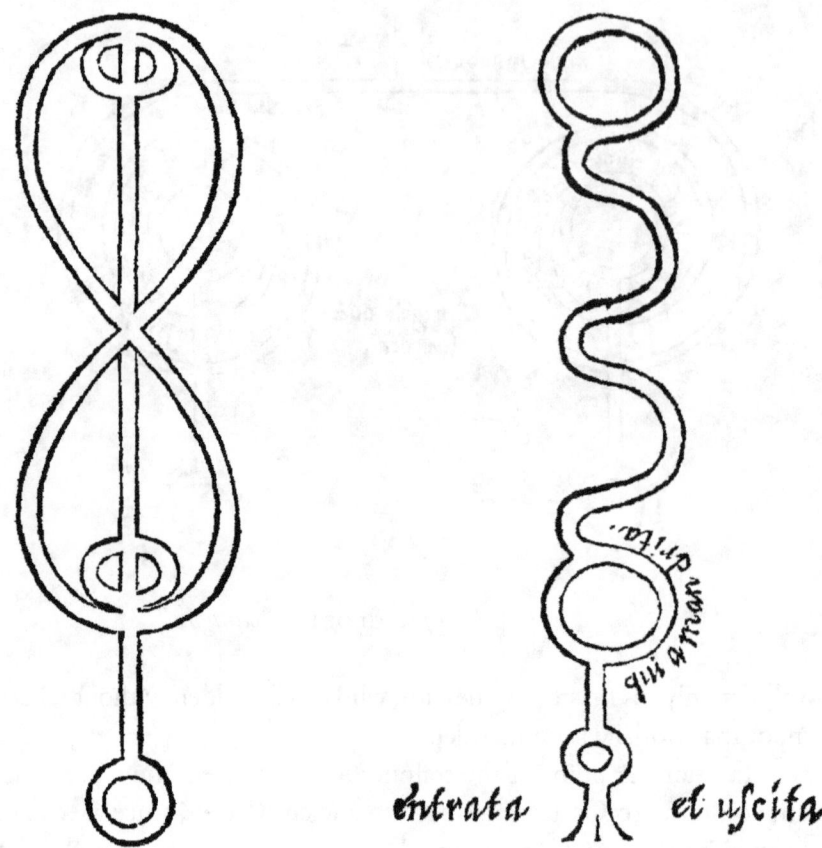

The 'tight-S' pattern "*esse serrato*"   The serpentine pattern "*serpeggiare*"

demonstrating the docility and the smoothness acquired by the horse and the skill of the rider.

Another innovative exercise is what Corte calls "*esse serrato*" (tight S). It is a path in the form of a figure eight, from which the rider comes up with a *repolone*, stopping the horse on the straight line. The author recommends covering it initially on a wider path, which is gradually reduced as the horse becomes accustomed and more dexterous in turning. Among other things, it is considered a prerequisite to the *repolone* (i.e. to the *passade*).

Finally, the last exercise introduced by Corte is what he calls "to snake" ("*serpeggiare*"), called the serpentine. This kind of training is suited to promote the balance of the horse and his obedience to the bit and to the legs. The author also considers it useful to avoid firearms shots in battles and skirmishes, and argues that horses, especially the most generous and noble, are pleased to do it. He adds that, unfortunately this exercise was generally neglected in the riding schools, where *courbettes* and *pesades* were mainly taught.

Training on the circles and on the serpentine, from Johann Jacob von Wallhausen, *Ritterkunst* (1614)

Corte is also the first author to mention the use of the work in-hand, with the rider on the ground who guides the horse with the reins. This way of training the horse will subsequently have a remarkable development, to teach to the horse the different exercises of dressage without the hindrance of the weight of the rider. Corte recommends it for training the horse to rein-back. If the animal resist the aids of the rider, he must get off the saddle and, taking in each hand the reins of the cavesson, he must push him "pleasantly" back until he understands what he has to do. As soon as the horse takes a few steps back, the rider must get back in the saddle and ask him to rein-back. If again he resists, the rider must repeat the exercise from the ground: "that you have to be very sure that doing so in two or three mornings, and even in less than an hour, you will have him at this."[379]

As for the rest, from the technical point of view the horsemanship proposed by Corte does not differ from that of his predecessors. Like them, he considers the voice aid very useful and says that it should vary in tone depending on the circumstances, suggesting on some occasions, such as the ordinary canter, to whisper to the horse[380]. An unexpected anticipation, at least four cen-

---

379) «*che ben devete essere sicuro, che così facendo in due ò tre mattine, e per aventura in men d'un hora lo haverete à questo.*» CORTE, 1562, p. 66v.

380) «*la qual voce medesimamente vi servirà nel galoppo ordinario insieme con l'andarli*

turies in advance, of the so-called modern "horse-whisperers"! However, even according to him, the voice should not be used with already-trained horses and in the presence of a select audience. The only exception being when the rider's voice marks the rhythm of school jumps. In general, Corte agrees with the idea that the aids—either of voice or of other kind—should be completely hidden, so that the horse seems to obey the rider by virtue of an occult art:

> But instead of the voice the other aids should stand in, which are most needed and masterly. Although, in the presence of these [the audience], it would be even better if the horse does well without any aid and that the rider proves a real covered art without forcing the horse to act with any aid.[381]

Like Fiaschi, Corte also does not seem to appreciate the *pesades* and the *courbettes*, which he considers dangerous for warhorses. Instead, he expresses a great esteem of the school jumps and boasts to have been the first to perform in Rome, in front of a selected audience, the so-called vigorous canter[382] on the *volte*:

> And I was the first one that did it in Rome, in the presence of many lords and knights, among whom were the illustrious Sir Giulio Orsini, who is no not only very well trained in this art but also an invincible captain of the militia. Also present was Sir Pietro Paolo Mignatelli, young man no less rich in goods of fortune, Knight with a really beautiful judgment in this art, my disciple and Benefactor. There were still two honorable and virtuous young gentlemen and brothers from Bologna, Sir Annibale del Giglio, of Sir Marc'antonio [sic], grandchildren of the very honorable Monsignor del Giglio, dear to the great Cardinal Farnese, and to the whole Court of the notables of Rome for its rare virtue, and there was also Sir Giovanbattista Pignatelli, very excellent horseman of the great Alessandro Farnese. I did it with a bay called Il Caraffa, who I trained in less than six months[383].

---

parlando sotto voce alcuna volta.» CORTE, 1562, p. 76v.

381) «*Ma in vece di voce deveno supplire gl'altri aiuti più necessarij, e maestrevoli. Benche meglio sarebbe ancora, che senza alcun aiuto, alla presenza di tali il cavallo facesse, e andasse bene; e che il cavalliero in questo dimostrasse una vera arte coperta senza sforzar il cavallo à fare con aiuto alcuno.*» CORTE, 1562, p. 76r.

382) It is a variant of the "one step and a jump," in which the horse jumps after two or three steps of canter, rather than at each stride. "In the vigorous canter, that is the way to call it rather than one step and a jump, because the jump is executed on the second and third step and not on the first, you have to be very careful to get the person most graceful and firm in the saddle, and with the legs as close to their place as possible." CORTE, 1562, p. 75v.

383) «*Et io fui il primo che lo feci in Roma presenti molti Signori, e cavallieri; tra i quali*

Notable was the presence in the audience of Giovan Battista Pignatelli, horseman of Alessandro Farnese. This is one of the most prominent figures of the Italian equitation of the sixteenth century, about whom we will talk diffusely in a later chapter.[384]

Unlike his predecessor, Corte does not dwell on the art of bridling and apologizes for not having enriched his work with the usual illustrations dedicated to various types of bit, because several of his friends hurried him to publish the book. Nevertheless, he considers the ability to choose the right bridle the "touchstone" of the true horseman and repeats the same information as the other writers about the use of the cannon, of the "*scaccia*" and of other mouthpieces.

The horses for the *palio* (racehorses)

Of particular interest is the chapter devoted to the horses for the *palio*, a kind of competition that, as we have already seen, at that time was very popular in Italy. The Barb, that is to say the Berber horses originating from North Africa, were considered the most suitable horses for this use, but were also appreciated specimens from Scythia, i.e. from the steppes of Central Asia. According to the author, in Italy the best horses were the Barb of the race of Mantua. However, Corte does not exclude that "in Italy can be found bastards and rustic horses absolutely perfect for this job"[385]. The latter, in his view, have the advantage of being generally more robust and suitable to the Italian climate and thus to require less care than specimens of other races, usually more delicate and with less spirit.

In any case, for racehorses Corte prescribes an extremely accurate treatment. They should be meticulously groomed and massaged every morning and their diet must be closely monitored. It includes, in addition to straw and barley, hot and cold mashes, which in the days before the race are enriched with eggs, or with herbal specialties, to be bought directly at the apothecary. In another place of his treatise, Corte also recommends to geld the horses in order to prevent the hardening of their nerves[386].

---

erano lo Illustrissimo Signor Giulio Orsino, il quale non è meno esercitato in quest'arte che invitto Capitano della militia. Ci era anco il Signor Pietro Paolo Mignatelli giovine non men ricco de' beni della fortuna, Cavallier veramente di bellissimo giuditio in quest'arte, mio discepolo, e Mecenate. Ci erano ancora due honorati e virtuosi giovani e fratelli gentilhomini Bolognesi, Messer Annibale del Giglio, di Messer Marc'antonio; nipoti dell'honoratissimo Monsignor del Giglio cariss. molto al gran cardinal Farnese, e à tutta la Corte de' maggiori di Roma per le sue rare virtù: eraci anco il Signor Giovanbattista Pignatello cavallarizzo eccellentissimo del grande Alessandro Farnese, lo feci dico con un baio chiamato il caraffa fatto da me in men di sei mesi.» CORTE, 1562, p. 75r.

384) See Chapter VIII.

385) «*si trovino alcuni cavalli bastardi, e villanotti in Italia à questo mestiere perfettissimi.*» CORTE, 1562, p. 98r.

386) See CORTE, 1562, p. 20v.

The training must be carried out over gradually increasing distances, until it reaches the length of the race, never letting the horse run as fast as he can, except for short sprints. Immediately afterward, the legs of the animal should be washed with lye and warm wine and he should not be returned to the stable until he is completely dry and groomed.

The day before the race, his tendons must be greased with marrow of deer and the legs must be washed with an infusion of dried roses, rosemary, sage, cedar leaves and chamomile. The morning of the race the cares intensify further and, just before the animal moves between the ropes of the starter, his legs, belly, and the penis and testicles should be greased with an oil of fine quality. The jockeys of this kind of races were little more than boys and, according to Corte, they should have the following characteristics:

> The boys running in the race must be small, dry, nervous, dexterous and spirited, of good intellect and memory, and in love with this craft[387].

As for the other breeds of horses, for war, tournaments or for the pomp of public cavalcades, Corte agrees with the opinions of his contemporaries, just showing to be slightly more indulgent towards the horses of Nordic origin. He denies that they are lazy horses and considers them to be rather shy and proud. He says that most of their shortcomings depend more on the incompetence of their masters than on a defective nature. As an example, he mentions the case of a horse he trained, which was ruined by his owner, a Roman nobleman, who continuously changed his bridle and ill-treated him in various ways. Centuries before us, he seems to describe the same bad habits that can still be seen today in many riding centers...

> ...the masters who are not able to ride should be patient to wait for [their horses] to be done [trained], or removed from the vice, which they have acquired because of bad manners and of excessive beatings, and they should not act like now does with me a Roman gentleman, who I do not want to name for good respect, that as soon as I have ridden and given a strong lesson to his fresian, gives another the same day and very often with another bridle, so if his mouth is spoiled, with his damage and further damaged by everyone that acts in this way, it should not be blamed the horseman, who, being an expert of the art, should be believed, and they [the masters] do not have to do what they do not know and what ignorant riders counsel them[388].

---

387) «*I ragazzi che gl'hanno à correre vogliono essere piccioli, asciutti, nervosi, destri, e animosi, di buon intelletto e memoria, e innamorati di tal mestiere.*» CORTE, 1562, p. 100v.

388) «...*i patroni che non sanno cavalcare habbino patientia in aspettare che [i loro ca-*

Corte shares the admiration of his contemporaries for the Spanish horses, which he defines as beautiful, enemies of blows and with the only flaw of being subject to suffer damage and diseases of the hooves. However, (and this is an innovation from his predecessors) he considers the Portuguese horses even better, showing particular appreciation for the Lusitanian riders who "make a great profession of having them fast and dexterous"[389].

The horseman, brother of the Courtier

The main purpose of Claudio Corte's work is not simply to bring together a compendium of the equestrian knowledge of the time but, far more ambitiously, to establish the figure of the horseman as a precise social role, borrowing the example canonized by Castiglione. He consecrates the third book of the treatise toward this aim. According to the literary model of the *Book of the Courtier*, this part of the treatise is written in the form of dialogues. The plotline from which these dialogues moves is a friendly dispute between Fra Prospero Ricco—Milanese gentleman, defined as a very honored and excellent rider[390]—and the author. The first challenges Corte, during a morning when they were riding in the garden of Augustino Ghisi[391], in the company of other riders. Prospero reproves Claudio to have entitled his work *Il cavallarizzo* (The Horseman) even if in the first two books he hasn't explicitly defined the features of this figure. The author, tired and self-absorbed from having ridden many horses, proposes to postpone the debate to the next day, giving him an appointment in the same place with the same company. The next evening the brigade meets again in the specified place. In addition to the

---

valli] siano fatti, over levati dal vitio, che tengano, e hanno acquistato per mala creanza e per soverchie battiture, e non faccino come fa hora con me un gentilhomo Romano, il quale non vò nominare per bon rispetto, che non più presto io ho cavalcato, e dato una forte lettione al suo frigione, ch'egli glie ne dà un'altra quel dì medesimo, e ben spesso con altra briglia, se se [sic] ne va di bocca poi suo danno adunque, e danno di ciascuno che così faccia, e non biasimo del cavallerizzo, al quale come è perito nell'arte sua devriano credere, e non persuadersi di fare quel che non sanno, e che da cavalcatori ignoranti sono consigliati.» CORTE, 1562, pp. 21v–22r. On the other hand, in Corte's peroration is evident a certain concern for his reputation as a horseman, which is threatened by the inconstancy of a horse owner who, instead of trusting his art, wants to do what he does not know, on the advice of incompetent people. Here it seems that the author takes the opportunity of a personal revenge on those who poked their nose into his work.

389) «*fanno gran professione d'haverli veloci, e destri.*» CORTE, 1562, p. 22r.

390) We know by the same Corte that he was page of Isabella of Aragon, then horseman of Alessandro Farnese (Corte, 1562, p. 4r). Prospero was the grandson of Giovanangelo di Carcano, a Milanese gentleman, who Corte counts among his teachers.

391) The 49th story of the first book of The Tales (1554) by Matteo Bandello is dedicated to a certain Agostino Ghisi.

two disputants, who in a cheerful atmosphere are ready "to come to blows through the language,"[392] there are Riccardo Mantoano, Giovan Battista Pignatelli, the Cavalier Seloro, Giovan Antonio Catamusto, Giovan Luigi Ruggiero, Giulio Orsini and Pompeo Colonna, who, one by one, kindly decline the invitation to assume the role of arbiter of the dispute, which is finally assigned to the same Prospero, in spite of the fact that he also a part of the case in the dispute.

The repartee between the two contenders is the most literary part of Corte's work. The author demonstrates his competence as a writer, announcing the completion of his treatise with a dizzying process of *mise en abyme* [curveball] which Jorge Luis Borges probably would have liked. In the first dialogue Prospero, who is in search of critical topics, notes that the author has not yet published the third book of his work, despite having announced it in the preface. Corte defends himself saying that many authors have published only part of their work, reserving the right to complete it later, in order to edit it better, or simply to verify the interest and the criticisms of the readers. But unlike him, since he published it in full. This statement obviously raises the bewilderment of his coversation partner:

>...But you claim to have published the third book.

>Yes, I say it.

>And what is that?

>It is this that we are discussing now.

>So you consider this argument that we do together the third book?

>Yes I do.

>It seems to methat one thing is to argue and another is to write, and from writing to get a book.

>You make me laugh. What else are the many books that you may find in the form of a dialogue? Aren't they nothing more than arguments between several people?

>Our discussion is therefore a dialogue and a book, and this book will be the third that you have promised.

---

392) «*a venir alle mani con la lingua.*» CORTE, 1562, p. 111v.

Yes, this is the third that I promised in the Preface.

And are you going to send it out?

Don't you see that while you keep on questioning me and I answer you I put it out or, to say the truth, we put it out?

So the book will consist of everything that I have asked and I will ask you about the subject that we have in hand, and of what you will answer to me? And others may not hear it [except] those few knights and gentlemen that are now listening here? If so, I think it will be printed in the air and not on the paper, as I think it will happen to your horseman, who, as you want him with so many virtues and conditions that he will fly in the sky, will remain in the air and those who will want to see him in action will have to contemplate him as Plato's ideas. But, joking aside, please tell me if sooner or later you are really going to print this discussion that we do now, from which you intend to do the third book?

To tell the truth it is already printed and there is nothing that you're asking me now that I did not foresee and printed in it.

And you printed it in the form of a Dialogue?

As a Dialogue.[393]

---

393) «*P. ... Ma voi dite di haver dato fuori il terzo libro. / C. Sì dico. / P. Et qual'è questo? / C. Questo che tra noi trattiamo hora è d'esso. / P. Che, questo ragionamento che noi facciamo insieme adimandate voi dunque il terzo libro? / C. Sì dimando. / P. A' me pare che altro sia il ragionare, e altro sia lo scrivere, e di poi scritto cavar fuori un libro. / C. Voi mi fate ridere, tanti libri che si trovano in dialoghi che cosa sono? Sono altro che ragionamenti tra più persone? / P. Questo ragionamento nostro adunque è un Dialogo e un libro, e questo libro sarà il terzo che havete promesso. / C. Sì, questo è il terzo ch'io promisi nel Proemio. / P. Et quando lo darete voi fuori? / C. Non vedete voi che secondo che mi andate interrogando, e io rispondendo lo veggo à cavar fuori, ò per più vero dire, voi e io lo caviamo fuori? / P. Adunque di tutto quello ch'io vi ho adimandato, e che vi adimanderò d'intorno al soggetto che havemo per le mani, e voi mi risponderete sarà composto il libro? e altri non lo intenderanno se non quei pochi gentilhomini e cavallieri, che qui hora ci ascoltano? Se così sia, credo, che rimarà istampato in aere e non in carta, come credo quasi che habbi ad essere del vostro cavallarizzo, il quale per volerlo con tante virtù e conditioni farlo volar al cielo rimarasse nell'aere, e nell'aere à chi vorrà vederlo in atto bisognerà contemplarlo peggio che le Idee di Platone. Ma senza burla di gratia ditemi da vero questo discorrere che noi facciamo hora, del quale voi v'ingannate di farne il terzo libro, lo farete voi stampare presto ò tardi? / C. A dirvi il vero di già è istampato, e non è cosa che voi*

Corte was therefore not only a good horseman. His interlocutor learns that he's become a literary character while he is disputing with him on the subject of a book of which he is already a protagonist! And Corte's literary culture is also evident through his many quotations from Cicero to Virgil and the more recent Castiglione and Ariosto. Corte considers art, music, architecture and literature as the terms of comparison of the equestrian art. On the other hand, fundamental assumption of Corte's treatise is that "if the horseman won't be a literate he will not ever ascend to that perfection to which every well born knight and gentleman is bound."[394]

When Prospero asserts that culture is not needed to ride well, the author replies that it is possible to be—as many are—a good rider even being an illiterate but, he adds, with a greater fatigue and less authority. The illiterate, in fact, lacks good manners. In addition, those who are educated know better the nature of horses, while the others go on blindly. Therefore, not only the rider must be skilled in riding and in all the other disciplines of the body—such as dancing, wrestling and fencing—but must also learn Greek and Latin from an early age, and he should also have a certain knowledge of music, at least to have a full cognition of rhythm[395]. Such high requirements provoke Prospero's reaction. So he exclaims: the one outlined by Sir Claudio is an abstract ideal, such as those of Plato, Xenophon, Cicero and the same Castiglione. No one—he adds—will ever meet such a rider. Not at all bothered, but rather flattered to be compared to the authority of these authors, Corte admits: I wanted to indicate a perfect model, in which those who want to really excel will have to try to approach.

Then the description continues. According to Corte, even before being learned, the true horseman must be born noble. In fact, even if the majority of those who practiced this profession were not aristocratic, the author considers the inheritance of blood fundamental, because—he says—it involves the desire to emulate the ancestors and to maintain the respect of the contemporaries. Here his argument reflects quite clearly the prejudices and social conventions of the time, even contradicting his own words, seeing that he previously pointed out that the skill in the equestrian art, combined with a proper and honorable behavior, is worthy as an instrument of emancipation, whose effectiveness is demonstrated by the example of many stableboys who became the horsemen of noble families. And on this point the author gets tangled in the strange theory that is not enough for the horseman to be noble, but he must also be nursed directly by his mother, because only in this way the child gets naturally the aristocratic manners of his parents! A very strange opinion, if one considers the widespread

---

hora mi adimandiate, che da me non sia stata prevista, e stampata in quello. / P. Et in Dialogo l'havete fatto stampare? / C. In Dialogo.» CORTE, 1562, p. 116v.

394) «*se'l cavallarizzo non sarà letterato non potrà gia mai ascendere à quella perfetione, alla quale è obligato ogni cavalliere, e gentilhuomo ben nato.*» CORTE, 1562, p. 114r.

395) See CORTE, 1562, 117v.

habit between the aristocrats of the time to put out to a wetnurse their offspring.

As the courtier, the rider must be beautiful, but not to the point of appearing effeminate. The beauty—and here is evident the debt to Castiglione's ideal—implies the supreme quality of the aristocratic in the old regime society: grace. This spontaneous mood must be associated with the virtues of prudence and patience—which to subdue the horses are much more effective than any violence—but also essential in dealing with men, especially for those who attend the not always benevolent rooms of the courts. On the other hand, however, a man who wants to be respected should in no way come to any compromise about his honor, a point on which the rider must indeed be "very bold and, so to speak, very impatient and intemperate."[396] The virtues—Corte never tires to repeat it—must be learned from childhood and it is the parents' responsibility to take care of the education of their children. To complete his personal decorum, Corte also requires the horseman to be married, "because the man who has neither wife nor children in the house can have little authority in the direction of important things."[397]

Finally, to all of these qualities must be added the worldly customs, typical of a society that made of the "civil conversation"[398] a way of life and of relationships. The rider must be a good speaker, but avoid flattery, actively seeking the conversation of gentlemen, but shrinking from all affectation. Furthermore, he should always have to be present when his prince rides a horse and, having full responsibility for all that belongs to the stables of his master, he must know how to command the workers of the stables (which Corte lists in their precise hierarchy, from the master to the stableboys) with kindness and love, but at the same time with firmness and good judgment. His dignity demands that he should be diligent, honest and of few words. In fact, while he must be a good conversationalist, the horseman should never talk too much in public of his art, displaying a certain gravity and reserve, which enhance his authority and *sprezzatura*[399].

---

396) «*essere fierissimo, e per modo di dire impatientissimo, e intemperato.*» CORTE, 1562, p. 122r.

397) «*che l'homo che non ha moglie, ne figlioli in casa, poca auttorità possi havere nel governo d'importanza.*» CORTE, 1562, p. 129r.

398) Twelve years after the publication of Corte's work, the art of conversation, which was already fully acknowledged in the *Book of the Courtier*, was explicitly codified in a treatise, *La civil conversazione* (The Civil Conversation, 1574), by Stefano Guazzo, which had a success that can be compared to that of Castiglione and is rightly considered one of the fundamental texts of the old regime society. See AA.VV., 1990. Another fundamental work in which, in those years, "it is argued about the manners to be kept or avoided in ordinary conversation" (Patrizi, 1993, p. 458) is the *Galateo* (1558) by Giovanni Della Casa.

399) A precept which echoes the ideal of measure and prudence typical of the sixteenth-century treatises on behavior: "The appropriate measure—said Giorgio Patrizi—is halfway between exaltation and humiliation: one must 'tell the truth humbly,' because his own truth should not be too much exhibited." Patrizi, 1993, p. 467.

For this reason it must take a lot of persuading to get him to touch the topic of riding.

> ...never forget that nothing could dishonor him as riding or talking a lot about horses and about the art itself in the presence of princes, or knights. And then it must take a lot of persuading before, on his own initiative, he ever meddles with talking about this art, or in riding horses.[400]

One can not help but notice how this reserve—which is about the facts, rather than talk—still identifies the true horseman compared with the many, too many, who are ready to dispense judgment and not required suggestions, never giving practical proof of the supposed competence they strut about!

---

400) «...*non mandi mai in oblio che poca cosa lo potrebbe dishonorare in presentia di prencipi, e cavallieri nel cavalcare, e nel parlar molto de' cavalli e dell'arte istessa. Et però lasciasi pregar molto pria che da se stesso s'ingerischi mai ne à parlar di quest'arte, ne à maneggiar cavalli.*» CORTE, 1562, p. 109r.

VII
The other Renaissance treatises

The number of treatises by Italian authors printed in the sixteenth century total eight. Four of these were written by authors of the southern regions of the Italian peninsula, testifying to the diffusion and the prestige achieved by the equestrian culture in the kingdom of Naples. It should be noted that even if the structure of each of these works was different from the others, they all present the same "rules of riding," that is to say that they all explain, more or less in detail, the same exercises (*pesades* and the different kind of "*maneggi*," i.e., the different way to perform the *passade*) and the same school jumps (*courbette*, *cabriole*, one step and a jump, exc.), demonstrating a considerable homogeneity of the equestrian practice of the time. So, if the printing of the treatises, granting a more wide circulation of the works, contributed to the institution of the literary genre and to set the rules of school equitation, it is also evident that riding was already well developed into a consolidated practice. It should also be considered that, moving from court to court, the best horsemen spread the equestrian doctrine in Italy and in Europe. This largely explains the strict compliance to exercises practiced, although it is likely that the authority immediately gained by the first authors—particularly Grisone and Fiaschi—had encouraged their followers to conform to their teachings.

Giovan Battista and Pirro Antonio Ferraro

The treatise of the Neapolitan Giovan Battista Ferraro, *Races, discipline of riding and other things relevant to this exercise* (*Delle razze, disciplina del cavalcare, et altre cose pertinenti ad essercitio così fatto*), printed in Naples, by Matteo Cancer, in 1560, is the third in chronological order of publication, after the texts of Grisone and Fiaschi. The work was reprinted ten years later[401] and then again published—revised and with a few additions—in the posthumous work of the author's son, Pirro Antonio, which appeared in Naples in 1602[402]. From what the son writes in this last edition we learn that Giovan Battista died the

---

401) *Del signor Giouan Battista Ferraro cauallerizzo napolitano libri quattro: de' quali si tratta delle razze, della disciplina del caualcare, e di molte altre cose appartenenti a si fatto essercitio*, in Campagna, appresso Gio. Domeninico [!] Nibio e Gio. Francesco Scaglione, 1570.

402) See FERRARO, 1602. Given the rarity of the work, for practical reasons, I have chosen to quote from this edition, which is much more common and easy to find even in electronic format through the Internet (see the final Appendix about on-line resources).

25th of October 1562. We also know that he was the first master of riding of Ottaviano Siliceo,[403] in turn, the author of another equestrian treatise, which we discuss later in this chapter.

The work is divided into four books. The first is devoted to breeding: from the quality of the pastures, to the selection of mares and stallions, up to the enclosing of foals in the stable. The second concerns the discipline of the horse, which is the taming of the foal and the technique of riding. The third and fourth are about the treatment of diseases. In particular, the third is about preventive and curative medicine and the fourth about surgery. These two parts were, in the words of Pirro Antonio, published in anonymous form as an appendix to some editions of Grisone's treatise.

According to Ferraro the horse has a warm, but at the same time, tempered nature. He is of great benefit to man for his many uses, "by means of him, human dignity shines, as (without him) it's difficult to deal with the decorum of the glorious operations"[404]. From the technical point of view, the text presents no novelty with respect to those of Grisone and Fiaschi. There are also some curiosities. When speaking of the breeding, Ferraro says that the favorable period for covering begins with the feast of St. George (23rd of April), "that being the patron saint of knights, it's better that this job starts on the day dedicated to him."[405] The covering season ends on the day of St. Peter (29th of June). The author contends that the semen quality of the stallion determines the sex of the foal. If it is viscous it will generate a male, while if it is fluid and cold it will produce a female. Then he recommends that the stallion not mate more than twice a day with the same mare,

> So that the stallion covering, so to say, with more zest will more easily produce his effect and the mare, not transformed into a whore [*imputtanita*], with more zest and ease will conceive.[406]

It's also interesting the description of the qualities of the good horse, all played on the edge of similarities:

> ...I had always liked that my horse has: the chest, animosity, and the back of the Lion; the body, the joints, and the eyes of the Ox; the mouth, the promptness, and the ears of

---

403) See SILICEO, 1598, p. 39.

404) «*suo mezo, l'humana dignità risplende, trattandosi (senza lui) malagevolmente il decoro delle gloriose operationi.*» FERRARO, 1602, p. 2.

405) FERRARO, 1602, p. 6.

406) «*Che lo stallone, con maggior gusto montando per così dire, con maggior facilità farà l'effetto suo, e la giumenta non imputtanita, con maggior gusto, e facilità concepirà.*» FERRARO, 1602, p. 10.

Giovan Battista Ferraro suggests to lead the colt by hand when he is haltered for the first time, in order to gently induce him to yield (1602).

the fox: the greed and the fatness of the pig, without which the natural heat it is hardly supported, and finally I wish that he would imitate the short walk of the woman having her determination and grace, lifting his foot as the cock while walking, being joyful and of pleasant appearance.[407]

Ferraro then proposes again the theory of the four humors, which depend on eating and drinking, even if he does not explain it as clearly and abundantly as Claudio Corte.

With regard to the taming of the foal, Ferraro is against the use of the so-called "judge" (i.e. the pole that is still used in some parts of Italy, especially in Tuscany and Lazio, at the center of the round pen and that can be considered a forerunner of the Pillar), to put the halter on foals for the first time:

> First of all I will tell you what you should avoid in any way, which is when a person trusting the foalers [*poleddrari*], to whom reasonably belongs to halter; who to discharge their arms invented to plant a very big pole in the middle of the fence, where the colts will be haltered, six or seven palms tall from the ground, which they call the judge; the effects it produces are bad for the poor foal, because when they tied him to the pole to halter him, they make him run on one side and on the other, so that it often happens that he's injured and that he breaks his neck more on one side than on the other and then he remains in that way.[408]

Therefore Ferraro suggests that the colt is instead carried out by hand after being haltered, to induce him gently to give up. Even better—he says—is to halter the foal and then let him go with the long rope, so that he gradually gets used to yield, by treading on it accidentally. The taming will then be carried out by a good horseman that, initially, will be helped by a man on

---

407) «...*vorrei sempre che il mio Cavallo havesse: Del Leone, il petto, l'animosità, e la schiena: Del bue, il corpo, le giunture, e gl'occhi: della volpe, la bocca, la sollecitudine, e l'orecchie: Del porco, la voracità, e la grassezza, senza la quale il calor naturale mal si sostiene; et finalmente vorrei, che egli imitasse il passeggiar corto della donna, havendo la sua determinatione, e leggiadria, alzando il piede nel passeggiare, come fa il gallo, essendo gioioso, e di piacevolissimo aspetto.*» FERRARO, 1602, p. 11.

408) « *Prima dirò quello che si haverà in ogni modo à fuggire; che è quando la persona confidandosi à i poleddrari à cui ragionevolmente appartiene lo scavezzare; i quali hanno inventato per discarico di loro braccia, piantare in mezo allo steccato, ove si allazzeranno i polledri, un palo ben grosso, alto sei palmi ò sette da terra, da loro giodice chiamato; dall'effetto che fa, giudicando malamente contra il povero polledro, al qual palo per incavezzarlo, l'infuriano, hora dall'una parte, e hora dall'altra, in modo che spesso avviene che il polledro si sfruscierà, e si incollerà (come si dice) cioè che rompendosi più dall'una parte che dall'altra, il collo rimanerà in quel modo.*» FERRARO, 1602, p. 26.

From Pirro Antonio Ferraro's *Cavallo frenato* (1602)

the ground, which must be skilled and not chosen from anyone who is in the stable. The first thing to teach the foal is, of course, to move forward.

As already in Grisone[409], we find in Ferraro also the theme of the difficulty to express in writing the correct position of the rider, "that can be seen and realized only with the practical act."[410] For the same reason he avoids explaining the use of the fingers, which can be learned—he says—only directly from a master. Despite the difficulty to clarify through words the details and nuances, the author argues that the rider should sit in the saddle straight and loose at the same time, rejecting all affectation, taking care to express his ease, even and especially with the expression of his face:

> the Rider must stand up straight, solid and loose on the Horse, however he must not look affected or angry, but with a cheerful rather than severe face; so it happened that many Riders looked more beautiful dressed (that is to say armed) than unarmed because under the visor of their helmet, whatever was their face, happy or sad, the affectation or mutation of the members of the face could not be seen [...]. I wish, therefore, that starting from the head, when the Rider is on horseback (as I said) shows more joy than melancholy in his face, so that it will not only bring a better view, but it will also show to the bystanders that he well possesses what he does, or is about to do, and that it is very easy for him.[411]

Then the author adds a consideration of common sense, which shows a different approach from Grisone's brisk methods. If groomed and trained properly, without violence and excessive force, the horse will live longer and will be suitable for every application:

> [by] treating the horse in the right way he will last a long season and finally making him work as it should be, and in the way I said, without any unreason-

---

409) See Chapter IV.

410) «*che solamente con l'atto pratico si può vedere, e toccare con mani.*» FERRARO, 1602, p. 40.

411) «*anchor che il Cavaliero à Cavallo dee star dritto, annervato, e disciolto, non dee mostrarsi però affettato, ò colerico, ma con volto anzi allegro, che severo; quindi avviene, che molti Cavalieri, sono riusciti, e riescono, più belli vestiti (dico armati) che disarmati, perché sotto la celata, qual sia stato il volto, allegro, ò malinconico, l'affettatione, ò mutatione di membri della faccia, che far si sogliono, non si è veduta [...]. Vorrei perciò, cominciando dal capo, che il Cavaliero posto à Cavallo (come ho detto) mostrasse più allegrezza, che malinconia nel volto, il che farà, che non solo apporti miglior vista, ma mostrerà a circostanti, che quel che fa, o havrà à fare il possegga bene, e che l'habbia facilissimo.*» FERRARO, 1602, p. 40.

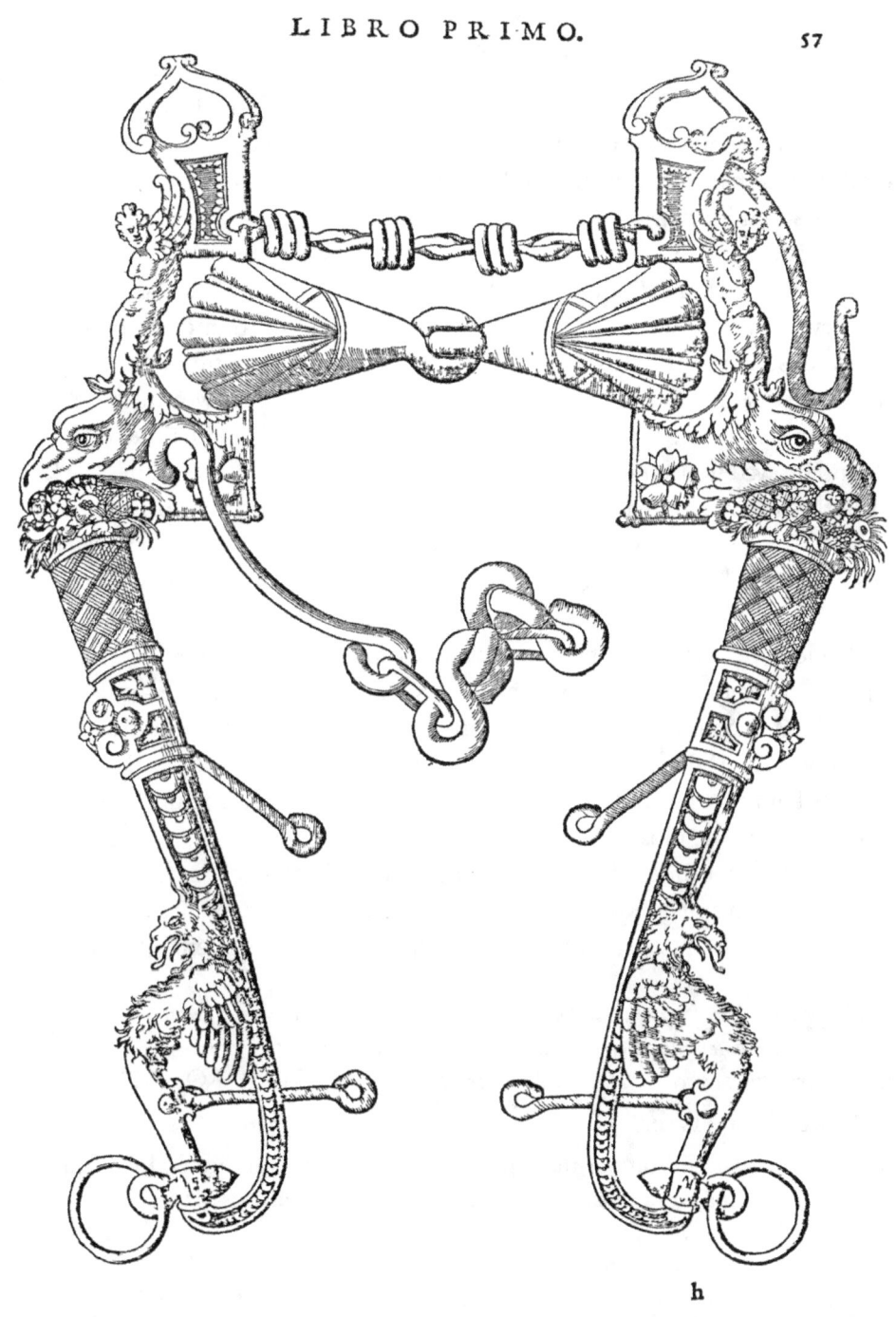

"*Scaccia*" bit, with chiselled shanks.
Pirro Antonio Ferraro considers the art of choosing the right bit
"the most difficult part of this profession."

able violence, nor excessive fatigue, he will be able to make any honorable and pleasant operation[412].

Finally, Ferraro reports about the "airs of fantasy" as the *ciambetta* (i.e. what we now call Spanish walk[413]), or the horse who works with the rider driving him with the reins tied to his belt, as the Spanish and Portuguese bullfighters still do today.

Even if printed in Naples in 1602, the work of his son Pirro Antonio, *Cavallo frenato* (Braked horse), should be considered fully a part of the sixteenth century's treatises tradition. In fact, it was published posthumously by the author's sons Giovanni Battista and Bernardino, but it was written by their father some decades earlier. In the dedication letter to Philip III, the two editors tell that their father went to Spain on a visit to the sovereign (which at the time was Philip II) and showed him some pen drawings of bridles of his own invention. The king liked them so much that he ordered the Neapolitan horseman to print them.

The author, however, could not see his effort accomplished because he was "surprised by untimely death." The work had a long gestation and was written in various drafts from at least twenty years before the publication date. In the Prologue of the first book, the same Ferraro said in fact that since 1577 he made a present of manuscript copies of his treatise to various Princes and lords – such as the king of Spain, the Duke of Ferrara, the Duke of Urbino and the Duke of Tuscany[414]. In 1586 he also gave the first printed edition to Philip II, even if it included only the illustrations of the bridles without the accompanying text. The work is in fact the most richly illustrated book on horsemanship ever published in Italy until that time. The drawings of the bridles are by the same author[415].

The seventeenth-century edition is divided into two parts. As we have already seen, the first is, with some additions and amendments, the work of

---

412) «*per trattarsi il Cavallo al dovuto modo, durerà lunga stagione, e finalmente per crearsi come conviene, e nella maniera detta, senza violenza alcuna fuor di ragione, né con soverchia fatica, sarà atto à ciascuna honorata, e piacevole operatione.*» FERRARO, 1602, p. 71.

413) See Chapter IV, n. 270.

414) The presence of one of these precious manuscripts is indicated by Sabina De Cavi in the Osuna Fund of the Biblioteca Nacional de España in Madrid (BNM mss. Riservato 10116), with the title *Libro di Mariscalcheria* (The Book of Farriery). The manuscript is decorated with a "magnificent allegorical frontispiece in pen and brown ink, with watercolors over traces of black pencil, it depicts Mars and Athena in an architectonical *portada*, with, in the center an unidentified heraldic escutcheon. The manuscript consists of 66 plates, an index (fols. 1r–3r) and two manuscript treatises. The pages of the plates have colored frames on the back (*verso*) and the bridles and the bits elaborated by Ferraro on the front (*recto*), finely painted with watercolor and sometimes silvered (fol. LIr). In one case, also appears a black pencil drawing depicting a walking horse (fol. XXv)." De Cavi, 2013.

415) FERRARO, 1602, p. 2.

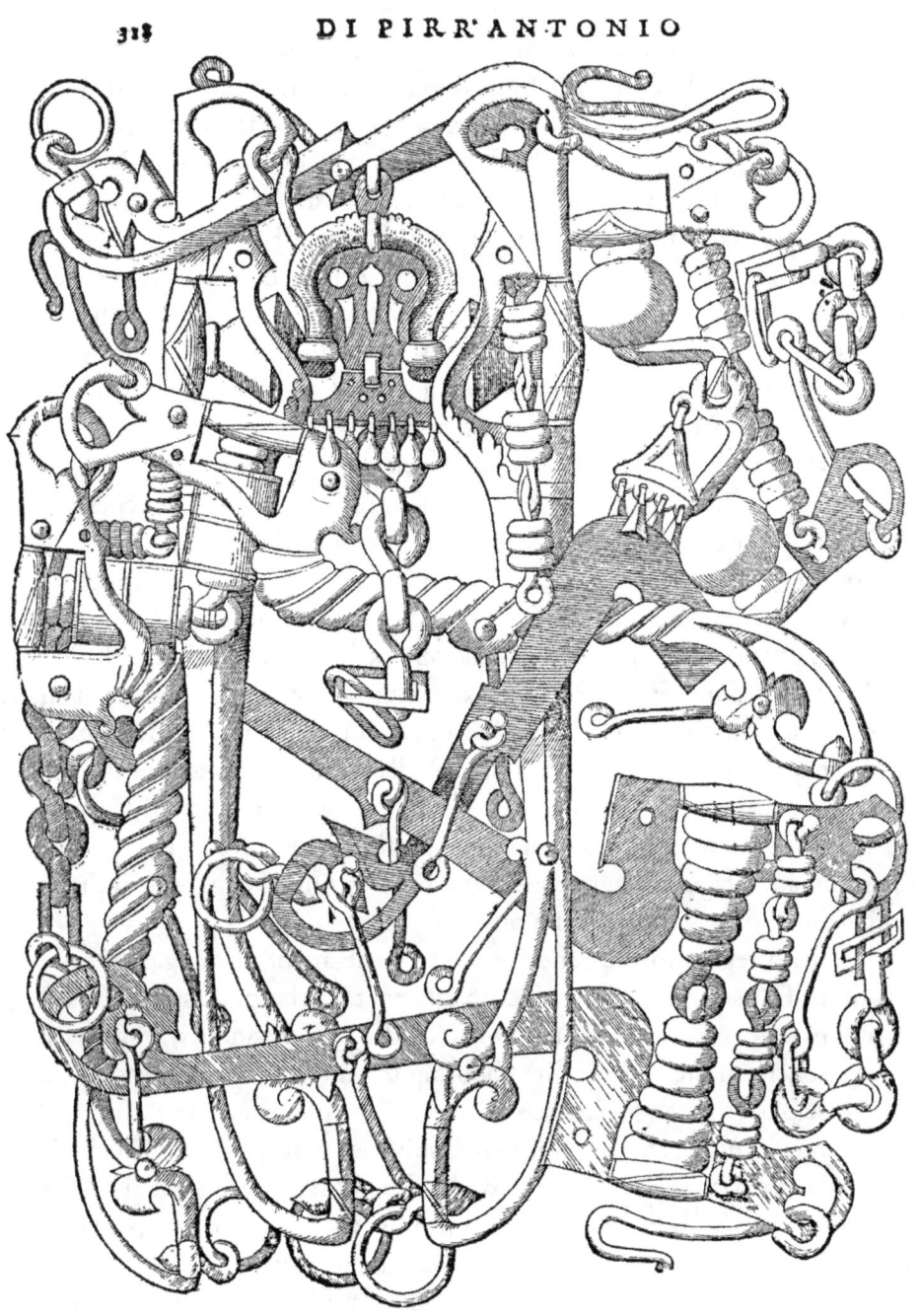

Pirro Antonio Ferraro, Hungarian and Polish bridles

the author's father, Giovanni Battista. The second is divided into four books. The first two describe ancient and modern bridles and others invented by the same author. The third and the fourth books are in the form of dialogues. In the third the author disserts the art of bridling with the Major Horseman of the king, Don Diego of Cordoba, while the fourth dialogue is with the Marquis of Sant'Eramo, Lieutenant of the previous interlocutor.

More than a treatise on horsemanship, that of Ferraro is a very detailed repertoire of bridles. It represents the clearest evidence of the importance attributed at the time to the selection of the right bit. In addition to those currently in use in Italy, there are also displayed some bridles used in the past and, for the sake of completeness and the delight of the readers, are also provided illustrations and explanations of exotic bridles like the Spanish, Arabic, Turkish and Polish. Even if he was aware that other authors have already dealt with the subject, the author aims to provide the most comprehensive repertoire of bridles ever written, since the art of bridling is considered "the most difficult part of this profession."[416] On the other hand, even in this case, the author is well aware that in such a delicate matter no one can believe that "just through my writings and drawings, or by others, one can absolutely bridle well."[417] The book, he says, can however aid the experience, providing accurate guidance, in order not to proceed by trial and error, with the risk of incurring mistakes which may harm the horses. For this, he tells the name of each bridle, shows its design and specifies its functions. The drawings are particularly important because they provide the size and especially the proportion of the parts, so as to ensure a clear guidance to those who have to order them and to the same craftsman who has to carry them out.

With regard to the general theory of the art of bridling, Ferraro does not differ from other authors. He notices that in the past, strong bits were mainly used to subdue the horse. A choice that he considers wrong, because, as the modern masters say, before choosing the mouthpiece: "the horse ought to be disciplined through the true doctrine."[418] Only when the animal will be fully trained can one choose a bit that is suitable to his physical characteristics and to the use to which he is destined. While choosing the bit one should keep in mind that to aid and to punish him it must use "less iron as possible," that is to say that the less severe bit should always be preferred. On the other hand, Ferraro explains that a heavy hand can cause damage even using a gentle bit. By way of example, he cites the case of Antonio Catamusto, famous horseman of his age who, according to the author, even if he used to ride his horses only with the cannon (that was the gentler bit used at the time), he corrected them

---

416) «*la più difficile parte di questa professione.*» FERRARO, 1602, p. 2..

417) «*con gli scritti, e co i miei disegni soli, ò di altri si possa assolutamente ben imbrigliare.*» FERRARO , 1602, p. 2.

418) «*si dee con vera dottrina disciplinare il Cavallo.*» FERRARO, 1602, p. 15.

Pirro Antonio Ferraro, Neptune and the Horse

with such violent "hand strokes" and "jerks" that pulled them back three or four steps, often injuring them on the bars and disheartening them, to the point that they lost their will to work.

Similarly, the author refutes the opinion of those who believe that the horse should always be ridden with the same bridle and considers variety in mouthpieces superfluous. Instead he considers the different types of bits useful to fit as much as possible to the morphology of the mouth of each specimen and to mitigate the problems and defects that may arise during the life of the animal. However, he specifies that one should not think

> that to curb well a horse there is a need for hundreds of bridles, but I declare, that this variety and quantity will at some point be useful, when one will do a perfect choice of each and do not apply them guessing, but with art, judgment, experience, and time, considering that the different qualities of mouths are more than the types of curbs[419].

This general premise is followed by the analytical treatment of the three essential parts of each bridle, namely: the shanks, (i.e. the outer levers of the bit), the mouthpiece (which is the part that the horse keeps in his mouth) and the curb chain (i.e. the chain secured with two hooks to the eye of the bit, which passes under the chin groove of the horse). Particular emphasis is given to the proportion of the parts that make up the shank. The author also explains in detail how to draw them, using ruler and compass.

Today Ferraro's work is more admired for the beauty of its illustrations than for the technical interest of the text. Some of the drawings, which show an intricate tangle of harnesses, already show a baroque taste. It is probably due to the protection of the king of Spain that the author and his heirs could print such a rich and expensive book. For at least a century, the *Cavallo frenato* represented the compilation of reference about the art of bridling. It was reprinted several times and had a considerable success abroad, so that Antoine de Pluvinel, in his *L'instruction du Roy en l'exercice de monter à cheval* (1625)[*The Maneige Royal*, Xenophon Press 2010], refers to the work of the Neapolitan horseman whoever is curious to know about the wide variety of existing bits:

> Many excellent riders have talked about the way in which we must bridle the horses and in particular Sir Pietro Antonio Ferrara [sic], Neapolitan Gentleman, wrote so worthily and with such great care and judgment, which is impossible to

---

419) «*che per frenare bene un Cavallo bisognasse un centinaio di briglie: ma ben mi dichiaro, che questa varietà, e quantità di esse, tutte potranno in un tempo servire, quando si farà perfetta elettione di ciascuna di quelle, e non si applicheranno à modo d'indovinare; ma con arte, giuditio, sperienza, e à tempo, considerando che più sono le diverse qualità di bocche, che non sono le spetie di freni.*» FERRARO, 1602, p. 16.

Rider mounted "*a la gineta*," i.e., with short stirrups, according to the typical use of Spaniards who had, in turn, borrowed this method from the Arabs.

do better. For this reason those who are curious to see a large number of mouthpieces of different shapes, can give a glance (if they want) to what he has brought to light[420].

Pasquale Caracciolo

The impressive work *La gloria del Cavallo* (The Glory of the Horse) by Pasquale Caracciolo, a Neapolitan gentleman, stands out among the treatises dedicated to the equestrian art after 1560. It is a veritable encyclopedia, which offers a truly remarkable synthesis of the equestrian culture of the time. "The structure of the work [...] covers all subject areas of the hippological and hippiatrical ancient, medieval and modern tradition, showing a formidable knowledge not only of this specialized segment but also of the entire classical library (as well as Italian): is a kind of classicist gentleman's macroapologue, of his dwelling with ease and profit among ancient and modern texts, in a back and forth of quotations that is never a superfluous display of erudition or accumulation of clichés."[421]

Born in Naples, Pasquale Caracciolo belonged to a noble and famous family. He lived during the reign of Philip II of Spain[422]. His brother, Don Petraccone, was the third Duke of Martina Franca. His treatise *La Gloria del cavallo* (The Glory of the Horse) was first published in Venice by Gabriel Giolito de' Ferrari in 1566. This first edition was followed by six more in the sixteenth[423] and seventeenth[424] centuries.

In the dedication to his sons, the author explains that, for his own pleasure and for the fondness he had since his birth for "this very noble animal," he collected an impressive body of news about the horse. Then he decided to order the information, to facilitate their consultation, but without even thinking about their publication. Nevertheless some manuscript copies of the text began to circulate and the author heard that someone intended to print the work without his permission and control[425]. In order to avoid the text coming

---

420) PLUVINEL, 1625, p. 143.

421) Quondam, 2003, p. 192.

422) It is the same Caracciolo who said it. See CARACCIOLO, 1566, p.141. Philip II of Habsburg (21 May 1527–13 September 1598), was king of Spain from 1556 to 1598, king of Naples and king of Sicily from 1554 to 1598, king of Sardinia and eighteenth king of Portugal and the Algarve, as Philip I from 1581 to 1598.

423) 1567–85–86–87–89 by Giolito and a second edition in 1589 by Nicolò Moretti, in Venice as well.

424) Ber. Giunti and Batt. Ciotti, Venetia 1608

425) Sabina De Cavi indicates the presence of one of these manuscripts, entitled

to light without proper review and without the fatherhood of the author, Caracciolo decided to publish it.

The first book of the treatise discusses the usefulness of the horse and his conformity and similarity to humans. In this regard for example the author, drawing on the authority of the ancients, says that horses share with man the desire of glory, as evidenced by the fact that "when they win [a race] they jump for their own joy, while lying down, grieving, when they lose."[426] He then lists a series of anecdotes that testify the attachment of famous historical figures to these animals. He also talks about the origins of cavalry and of duels, discusses the presence of the horse in art and describes triumphal chariots. Finally the author considers different theological and allegorical interpretations of the horse and talks about devices, that is to say, coats of arms, medals and insignia of chivalry.

The second book first lists the various names given to the horse by the various peoples of the world and then the proper names and surnames that refer to the horse. Then he goes on with the description of the equestrian games, especially the ancient ones, and of tournaments. Caracciolo then talks about the different types of horses, about their uses and about the origin of the chariots. He dwells on horses made famous by the stories of the writers and mentions the use of the horse in the carriage of the mail. In this regard it is interesting to note that at the time the mail system was already very efficient, since "in thirteen days one comes from England to Rome and from Lyon of France in five or six."[427] He then refers to the mythical origin of the horse, by means of Neptune, and to the myths of the Centaurs and of the Amazons. The book is concluded recalling famous ancient and modern riders and horse trainers.

The third book begins with an accurate description of the morphology of the horse, of his qualities and physical defects, providing an interesting overview of the anatomical knowledge of the time. The author insists on the necessity of long experience to evaluate each specimen and offers a number of suggestions for a correct estimate of the horse to buy, also adding a list of the

---

Discorso de' freni, et de' maneggi (Discourse about bits and exercises, BNE, ms 7802), in the Osuna Fund of the Biblioteca Nacional de España in Madrid. Prepared in a fair copy "this little treatise (the fifth book or appendix to *La Gloria del Cavallo*), has a total of fourteen illustrations of equestrian choreographies, drawn in pen and brown ink over traces of black pencil with yellow watercolors." The manuscript includes as a premise to the treatise, the author's correspondence with the "spanish horseman," Juan Arias Davila Puertocarrero, II Count of Puñorostro (secc XVI–XVII), a resident of Rome, with whom the Neapolitan entertained a correspondence in 1567/68. De Cavi, 2013.

426) «*che vincitori saltando s'allegrano; vinti giacendo si dogliono.*» CARACCIOLO, 1566, p. 3.

427) «*in tredici dì si viene da Inghilterra a Roma, e da Lione di Francia in cinque o sei.*» CARACCIOLO, 1566, p. 116.

main tricks used by livestock traders to hide imperfections and vices. For example, some bind the tail of the horse to the harness to prevent him from shaking it, or they immobilize it with an iron hidden between the hairs, or they cut a nerve. Or others that warned of the suspicious nature and reluctance of certain specimens, stimulate them with the spurs and animate them with care, without being seen, thus preventing their refusal. Others hide the physical defects of the horse with appropriate saddles and harnesses, and remedy the insensitivity of the mouth with modified bits, perhaps coated with honey and salt, so that the horse chew the mouthpiece, as if he accepts it. Caracciolo then suggests a thorough examination of the mouth and teeth, from which one can infer the age and state of health of the animal. Then he switches to the care of the stallion and of the mares and to the criteria of proper breeding. An appendix is specifically dedicated to mules, which were, at the time and for many centuries, still very popular, not only for working in the fields and transport, but also as riding mounts. He concludes by examining the medicinal use [parts and fluids from the horse's body were used as medication at the time] which were made at the time of the different parts of the horse's body and of his humors (blood, saliva, sweat, urine).

The fourth book opens with a dissertation about the colors of the horses' coats, followed by a section on the hairs and how they are formed and how they change. Therefore he proposes the theory of the relationship between the coat's color and the qualities of the horse that we have already seen shared by other authors. The book goes on with an extensive discussion on the influence of the stars and planets on the nature of the horses, which summarizes the astrological theories popular at the time:

> since it is necessary (as written by Aristotle) that this lower world continuously receives his virtues and its governance from the supernal motion, and although all horses are subject to Mars, they also participate of the others.[428]

Caracciolo then lists the characteristics of the seven "planets" [known at the time] (The Moon, Mercury, Venus, Sun, Mars, Jupiter and Saturn), corresponding to the seven ages of man: "infancy, childhood, adolescence, youth, manhood, old age, and decrepitude."[429] According to Caracciolo, each planet affects specific body parts of the animal (eg. Saturn the right ear, the spleen, the bladder, the phlegm and the bones; Jupiter the touch, the lung, the ribs, the cartilages, the arteries and the semen, etc.), though—he adds—the authors do

---

428) «*poi che necessario è (come Aristotile scrive) che questo mondo inferiore da i superni moti riceva continouamente le sue virtuti, e'l suo governo; e benché tutti i Cavalli siano soggetti à Marte, tuttavia essi partecipano ancor de gli altri.*» CARACCIOLO, 1566, p. 280.

429) «*infantia, pueritia, adolescenza, gioventù, virilità, vecchiezza, e decrepità.*» CARACCIOLO, 1566, p. 280.

Pirro Antonio Ferraro, Armed rider

not agree on the exact correspondence of their influences. The planets also exert a more general influence on the "complexion" of the animal. Thus, for example, the Moon "makes the animal phlegmatic, mutable and inconstant, not uniform in the eyes; greedy eater, dangerous in the water, unfit to discipline and easy to fall ill,"[430] while Venus "gives a lot of grace and loveliness to creatures; especially in their eyes and makes them lovable, witty, lascivious and friends of harmony; with a temperate complexion when she [Venus] is Western."[431]

The effect produced by the power of the stars then changes depending on the position they assume in the twelve houses of the zodiac. Even the signs of the zodiac determine the characteristics of the animal born under their influence. So the horses born under Aries "are agile and strong: with a fleshy body, thick hairs, small ears, long neck, and thin head,"[432] while Gemini brings "vexed animals, but little lasting in anger: sterile, but eager of high things; virtuous, docile, beautiful, lucky, sanguineous, and of good constitution, because in the month of May the blood is more refined in everyone."[433] The combination of the influences produced by signs and planets, depending on the astral configuration present at the time of the birth, causes complex effects that the author himself admits are "very difficult to investigate: being necessarily subject to many subtleties of Astronomical rules, and many minute but very important circumstances, which can be hardly understood more through divine inspiration than through art."[434] Caracciolo, however, concludes that, though powerful, the influence of the stars cannot counteract the effects produced by man who, according to his ability and doctrine in the care and training, can ruin the most gifted specimen, as well as improve and correct the most disadvantaged:

> I do not deny already, that it does not consist of man's free will to use well or badly his instrument: because every day you see a good horse becoming better under a good Rider, than under another: and if he will be less good, certainly he

---

430) «*fa l'animal flemmatico, mutabile e incostante, disforme d'occhi; mangiator ingordo, pericoloso in acqua, poco atto alla disciplina, e facile ad infermarsi.*» CARACCIOLO, 1566, p. 281.

431) «*Dà alle creature molta gratia e venustà; massimamente ne gli occhi, e le rende amabili, spiritose, lascive e amiche dell'armonia; con temperata complessione, trovandosi ella [Venere] Occidentale.*» CARACCIOLO, 1566, p. 282.

432) «*riescono agili, e gagliardi: col corpo carnoso, crini folti, orecchie picciole, collo lungo, e testa asciutta.*» CARACCIOLO, 1566, p. 289.

433) «*animali corrucciosi, ma poco durabili all'ira: sterili: ma disiderosi di cose alte; virtuosi, docili, belli, fortunati, sanguigni, e ben complessionati, perché nel mese di Maggio si trova in tutti il sangue più affinato.*» CARACCIOLO, 1566, p. 289.

434) «*difficilissimi da investigare: bisognandosi molte sottilità di regole Astronomiche, e molte minute, ma importantissime circostanze, le quali più per ispiratione divina, che per arte si possono à pena comprendere.*» CARACCIOLO, 1566, p. 294.

will not go with so much disorder and danger, if he is held by a learned maker, than if the brake is in the hands of a fool and inexperienced[435].

To complete the description, he then examines the horse markings, such as socks, whorls and stripes, which were considered evidence of certain attitudes. Finally, he gives an overview of the influences that the different geographical conditions of the countries in which the horses are raised have on their qualities and discusses the major breeds, especially the Italian and the Spanish.

The fifth book is the one properly dedicated to the equestrian art. Even in this case, the "rules of riding" described are the same of those indicated by other Renaissance authors. Caracciolo starts from what is required of a good rider:

> To whom, as for the Orator, besides the Art, are required the Imitation and the exercise, and above all the desire to achieve excellence: things that are so effective in every profession, that no one should distrust himself when, left the vain games and the idleness contrary to virtue, he practices all the time, learning: and so much more for a Noble man, whom having to surpass the other in every praise, as he surpasses them in dignity, with more ardor he will have to strive to acquire the perfection of this very honorable profession, in which the military glory mainly consists.[436]

Dedication and exercise must associate with experience and expertise, in order to know how to evaluate the nature of the different specimens and to modulate consequently their training to their aptitudes:

> ...certainly if horses would be limited to that for which they are inclined by Nature, each would be the most excellent in his operation.[437]

---

435) «*Non niego io già, che non consista nella libera volontà dell'huomo di adoperare ò bene, ò male il suo strumento: perché si vede tutto il giorno, un cavallo buono sotto un buon Cavaliere venir migliore, che sotto un'altro [sic]: e s'egli sarà men buono, certamente non andrà con tanto disordine, e pericolo, se lo regga un dotto artefice, quanto se il freno sia in mano di uno sciocco, e inesperto.*» CARACCIOLO, 1566, p. 293.

436) «*A cui non altrimenti, che à l'Oratore si richiedono oltra l'Arte, l'Imitatione, e l'essercitio; e sopra tutto il disiderio di conseguir la eccellanza: le quai cose in ogni professione son tanto efficaci, che niuno dee diffidarsi di se medesimo, quando lasciati i vani giuochi, e gli ocy contrari alla virtù, di continuo si esserciti imparando: e tanto maggiormente un'huomo [sic] Nobile, il qual dovendo avanzar gli altri in ogni lode, come gli avanza in degnità, con più ardore devrà sforzarsi di acquistar la perfettione di questo mestiere honoratissimo, nel qual principalmente consiste la gloria militare.*» CARACCIOLO, 1566, p. 327.

437) «*Che certamente se i Cavalli si astringessero à quello solo, à che dalla Natura si riconoscono inchinati, ciascuno riuscirebbe nella sua operatione eccellentissimo.*» CARAC-

Caracciolo says that it makes no sense to impose on a Turkish or on a Berber horse, born to run like the wind, the strict discipline of the *manège* and of the school jumps, as well as it's senseless to expect from a nice and quiet horse to trot and canter like a racehorse. One can help nature with training and discipline, but the idea of distorting and contrasting her is a vain and rash thought. Also for this reason, Caracciolo recommends pleasantness and rejects any excess in punishments. He also recommends taming the colt only when he is strong enough to withstand the job. He then talks largely about bridles and their use in function of the characteristics of the mouth of the horse and of its possible defects. Then he describes the different school exercises and stresses the affinity between riding and music, ending his detailed description talking about the training of the horse for fighting.

The sixth book is devoted to military horsemanship: from the equipment to the selection of the troops, up to strategy and to the exercises needed to keep the party always ready for war. Finally, the remaining four books are devoted to the prevention and treatment of diseases, starting from the grooming and the diet, passing then to the care and to surgical operation.

Marco de Pavari

The case of Marco de Pavari is quite original, compared to those of the other authors of the second half of the sixteenth century. Of this Venetian horseman we have a treatise, in a bilingual edition both in Italian and French, printed in 1581, in Lyon, France, by the printer and bookseller Jean de Tournes, entitled *Escuirie de M. de Pavari vénitien*. It is a folio volume of about sixty pages, in which the Italian and French texts are side by side in two columns. The text is enriched by fourteen full-page plates depicting different models of bits.

The fact that the dedicatory letter of the treatise is signed by the publisher Jean de Tournes suggests that probably de Pavari did not edit himself the printed edition of his work, and that the publisher provided the translation and the printing of the orginal manuscript, after the author had already left Lyon, or perhaps when he was already dead.

Mario Gennero, who has the merit of having edited with Patrizia Arquint a modern edition of this treatise, tells us that there are no other news about the author apart from the few that can be found directly in the text. His Venetian origin is indicated on the title page and the name can be found in the extract of the privilege. Let us add that, in this case, "Venetian" does not necessarily mean "from the city of Venice." The term designated the citizens of the Republic of Venice and it could be that the author came from a minor center on the mainland. Even if it was mainly a maritime power,

---

CIOLO, 1566, p. 328.

Mounted harquebuser, from Flaminio Della Croce,
L'essercitio della cavalleria (1625).
The advent of firearms stimulated the evolution of equestrian practices.

the Republic of Venice held the arts of chivalry in particular esteem for their importance in the military field, and—as we shall see in the next chapter—in many cases the government directly encouraged their practice. From the dedication letter of the treatise we also know that de Pavari was horseman of François de Mandelot[438], lord of Passy and governor of Lyons, Forests and Beaujeaulais. Lyon was a very important center of trade, and—as evidenced by Matteo Bandello in his *Novelle* (1554)—between the European cities of the time was the one in which "maybe there are ordinarily more Italians [...] that in any other known place out of Italy."[439] The presence of Italian horsemen in France was, at that time, absolutely ordinary. Many riders in the service of the king of France were Italians.[440]

The work is particularly rare and is not mentioned by other Renaissance authors, which instead show good knowledge of their other predecessors, in particular Grisone and Fiaschi. But this is a text which, despite its relative brevity, is extremely interesting, because it offers a much more modern and fresh approach to training. We could say that de Pavari is a kind of Monty Roberts before its time. He dedicates the greater part of his treatise to the rehabilitation of horses that became resistant or rebellious because of mistreatment. Judging by the often hasty methods popular at the time and witnessed from works like the one by Grisone, it is easy to imagine that the problem was quite widespread. De Pavari suggests rehabilitating them with gentleness and caresses, given

> that gentleness earns more than desperation: which you too can learn to be true, that desperation leads them [the horses] to do all this bad wills and not gentleness, which does not do this, but mitigates them and draws them to itself [i.e. to gentleness].[441]

---

438) Coming from a family of small nobility, he was born in Paris in 1529 and was assigned to the profession of arms. Admitted among the pages of Jacques de Savoie, duke of Nemours, later he became chamber gentleman of the king and lieutenant of the Duke of Nemours. He participated in the wars against Charles V, distinguishing himself at the siege of Metz (1552) and in the campaign of Italy (1555). At the side of the Duke of Nemours, he participated in the liberation of Lyon occupied by the Protestants, during the wars of religion. The king appointed him in his private council and then Lieutenant-General of the Duke of Nemours in Lyon. When the latter renounced the office of governor (1571) he succeeded in his role, while still retaining it until his death in 1588.

439) «*ove forse sono più ordinariamente italiani [...] che in qual altro luoco fuor d'Italia si sappia.*» Bandello, 2011, I, 50, p. 219.

440) The historian Jean-François Dubost lists twenty-four Italian horsemen in France, between the Sixteenth and the Seventennth centuries... See Dubost, 1997, p. 108.

441) «*che la piacevolezza guadagna assai più della disperatione: il che potrete conoscere*

The approach of de Pavari is aimed at avoiding trauma to the horse which could spoil his good disposition towards man, or to cancel their symptoms, since he has already suffered at least one trauma as a result of the brutality with which he has been handled. For this reason, for example, he recommends to place an experienced horse side by side to the colt in order to calm him in the first phase of the taming and to use only the cavesson in the first period of training in order not to damage his mouth with the bit. Therefore he emphasizes the importance of caresses, to calm and give a prize to the animal, and the need to take care not to expect too much from a young and untrained specimen, not to bother him. Similarly he suggests giving with the hand when the horse tends to escape, rather than trying to stop him with an excessive use of the bit:

> But these, on the contrary, as they have the mouth or the chin groove broken, as soon as they lose their energy they transport you and escape as a lost and very broken and slack thing, and as you think to stop them pulling the bridle, the more they transport you. So that when they show such a bad will you must do the opposite and you must give, that is to say to loosen the hand little by little and then to collect it in the same way, so that they will lose that bad will and they will stop.[442]

He then adds that if this expedient method does not work, rather than clinging to the reins, it's enough to put the horse on a tight *volte* to stop his flight. He then suggests a trick: to distract the horse from his desire to escape the rider can give him a branch of willow, full of leaves, letting him eat them, but without giving it completely, but holding it, in order to divert him from his intention.

De Pavari says that the horses which refuse to turn to one side, or which recoil instead of going forward, should always be won with gentleness. He also prescribes using a milder bit, the cannon, and the cavesson and to ride them without spurs, instead of beating them, ensuring that the girth is not too tight.

---

anche voi esser vero, che la disperatione li conduce a fare tutte queste cattive volontà, e non la piacevolezza, la quale non fa questo, ma li mitiga e li tira a sé.» DE PAVARI, 1581, [42] p. 31.

442) «*Ma questi, per il contrario, come hanno la bocca o il barbozzo rotto, non mancano per poco che manchi lor la lena di trasportarvi e andarsene come cosa perse, e cosa molto rotta e molle, e come più penserete di tirar la briglia per ritenerli fermi, a l'hora più vi trasportano. Per il che bisogna fare il contrario quando si mettono in tal cattiva volontà, e ve li bisogna dare, cioè allentare, la mano poco a poco, e, raccogliendola per il medesimo, essi perderanno quella volontà cattiva, e verrannnosi a fermare.*» DE PAVARI, 1581, [31] p. 27.

And if you love this virtue I urge you to proceed with gentleness, which dominates everything, that if you will do the opposite you will not acquire anything but the blame of the people who are worthy and expert.[443]

Nevertheless, in de Pavari's treatise there are also glaring contradictions, which now make us shudder, as when, in obedience to a widespread use of the time, he suggests to cut the tongue tip with a razor to those horses that have the habit of keeping it out even when they are harnessed and mounted.

From the technical point of view, the equitation proposed by de Pavari is consistent with that of his contemporaries: focused on the different types of "*passade*" and on the school jumps. The second part of his treatise is dedicated to the art of bridling and contains a description of the different types of mouthpieces, according to the different morphological and attitude problems they are supposed to solve.

Ottaviano Siliceo

One of the last treatises published in the sixteenth century is the one by Ottaviano Siliceo, printed in Orvieto, by Antonio Colaldi, and Ventura Aquilini, in 1598, under the title *Scuola de' cavalieri di Ottaviano Siliceo gentilhuomo troiano, nella quale principalmente si discorre delle maniere, & qualità de cavalli, in che modo si debbono disciplinare, & conservare, & anco di migliorare le razze* (School of riders by Ottaviano Siliceo, Trojan gentleman, which mainly talks about the manners and qualities of horses, and about how they should be disciplined and preserved, and also about how to improve the breeds). It is a very rare book, divided into five parts: the first deals with the proportions of the horse and its breeding, the second is about his education, the third reviews the faults in training and the ways to remedy them, the fourth concerns bits and the different mouthpieces, the fifth is about races, shoeing, jousts and tournaments[444].

The book is dedicated to Cardinal Pietro Aldobrandini[445], nephew of

---

443) «*E a ciò vi essorto se amate questa virtù, cioè di procedere con piacevolezza, la qual domina ogni cosa, che, se farete il contrario, non acquisterete che biasimo fra persone che saranno degne di essa e che se ne intenderanno.*» DE PAVARI, 1581, [60] p. 38.

444) See Deblaise, 2002, pp. 263–264.

445) He was born in Rome in 1571. Pope Clement VIII made him a cardinal in 1593. At the beginning of the Seventeenth century, he was Archbishop of Ravenna and Cardinal Commendatory Abbot of Sant'Ellero in Galeata. He played an important role in the events that led to the signing of the Treaty of Lyons in 1601: it was he who persuaded Henry IV of France and Charles Emmanuel I of Savoy to finish the war for the possession of the Marquis of Saluzzo. The poet Giovan Battista Marino

Pope Clement VIII[446], and a relative of Giacomo Aldobrandini—Bishop of Troy and Apostolic Nuncio to the kingdom of Naples. The vicar of the bishop was the Archdeacon Felice Siliceo, grandson of the author. The treatise was printed after the author's death by Giovan Battista Siliceo, Octavian's nephew and brother of Felice. In the text Ottaviano says that Giovan Battista Ferraro was his first master. From the text[447] we also learn that he served in the ranks of the Imperial Army of Charles V and participated in the Battle of Pavia. The author also claims that he took part in the war of Siena, which ended with the Battle of Scannagallo (2 August 1554), and that he also fought in Germany.

Alessandro Massari Malatesta

The treatise entitled *Compendio dell'heroica arte di cavalleria* (Compendium of the Heroic Art of Chivalry) by Alessandro Massari Malatesta was also printed in the late sixteenth century. We know of two editions of this book: one in 1599 and the other in 1600. Both were printed in Venice, at the request of Francesco Bolzetta, bookseller in Padua[448]. The author was born in Tivoli, near Rome, and was the son of Ferrante, who was general war auditor of Pope Paul IV and fought in Germany.[449] Alexander was in the service of Luigi Carafa, Prince of Stigliano, to whom the work is dedicated. The author claims to have practiced the arts of chivalry with the horseman of the Prince, "the most excellent and incomparable Master of horses Sir Silvio de Florio."[450] As we have already seen in the first chapter, the principles of Stigliano were large landowners, famous for their well provided stables and for the quality of their herds of horses. From the words of the same author we also know that at the time of the publication of his treatise, in 1599, Massari Malatesta resided in Padua, where he taught as a master in horse riding[451]. In the Venetian city he definitely had contacts with the Academy of Oplosifisti[452], which he explicitly mentions. He also published other works on chivalry, starting from the *Tractatus de modo equos fraenandi. Cum diversorum fraenorum variis fi-*

---

worked for him for many years. He died in 1621.

446) Ippolito Aldobrandini (1536–1605), was the 231ˢᵗ Pope of the Catholic Church (J from Jan. 20, 1592).

447) See SILICEO, 1598, p. 17.

448) The work was then also reprinted in Danzig, by Andrea Hunefeldi (Andrzey Hunefeldt), in 1610.

449) See Ilari, 2011, pp. 254–255.

450) «*l'eccellentissimo, e incomparabile Maestro di cavalli il Signor Silvio de Florio.*» MASSARRI MALATESTA, 1599, dedica.

451) See MASSARI MALATESTA, 1599, pp. 41r e 42r.

452) See Chapter VIII.

guris quibus ad praesens omnes bellicosi populi utuntur etc. (Treatise on how to curb horses), printed in Venice in 1607, then translated into Italian with the title *Della ragione e modi d'imbrigliar Cavalli: con una copiosa raccolta di varie figure di Briglie, cioè, di Morsi, Guardie, Barbazzali, e Capezzoni* (About the reason and ways to bridle horses: with a copious collection of various pictures of Bridles, that is to say Bits, Shanks, Curb Chains and Cavessons), published in Rome by Stefano Paolini, in 1613. He also published the *Trattato universale della vera arte militare...: Dove si descrivono tutte le militie del mondo, dal principio d'esso, sin'hora, etcome dovrebbeesser'una perfetta militar disciplina in tutte le sue parti* (Universal treatise on the true military art...: in which are described all the armies of the world, from its beginning until now, and on how a perfect military discipline should be in all its parts), printed in Turin, by Giovanni Antonio Seghino, in 1623.

The work by Massari is a true synthesis of the previous equestrian treatises. The author mentions both the authors of the classical era and the moderns, saying that he does not want to deviate from their teachings, but that he added to his works the precepts relating to fighting on horseback. In fact, from the technical point of view, the text presents no novelty but it is particularly interesting because it provides an overview of the use of the horse for military purposes, both in war and in tournaments. The work is also valuable because it contains a lexicon of the equestrian terminology of the time, which is very useful to clarify the meaning of many technical terms used by other Renaissance authors, which today are difficult to interpret. Another peculiarity of the text is that it provides a brief overview of the different equestrian cultures of the world known at the time, from Asia, to Africa and Europe, demonstrating a singular curiosity and the extent of the author's cultural horizons. Among other things, for example, by reviewing the main horse breeds, Massari describes—even if only by hearsay—the "very chosen" Mexican horses, who at the time would have been a rarity[453].

The author first distinguishes between single and battle combats. The single combat could be carried out by "armed" or "unarmed" knights, i.e. with or without armor. Even the horses could be protected by shaped metal plates, which protected their head and body. He suggests that the rider choose the armor carefully, which, in addition to being resistant to assure protection should above all be comfortable to allow the movements. He also says that it's better to avoid grating visor helmets, which proved to be poor protection in the tragic accident that cost the life of Henry II of France, mortally wounded in a tournament by a splinter of the Lord of Montgomery's lance[454]. In lance fighting, in fact, the stroke was aiming to the opponent's head. Massari then suggests choosing a helmet with small openings on the visor. As for offensive weapons, the author expresses his preference for the gun, even if it was only effective against the armors at a very close distance, using ogive bullets. The sword was

---

453) MASSARI MALATAESTA, 1599, p. 24r.

454) See Chapter I.

double-edged, neither too long nor too short, while the lance had to be "strong, thick, maneuverable and with long proportion."[455] Maces and axes were considered to be instead more as duel weapons than to fight in wars, because they were heavy and inconvenient to use. Finally, he mentions assagais ("*zagaglie*'"), a sort of javelin, with one or two points, used by the Moors and the Spaniards.

Massari underlines the importance of the horse's agility and obedience to dodge the opponent and immediately gain the advantage to hit him, both in combats with the gun and with the lance. With the gun, the knight had to induce the enemy to fire first, escaping the bullet with a skilful twist of the torso, or by using a quick change of direction of the mount. This then allowed him to shoot in turn at the time when he was at the side of the opponent, aiming at the head, or at the kidneys, or at the back, turning the horse to the right to keep him close to the opponent. The author suggests to fire only when the gun barrel is practically in contact with the opponent's armor. Similarly, the horse's ability to quickly turn was also essential in the combat with the lance, because it allowed for immediately attacking the opponent from behind with the sword, trying to hurt him in the neck, or at the point where the armor left the kidneys uncovered. Taking advantage of the speed of his horse, the knight had to try going around his opponent to be on his left side, in order to be more distant from his sword and to be able to better offend him.

Even in "disarmed" combats, that is to say without armor, the technique recommended by Massarri is to dodge the first encounter, to rapidly turn the horse and gain the advantage. In any case, the choice of a horse of adequate quality remains essential:

> As the fights that are done on horseback aim to different purposes, they are also made in various ways, and on this subject I advise you that these fights consist of two virtues: the value of the Knight and the perfection of the horse. And being that we have already talked of both, I will say that the fighting Knight must always use a generous horse, choosing him of good girth and size[456].

The characteristics of the horse had to be evaluated according to the needs of the different specialties of the cavalry of the time, which included riding arquebusiers, light cavalry armed with a lance, heavy cavalry with lance and gun and knights with armor, but armed with gun and sword.

---

455) «*forte, grossa, nervosa e con lunga proportione.*» MASSARI MALATESTA, 1599, p. 9v.

456) «*I combattimenti, che si fanno a cavallo si come si terminano in diversi fini, così anco si fanno con vari modi, sopra di che si deve avvertire, che questo combattimento consiste in due virtù, nel valore del Cavaliero: e nella perfettione del cavallo. Et essendo che dell'uno, e dell'altro ne habbiamo discorso, Dirò che il Cavaliere combattente deve servirsi sempre in fattioni di generoso, e forte cavallo, scegliendolo di buona vita, e taglia.*» MASSARI MALATESTA, 1599, p. 12r.

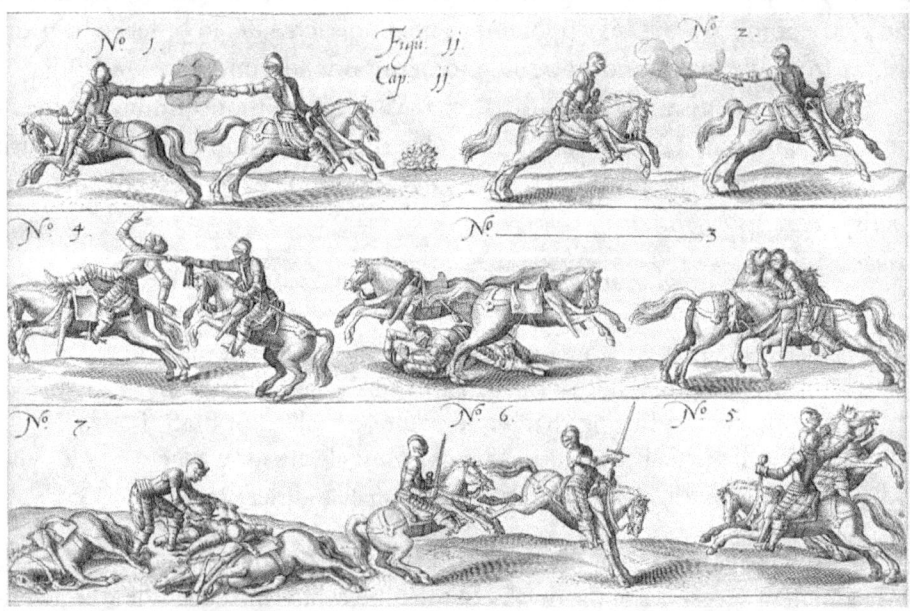

Techniques and weapons of combat on horseback from the treatise by Jacob von Walhausen, *Ritterkunst* (1614)

Massari then distinguishes the different ways of fighting of Germans and French. According to him, the main feature of the Germans was discipline, while the French were characterized by impetus. In other words the German cavalry was able to maintain the ranks close and neat, but this partly damaged their impact force, which was instead the winning feature of the French. The author then recommends to the Italian armies to take the better of these two tactical attitudes, combining order and vigor. With regard to the fight between cavalry and infantry, the technique consisted in breaking into the enemy's ranks, turning the horse to the left and to the right to sow confusion. The author also suggests resorting to the leaps and kicks of the horse if the knight finds himself surrounded:

> being surrounded [the knight] will free himself forcing the horse to make high jumps and kicking, turning somewhat to the right and to the left; that being the way to open and route the enemy, he will save himself letting the horse go out of the hand.[457]

The knight then always had to have a substitute horse, which was brought onto the battlefield by an equerry and which remained at his disposal in order to guarantee him a fresh mount.

Also Massari's precepts about the chivalrous trials, such as jousts and tournaments, are very interesting. The jousts consisted of forms of equestrian skill-at-arms in which the knight had to hit a target with his weapons. This is the case, for example, of the ring jousts, in which the knight had to insert the tip of the lance into a ring suspended from a support, while galloping at a charge. Another kind of joust was the so called "Quintain," which consisted in hitting with the lance the shield held by a rotating manequin, trying to avoid the blow of the mace attached to the other arm of the same dummy. Another skill trial was called "breaking lances" (*romper lance*). The knights had to charge on a straight line, put the lance on their arm and then, pointing it in a marked area of the field, break its tip on the ground. There were also races with the gun, in which the rider fired against a target while charging. Another trial was the so called "race to the encounter" ("*corsa all'incontro*"), namely the competition between two knights in armor facing each other with the lance, separated by a wooden barrier, or fence (know as "tilt barrier"). When the fighting was held without this barrier, the contention between the two knights was called combat in "open field." It was, of course, a much more dangerous kind of combat, in which the contestants faced each other with lance and sword, as in the tourna-

---

457) «*essendo circondato [il cavaliere] vedrà di sbrigrasi con sforzare il cavallo alto con salti, e calci, girandolo alquanto a destra, e a sinistra; che havendosi aperta la via, e sbaragliati i nemici con lasciar partire dalla mano il cavallo, si renderà salvo.*» MASSARI MALATESTA, 1599, pp. 13v–14r.

ment held in 1565 in the Belvedere courtyard of the Vatican, which the author mentions as a renowned example[458].

Massari distinguishes all these trials from tournaments, which were instead fighting between many knights:

> The word "Tournament" is taken from going and turning around, which is done in a show and in a exhibition on horseback, involving many Knights, nor can any chivalrous game be called tournament, if not at least with three Knights, which otherwise would be called singular combat.[459]

He then explains that the tournaments were set up with a real dramaturgy, which dealt with the exercises of the horses, the disposition and the movements of the riders, the scenery and the narrative framework in which the fights took place. The complexity of the equestrian choreography, more than any other chivalry trial, required just perfectly trained horses:

> whenever a Knight, both for his mistake or that of the horse, does not match with others in harmony, measures and order, not only causes discomfort, but great disorder: nor in any place, time, or action (not talking of warfare) the virtues held by a knight on horseback are more noticeable than in the Tournament.[460]

The movements of the riders and the exercises performed with their mounts were a real "horse ballet" (as defined by the same author, describing a tournament he conceived and held in Padua in 1599). In short, during the Renaissance, the tournament represented the highest expression of the chivalrous value and skill.

---

458) See Chapter VIII.

459) «*Torneo parola presa dall'andare, e girare intorno, che si fa in spettacolo, e mostra a cavallo, dove intervengono più Cavalieri, né si può far gioco cavalleresco e darli nome di Torneo, se non in tre Cavalieri almeno, che altrimenti sarebbe chiamato abbattimento singolare..*» MASSARI MALATESTA, 1599, p. 46r.

460) «*quando un Cavaliero, o sia suo, ò pur errore del cavallo ogni volta, che non corrisponde con gli altri di consonanza, di misure, e d'ordine, non solo causa disconforto, ma disordine grande: né in alcun luogo, tempo, ò attione (non parlando del guerreggiare) si nota più la virtù esercitata di un Cavaliero a cavallo, che nel Torneo.*» MASSARI MALATESTA, 1599, p. 46v.

VIII
Giovan Battista Pignatelli and the riding academies

Although we do not have any book by him, speaking of the equestrian art in the Renaissance, we cannot ignore the figure of Giovan Battista Pignatelli. He was one of the most famous and celebrated Italian masters of riding of the time, whose legendary reputation has come down to us mainly through the works of his many and, in turn, distinguished foreign students. If, in fact, the Italian authors of his time do not fail to mention his skill, are especially the foreign ones who celebrate his memory as a true founder. In the wake of his international success Pignatelli has become the very symbol of the Renaissance equitation of the Italian school and, from having been a skilled horseman among many others, he is turned into a leading authority. Key drivers for his popularity were his two most famous disciples, the French Salomon de la Broue[461] and Antoine de Pluvinel[462].

After an apprenticeship with the Italian master, La Broue wrote the first French treatise on horsemanship, which appeared in 1593 in La Rochelle with the title *Preceptes Principaux Que les bons Cavalerisses doivent exactement observer en leurs Escole*, then reissued in a revised and expanded version in 1610 under the title *Le Cavalerice françois*.[463] Pluvinel was a personage of great importance at the court of France and master of riding to King Louis XIII, as well as author of one of the most famous treatises on equitation of all times, which appeared posthumously in a first version in 1623, with the title of *Le maneige royal*, [*The Maneige Royal*, Xenophon Press 2010] and then published again in a new revised and corrected version in 1625, entitled *L'instruction du Roy en l'exercice de monter à cheval*.[464] Both authors recognize an important tribute to their master, Pignatelli. La Broue, in fact, writes:

---

461) He was born around 1530 and died around 1610. He was first page of the Earl of Aubijoux, then horseman of the Duke of Epernon. He became ordinary horseman of the Great Royal Stable under Henry III.

462) He was born in Crest, in the Dauphiné, according to some authors in 1552, according to others in 1555. He went to Italy very young and on his return he entered the service of King Henry III, who recognized on him many privileges and positions of prestige, as did his successor Henry IV. He was a master of riding of the Dauphin, the future King Louis XIII. In 1594 he founded an academy, inspired by the model of the Italian ones (see below in this chapter). He died the 24th of August 1620.

463) LA BROUE, 1610.

464) PLUVINEL, 1625.

Louis XIII (on horseback) trained by Antoine de Pluvinel (right, with the whip raised), from Antoine de Pluvinel, *L'instruction du Roy en l'exercice de monter à cheval* (1625)

> And among all the worthy masters that I met, I ascribe the highest praise to Sir Giovan Battista Pignatelli, whose memory must be forever honored among the men of horses, as that of who first invented the justness of our schools [i.e. of our exercises] and began to show us the true order and the finest proportions of all our low, medium and high airs[465].

His words are echoed by Pluvinel, who nevertheless points out that he learned from him only part of what he knows:

> ... Sir J. B. Pignatelli, Neapolitan gentleman, the most excellent Horseman that has ever been in our century and in previous years, from which I learned a part of what I know during the six years that I spent with him[466].

The works of both authors had a huge success and contributed significantly to impose the prestige of Pignatelli.

---

465) LA BROUE, 1610, II, p. 5

466) Cfr. Monteilhet. 1979, pp. 232–233.

An uncertain biography

Unfortunately we have little information about Pignatelli from the documents and chronicles of the time. According to André Montheilhet[467], who however does not motivate the indication of these dates, he was probably born around 1525 and died before the end of the century. Also according to the same author he belonged to the same noble Neapolitan family of Calabrian origin from which afterwards descended Pope Innocent XII (1615–1700) and St. Giuseppe Pignatelli (1737–1811). However if it was so, it is difficult to imagine why historians and chroniclers, who wrote extensively on what was once one of the oldest and most powerful families of the kingdom of Naples, did not mention the figure of such a famous horseman.

We can get some information about him directly from the same equestrian treatises of the Renaissance and the Baroque period. We find the most abundant news in the *Cavallo Frenato* by Pirro Antonio Ferraro[468]. From this source we learn that Giovan Battista Pignatelli was a pupil of Alessandro Conestabile,[469] a horseman in the service of various principles. Ferraro says also that when Pignatelli became old he finally retired at the house of another horseman, a certain Serpentino, who had been Ferraro's master[470]. From the book by Claudio Corte, however, we know that Pignatelli served in Rome as "very excellent horseman of the great Alessandro Farnese,"[471] The author describes him as a "Neapolitan gentleman, and really no less facetious and courteous, and very rare in the profession of riding."[472] However, it is difficult to determine a possible dating of this

---

467) PLUVINEL, 1625, p.30.

468) FERRARO, 1602.

469) Not of his brother Giannetto, as erroneously considered Monteilhet, 1979, p. 232 and Mario Gennero, in Gennero 2001 e Gennero 2002.

470) «*M. Alessandro [Conestabile] suo fratello, il quale visse con l'Illustrissimo Prencipe di Bisignano [...]: Costui si fè perfetto in casa del Conte vecchio di Consa, dopo il quale hà pur servito gran tempo il Sig. Conte di potenza, havendo fatto in sua casa, oltre gli altri Cavalli di gran finezze, un sauro, saltatore sì disposto e gagliardo, che faceva pagura [sic] à molti Cavalcatori, il qual per lui mandò a presentare al Reverendissimo Farnese: Di sua scuola sono usciti, il sig. Gio: Battista Pignatello e M. Leonardo suo nipote, il quale si è collocato con Bisignano, fendose il suo Zio, per infirmità, e ricchezze ridotto al fine à riposarci in sua casa giuditiosamente di M. Serpentino, il quale fu mio maestro...*» FERRARO, 1602, pp. 67–68.

471) «*cavallarizzo eccellentissimo del grande Alessandro Farnese.*» CORTE, 1562, p. 75r. We know from Ferraro that a famous horse trained by Alessandro Conestabile, Pignatelli's master, was presented to Alessandro Farnese. It is therefore conceivable that the "Great Cardinal" knew the Neapolitan horseman and his students. This could have created the contact, following which Pignatelli entered the service of the high prelate.

472) «*gentilhuomo napoletano, e veramente non men faceto, e cortese, che nel mestier del cavalcare molto raro.*» CORTE, 1562, p. 111v.

Giovan Battista Pignatelli took part in the great tournament fought in the courtyard of Belvedere in the Vatican, March 5, 1565.

phase of Pignatelli's activity in Rome. On the basis of what Corte says, it seems possible to consider it close to the writing and publication of his book, that is to say around 1560.

Another evidence of the presence of Pignatelli in Rome comes from the papers of the Archivio Storico Capitolino in Rome. Elizabetta Mori has in fact tracked down the name of the Neapolitan horseman in the barn's inventory of the Dukes of Bracciano, where he is cited among the people in the service of the Orsini family, from the 1540s to the 1570s[473]. According to Mori, Pignatelli was riding master of the Duke of Bracciano, Paolo Giordano Orsini, who possessed a sumptuous stable, overflowing with precious harnesses, with ornaments in gold, silver, silk, velvet and brocade, regularly surveyed in the inventory kept in the family archive.

The presence in Rome of a horseman named Giovan Battista Pignatelli—a circumstance hitherto ignored by historians of equitation—is also indicated on the occasion of the grand tournament fought in the courtyard of Belvedere in the Vatican under Pope Pius IV, to celebrate the wedding of Annibale Altemps and Ortensia Borromeo. Two chronicles[474] meticulously report the events of that memorable 5th of March 1565, in which twelve teams of knights faced each other after marching with great pomp in the beautiful theater built for the occasion. The tournament was an event of great importance. According to one of the reporters, Blado, not less than thirty thousand people attended the show, including the pick of the Roman aristocracy and twenty-two cardinals. The same Pope gave the start to the parade of riders, appearing from a window of the Borgia tower, while trumpets and drums resounded. So, the knights began to make their entrance on the field, in an order drawn by lot. The fourth team was led by Domenico Massimi[475]. Preceded by a timbal player, it included four seconds and six knights in splendid green armors with golden profiles, all accompanied by pages and footmen in gaudy and exotic costumes. Among the riders there was also a certain Giovanni Battista Pignatelli, who is probably the same sublime horseman, whose name will go down in history as one of the greatest masters of the Italian equitation of the Renaissance[476].

---

473) Mori, 2011, p. 38–39. Pignatelli is mentioned in *Inventario della stalla di Bracciano*, first half of the sixteenth century, Archivio Storico Capitolino, Archivio Orsini, I, b. 414, fasc. 2, inv.n. 3 7.

474) Blado, 1565 e Cirni, 1565. Both reprintend in Tosi, 1945, pp. 126–164.

475) Domenico Massimi (1531-1570) was marshal of the Roman people (1547). He was with the Colonna in the siege of Ostia and in the battle of Palliano, during the war of Paul IV against the Spaniards (1557, see Chapter VI, n. 350). With the ascent to the papacy of Pius IV he became master of field and cavalry general of the Papal State and later governor of Ancona (1565). In 1566 Pius IV appointed him Earl of Cicicliano. He also commanded a papal galley against the Turks. Wounded in a shipwreck near the island of Candia, died in Lecce in 1570.

476) Blado, 1565, in Tosi, 1945, pp. 137–138.

It must be said that in the report of the party held in the Apostolic Palace after the tournament, Pignatelli is not mentioned anymore. The prizes awarded by the masters of the field went to other riders. The captain, Giovan Battista Tosi[477] from Palombara, in Bernardino Savelli's[478] quadrille, won as first prize, a cross with four emeralds, four rubies and two diamonds, for being the best to break the first lance, and a pendant with a diamond, a ruby and six pearls, as second prize, for having broken all three lances better than others.

All these testimonies, so far neglected, that signal Giovan Battista Pignatelli in the service of some of the most prominent families of the Roman nobility, suggest that, at least at this stage of his maturity, the activity of the great Neapolitan horseman was mainly in the capital of Christianity rather than in Naples. This is also confirmed by what Luigi Contarino wrote, in 1569, in his dialogue *La nobiltà di Napoli* (The Nobility of Naples). After listing the many famous riders coming from the Reign, the author concludes: "I could tell you many others who are competent in this, as Giovan Battista Pignatello in Rome, Roggiero in Sicily, Sanseverino in Milan."[479] On the other hand, in the sixteenth century, in Rome there were many who could appreciate his great skill as a teacher and trainer. The Roman nobility lived in the cult of the arts of chivalry, so that visiting the eternal city Montaigne wrote in his diary: "there is nothing that the nobility of the place can do better than riding."[480]

From the authors of the time we know that Pignatelli practiced as a riding teacher in Naples mainly in his old age. We have a direct testimony from Giovanni Paolo D'Aquino[481], horseman of Neapolitan origin, who in his treatise *Disciplina del cavallo con l'uso del piliere* (Discipline of the horse with the use of the pillar, 1630) says he was a "very good friend" of Salomon de La Broue, when he was in Naples with Pignatelli, and that he then met also Pluvinel[482] in France. According to him, the two French gentlemen would have learned the technique of the use of the pillar from the Neapolitan master, and then refined it, and publicize it in their works.

---

477) Of ancient Milanese family, Captain Palombara was in connection with the Este, with the Pio di Savoia and the Medici, who had him as captain of the cavalry of Arezzo. He was then commanding officer of the cavalry of the Church's militia under Pope Paul IV, Pius IV, Gregory XII and Sixtus V. In 1557 he was appointed captain of a company of 250 soldiers.

478) He came from the family of the lords of Palombara, Dukes of Castel Gandolfo and of Ariccia and princes of Albano. He was appointed Marshal of the Holy Church and guardian of the conclave by Pope Gregory XIII (1575). Sixtus V made him Duke of Castel Gandolfo and Marquis of Rocca Priora (1580).

479) Contarino, 1569, p. 33.

480) Montaigne, 2010, p. 250.

481) See Chapter IX.

482) Cfr. D'AQUINO, 1636, p. 5.

Use of the pillar, in Antoine de Pluvinel, *L'instruction du Roy en l'exercice de monter à cheval* (1625)

Sir Gio. Battista Pignatello our Neapolitan Gentleman, one of the first men of his time in this exercise [of riding], when he came to an age when he could no longer ride, he used to give lessons at his home into an open place, where a tree was planted, which sometimes he used with some horses of bad will, in the same way in which a man stands on the ground in the middle of the *volte*, holding the rope of the cavesson in his hand; at the time Sir de La Broue and Sir de Pluvinel, French Gentlemen were his disciples, who observed very well the good effects caused by holding the horses in this subjection; they then returned to France, and having already become Masters of good quality, they ordered to plant in the ground a pole, round and tall as a man, and they used this Pillar without distinction with all horses...[483]

---

483) «*Il signor Gio: Battista Pignatello nostro Getilhuomo Napolitano, uno dei primi huomini del suo tempo in questo esercitio, quando fù in età, che non poteva più cavalcare, dava lettione in casa sua in un luoco discoverto, dove era piantato un'arbore, del quale si serviva alle volte con alcuni Cavalli di mala voluntà, dell'istesso modo quando un'huomo*

The argument that dates the teaching of Pignatelli in Naples around 1540[484] is therefore to be rejected. If the Neapolitan horseman began to teach in Naples when he was already so old that he could no longer ride, it had to be after his participation in the tournament of Belvedere (1565). Also because, while admitting that Pluvinel attended the school of the Italian master when he was very young (ten years old, as some argue[485], but more likely sixteen, as claimed by others[486]), having regard to his date of birth, he could not stay in Naples with Pignatelli before 1562, or better still probably around 1568–69 (if not even in 1571).

It should also be noticed that in his *La Gloria del Cavallo*, Pasquale Caracciolo merely cites Pignatelli in a list of the most eminent Neapolitan riders, of noble origin, of whom—as we saw in Chapter IV—the only two who deserve a special mention were Federico Grisone and Giovanni Berardino delle Castella[487]. This confirms two things. The first is that actually Pignatelli was of noble origin, and the second is that he was considered by his contemporaries definitely a great rider, but not yet the absolute founder as he would later become in the works of his pupils.

Pignatelli was also a skilled horse trainer. This is first of all testified by Pirro Antonio Ferraro, who also gives a precise temporal indication, which allows us to place the activity of the Neapolitan master in the second half of the sixteenth century. In the third book of his treatise—written in the form of a dialogue between the author and Don Diego de Cordova, "great horseman of His Majesty"—speaking of bits that allow "freedom to the tongue," Ferraro recalls a dispute held with Pignatelli, about a mouthpiece invented by the latter. Hearing the name of the Neapolitan master, Don Diego intervenes asking:

> D.D.
> Tell me please (since you named me Pignatello) isn't he the one whose name I heard so celebrated in the universe, by whom (as I heard) was trained the chestnut Torremaioré,

---

[sic] *stà in terra in mezzo alla volta, e tiene la corda del capezzone in mano; furono a quel tempo suoi discepoli il signor della Broue, e il Signor di Pluvinel Gentil'huomini Francesi, i quali osservorono molto bene i buoni effetti, che causavano il tenere i cavalli in questa suggettione, ritornorono in Francia, e fatti già Maestri di molta qualità, fecero piantare un palo in terra tondo, e alto quanto un'huomo [sic], e si servirono indifferentemente con tutti i Cavalli di questo Piliere..."»* D'AQUINO, 1636, p. 4.

484) See Christian, 1907; Mennessier de la Lance, 1915–21; Saurel, 1971; Monteilhet, 1979.

485) As instead stated by Antonelli, 1992, p. 180 e Hernando Sánchez, 1998, p. 280.

486) See Tucker, 2007.

487) See CARACCIOLO, 1566, p. 142.

on which you gave lesson to His Highness the Prince Ladislaus, brother of his Majesty the Emperor Rudolf, the first time that you came to this Royal Court in the year 1578, which Horse was certainly [fit for] a great Lord, suitable to every kind of exercise.[488]

Ferraro adds that it is wrong to cite just one of the many excellent horses trained by Pignatelli and remembers a black horse that belonged to Don Juan of Austria[489], injured in a bullfight, a bay sent as a gift to the king of Poland and another given to Philip II of Habsburg when he was prince of the kingdom, by the Viceroy Pietro di Toledo on behalf of the city of Naples. The list also includes a horse owned by Cardinal Carafa, nephew of Pope Paul IV, donated to the king of France, and another owned by the Cardinal Farnese, sent to his namesake Alexander Farnese, Duke of Parma[490]. In short, all famous horses destined to owners of great prestige, that only a great horseman could train. So much so that Ferraro concludes:

> it's useless to list all the horses he trained, because they are countless and also in part because owing to my age I don't know them all, but what I can say is: "his efforts give fame to the riding schools of the Principles"[491].

According to D'Aquino, Pignatelli kept on training horses even when he was very old and he could not ride anymore. So he directed his assistants, sitting on a chair in a corner of the arena.

> Sir Gio. Battista Pignatelli trained more Horses commanding from a chair than operating[492].

---

488) «*D.D. Ditemi di gratia (poiché mi nominate il Pignatello) non è egli pur quello, il cui nome s'intende tanto celebrare per l'universo, dal quale (per quant' io odo) fu dottrinato il sauro Torremaioré, sopra del quale davate lettione all'Altezza del Prencipe Ladislao, fratello della Maestà dell'Imperador Ridolfo, la prima volta che veniste a questa Real Corte l'anno 1578, il qual Cavallo, certo era di gran Signore, atto ad ogni sorte di maneggio.*» FERRARO, 1602, p. 260.

489) Don Juan de Austria, (1547–1578), the illegitimate son of Emperor Charles V, was a commander and Spanish diplomat. He commanded the fleet of the Holy League which defeated the Ottomans in the Battle of Lepanto in 1571.

490) Alessandro Farnese, third Duke of Parma and Piacenza, fourth Duke of Castro (1545–1592), was one of the greatest leaders of the sixteenth century. He was sent as a hostage to the court of Spain by his father Ottavio after the Treaty of Ghent (1556). He participated as a protagonist in the battle of Lepanto (1571) and was sent to Flanders, where he distinguished himself as a leader and as a fine politician.

491) «*le sue fatiche illustrano le gran Cavallerizze di Principi.*» FERRARO, 1602, p. 260.

492) «*il Sig... Gio: Battista Pignatelli fece più Cavalli commandando da sopra una seggia,*

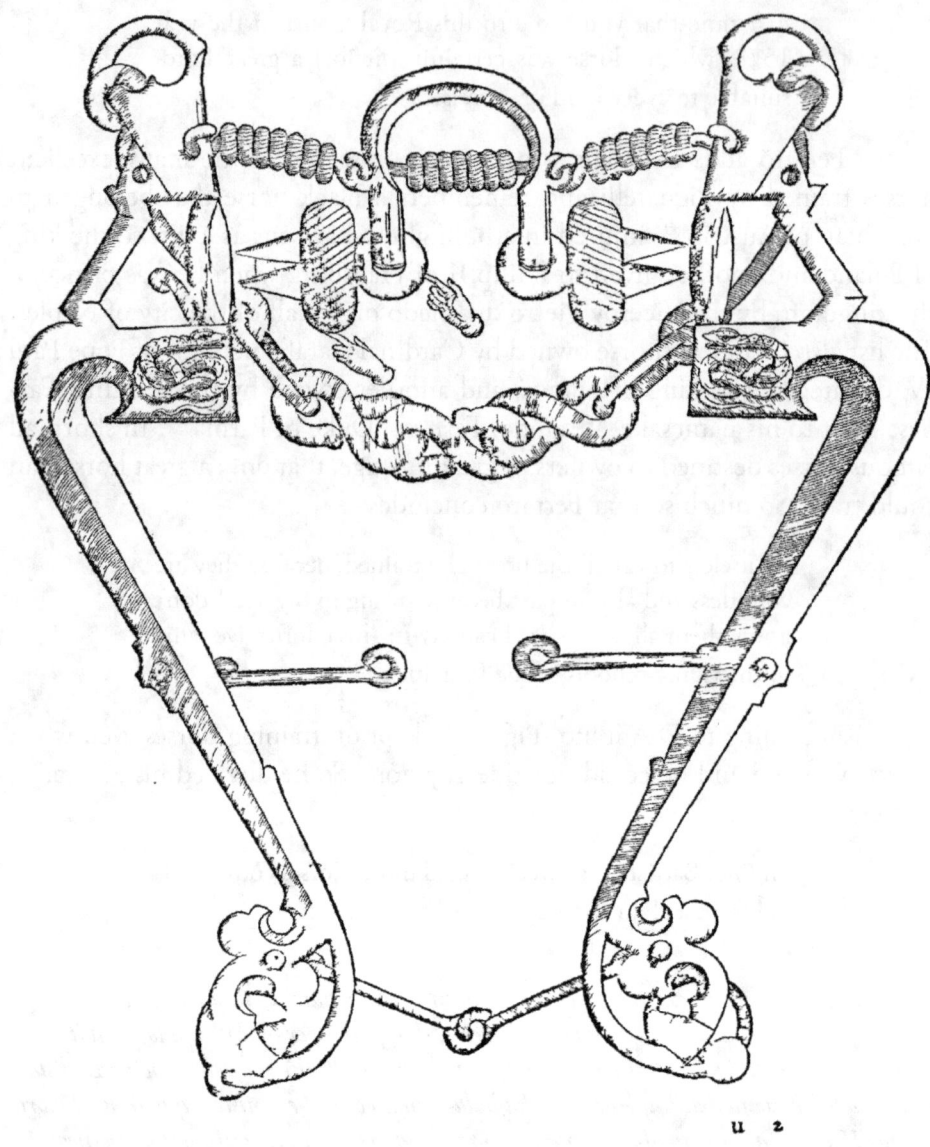

Pirro Antonio Ferraro, the Pignatelli bit.
The mouthpiece designed by the Neapolitan maestro gave greater freedom
the tongue of the horse.

---

che operando.» FERRARO, 1602, p. 59.

Pignatelli's legacy

There is a big debate between the historians of equitation about the legacy of Pignatelli's teaching, which they tried to reconstruct through the subsequent testimonies of his pupils. According to André Montheilet[493], the Neapolitan master represents a gap between the equitation of the Italian school of the Renaissance, that the author considers implicitly more crude and brutal, and the Baroque school, that developed mainly in France and tended toward an increasing stylization of the airs and to a gradual emancipation of the training of the horse from military purposes. What has been considered the main feature of Pignatelli's teaching is the use of a non-coercive method of training, an attitude that was particularly underlined by his students in France. According to Pluvinel, his master insisted in particular on the need to be stingy with blows and lavish with caresses.

This inclination to patience and kindness is highlighted also by Salomon de La Broue, who recalls how his teacher used mainly the bit that, at the time, was considered the lighter, the so-called simple cannon, drawing for this reason some blame, because he disdained the use of more complicated mouthpieces, on which there was much talk in the Treatises:

> Several envious or not very skillful often blamed that great and important character, Sir Giovan Battista Pignatelli, since he wasn't very dedicated to the diversity of the bridles and cavessons and they nearly pretend that one could think that he ignored their effects. On the contrary, what once made me admire his knowledge and that moved me the most to seek and to serve him, is the thought that, as he made the horses so obedient and so easy to manage and showing so beautiful airs in his school without however commonly using any other bit than an ordinary cannon and a common cavesson, his rules and his experience should have much more effect than the ways of those that apply so much to the artifice of an infinity of bridles and of some peculiar secrets mostly useless, to which however they resort when they lack the most beautiful and major means of the art.[494]

La Broue talks of simple cannon bit, but the Neapolitan master gets credit for the creation of a specific type of mouthpiece, called *"alla Pignatelli."* Peculiar to this bit was to let the tongue of the horse free through a port, called *"chiappone."* To tell the truth, this kind of bit was already widely in use during the Renaissance and it was already presented, although with some differences,

---

493) Monteilhet, 1979, p. 233.

494) LA BROUE, 1610, p. 18.

LIBRO SECONDO.

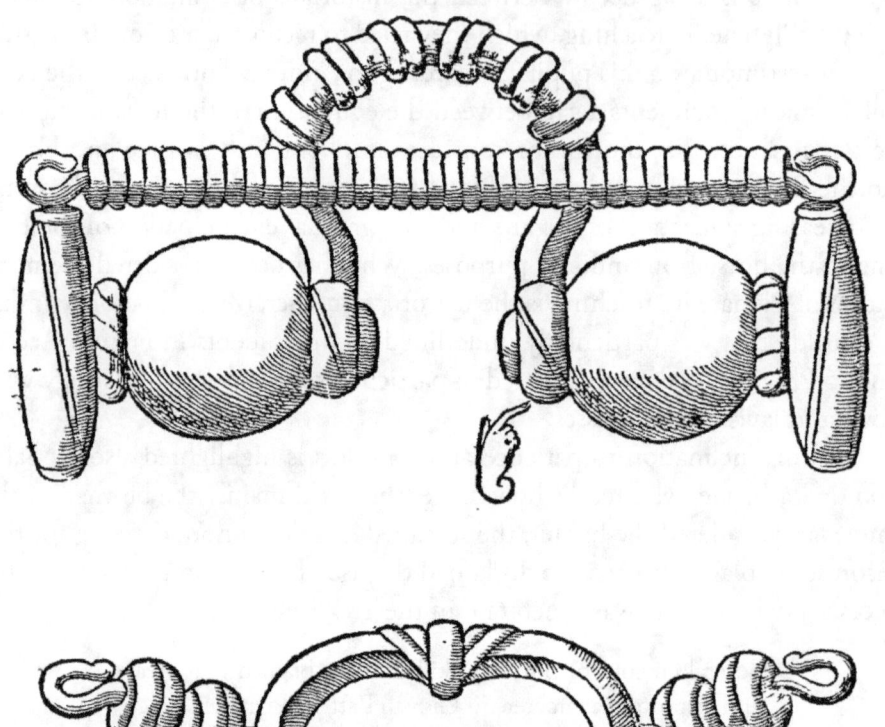

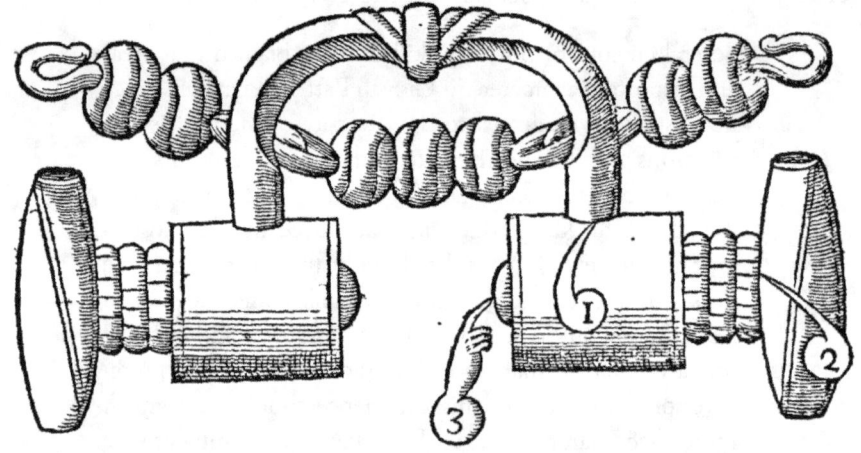

Pirro Antonio Ferraro, other kinds of Pignatelli's mouthpieces. The master had to change his bit to make the ties between the parties that made up the mouthpiece stronger.

in the treatises of Grisone, Fiaschi and others[495]. According to Pirro Antonio Ferraro, Pignatelli reworked this bit several times to remedy some weaknesses of the ties that held the parts together and to get a more effective action on the bars[496]. The author emphasizes how the function of the "*chiappone*" (namely the port) was precisely to ensure freedom to the tongue of the animal, with the result of obtaining a more gentle action, but without offending the palate.

> This figure of bridle, called *Pignatella*, was invented by S. Gio Battista Pignatello that so singularly practiced in that doctrine; the purpose of his invention was to give freedom to the tongue and that "*chiappone*" (the port) going back with the pulling of the bridle, as it is known, did not have the strength to offend the palate, to avoid that the horse could get subjugate or overbent[497].

This bit had considerable fortune and we find it represented in the treatise by William Cavendish, Duke of Newcastle *Methode et Invention nouvelle de dresser les chevaux* (1657, Method and new invention on how to train horses), with a slightly different form from the one that we find in Ferraro's book, but always with the "*chiappone*" to ensure freedom to the tongue of the horse.

Finally, Pluvinel attributes to Pignatelli the invention of some exercises (the "*volte* from quarter to quarter" and the "square *volte*") in which (particularly in the second) we can see the use of the work "on two tracks" already during the Renaissance, to improve the balance and the elasticity of the horse.

> [in the square *volte*] the horse should proceed by the side, at a walk, on a square instead of a circle, and he has to go along the four corners doing *courbettes* and, at the discretion of the rider, change what he has done at a walk, doing it in *courbettes* by the side: and I think this is the best lesson to adjust all the horses on the *voltes* and mainly those who are very impatient, who usually do like rabbits on the run, that go on one side and on the other.[498]

---

495) Therefore the adoption of a bit which allowed freedom to the tongue of the horse is not that "revolutionary" as stated by Mario Gennero in Gennero, 2001 and Gennero 2002. Similarly, has no historical foundation the claim of the same Gennero who attributes to Pignatelli the invention of the cavesson, whose use is widely documented by the authors of much earlier epochs, as Ruffo of Calabria. The ancient Greek cavalry already use a sort of cavesson, in association with the bit called *psalion* (see. Anderson, 1961, pp. 60 e ss.).

496) FERRARO, 1602, p. 156.

497) «*Questa figura di briglia, che Pignatella si dice, fu dal S. Gio Battista Pignatello ritrovata, che tanto singolarmente in quella dottrina si esercitò; il fine della sua invenzione fu, perché porgesse libertà alla lingua, e che il chiappone facendosi addietro al raccorre che si fa della briglia, come si sà, non avesse forza di offendere il palato, con la qual offesa, potrebbe il cavallo soggiogarsi o porsi più sotto.*» FERRARO, 1602, p. 154.

498) PLUVINEL, 1625, p. 144.

In fact, from what we have seen so far, it seems pretty obvious that these few prescriptions handed down from the texts of the time do not have any particular innovative feature compared to the dictates of the Italian school, expressed in the Renaissance equestrian treatises. Even the much-emphasized kindness of Pignatelli is perfectly in line with the teachings handed down by the authors of the sixteenth century. Even the ill-famed Grisone—who even devoted a part of his work to absurd tortures to be imposed on reluctant and rebel horses—recommended proceeding first with pleasantness and caresses. Exhortation unanimously shared by the other authors of the time, all of whom also prescribed the use of the ordinary cannon bit for the training and stressed that the use of other mouthpieces should be decided only in cases in which specific problems arose. This fact leads us to think that the evaluation of the equestrian figure of Pignatelli done by historians has been largely influenced by the excellent propaganda made by his students, rather than based on objective facts[499]. By saying this I do not want to reduce the fundamental importance of his teaching, but rather to point out that through his mediation is the full legacy of the Italian tradition, and not an innovative variation, which was transfused into the equestrian culture of the whole of Europe.

"L'arte veterale"

Giovan Battista Pignatelli didn't publish any book, but a manuscript tradition has given us a treatise on his behalf, entitled *L'arte veterale*[500]. It is a compendium of "*beautiful secrets*" on the treatment of the diseases of the horse, which are the expression of a still medieval knowledge, partly made of empirical observation and in part of real superstitions. Although in the explanation of the remedies are often repeated formulas like "and it is a thing experimented and true," or "and this has been proven time and again," it is really hard to believe in the efficacy of treatments that resorted to amulets, bloodletting and prayers. Moreover, the work has a disorganized structure and seams to be instead "a series of notes, of 'handouts' written for the students, perhaps, in the perspective of a future publication then never done."[501] We cannot exclude that the text was written by one of the disciples of the Neapolitan master on the basis of his teaching. The work, however, had a certain issue and we know at least nine manuscripts preserved in Italian, French and English libraries. In any case, the knowledge of Pignatelli in the veterinary field "does not deviate from

---

499) Besides the already mentioned Montheilet e Gennero, see also Franchet d'Espèrey, 2002.

500) *L'arte veterale* (Pignatelli's book about the care of the horse) was meritoriously reprinted by Mario Gennero and Patrizia Arquint. *See* Pignatelli, 2001.

501) Gennero, 2001, p. XXVII.

what was written or published before him. It doesn't give any contribution to the advancement of veterinary science."[502]

The work also disappoints the many who have fantasized about a text that could finally summarize the valuable lessons of Pignatelli[503]. Hypothesis that is not only imaginary, seeing that someone has actually spoken of a book about the equestrian art written by Pignatelli. This is the case of Manoel Carlos de Andrade, who—in his treatise *Luz da liberal e nobre arte da cavallaria* (1790), the real monument of the Portuguese equestrian art—states that even if horse riding was protected and cultivated by kings, princes and nobles, unlike other arts and sciences it was handed down by few written texts:

> Only Pignatelli, of Italian Nation, very famous Master of the Academy of Naples, was the first to embark on the job of writing about the Art of Chivalry *a la brida*[504], even if very briefly. He gives us a good method to have foals and to instruct the Beginners to the lesson: he was the inventor of the circle on two tracks, which was later perfected by La Broue, who also wrote on this subject.[505]

The text is quite ambiguous. The fact that de Andrade considers Pignatelli the first that wrote about the Equestrian Art can make us suspect that he confuses him with Grisone, even if the description of the work does not match with *The Rules of Riding*, which does not explain in detail any method for beginners, nor is it specifically committed to the care and breeding of foals. On the other hand, if a manuscript about riding by Pignatelli would have circulated before the publication of Grisone's work, it is unlikely that it could escape the notice of other Renaissance authors, who instead were very attentive to their predecessors and never failed to mention them in their treatises. Furthermore, even if we do not know the dates of birth of Grisone and Pignatelli, it is reasonable to think that—as explained above—Pignatelli belonged to a later generation than Grisone. The quote from de Andrade is then probably not trustworthy, at least with respect to the primacy of the text attributed to Pignatelli.

---

502) Gennero, 2001, p. XXX.

503) The dream of the publishing of a treatise on horsemanship by Pignatelli inspired a nice novel by Philippe Deblaise. See Deblaise, 2009.

504) During the Renaissance, two main riding techniques were distinguished: the so-called riding *a la brida* and the *gineta*. In the first, *a la brida*, the rider rode with very long stirrups and with his legs almost straight, while in the second, *gineta*, which resulted from an Arabian influence and was especially in use in Spain, the stirrups were adjusted shorter and the rider rode with bent knees. The riding *a la brida* was suited to European heavy cavalry chargers, while the *gineta* allowed for greater agility and was more suited to the incursions of the light cavalry and to bullfighting.

505) DE ANDRADE, 1790, p. 3.

But there is another significant track. At the turn of the eighteenth and nineteenth century, Jean Baptiste Huzard[506], humble son of a blacksmith who later became one of the most important veterinarians of France, put together an extraordinary private library about science, agronomy and especially horse riding. He had over 40,000 volumes. The section dedicated to equestrian was the largest and the best-stocked and included almost everything ever published on the subject up until 1837. It was so complete that its catalog is still used today as a bibliographic source. In this valuable book list, at number 4380, is listed a manuscript dated around the end of the seventeenth century, of 84 cards, containing many colorful designs, with their captions, entitled: *Libro d'Imbocature de' Cavalli, del sig.re J.-B. Ta Pignatello, dove si può imbrigliare ogni sorte de Cavalli e conoser le boche di quelli, et ancora ci è agiutato le libre dei sig.ri Silvio, Lelio, Michaello, Baltazardo, Don Ottavio Monacho, et del sig. re Alexandro Massari, de loro inventione, et ancora del Scanio Napolitano* (Book of Horses Mouthpieces by Sir J.B. Pignatello, where you can harness all sorts of horses and know the mouths of those, and also there is added the books by Sir Silvio, Lelio, Michaello, Baltazardo, Don Ottavio Monacho, and of Sir Alexandro Massari, of their invention, and more by Scanio Napolitano). Sadly, the collection of books patiently put together by Huzard was dismembered and sold in three auctions in 1843. Part of the fund, including the manuscript we are talking about, was bought by Baron Curnieu and was then sold in a new auction, held in Paris, February 25, 1986. The manuscript attributed to Pignatelli is now preserved in a private collection in Portugal. Mario Gennero rightly complains that "no Italian institution attempted to acquire it."[507] Judging by the title and by the brief description given in the catalog it seems unlikely that it contains a real treatise, but that it consists rather in a repertoire of mouthpieces. The title also refers to the addition of other works, but it seems impossible that all can be contained in the few dozen of pages of the manuscript. Among the names of the authors mentioned you can recognize that of Alessandro Massari Malatesta, author of the *Compendio dell'eroica arte di cavalleria* (Compendium of the heroic art of chivalry, 1599)[508].

---

506) He was born in 1755 and he was son and grandson of blacksmiths. He studied at the Ecole d'Alfort and soon became a well-known veterinarian, while maintaining his activity in the forge of his father. Starting from 1785 he became a consultant of various courts of justice, particularly in the field of redhibitory defects of horses and of other domestic animals. He was a passionate bibliophile. Together with his wife, he founded a library and publishing house which then gave birth to the famous Bouchard-Huzard library, specialized in publications about veterinary, nature and agriculture. He possessed a rich library, dedicated to veterinary sciences, agriculture and horse riding. He died the 1st December 1838.

507) Gennero, 2002, p. 155.

508) See Chapter VII.

The mystery of the Academy of Naples

The passage dedicated to Pignatelli by de Andrade continues celebrating the prestige of the Neapolitan master and recalling the importance of his teaching and the influence he had on his two most famous French pupils:

> La Broue composed a folio volume, which contains the main maxims of Giovan Battista Pignatelli, his Master, and of the Academy of Naples. This school reached such a high reputation in his time, so that it was deemed to be the best in the world; so much so that all the nobility of Italy, Naples, France and Germany claimed to have taken lessons from such an excellent Master. Pluvinel went from France to Naples, and was himself a disciple of Pignatelli, and accompanied Henry IV the Great, king of Navarre, when in 1589 was called to succeed to the Crown of France, and was his Horseman, and Master of Louis XIII, the Just[509].

De Andrade makes a reference that we had not encountered in the texts from a previous era, but that the subsequent historiography on horse riding acquired and is now in common usage to such an extent as to be considered an indisputable fact. Speaking of Pignatelli, the Portuguese author describes him, in fact, as a master of the Academy of Naples. Actually, he is not the first to attribute him this title. The text of the Portuguese author resumes, in fact, almost to the letter what François Robichon de La Guérinière wrote about Pignatelli in his fundamental *Ecole de cavalerie* (1733) [*School of Horsemanship*, Xenophon Press, 1992]:

> Sir de La Broue lived under the reign of Henry IV. He composed a work in folio that contains the principles of Giovan Battista Pignatelli his Master, who held in Naples Academy: This school had such a great reputation that was considered as the first in the world. All the nobility of France and Germany, who wanted to perfect in Chivalry, was obliged to go to take lessons from this illustrious Master.[510]

It is probably the great authority of the work by La Guérinière to affirm the reliability of this version and to pass it down to the following historiography. However, it is suspicious that none of the authors of the Italian Renaissance—although they certainly should have a more accurate and direct knowledge of the facts than the the great French horseman about a century and a half later—ever expressly mention an Academy of Naples in which horse riding was taught; neither qualifies Pignatelli (or Grisone, seeing that he as well was honored by many

---

509) DE ANDRADE, 1790, p. 4.
510) LA GUÉRINIÈRE, 1733, pp. 60–61.

historians of this title) as a master in this academy. Even more suspicious is that neither La Broue nor Pluvinel, who were personally students of Pignatelli, claim to have attended an academy, but they speak of the Neapolitan horseman just as their master. Furthermore, the existence of this academy is not demonstrated by any known document of the time. In fact, if you consult the impressive history of the academies of Italy by Michele Mayländer[511]—the widest and documented repertoire on the matter, which lists 2050 Italian academies, from the fifteenth to the nineteenth century—it turns out that none of the 177 Neapolitan academies mentioned may be in any way traced back to the figures of Pignatelli, or Grisone, nor to the teaching of riding in Naples in the sixteenth century.

The solution to this little mystery—which is likely to provoke a debate between the experts—is to be found by following cultural cues. First of all, by clarifying what the word "academy" really means. This term, in fact, designates a specific type of cultural institution, which had its heyday during the Renaissance, especially in Italy. The *Vocabolario della Crusca*[512] (1612) defines it an "assembly of studious men," but as Amedeo Quondam specifies better "the academy is born as an institutional form only when [...] it gives to itself a set of rules (written or spoken: in some way codified and implicitly/explicitly accepted)."[513] The academy, in short, is not simply a group of experts in a specific field of knowledge, who come together to discuss and explore their interests and perhaps to disclose them. The identity of the academy is structured around four founding moments: the choice of a name for the academy, the names of its members, the invention of a device (i.e. a coat of arms) and the development of a Statute. Usually, "the first act of the academy, when it wants to adopt a structured organization (spoken or written, that is), or at least notify—to others—its existence is to develop a mark of identity, a brand for immediate recognition of its individuality as an academy."[514] This mark of identity is first of all the proper name that distinguishes it and in the past was often strange or curious. Closely linked to the identification through the name is then the definition of the device, namely the emblem that synthesizes in visual form the identity of the group. Usually then, to the members of the academy are given pseudonyms in turn, that identify them as members of the group, and which are usually related to the name of the academy, or at least referred to the same semantic field.

The academies are born as places where learned people in a given field of knowledge come together and debate on the subject of their interest. Therefore, they are initially mainly places of cultivated conversation and only in the seven-

---

511) Maylander, 1926–30.

512) The *Vocabolario degli Accademici della Crusca* was printed in Venice in 1612. In a politically and linguistically divided Italy, it represented, for centuries, the most precious collection of the common language and an indispensable tool for all those who wanted to write in good Italian.

513) Quondam, 1982, p. 827.

514) Quondam, 1982, p. 828.

teenth century begin to turn into institutions of superior education. In the first phase, in statistical terms, private academies prevail over public ones. The relationship between academic circles and political power varies significantly, ranging from approval and support (including from the financial point of view) to an open hostility.[515] The ways of financing academies vary greatly: in some cases the resources come from the munificence of a prince, or of other noble patron, but in others they come from the collection of membership fees. With regard to the fields of interest, in Italy the literary academies prevail (in the sixteenth century they represented 72.6% of those surveyed by Maylander), followed by those dedicated to the knightly exercises of the nobility, the ones dedicated to theater, the scientific, the musical, the colleges, the juridical-legal and finally the ecclesiastical academies[516].

As for the academies devoted to the knightly exercises it is possible to distinguish four basic types:

1) the special academies inside the *seminaria nobilium*, namely the colleges reserved for aristocrats, mainly managed by the Society of Jesus;

2) the academies of knights, reserved exclusively for nobles, which are dedicated to the humanities and to the arms at the same time;

3) those academies that, excluding from their horizons the humanities are autonomously reserved to the knightly exercises, or rather to the art of chivalry par excellence, that is to say: to horseback riding;

4) the academies which put the study of mathematics, applied to the art of War, beside equitation, which remained the central discipline[517].

During the Renaissance the academies flourished in Italy, where they had a vivacious development and dissemination. As noted by Amedeo Quondam that of the academies is in fact "mainly an Italian story [...]. On an entirely European scale: one of the sharper and more scattered macrosigns of the Italian primacy between the fifteenth and sixteenth centuries."[518] A cultural institution so typically Italian that, under the entry *Académie* of the *Encyclopédie*, d'Alembert wrote:

> Italy alone has more academies than the rest of the world. There isn't a town of a certain importance in which there aren't enough scholars to form an academy and that, as a matter of fact, do not form one[519].

---

515) See Quondam, 1982, p. 861.

516) See Quondam, 1982, pp. 871–874.

517) I draw on the analysis from Quondam, 1982, the typology is proposed in Del Negro, 2008, p. 35.

518) Quondam, 1982, pp. 824–825.

519) D'Alembert 1715–65, p. 56.

Italy, then, is the country of the academies and is perceived as such by the Europeans of the eighteenth century. Here, then, is a first significant clue to our investigation.

The knightly academies in Italy

According to Maylander's repertoire, which refers to the only evidence given by the late sixteenth century historian Giovanni Bonifacio,[520] the first knightly academy was founded in 1518 in Treviso,[521] where "after bringing several Professors of letters, and teachers of singing, playing, fencing, dance and riding, the members attended to noble studies and knightly exercises."[522] If this first attribution may appear a testimony still too fragmentary, the primacy still has to be assigned to a Venetian academy, the one of the *Costanti* of Vicenza, of which we have more extensive and reliable data. It is an academy of arms and letters, active between 1556 and 1568. Founded by forty noble members, it was ruled by a prince, assisted by two counselors, two censors, a contradictor and other notables. There were practiced "virtuous exercises" as much in the field of arms as in that of letters and it was distinguished especially for the organization of various jousts and tournaments in the city.

Ten years later, in 1565, the governor of Verona, Astorre Baglioni,[523] wanted the establishment of a military academy, in order to give a place for the young nobles of the city where they could practice the use of arms and horseback riding, to keep them from idleness and to make them ever-ready to serve the republic. It was composed of sixty nobles who—after having established a statute and a government, formed by four of the notables of the city—procured themselves weapons and horses and trained all in the same place. We don't know its duration, but it was probably already closed in 1570. They tried to obtain recognition by the Venetian government but it was not granted, as happened later to the Academy of Rovigo, founded in 1594 which lasted less than a year because of disagreements among the knights and their own protector, the mayor and captain Benedetto Tagliapietra.

Despite the difficulties encountered by the knights of Verona and Rovigo in getting support from the public power, the Venetian rectors of the mainland had a fairly active role in the promotion of knightly academies between the mid-sixteenth and the early seventeenth centuries. The knightly

---

520) Born in Rovigo the 6th of September 1547 and died on the 23rd of June1635.

521) About the knightly academy see Antonelli, 1997, Antonelli 1992 and Del Negro, 2008.

522) Maylander, 1926–1930, Vol. I, p. 527.

523) 1526–1571. Military man and leader, between 1556 and 1558 he was in the service of Venice. He participated in the supervision of the works of fortification of the Venetian states and was governor of Verona.

academies played an important political and social role, both in the military training of the army, and in contributing to the process of transformating the old feudal nobility into modern court aristocracy. The academies provided a place to cultivate the exercise of arms – which were considered central to the noble ideology founded on the concepts of honor and social standing. It should also be considered that the evolution of the art of war progressively subtracted military function from the nobles. At that time, the growing strategic importance of firearms and infantry caused to the nobility, the frustration that comes from being nominally knights but with little chance, if not in carousels and tournaments, to prove themselves to the world. So, the academy and especially the carousels and the tournaments were necessary for this reason: not to lose the identity of the nobles and warriors. Training with weapons and in the equestrian practices served the nobles precisely to recognize themselves as such[524].

Of particular importance, from this point of view, were the academies of Padua. There, four knightly academies follow one another in a period of about forty years: that of the *Gimnosofisti*, founded in 1564 by Sperone Speroni[525]; that of the *Oplosofisti*, that opened in 1581 and which included among its founders Giovanni VII Lazara[526]; that of the *Ascritti*, founded in 1600; and finally the *Accademia Delia*, founded in 1602 which survived until 1801. In the Venetian city the exercises of chivalry enjoyed special prestige and the riding schools were attended not only by local nobles, but also by many foreign gentlemen who studied at the university, one of the oldest and most prestigious in Europe. An international prestige well-evidenced by the fact that when he came to Padua, during his trip to Italy in November 1580, Michel de Montaigne spent a whole day visiting the schools of fencing (another discipline of chivalry practiced at a high level in the city), of dance and of horseback riding[527].

In the south of Italy, Don Garcia de Toledo[528], Viceroy of Sicily and son of the viceroy of Naples Pedro de Toledo[529], gave a decisive impulse to the

---

524) Antonelli, 1997, p. 194.

525) Philosopher and writer (1500–1588), he was very young professor of logic in the University of Padua. Friend of Torquato Tasso and sharp debater, was the author of the tragedy *Canace* (1546), which caused a sharp controversy with Giovan Battista Giraldi Cintio (1504–1573).

526) He was born in 1560 and died in 1639. He was one of the ablest champions of the tournaments of his time.

527) See Montaigne, 2010, pp. 200–201.

528) García Álvarez de Toledo y Osorio (1514–1577), was the fourth Marquis of Villafranca, the first Duke of Ferrandina and first prince of Montalbano in the kingdom of Naples, as well as viceroy of Sicily and Catalonia.

529) Don Pedro Álvarez de Toledo y Zúñiga (1484–1553) was Marquis of Villafranca

establishment of an academy in Palermo, made up of a hundred knights to be used in the militia in case of war and to engage in times of peace in jousts and tournaments, on the occasions of public celebrations[530]. As the members of the *Academia Delia* of Padua, also the academics of Palermo practiced in the study of mathematics, as well as geography and nautical science. During the meetings discussions were also held on political issues and about the duties of a true nobleman. The academy was called *Congregatione della felice Città di Palermo* (Congregation of the happy city of Palermo) and was founded in 1556. It lasted until the end of the sixteenth century. Its statute regulated minutely the tasks, the meetings, the ceremonies and the devotions, and fixed the requirements for the aspirants, as well as how to behave in the presence of the Viceroy. Academics practiced daily for two hours in the riding arena, divided into two classes. The session of the most experienced was open to the public, while the extraneous could not be present to that of the novice riders[531].

Ferrara also had his own academy of letters, arms and music. It is believed it was active between 1570 and 1580. According to Maylander[532], its characteristics were similar to that of other academies of nobles as that of the *Scelti* in Parma, of the *Filotomi* in Verona and the *Delia* of Padua, but with a stronger focus on music. Cesare Fiaschi was not one of its members, even if he is frequently considered—as is the case with Grisone and Pignatelli—as the founder of an academy of exercises of chivalry. In fact, there is no trace of such an academy among the 52 surveyed in Ferrara by Maylander. In the five volumes of his work he reports, throughout Italy, 19 academies of noble knights in the sixteenth century, 13 in the seventeenth and only 2 in the eighteenth[533].

---

and, from 1532 to 1553, Viceroy of Naples on behalf of Charles V.

530) See Antonelli, 1997, pp. 192–193 and Hernando Sánchez, 1998, p. 281. Maylander, 1926–30, vol. I, p. 523.

531) See Antonelli, 1997, pp. 192–193 and Hernando Sánchez, 1998, p. 281.

532) See Maylander, 1926–30, vol. III, p. 417–418.

533) See Quondam, 1982, p. 872.

Academy or riding school?

After six years in Naples, with his master Pignatelli, Antoine de Pluvinel was brought back to France by M. de Sourdis, first horseman of the future King Henry III[534]. We find evidence of this episode in a work of René de Menou de Charnizay[535]—a personal friend of Pluvinel—that deserves to be mentioned because it confirms that the sources historically close to Pluvinel's stay in Naples do not speak of any Neapolitan academy, but simply of the School of Pignatelli:

> On his return from Poland, the King Henry III, finding his great Stable poorly served of good horses, sent to Italy his first horseman, Sir de Sourdis, to bring him back the more excellent and better trained; which he did [...]. Sir de Sourdis brought with him Sir de Pluvinel, Gentleman of the Dauphiné, which until then had been at the School of Sir Giovan Battista Pignatelli[536].

Back home, Pluvinel came in turn into the service of Henry of France, and after the latter's death in 1589, he entered the service of his successor Henry IV[537], who gave him many prestigious positions, appointing him as the king's horseman, guardian of his own illegitimate son César de Vendôme and lieutenant governor of the Dauphin, the future Louis XIII[538]. One of the most important aspects of this job was just educating the heir to the throne in the equestrian art[539]. In 1594, Pluvinel founded in Paris, near what is now the

---

534) Henry III of Valois (1551–1589) was king of Poland from the 1st of May 1573 to the 18th of June 1574 under the name of Henry V of Poland, and then king of France from 1574 to 1589.

535) Born in 1570 and died in 1651. He edited the first edition (actually, much criticized by the students of the French master) of Pluvinel's treatise, entitling it *Maneige royal* (Paris, Guillaume le Noir et Melchior Tavernier, 1623).

536) MENOU DE CHARNIZAY, 1650, Preface.

537) Henry IV of Bourbon (1553–1610) was son of Anthony of Bourbon and of Queen Jeanne III of Navarre. In 1572 he inherited the crown of Navarre by his mother, becoming Henry III [he was Henry III of Navarre, then he became Henry IV of France] of Navarre. In 1589 he ascended the throne of France. He was the first French monarch of the Bourbon branch of the Capetian dynasty.

538) Louis XIII of Bourbon, called the Just (1601–1643), was King of France and Navarre from 1610. Eldest son of Henry IV and Marie de Medici, he became king when he was nine years old after his father's murder. Given his young age, the regency was exercised by the mother, until 1617 when, with a coup, the king regained the throne, depriving her of the power and forcing her into exile in the castle of Blois.

539) About Pluvinel's biography, see Tucker, 2007, pp. 162–164.

Place des Pyramides, one of the first riding academies of France[540], inspired by the model of similar Italian academies of nobles.

Finally, here is our second clue. One of the most famous students of Pignatelli returned to his homeland and founded an academy similar to the Italian ones. It is not difficult to conclude that, a century and a half later, La Guérinière imagined that in doing this, Pluvinel must have been directly inspired by the school of his Neapolitan master. Especially considering the fact that Pignatelli lived in what the French considered "the country of the academies." Hence was likely born the legend of the mysterious "Academy of Naples," mentioned in all the books about the history of equitation from the eighteenth century onwards, even if no one has ever proven its existence on the basis of documents of the time. Until proven otherwise, the solution of our mystery is so, probably, that Pignatelli, as well as Grisone before him, taught in a private school (that is to say in what at the time were called "*cavallerizze*," i.e., riding schools) as there were many at the time in Italy. Then, the Academy of Naples, (as well as the one that Cesare Fiaschi would have founded in Ferrara) seems more likely an historical mistake than a demonstrable reality.

---

540) For most historians of equitation, Pluvinel's Academy was the first ever in France. Corinne Doucet, who has dedicated a large and documented study on this subject, believes instead that similar institutions preceded it. Surely, in cities such as Caen and Rouen, there were already riding schools, that were invariably entrusted to Italian riding masters. See Doucet, 2007, pp. 40–41.

IX
Cantering through four centuries of history

From the early decades of the seventeenth century Italy quickly looses the hegemony that it hitherto had in the equestrian field. Soon, authors of other countries make their way on the road traced by Italian riders and writers. Many of the new foreign authors were, nevertheless, trained in Italy. The great monarchies, especially the French one[541], held in particular esteem the prestige that came from the knightly arts and encouraged the publication of books dedicated to horseback riding and the opening of schools where the pick of the aristocracy were cultured, not only in the exercise of riding, but also in all those disciplines which completed the education of the modern gentleman. As early as the sixteenth century, Spaniards such as Pedro de Aguilar[542], Englishmen such as Gervase Markham,[543] and Germans such as Georg Engelhard von Löhneysen[544], wrote treatises on horsemanship. But mainly the French stood out. Their primacy is established in continuity and then, in opposition to that of the Italian masters.

We have already seen that the author of the first French treatise on horsemanship, Salomon de La Broue, was a pupil of Giovanni Battista Pignatelli, as was Antoine de Pluvinel. The opening in Paris of the academy directed by the latter marks a critical step. From that moment on, the young transalpine aristocrats no longer had to make the obligatory trip to Italy to learn the practice of chivalry. "Now—exults, already in 1595, Alexandre de Pontaymery[545]—we can finally forget that path, and take the road to the academy of Sir de Pluvinel."[546] The birth of schools like that of Pluvinel, and those in Rouen and Toulouse, raised the alarm of the Venetian ambassador, Pietro Duodo,[547] who in his report from France to the Senate of Venice, in 1598, expresses his concern that the new

---

541) See Roche, 2011.

542) DE AGUILAR, 1572.

543) MARKHAM, 1593 e 1607.

544) ANONIMO, 1588 e LÖHNEYSEN, 1609.

545) Poet and essayist (?–1618). He was a Calvinist gentleman of the Low Dauphiné, lord of Focheran. In his early youth he stayed in Italy for instruction in the use of weapons and riding, returning from this experience with a fierce dislike for Italians.

546) Pontaymery, 1595, pp 2r, 3r. Treva J. Tucker collects many citations of this kind from authors writing between the beginning and the middle of the seventeenth century. See Tucker, 2007, p. 119.

547) Duodo, 1598, p. 103.

transalpine institutions could dissuade the young French aristocrats from coming to Italy and that the city of Padua, famous for its knightly academies and its university, may be damaged for this reason[548].

Although La Broue and Pluvinel are placed in a line of continuity with the Italian tradition, and in their works they bestow a tribute to the expertise of their master, handing down to posterity his fame, other authors began instead a systematic denigration of the Italian horsemen. This, combined with the changing of the historical and political conditions of the Italian peninsula, contributed to diminish the prestige of Italian horsemanship. This is the case, for example, with Pierre de La Noue, who in his *La cavalerie françoise et italienne* (The French and Italian cavalry, 1620) proposes a kind of summary "of what the French and Italian knights practice today for the perfection of the horse and the fulfillment of their praises."[549] Today, we can consider it a type of comparative analysis in which the author does not spare barbs to his Italian colleagues, arousing a controversy destined to last over the years. In fact, seventy years later, the words of de La Noue still burned the Italian pride, if Nicola Santapalina—who was riding master of the Grand Duke of Tuscany, Cosimo III de Medici[550]—wrote in the work that was published in 1696 by his son Nicola:

> "in the same [work] he [De la Noue] speaks badly of the Italian Horsemen, saying, among other things, that in the sixteenth century between the horsemen and riders who were in Italy at the time, there were not three who knew how to write their name, so that he concludes that from such rude people one can expect little good"[551].

That, from the French, was a curious and openly disparaging accusation, given that Italy had been, for at least a century, a real center of equestrian culture radiating across Europe. The Italian riders had given the first and de-

---

548) Born in Venice in 1554, he moved to Padua to improve his education. Author of scholarly works, he devoted himself to politics and participated in various diplomatic missions of the Republic of Venice. In 1594 he was appointed ambassador to France, from where he returned to his homeland in 1597. Subsequently he held the same position at the imperial court of Rudolf II and at the English court of James I. On February 4, 1607, he was elected captain of Padua, where he remained until 1609. He then returned to Venice, where he died the following year.

549) LA NOUE, 1620, dedication *Aux cavaliers*, p. 2.

550) Son of Grand Duke Ferdinando II de 'Medici and Vittoria della Rovere, he was Grand Duke of Tuscany from 1670 to 1723.

551) «*Costui [De la Noue] nella medesima [opera] sparla malamente de Cavallerizzi Italiani, dicendo trà l'altre cose, che in cinquecento trà Cavallerizzi, e Cavalcatori, che dovevano essere in Italia al suo tempo, non ve ne erano tre, che sapessero scrivere il suo nome, onde da gente così rozza inferisce potersi sperare poco di buono.*» SANTAPAULINA, 1696, p. 13.

cisive impulse to the achievement of the equestrian treatise as a literary genre. Santapaulina gives a sharp reply to De la Noue's insinuation:

"But, even if it does not deserve that we take too much trouble of what is said by an Author of that sort, I can guarantee that at the time that he wrote his work, in the city of Naples alone, there were more than forty Titled, Knights and Gentlemen, that made the occupation, for their liking, or to instruct others, and that each one of them had more than one assistant and an horse-dealer, who could teach this Author [De la Noue], not only how to ride, but also about good manners, and while we're on the subject, I don't want to forget to say that for many and many years up to the present, nearly all the Princes of Europe, for the service of their person, or to teach their children, returned to Italian Horsemen, or Italian Scholars, [this being] a clear sign that even if we do not have the fortune to satisfy Pietro della Noüe [De la Noue], we have been chosen by the first monarchs and princes of Europe over and above their own subjects [as preferred master riding teachers]."[552]

The main argument used by detractors of Italian horsemanship was, however, the supposed brutality of the training methods practiced in Italy. An accusation that—as we have already seen—weighed especially on Grisone's book (in which, to be fair, has a certain foundation; this criticism was then generalized to all Italian riders. This was the predominant and lasting prejudice that horsemen of other European countries used to prevail over their competing their Italian colleagues. It should not be forgotten that skill in the disciplines of chivalry brought horsemen lucrative, prestigious positions in the major European courts. That this criticism was instead used as a kind of "pretext" is clear when we consider the insistence by all of the Italian authors on the importance of "pleasantness" and "rewarding" in the training of the horse. Indeed, foreign authors were certainly not immune from recommending methods that today look very violent. One outstanding example, to correct a horse that has a tendency to lie down during the fording a stream, de La Noue suggests breaking a flask filled with water on his head...[553]

---

552) «*Ma, se bene il detto d'un Auttore di tal farina non merita, che ce ne pigliamo troppa briga, posso però assicurare che nel tempo, che scriveva costui la sua opera, nella sola città di Napoli vi erano più di quaranta tra Titolati, Cavalieri e Gentiluomini, che facevano il mestiere, chi per suo gusto, chi per istruire altri, ciascheduno de quali haveva più d'un Ajutante, e d'un Cozzone, che potevano insegnare à quest'auttore, non solo di cavalcare, mà di buona creanza altresì, e già che siamo a questo proposito, non voglio lasciar dire, che da molti, e molti anni à questa parte quasi tutt'i Prenicipi dell'Europa per servizio della loro persona, o per ammaestrare i figlioli s'hanno per lo più servito di Cavallerizzi Italiani, ò di Scolari Italiani, segno evidente, che, se non abbiamo fortuna di soddisfare à Pietro della Noüe, l'abbiamo havuta nell'esser stati anteposti fino a propri sudditi dalli primi Monarchi e principi dell'Europa.*» SANTAPAULINA, 1696, p. 13.

553) "I find that there is no better remedy to correct the horse that has a natural inclination [to lie down in the water] than breaking a glass bottle, covered with a wicker

In any case, once exhausted, the revolutionary thrust of the Renaissance of the Italian culture lost its shine in the field of equestrian, but this does not prevent the occurrence of significant experiences and the publication, for at least another three centuries, of many books of considerable historical and technical interest. A history rich and complex that we can only briefly summarize here, citing only some of the most significant examples and referring back, for a more complete picture of the Italian equestrian literature, to the bibliography of the treatises about horsemanship, that you will find at the end of this book.

The Delia academy in Padua

Among the most significant equestrian experiences of the seventeenth century surely stands out the case of the Delia Academy of Padua, a true paradigmatic institution of the Italian model of riding school. There, the disciplines of chivalry were associated with the study of mathematics and whose activities, despite ups and downs, continued for about two centuries. Pietro Duodo—who we have already mentioned and who was ambassador of the Republic of Venice in France and who later became captain of Padua—gave the decisive impulse to its founding, in 1608. He encouraged the initiative of twenty nobles from Padua, who wanted to set up an academy on the model of that of the *Ascritti*[554], and he probably did it to counteract the feared effects of the opening in Paris of Pluvinel's Academy. In the deed of the academy, it was provided to take a horseman and a fencing-master, whereas in a subsequent deliberation, it was decided also to recruit a mathematician. The aim was not only to train in the exercises of chivalry, but also in the disciplines of military theory. In addition to the essential elements of Euclidean geometry, the program presented by the first mathematician of the academy, Ingolfo Conti, included also geography, mechanics, strategy and military instruments, the study of the fortifications, the use of the compass, up to a "treatise on the virtues of the knight and of the captain."[555] In addition to providing a place of military training for the nobility of Padua, in the service of the city and of the Republic, the Academy also had a political purpose, bringing together the turbulent Venetian aristocracy in a partnership that favored internal harmony. It also ensured recognition of the knightly virtues of the nobility of Padua by foreign knights, both with the organization of jousts and other shows,

---

or straw hurdle and filled with water, between his ears when he shows the intention to lie down ..." LA NOUE, 1620, p. 82.

554) See Chapter VIII.

555) See Del Negro, 2008, p. 48. About the Delia Academy, see also Antonelli, 1997; Mazzarolli Ancillotto, 1931 and Orefice, 1966.

and by allowing the horsemen to impart "private" lessons in the afternoon. The students of these "extra" lessons were mostly noble from the Venetian hinterland, but also Germans and Italians coming from other regions.

At the beginning, the Academy was supposed to last five years, but thanks to the contribution of Duodo, who provided the fuunding, it continued. To house the school a permanent building was then built. In 1609, to finance its activity, the Venetian Senate granted to the academy the earnings of a penny for every pound concerning fines imposed by the rulers of the city of Padua. This form of "public taxation" was added to the annual fees that the sixty some members had to pay, thus ensuring the Academy considerable financial backing. At least in the early years, the salary of the Academy's horseman (which was higher than that of the mathematician) equaled that of one of the most important professors at the University of Padua. The Academy was run by a "bank" (composed by a prince, four councilors, a mayor and a co-director), which was renewed every four months and to which belonged, among other things, the processing of the membership applications, in which the aspirants had to prove to be gentlemen of Padua. Starting in 1658, a rule was passed that required the aspirants to posses adequate fortunes, to have attained the age of twenty years, to be legitimate children (and in turn, their fathers and grandparents had to be legitimate children of thier parents) and nobles of high rank from at least three generations.

Over the years, however, the enthusiasm of the members began to decline. The total number of sixty members was only rarely reached throughout the history of the Academy. Soon, the economic difficulties began, both for the progressive reduction of the proceeds from fines, and especially for the poor punctuality of the academics in paying their dues. So much so that, in 1682, the horseman, the fencing master and the mathematician had to be discharged. Only ten years later, the Doge Francesco Morosini[556], in appreciation for the participation of many Paduan nobles in the wars against the Turks, ordered the Venetian Senate to grant a fixed subsidy of 800 ducats to the Academy. In 1710, however, the number of members began to decline again. In 1725, the Venetian government subsidy was suspended, to be reinstated only two years later, but halved.

In fact, only some of the academics actually practiced riding. In 1612, about one third of them possessed one or more horses, while the remaining used the three school horses that the riding master was obliged to maintain[557]. In the following years the situation remained more or less the same and the reports of the various princes that followed in succession at the helm of the institution complained about the poor participation of members. The

---

556) Francesco Morosini (1619–1694), was Doge of Venice from 1688 until his death.

557) See Del Negro, 2008, p. 56

Use of the single pillar (William Cavendish, *Methode et invention nouvelle de dresser les chevaux*, 1657)

academics were even less assiduous in the practice of fencing, in spite of the fact that this art was the knightly exercise for which Padua was very famous. Among the fencing masters of the Delia was Francesco Ferdinando Alfieri, author of treatises that had a wide circulation in Europe[558].

The riding masters of the Academy were mostly people from outside of Padua, especially those of Neapolitan and Tuscan origin: in particular, during the seventeenth century, there were eight Neapolitan (including the two Santapaulina, grandfather and grandson) and three Tuscan (including the two Palmieri, father and son). "The most significant exceptions to this rule were represented by two nobles of Padua: Antonio Capodivacca, in office from 1622 to 1631, when he died of plague, and Duse Buzzacarini, who taught from 1718 to 1722: in both cases the choice to turn to academics was probably dictated by the fact that they were satisfied with lower salaries than those commanded by foreign riders."[559] Among the shows organized by

---

558) See in particular Alfieri, 1640, famous work, enriched with fine etching prints of the school of Jacques Callot, subsequently reprinted under the title *L'arte di ben maneggiare la spada* (1653, The art of well handling the sword).

559) Del Negro 2008, p. 60.

the Academy, let us mention a great carousel/joust held in 1610, in which thirty-four academics performed a representation of allegorical subject, with theatrical machines, chariots and music. The following year it was the turn of a "*caracollo*" in Prato della Valle (the main square of the city), on the feast of the patron saint. Many members of the Academy also took part in the great cavalcade through the city, which promenaded to meet the general superintendent of the Mainland, Pasqualigo[560]. Between 1613 and 1620 were held many jousts, quintane and races of the ring. In 1636, the academics performed the interludes between the actions of a real theater, *L'Ermiona* by the Marquis Pio Enea Obizzi (1592–1674). Two years later in 1638, a new joust open to the Paduan nobility was organized, while in 1643, another knightly theatrical invention of the Marquis Obizzi: *L'amor pudico* (The chaste love) was staged. After the fervor of the early years, however, these events decreased drastically in number and were progressively reduced to just the cavalcades on the feast of St. Anthony. Finally, after 193 years of history, the storm of the Napoleonic Wars and the cession of the Republic of Venice to Austria, on the 30th of July 1801, the Academy was closed[561].

D'Aquino, Santapaulina and the seventeenth-century treatises

Two of the horsemen of the Delia Academy published two equestrian treatises that are among the most significant of the Italian production of this genre in the seventeenth century. The first is the Neapolitan Giovanni Paolo d'Aquino, who was riding master of the Delia between 1636 and 1638. He published in 1630 the dialogues, divided into six days, entitled *Disciplina del cavallo con l'uso del piliere* (Discipline of the horse with the use of the pillar). The other is Luigi Santapaulina, who was riding master of the Delia from 1692 to 1700, and in 1696 he published a book entitled *L'arte del cavallo* (The Art of the Horse).

The treatise by d'Aquino is of particular interest, because it is dedicated to the technique of the single pillar, which specifically characterizes the training of the horse in the seventeenth century. Already described in the treatise of Pierre de La Noue, this technique received its consecration in those which are probably the two most beautiful books (at least from the iconographic point of view) ever devoted to the horse, namely the aforementioned

---

560) See Del Negro, 2008, p. 62.

561) The legacy of the Academy was, however, at least in part, inherited by New Riding Society of Padua that, since 1830, used the site of the Delia (the original building was largely destroyed by a fire in 1798)… Its activity continued until the Second World War.

Portrait of Nicola Santapaulina
(from Nicola and Luigi Santapaulina, *L'arte del cavallo*, 1696)

L'instruction du Roy en l'exercice de monter à cheval (1625) by Pluvinel[562], and the splendid treatise of the Duke of Newcastle, *Methode et invention nouvelle de dresser les chevaux* (1657, Method and New Invention of training horses) [563]. It consisted of the use of a pole, "round and as tall as a man,"[564] to which the rope of the cavesson was tied to exercise the horse on the circle, first without and then with the rider on saddle. The author, who met Salomon de La Broue and Pluvinel when they were with Pignatelli in Naples, said that he later went to France to visit them. He found, however, that La Broue—of whom he says he was "close friend" at the time of his Neapolitan period[565]— was already dead, so instead, he met Pluvinel. From the latter—whom he found "far greater than what was proclaimed by his fame"[566]—he learned the art of the pillar, and stayed with him "until I had complete knowledge and practice of this use."[567] According to d'Aquino, however, the origin of the technique of the pillar was Italian. The two French riders would have learned it from their master Pignatelli. As we have already seen, d'Aquino says that Pignatelli used a tree planted in his riding arena as a pillar, to reduce to perfect obedience "some horses of bad will,"[568] when he was no longer in the full vigor of his forces[569].

The popularization of this tool by the French authors was initially greeted with some skepticism, so that according to d'Aquino, many horsemen blamed its use. In fact, we have already seen that a few decades earlier, Giovan Battista Ferraro[570] criticized the use of a pole, called "judge," to tame colts. The use of the pillar by the French masters was, however, a much more refined technique and, above all, free from violence. In addition to the single,

---

562) Illustrated by the Flemish engraver Crispijn van de Passe (1597–1670)

563) William Cavendish (6th December 1592—25th December 1676), was a member of the court of James I and a personal friend of Charles I. During the English Civil War he was appointed general of the Royalist forces. Following the defeat at the Battle of Marston Moor (1644), he went into exile in Germany and then in Holland, where he wrote and published his book (NEWCASTLE, 1657), masterfully illustrated by the Dutch painter and engraver Abraham van Diepenbeeck (1596–1675). After the Restoration of Charles II, he returned to England and was named Duke.

564) We quote here from the second edition of the treatise: D'AQUINO, 1636, p. 4.

565) D'AQUINO, 1636, p. 4.

566) «*molto maggiore di quel che predicava la sua fama.*» D'AQUINO, 1636, p. 5.

567) «*insino à tanto, che non hebbi di questo uso intiera cognizione, e prattica.*» D'AQUINO, 1636, p. 5.

568) D'AQUINO, 1636, p. 4.

569) See Chapter VIII.

570) See Chapter VII.

What today we call *terre à terre* at the time was called
"galoppo a mezz'aria" (mid-air canter)
(from Giovanni Battista Galiberto, *Il cavallo da maneggio*, 1650)

two pillars were also used to train the horse to the piaffe[571], and to perform *pesades*[572] and *croupades*[573].

D'Aquino's book stands out as an extremely modern conception of training. For example, he insists on the need to first gain the complicity of the animal, using "good judgment, to know how to change actions from moment to moment as needed, and work the brain more than the legs, back and mouth of the Horse."[574] From the technical point of view, it also stands out for the adoption of exercises already modern, such as the half-pass[575] ("*fiancheggiare*" in the terminology of the author) and the head to the wall[576], but above all an exercise which prefigures what would later become the real cornerstone of modern dressage: the "shoulder-in."[577] The canonical definition of this exercise will only come a century later, in the *Ecole de cavalerie* (1733) by François Robichon de La Guérinière, who is considered its "inventor," but in the words of d'Aquino it's possible to recognize already some of its characteristic features:

> once placed the Horse to the pillar, you will make him go by the side with the shoulders and with the haunches together, making the shoulders precede a little, and when he will go easy, then you will stimulate him more, so that he brings as much the shoulders as the haunches with the front always to the Pillar, and in the same time helping him with the opposite leg and with the hand.[578]

---

571) See Chapter III, n. 216.

572) See Chapter IV.

573) See Chapter I, n. 41.

574) «*il buon giuditio, per saper cambiare di momento in momento le attioni secondo il bisogno, e travagliare più tosto il cervello, che le gambe, la schena e la bocca del Cavallo.*» D'AQUINO, 1636, p. 7.

575) Exercise in which the horse moves forward and sideways at the same time, proceeding slightly curved around the inside leg of the rider, looking in the direction of the movement. The forehand must precede slightly the hind end and the outside legs cross in front of the inside legs.

576) Also called *travers* [hauches-in], is a lateral movement, in which the horse proceeds slightly curved around the inside leg of the rider, keeping the forehand on the track and bringing the croup towards the inside of the arena.

577) It is the easier lateral movement for the horse and for this reason it is taught first. The horse proceeds curved around the inside leg of the rider, with the forehand positioned slightly inside the arena, moving in the opposite direction to that in which he is bent.

578) «*messo il Cavallo al piliere, si farà andare di costa con le spalle, e con l'anche insieme, facendo, che le spalle procedino un poco, e quando andarà facile, si solleciterà dapoi maggiormente, che porti tanto le spalle, quanto l'anche con la fronte sempre al Piliere, e in un istesso tempo aiutarlo con la gamba opposta, e con la mano.*» D'AQUINO, 1636, p. 33–34.

In short, it is an exercise very similar to the shoulder-in on the circle—made easier by the use of the pillar—with the front legs that move on an innermost track ("making the shoulders precede a little") with respect to the haunches. Note the distinctive role attributed to the outside hand and leg. Compared to the shoulder-in, however, no attention is paid to the lateral flexion of the horse. The same exercise is shown both in Pluvinel's and in Newcastle's treatises. According to d'Aquino, it is useful to obtain the engagement of the hindquarters, especially "for a horse that had a hard and tardy motion of the haunches."[579] making him instead "loose and fast."[580]

Although it isn't as much innovative from a technical point of view, the work published by Luigi Santapaulina still has a great historical importance. Descendant of a true dynasty of Neapolitan riders, he was the grandson of Gerolamo—who was himself horseman of the Delia from 1652 to 1654—and son of Nicola, who followed his father in Padua as an assistant, but then left to open a riding school in Venice. Even Luigi [Nicola's son], who had been in the service of Queen Christina of Sweden[581], enjoyed the reputation of skilled horseman, so much so that the academics invited him to take the job at the Delia promising him generous pay[582]. As a matter of fact, the period of his stay coincided with a period of renewed splendor of the Academy, which was shown especially by the spectacular cavalcades in honor of the patron saint.

The work published by Luigi is divided into three books. In the first two are the collected writings of his father, Nicola, about "the art to reduce the horse to complete perfection," while the third, whose author is the same Luigi, is dedicated to "how to use the horse in war and in feast." This third book provides an interesting overview of the equestrian games of the seventeenth century. Regarding the use of the horse in war it is noteworthy that Santapaulina already describes a modern cavalry, in which the lance has given way to the gun. As for the feasts and, as he writes, the "Theatres," Santapaulina mentions the cavalcades and what he calls the "*feste di operazione*" (namely: feast of operation), that is to say the carousel, the battle (synonymous of tilt-joust, or combat at the barrier), the feigned battle (in which guns are used loaded with blanks and swords without a cutting edg-

---

579) «*per Cavallo, c'havesse il moto dell'anche duro e tardo.*» D'AQUINO, 1636, p. 37.

580) «*sciolto, e presto.*» D'AQUINO, 1636, p. 38.

581) Christina of Sweden (1626–1689), was Queen of Sweden from 1632 (with full powers from 1650) to 1654. She was secretly converted to Catholicism and abdicated in favor of her cousin, Charles Gustav. She left Sweden incognito and reached Rome, where she was received with great honor by Pope Alexander VII. In Rome she held her own private courtyard, enlivened by intrigues, parties and love affairs, but also by wide intellectual relations.

582) See Mazzarolli Ancillotto, 1931, p. 57.

es), the open field (although the author declares it fell into disuse), the joust (a term referring to any "operation" with the lance: the meeting, the stroke of the Saracen or Quintane, and the race of the ring), the game of heads (in which the knights used the gun, the mace, the dart and the sword against templates, mostly in the form of monsters), and the ballet. In the words of the author the horse appears clearly as a symbol of the noble's identity, at the center of a complex etiquette made of social and behavior rules, but also as a means of seduction and of expression of virile resoluteness. We find a clear example of this last connotation in the description that the author makes of the so-called "cavalcades," i.e. the processions that took place in special occasions and feasts, and during which the riders had to follow a strict order and performed high school exercises to demonstrate their value and as sign of gallantry towards the ladies. It should be noted that, even if we are more than a century and half after the *Book of the Courtier*, we find in this passage the same code of the "*sprezzatura*" [studied nonchalance, perfect conduct or performance of something (as an artistic endeavor) without apparent effort] and the same disapproval for the affectation theorized by Castiglione:

> [in the Cavalcades] it is necessary to observe the parity, that is to say to go matched with the partner, given the fact that in the Cavalcades the riders should go two by two, and only the prince, if there is one, goes alone; then, going two by two, the rider should respect the parity not only with his companion, but also with those who are in front and behind, since this is what makes a nice view in a Cavalcade, and not always tormenting the poor horse, or performing *courbettes*, if there are horses that are able to do this exercise. But once made a straight line of six or eight *courbettes*, the rider should go back to walk and regain the right distance. And the rider should bear in mind that, performing co*urbettes*, he must put his hat on, and not keep it in his hand or under his arm, as many do, because it is ugly to see. More, when he wants to make a straight line of *courbettes* addressed to a carriage, or to the ladies appearing at a window, he must spur the horse before reaching there and, when he is in front, stop and take off his hat to greet, and this will be the sign that the exercise was done for them; and do not do as the many who keep on making *courbettes* even when they have already passed by, which is a mistake, because they [the *courbettes*] must be performed in front of the person to whom they are dedicated. In the cavalcades the rider should not keep the whip up, as in the school, but down on the right shoulder of the horse, and he should hold it now in the right hand, now in the left, and especially in this when he greets, because he has to hold the

Hat with the right [hand] and put his hand on the side, bow not straight, because if the horse raises his head he can break the riders nose, but on the side towards the person he wants to say hello. He should also pay attention to be with as much ease as possible and without affectation.[583]

The treatises dedicated to horse riding by Italian authors, published in the seventeenth century, are about fifteen in number[584]. In general, apart from that of d'Aquino, they do not propose any particular innovations from a technical point of view and refer mainly to the doctrine of the horsemen of the Renaissance, in particular to Grisone and Fiaschi. Of some interest is the book by Francesco Liberati, *La perfettione del cavallo*, (1639, The perfection of the horse), which more than a treatise about riding is a work dedicated to the care of the horse, further enriched by an extensive catalog of the many "*razze*," i.e., stud farms, of the peninsula with many plates showing their different brands. Of great value also is *Il cavallo da maneggio* (1650, The riding horse), by the Neapolitan Count Giovanni Battista Galiberto, Colonel and master of horse riding in the service of the king of Hungary and Bohemia Ferdinand IV[585], son of the emperor Ferdinand III, to whom the work

---

583) «*in queste [cioè nelle Cavalcate] devesi solamente osservare l'uguaglianza, cioè andar del pari col suo compagno, dovendosi nelle cavalcate andar a due, e solamente il Prencipe, se vi è, va solo; andando dunque a due, devesi osservar l'uguaglianza non solo del compagno, ma anco di quelli che sono avanti, e quelli di dietro, essendo questo quello, che fa il bel vedere in una Cavalcata, e non il tormentar sempre un povero cavallo, o in corvette, avendo Cavalli, che facci tal operazione, ma, fatto il suo dritto di sei, o otto tempi, tornar a pigliar il passo, e rimettersi nella sua distanza; e si avverta, che, chiamando il Cavallo in corvette, si deve metter il cappello in testa, e non tenerlo in mano, o sotto il braccio, come fanno molti, perché fa bruttissimo vedere; di più, quando si vuol far un dritto di corvette ad una Carrozza, o a una finestra di Dame, si deve chiamare il cavallo prima di arrivarvi, e quando si è in faccia, fermarsi, e cavarsi il Cappello con salutare, e questo sarà il segno, che son fatte per loro; e non fare all'uso di molti, i quali seguitano a far corvette, anche dopo passate, il che è errore, mentre si devono sempre fare in faccia alla persona per la quale si fanno: Nelle cavalcate ancora non si deve tener la bacchetta alta all'uso della scuola, ma bassa calata dalla spalla dritta del cavallo, e si tiene ora nella man dritta, & ora nella manca, e particolarmente in questa, quando si saluta, dovendosi con la dritta pigliar il Cappello, e con esso, messa la mano in Fianco, inchinarsi non dritto, perché, se il Cavallo dà un alzata di testa, vi romperà il naso, ma alla banda verso la persona, che volete salutare. Si deve anche procurare di star con più disinvoltura, che sia possibile, e senza affettazione.*» SANTAPAULINA, 1696, p. 176–177.

584) See Bibliography of the equestrian treatises.

585) Ferdinand of Habsburg (1633–1654) was the eldest son of Emperor Ferdinand III (1608–1657). He was appointed to succeed his father as early as 1652. On the 31st May 1653 he was elected king of the Romans and was crowned on the 18th of June. Being still alive, his father Ferdinand III retained the title of Emperor, reserving for his son only the governance of a part of his personal domains. He died of smallpox the

is dedicated. The book, published in Vienna, is divided into three parts. The first deals with the proper conformation and knowledge of the horse, with a discussion on which should be considered the best breeds and the best coats; the second is about the taming and the riding exercises; the third talks of diseases, defects and their cures. It is enriched by interesting full-page copper engravings, mostly illustrating the various school airs. It proposes the classical exercises and school jumps of the Renaissance tradition.

Survey of eighteenth century Europe

The eighteenth is still a century of French hegemony, although in the equestrian field begins to manifest the Franco-German dualism, which will result soon in open rivalry between the two cavalries. In French is still the most important work published in the eighteenth century: the aforementioned *Ecole de cavalerie* (1733) by François Robichon de La Guérinière (1688–1751)[In English, *The School of Horsemanship Part II*, Xenophon Press, 1992], destined to become the veritable Bible of classical riding and still considered the foundation of high-school riding and of modern dressage. It is a book that summarizes in a very clear synthesis the equestrian tradition of previous centuries, transcending it in an innovative program of rational gymnastics that allows the harmonious physical development of the horse and his training to the most sophisticated school airs.

A native of Lower Normandy, La Guérinière was a pupil of Monsieur de Vandeuil and graduated in 1715 as a royal horseman. He then moved to Paris and for fifteen years directed a riding school, soon gaining a high reputation. In 1730, Prince Charles de Lorraine, "Gran squire" of France, called him to direct the royal *manège* of the Tuileries, an assignment he held until his death. He was also the author of a second book, the *Éléments de Cavalerie*[586], which summarized the doctrine expounded in his previous book. The treatises of La Guérinière reached a very wide circulation and their absolute authoritativeness was immediately recognized. So much so that even the renowned Spanish Riding School of Vienna (the *Spanischen Hofreitschule*, founded in the sixteenth century by the Habsburgs) assumed the doctrine of the French horseman, claiming even today, to be one of its most faithful interpreters.

In addition to La Guérinière, in the eighteenth century there are many other French authors who wrote important treatises on horsemanship. Among others we recall Gaspard de Saunier[587] (educated at the Royal Academy of the pages, he was inspector on behalf of Louis XIV of the royal stud farms of Saint Lég-

---

year after his coronation.
586) LA GUÉRINIÈRE, 1740.
587) SAUNIER, 1734; 1749; 1756.

Ecole de cavalerie (1733) by La Guérinière
[Xenophon Press 1992] is the most important equestrian treatise
published in the eighteenth century.

The German engraver, Johann Elias Ridinger, published many books about horseback riding.

er), Claude Bourgelat[588] (father of equine veterinary medicine in France, founder of the veterinary colleges of Lyon and author of a treatise on cavalry), Louis Charles Dupaty de Clam[589] (equerry to the king and musketeer, and also member of the Academy of Science and Humanities of La Rochelle), Mottin Augustin de la Balme[590] (cavalry officer, who died in America, fighting for the American Revolution), Pierre François de Montfaucon de Rogles[591] (ordinary horseman of the Little Stable, who bequeathed in his *Traité d'equitation* the doctrine of the so-called School of Versailles, which was founded in 1680 with the building of the Petite and Grande Écurie du Roi in the palace of Louis XIV).

In the same period, many German-speaking authors published books devoted to the disciplines of chivalry, some of which were translated, managing to overcome the language barrier that, to a certain extent, had hitherto limited the circulation of their treatises. First of all, the wonderful engravings by Johann Elias Ridinger[592] (1698–1767) aroused great admiration. He is considered one of the best German engravers of animals, especially horses, dogs and hunting scenes. He founded his own printing office in Augsburg, where he published most of his works. His famous scenes of the riding school became a source of inspiration not only for the German riders. The engravings were accompanied by explanations of the different exercises, generally in German and French.

The production of Baron von Sind[593] (1709–1776), colonel of cavalry and First Squire of the Elector of Cologne, is also remarkable. In the space of just four years, between 1766 and 1770, he published a dozen works, some of which were also translated into French and obtained great success. The author ranges from the precepts of school equitation to the treatment of diseases of the horse, the art of harnessing and the tactics of cavalry.

It is worthwhile, to mention the treatise by Ludwig Hünersdorf[594] (1748–1813), horseman of the Prince of Hesse and later to the Duke of Brunswick published at the end of the century (1791); his book about the training of the horse was very popular and had many translations, including one in Italian, in 1826, translated by Federico Palmieri, (a lieutenant in the cavalry of Frederick II of Bourbon) which was reprinted several times.

In contrast, at the time the production of books about horse riding remains rather limited in the Iberian Peninsula, where however some notable works

---

588) BOURGELAT, 1744.

589) DUPATY DE CLAM, 1769; 1771; 1776.

590) MOTTIN DE LA BALME, 1733; 1776.

591) MONTFAUCON DE ROGLES, 1778.

592) RIDINGER, 1722; 1734; 1752; 1760; 1761; 1761; 1775.

593) SIND, 1766; 1766;1766; 1768; 1768;1769;1770; 1770.

594) HÜNERSDORF, 1791.

were printed. As the *Manejo Real* (1733) by Manuel Alvarez Ossorio y Vega[595], but especially as the aforementioned masterpiece by Carlos de Andrade, *Luz da liberal e nobre arte da cavallaria* (1791), an expression of the equestrian wisdom of the "Picaria Real," the school of the Portuguese royal court, founded by King José I. The book, which is enriched by beautiful engravings, demonstrates a clear influence of the teachings of La Guérinière on Portuguese horsemen and proposes an interesting synthesis between the European school and the local Portuguese tradition, mainly developed through the practice of bullfighting on horseback[596].

The Italian Treatises of the eighteenth century

The situation in Italy was very different. The Renaissance splendor of the Italian cavalry, which kept its leadership during the seventeenth century, at the turn of the new century seemed to have lost its momentum. Of course, the historical and political conditions of the country, largely subjected to the domination of foreign powers, played a decisive role in discouraging the practice of the arts of chivalry. This situation affected, of course, the production of works dedicated to horse riding, which decreased in this century. In all, they number a dozen, but the authors who wrote them are even less in number. Yet some of these works had a certain value. This is the case, for example, of the *Pietra di paragone dei cavalieri* (The Touchstone of the Knights) by Giovanni Giuseppe d'Alessandro, Duke of Pescolanciano, which is—together with Cesare Fiaschi's masterpiece and Pirro Antonio Ferraro's treatise—one of the most elegant Italian books dedicated to horse riding.

Born in Pescolanciano (now town in the province of Isernia) in 1656, Giovanni Giuseppe[597] succeeded his older brother Geronimo, who died prematurely. The knightly traditions were already lively in his family. Before his birth, in the fiefdom of Pescolanciano, his paternal uncle Giovanni started a stud farm of "jumping" horses[598], much appreciated and demanded by the best riders in Naples. Joseph spent his youth in the family home in Naples, soon attracting the attention of the viceroyalty for his critical attitude towards the Spanish rulers. So much so that, in 1705, he was arrested and imprisoned, on suspicion of being involved in an anti-Spanish plot. He was pardoned and released two years later by Count Daun[599], commander of the Spanish-Habsburg

---

595) OSSORIO Y VEGA, 1733.

596) About the relations between the Portuguese and the French horsemanship tradition, see Bragance, 1976.[*Dressage in the French Tradition*, Xenophon Press, 2011].

597) See Vigilante, 1985.

598) That is to say selected for their aptitude in the execution of the of school jumps.

599) Wirich Philipp Lorenz von und zu Daun (1669–1741), was imperial field mar-

Sig.^r Gennaro Cristallino

The book by the duke of Pescolanciano is enirched by a gallery of plates of the best Neapolitan riders of the time.

troops who settled in Naples, after the capture of Gaeta, in the War of the Spanish Succession. The life of an Italian nobleman at the time was not always easy. Shortly after, his own liberator returned and sent him to prison again. Once he regained freedom, the duke retired to his fiefdom in Molise, where, however, he continued to have problems with the Habsburg authorities. He finally died in Naples in 1715.

Lover of the knightly virtues, Giovanni Giuseppe made many improvements to the Castle of Pescolanciano, building large stables, but also demonstrating an acute intellectual sensitivity, collecting a considerable picture gallery and hosting intellectuals and poets. By the end of the eighteenth century, Eustachio d'Afflitto wrote about him:

> "he had the reputation of being a major expert in the knightly arts. Whence I herd our knights say that, with respect to the quarrels of sword and the qualities of a horse, people turned to him as to an oracle"[600].

He poured this expertise into his book, printed in Naples in 1711. A curious work, in which the traditional form of the equestrian treatise is alternated with sonnets and madrigals (mostly dedicated to the exaltation of the horse and of the knightly arts, such as fencing, but also of amorous inspiration), which show a clear influence of Giovan Battista Marino's works[601]. The author demonstrates, however, extensive knowledge of the Italian books dedicated to horse riding, citing the classics, Grisone and Fiaschi, but also more recent authors, such as Ferraro, Galiberto, de Gamboa and Lorenzino Palmieri[602].

The work is divided into five books. In the first are presented the "rules of riding," that is to say it talks about the correct position in saddle, the use of spurs, the aids and punishments, the taming and the different exercises. There are also recommendations on the management of the "*razze*" (the stud farms) and of stables, with chapters devoted to the tasks of the Master of the barn and of the bailiff. The second book is about the rules of "the very difficult job of bridling"[603] and summarizes the precepts contained in the sixteenth and seven-

---

shal. He fought in the War of the Spanish Succession (1701–1713/14), distinguishing himself in the defense of Turin, in 1706. The following year he conquered Gaeta and in 1713—after the Peace of Utrecht, in which Spain ceded the kingdom of Naples to Austria—was appointed viceroy of Naples.

600) «*fu in riputazione di esser intendentissimo delle arti cavalleresche. Onde ho inteso a dire da' nostri cavalieri, che nelle contese di spada e del merito di un cavallo, a lui come ad oracolo si ricorrea.*» D'Afflitto, 1782, Tomo I, p. 211.

601) Italian poet and writer (1569–1625). It is considered the most representative of Baroque poetry in Italian.

602) See the Bibliography of the equestrian treatises.

603) «*del difficilissimo mestiere dell'imbrigliare.*» D'ALESSANDRO, 1723, p. 65 [we

Portrait of Carlo Miroballo
(from *Opere di Giuseppe d'Alessandro duca di Pescolanciano*, 1723)

teenth-century treatises about the choice of the bit. The third book shows the images of bits accompanied by captions that explain their functions. The fourth contains the geometric patterns representing the plans of different exercises, but also several sonnets. The most interesting part is, however, the gallery of portraits of the most illustrious Neapolitan knights of the time, represented in beautiful copper engravings, which are also supplied with synthetic biographical notes. They are followed by the portraits of the "players of sword," that is to say the best fencers among the Neapolitan nobles. The fifth book, finally, is about the breeding and care of the horse. Eight years after the death of Duke Giuseppe, his son Ettore reprinted the work of his father, enriching it with other compositions of the author and a series of tables of physiognomy drawn from the work of Giovan Battista della Porta[604]. Finally, at the end of the treatise were inserted eleven plates, which bear the brands of the best stud farms of the kingdom of Naples.

In fact, the interest of Pescolanciano's work lies primarily in the aesthetic value of the engravings, while from the technical point of view it doesn't present any innovative feature in comparison with the previous Italian tradition. But, above all, the author proves to be unaware of what was proposed in the field of equestrian art in other countries, by masters such as Pluvinel and Newcastle. It is a different case with the books by Niccolò Rosselmini (?–1772), a patrician of Pisa, chamberlain of the Grand Duke of Tuscany and superintendent of the stud-farms of the Grand Duke in San Rossore, as well as director of the riding school of Siena. In particular, his *Dell'obbedienza del cavallo* (1764, On the Obedience of the Horse) has features of striking originality and anticipates, even if still in quite an approximate way, the approach and themes that would be destined to revolutionize modern horse riding at the beginning of the twentieth century.

In his treatise, Rosselmini proposes a method by which, according to him, anyone (even a young man at an early age) can reduce a horse to complete obedience, without taking any risk or encountering any resistance of the animal. Already in this regard, the author proves to be an innovator not only with respect to the Italian context, but also in Europe. The notion of "training method," introduced in the equestrian field by Newcastle a century earlier, will in fact be particularly fortunate in later years, in which different authors, both German and French (as Hünersdorf, Baucher, Steinbrecht, Plinzner[605]), will offer their "systems" to reduce the horse to obedience. Rather than rely on the authority of the classics, Rosselmini says his system is different "from the universal opinion, [...] for a long time espoused"[606] even by himself. Despite this, it is a

---

604) Giovanni Battista della Porta (1535–1615), philosopher, alchemist and playwright, published in 1586 the *De humana physiognomonia* in four books.

605) See below in this chapter.

606) «*dall'universale opinione, ...per lungo tempo abbracciata.*» ROSSELMINI, 1764, p. 13.

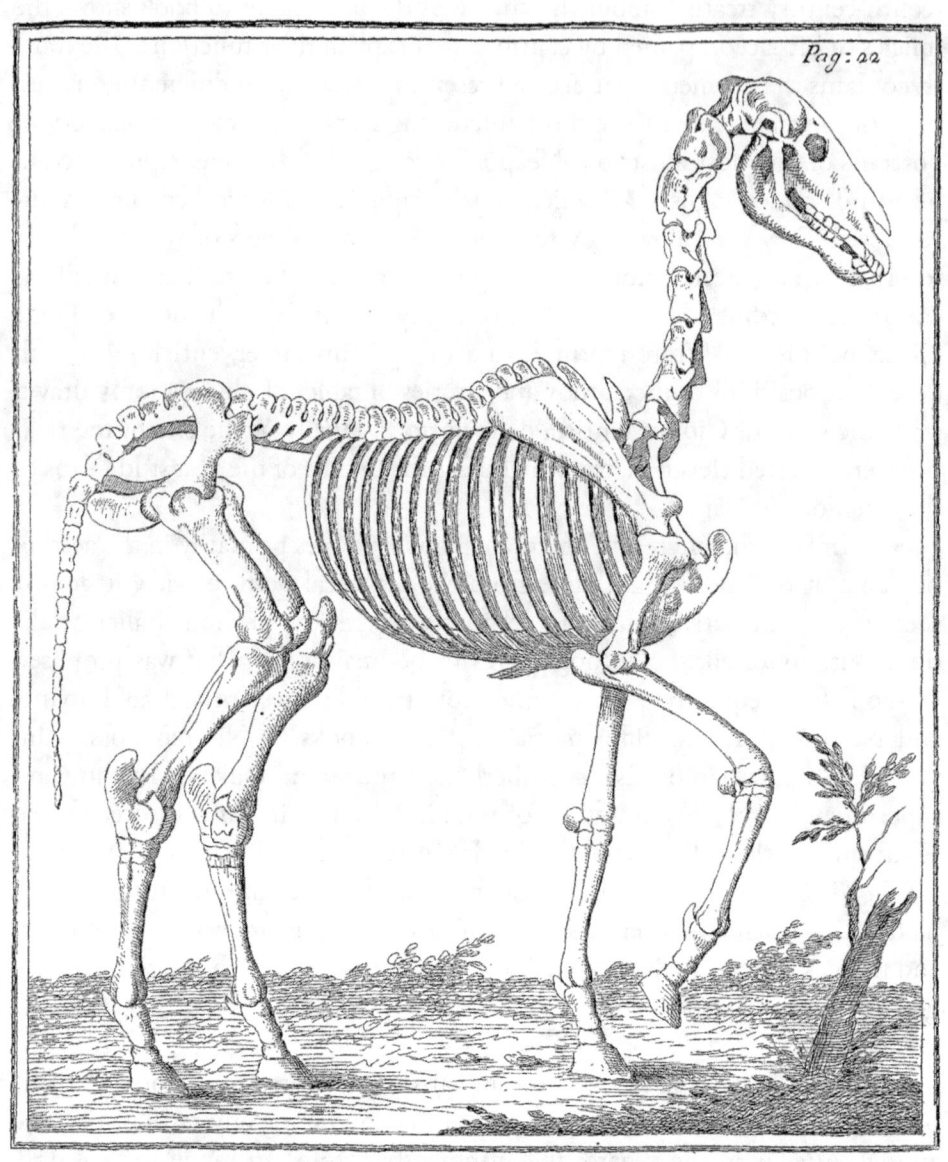

Niccolò Rosselmini says that his training method comes from the observation of the physiology of the horse.

simple process, because it conforms to the character, but especially to the physical conformation of the horse. It is based on the experience gained through years of observation "over the various motions of the Horse,"[607] which revealed to him the true function of the equine "machine" and then also disclosed which are the actions to which "the Horse can adapt and those by which the same mechanism [of the horse] is naturally disgusted and to which it opposes."[608]

In this new attention to the functioning of what, on the basis of the philosophy of Descartes[609], Rosselmini calls the "machine" of the horse we recognize the interest of the Enlightenment for the observation of natural phenomena and the confidence in science's ability to address and solve any kind of problem. A trust that we find not only in the treatise published a few years later by the French Dupaty de Clam, *La Science et l'Art de l'Equitation* (1776), but that anticipates by about two centuries the modern theories of biomechanics, which still today intend to perfect the equestrian practice through the study of the morphological structure and the dynamics of the motion of the horse[610].

Obviously, the conclusion to which the author came after his observations was that the rules taught until then in riding schools (the same to which he had already dedicated two books[611]) were wrong, because they were adverse to the true nature of the horse[612]. To demonstrate the effectiveness of his system, Rosselmini holds his son up as an example. In fact, the authors assures that even if the boy was "of gentle and weak rather than robust body,"[613] when he was just twelve years old, using his precepts he managed, in just two years (during which he had smallpox as well!) to train horses "as could have done a professor already skilled in the art."[614]

The description of the equine "machine" bewilders the modern reader.

---

607) «*sopra i vari moti del Cavallo.*» ROSSELMINI, 1764, p. 14.

608) «*per cagion di esso [meccanismo] adattar si possa il Cavallo, e da quali il meccanismo medesimo naturalmente ripugna e si oppone.*» ROSSELMINI, 1764, p. 14.

609) According to Descartes (1596–1650), in fact, the bodies of animals are nothing more than complex machines, in which bones, muscles and organs could be replaced by pulleys and pistons.

610) The publications in this field are innumerable. To get an idea of this kind of approach to riding, you can consider the activities of the International Society for Equitation Science (ISES): http://www.equitationscience.com/.

611) See Bibliography of the equestrian treatises.

612) It is worth noting that this assumption, a bit arrogant, is the basis of all "riding methods," from that of Rosselmini, to the following of Baucher and Caprilli, up to those of the "whisperers" and supporters of today's "natural horsemanship."

613) «*di corpo gentile, e gracile, piuttosto che robusto.*» ROSSELMINI, 1764, p. 14.

614) «*come fare avrebbe potuto un professore già provetto nell'arte.*» ROSSELMINI, 1764, p. 15.

Rosselmini writes: "the horse is a heavy bulk machine, and in the quadrilateral base supported by four feet, two similar of a steady column, and two formed with different angular shapes a little arched, less robust than the first, because flexible and springy"[615]. It is animated by a "motive power" that "is in a way similar to a kind of intelligence"[616] which makes it obedient to the orders of the rider. Anyway, the author does not dwell on the nature of this motive power (which he called indifferently "spirit"), leaving the investigation to the metaphysical researches of philosophers. More important to him is to show that the structure of the horse-machine assigns to the front legs the basic function of supporting the weight, while to the hind that of regulating the action of the body. It is because of these remarks that Rosselmini maintains that the training should develop the support capacity of the front legs and the elasticity of the hind, in open contradiction of the rule hitherto universally applied to train the horse to balance the weight over the haunches, engaging the hind legs under the body, in order to balance the additional weight of the rider and ensure greater mobility.

Even if expressed in a rather difficult prose, Rosselmini's theory is markedly innovative and anticipatory of subsequent acquisition in the field of equestrian art. Today, in fact, all agree that, in a state of natural balance, the horse's front legs actually support a greater weight than the hind end (because they also support the head and neck of the animal), and that this condition is likely to be further accentuated with the additional weight of the rider. Starting from a similar observation—as we will see in more detail—a century and a half later, Federico Caprilli will develop a way to ride inspired by the natural balance of the horse, which would revolutionize modern horse riding, allowing results hitherto unimaginable in jumping obstacles. Rosselmini also shows a good knowledge of the European debate in the equestrian field. In particular, he declares to be an admirer of the Duke of Newcastle, from whose precepts he says he drew his inspiration. According to Rosselmini, in fact, even if as everybody else at the time Newcastle professed the need to shift the weight onto the hind legs of the horse, the English nobleman actually proposed unknowingly an opposite doctrine.

---

615) «*il Cavallo è una macchina di mole pesante, e nella base quadrilatere sostenuta da quattro piedi, che due formati a similitudine di colonna stabile, e due formati di diverse figure angolari un poco arcate, meno robuste della prima, perché flessibili e molleggianti.*» ROSSELMINI, 1764, p. 15.

616) «*ha un non so che di analogo ad una tal qual specie di intelligenza.*» ROSSELMINI, 1764, p. 17.

Between two epochs: Federico Mazzucchelli

Between the two centuries lies another extremely significant work by an Italian author. These are the *Elementi di cavallerizza* (1802, Elements of Riding)[617] by Federico Mazzucchelli. Descendant of one of the most prominent families from Brescia, the younger son of the Earl Gianmaria[618], Federico was born in 1747. He studied in Rome, showing even in those early years his passion for riding horses. Dating back to that period is a letter he addressed to his father complaining that, due to riding continuously, all of his trousers were consumed. He then prayed his father to give provision to the leather dealer to bring different sets of trousers in black leather.

At a later age he was an ardent Jacobin, so that in May 1794, he was arrested leaving the city theater, on charges of having participated in political meetings. Together with Carlo Arici (who called himself ex-noble), Mazzucchelli was in fact the most resolute leader of Jacobin coterie, which met in Brescia in the circle named Good Friends. He was sentenced to remain imprisoned in the Castle of San Felice until the end of September. Prison, however, did not discourage his political passion. Three years later, while Napoleon was approaching, as chairman of the Supervisory and Police Committee, he signed a proclamation to all people of free Italy, in which was extolled the unity of an Italian Republic, that the naive young noble hoped would be realized with the help of Bonaparte. The story would soon completely disillusion him. He resigned from all political functions and returned to his beloved horses. He died in 1805. Even his death was in the sign of equitation since, as it is written in his obituary which appeared in the "Giornale dell'Italiana Letteratura" (Journal of the Italian Literature) of Padua, he died while he was riding:

> "Passionately devoted to his art, he died in the very act of exercising it, since being hit by a fierce apoplectic accident while he was riding, he left the life in the same riding arena in the 28th of January 1805, with pain of his friends and of every educated person that knew him"[619].

---

617) The work was reprinted and expanded in 1805, with the title of *Scuola equestre* (Equestrian School).

618) Historian and writer (1707–1765), famous, among other things, for his monumental *Gli scrittori d'Italia, cioè, Notizie storiche e critiche intorno alle vite e agli scritti dei letterati italiani* (1753–1763).

619) «*Appassionato per l'arte sua morì nell'atto stesso d'esercitarla, poiché colpito essendo a cavallo da fierissimo accidente apopletico [sic] lasciò la vita nella cavallerizza medesima a' 28 di gennaio 1805, con dolore degli amici, e d'ogni colta persona che il conosceva.*» ANONIMO, 1805, p. 282. The date of the death is confirmed also in Moschini, 1806, Vol. 1, p. 85. According to Agliardi, 2008, p. 25, instead, the year of his death would be 1804.

Federigo Mazzucchelli (1747-1805) came from one of the most prominent families from Brescia.

The date of his death definitively disproves the hypothesis of his alleged relationship with François Baucher[620]. It was General Decarpentry, author in 1948 of a famous biography of the French master [*Baucher and his school*, Xenophon Press, 2011], who formulated it. During his younger years, in fact, François Baucher did his riding apprenticeship in Italy following an uncle who was in charge of the stables of Prince Camillo Borghese[621]. In this regard, Decarpentry suggests that, during that period, the curiosity of the young Frenchman may have been attracted by the teaching of the Italian rider Federico Mazzucchelli that, he said, at that time, "practised" at an unidentified Academy in Milan. On the other hand, he properly takes care to clarify immediately the nature of this speculative argument, concluding:

> "Nothing can, however, say that he may have received his teaching and if the birth of his talent was affected by that, we do not know to what extent."[622]

What was formulated only as a hypothesis was, however, soon turned into a certainty by many historians of equitation[623], who do not hesitate to consider Baucher to be one of Mazzucchelli's pupils. In fact, the encounter between the two horsemen could not have taken place simply because, at the time of the young Frenchman's stay in Milan in 1810, the Earl Federico Mazzucchelli from Brescia had already been dead for five years.

The work of Mazzucchelli has several points of interest. First, it shows a significant evolution of equestrian practices in Italy. It presents an articulated exercise program to develop harmoniously the horse from the physical point of view, but also a set of necessary care to gain its good disposition to work and its obedience.

---

620) See *infra* in this chapter.

621) Camillo Filippo Ludovico Borghese (1775–1832). He was the second husband of Napoleon's sister, Pauline Bonaparte, whom he married in 1803. Starting from 1808 he became governor of Piemonte.

622) Decarpentry, 1948, p. 14. The French author demonstrates a rather superficial knowledge of Mazzucchelli's work, tinged with the traditional prejudice against the brutality of the classical Italian school. Mainly inspired by the illustrations of the book, he states that the Italian author "in his training pushed to the extreme the minutiae and the rigors that the Neapolitan School spread throughout Italy during the eighteenth century. His horses were prepared with the lunge and the long reins for a long time, with all sorts of side reins, worked in hand and among the Pillars with the participation of a large number of helpers and with great reinforcement from whips, lashes and indented cavesson." Decarpentry, 1948, p. 14, n. 1.

623) See, for example, Montheilhet, 1979, p. 207.

The book by Mazzuccheli is one of the first in which the technique of the "long reins" is shown.

"Since [the horse] is to be considered as a physical being and as a moral being, being capable of feeling and understanding, he is also capable of perfectibility, so education should embrace the means which tends to refine the one and the other of these two beings."[624]

In this statement is evident a new attitude towards the animal, no longer conceived as a brute, or a machine, to be submitted (even by violent means) to the will of the rider, but as a companion from whom to obtain complicity.

The work opens with a careful analysis of the conformation of the animal and of the characteristics of a good saddle horse. It also gives precise information about the care of the animal, from hygiene to nutrition and shoeing. Then the entire progression of the training is exposed, from taming up to high school airs, according to a method already very close to that of modern dressage. The author

---

624) «*Siccome [il cavallo] è da considerarsi come un essere fisico, e come un essere morale in quanto che capace di sensazione, e di comprensione è pur capace di perfettibilità, così l'educazione abbraccia i mezzi, i quali tendono a perfezionare l'uno, e l'altro di questi due esseri.*» MAZZUCCHELLI, 1805, Tomo I, p. 57.

puts special emphasis on the efficacy of two-track exercises for improving the balance of the horse, the looseness of the joints and the symmetrical development of the musculature. The work is also enriched by beautiful copper engravings[625] that illustrate the exercises and show the work in the arena. It should be noted that in these illustrations is highlighted the usefulness of the work "in-hand," that is to say with the horse not mounted, but trained by the horseman and his assistants from the ground, in order to make him learn the different exercises without being burdened by the weight of the rider. In this sense, the book is notable for being one of the first showing the work on the long reins, with bridle and a particular type of "lever" cavesson[626], by means of which the horseman drove the horse from behind as if it was attached to a carriage. Particularly interesting is also the chapter "on how to ride in the English way and on the horseraces practiced in England"[627] that testifies to the increasing influence of the British school of equitation, which—as we shall see—in the following years will develop into real anglomania. Mazzucchelli proves to be open to innovations from across the Channel, such as the use of the rising trot[628], but considers them primarily useful to adapt to the physical conformation of English horses, more long-limbed and suitable for races, compared to the riding horses used in Europe. Another part of the book that had a good success was the one "on equitation suited for women,"[629] describing sidesaddle riding. This chapter was independently translated and printed in France[630].

A century of challenges

It was from the mid-eighteenth century that the English culture, and the British way of life, began to exert a growing influence in Europe, especially in France. From clothing to food, from games to sport (but also in literature and politics) England became a model of modernity to imitate by a society that wanted to emancipate from the legacy of the old regime. Riding was no exception and indeed played a crucial role in spreading the British fashion. In the domain of equestrian art, in fact, across the Channel different practices developed, which

---

625) Similar to a kind of *hackamore* [a type headgear which does not have a bit.]

626) From the workshop of the brothers Bordiga, based on drawings by Basil Lasinio. See Peco, 1998, p. 86.

627) MAZZUCCHELLI, 1805, Tomo II, pp. 274 e ss.

628) That is to say, with the rider that follows the movements of the horse rising and sitting in the saddle, following the rhythm of the gait.

629) MAZZUCCHELLI, 1805, Tomo II, p. 293 e ss.

630) With the title of *Petit traité d'équitation à l'usage des dames. Extrait du traité complet de Mazzuchelli. Traduit de l'italien par L.-B. Quatteri* (Paris, impr. de Thibaud-Landriot, 1827).

gradually began to spread in Europe. While the rest of the Continent was fond of the stylized riding exercises and of the baroque figure of Iberian horses, in England, as early as the seventeenth century, grew a passion for speed races and horse riding in the countryside. For these needs, in the late sixteenth century, began the slow selection of a new breed of horses: agile, spirited, fast. The Thoroughbred was less suited to the deliberate slowness of academic exercises, but was perfect to compete with the wind on the turf at Newmarket. They were equally well-suited for chasing fox or deer over English estates, scattered with natural obstacles which had to be forded.. The European horseman-courtier was transforming into the modern sportsman. Lace and silk stockings were abandoned; the new gentleman did not disdain to appear in public in his riding clothes, complete with spurs and whip, giving the self-image of a rich, dynamic and sophisticated man[631].

This fashion—along with the changing needs of military cavalry, on the basis of the evolution of armaments and strategies—introduced deep changes in European equitation. Meanwhile, after centuries of absolute dominance, the Iberian breeds, the Andalusian and the rarest Lusitano, were quickly supplanted by English horses. To get an idea of the dazzling rise of this new breed, even in Italy, we may consider that, in 1784, the Italian writer Vittorio Alfieri (1749–1803)[632]—who was a great horse lover[633]—traveled to England to buy fourteen horses, for racing, riding and carriage and he returned home, crossing the Alps with his herd like a modern day Hannibal[634].

Competitions and horse race betting began to spread in continental Europe, while the academic horse riding was threatened by the growing passion for country riding, which involved the crossing of natural obstacles. Since then the knightly daring was not expressed any longer in tournaments and carousels, now fallen into disuse, but in reckless jumps over fences, ditches and boundary walls, while fox hunting. It was from this new type of horse riding that the sport of show-jumping gradually developed, as it is still practiced today.

In the eighteenth century the equestrian culture is dominated by some very famous figures. After the upheavals of the Revolution and the whirling Napoleonic adventure, the main institutions of French equitation changed. In 1814, the royal stables of Versailles, whose school had been abolished in 1793, resumed their activities, under the direction of Pierre Marie d'Abzac (1744–1827).

---

631) See Roche, 1989 e Roche, 2011.

632) Vittorio Amedeo Alfieri (January 16, 1749—October 8, 1803) was an Italian playwright, poet and writer and is one of the most prominent figures of the Italian literature of the eighteenth century.

633) So much to say in his autobiography: "without horses I'm not even half." («*io senza cavalli non son neppure mezzo…*»). Alfieri, 1967, p. 123.

634) Alfieri, 1967, pp. 214–219.

It went on until 1830, when the abdication of Charles X[635] and the accession to the throne of Louis Philippe[636] obliterated the old monarchy. The role of guardian of the French equestrian tradition was then hired by the *École de cavalerie* of Saumur, born from the original core of the royal mounted carabineer's school, created in 1763. The last director of the School of Versailles was Antoine Henri Philippe Léon Cartier d'Aure (1799–1863), figure of transition between the old and the new doctrine, a promoter of a synthesis between a simplified version of the academic tradition and the new country equitation[637], as well as the protagonist of a famous dispute with the new rising star of the transalpine equestrian scene: François Baucher (1796–1873). The latter was one of the most significant and controversial figures of the nineteenth century.

Of humble origins, Baucher was born in 1796 in Versailles and learned the art of riding from his uncle who, as we have already seen, he followed for a period in Italy. Back in France, he became squire of the Duke of Berry[638] then, in 1820, he took over the direction of two riding schools in Havre and Rouen. In 1833 he published the *Dictionnaire raisonné d'Équitation*[639], in which he set out the foundations of his new method. The same Baucher told that, by mounting a horse who was heavy on the hand, he noticed that opposing the resistance of an equal tension of the reins, sustained by hands held in a fixed position, the animal was brought to yield the tension of jaw and neck and, consequently, to relax the whole of his muscles. From this finding, the French master moved to develop a training method based on jaw and neck flexions, first executed at the standstill, with the rider on the ground, and then at walk, with the rider on horseback, to quell every resistance of the animal. In an effort to prove himself an absolute innovator, Baucher flatly refused the principles of what classical riding was up until then, especially the fundamental doctrine of La Guérinière.

In 1834, he returned to Paris, where he became the director of a riding school in the Rue Saint-Marthin, not far from the one where Count d'Aure taught. Baucher also agreed to perform in the circus of the Champs Élysées, where his extraordinary ability quickly made him very famous. In the following

---

635) Charles X of Bourbon (1757–1836), was king of France from 1824 to 1830. After the uprising of the Three Glorious Days (27–29 July 1830), caused by the Ordinances of Saint-Cloud—with which the Parliament was dissolved, a new electoral law was promulgated and censorship tightened—was forced to abdicate in favor of his nephew Henry d'Artois, under the tutelage of his cousin Louis-Philippe d'Orléans.

636) Louis Philippe Bourbon d'Orléans (1773—1850) was king of France from 1830 to 1848. Initially appointed regent to the young Henry V, shortly after took the throne under the name of Louis Philippe I.

637) See especially D'AURE, 1834.

638) Charles Ferdinand de Bourbon, Duke of Berry (1778–1820), was the second son of the future king of France, Charles X.

639) BAUCHER, 1833.

years, he published several books, in which he continued to explain his principles thoroughly, but it was in 1842, with the publication of his *Méthode d'équitation basée sur de nouveaux principes*[640], he had an instant and dazzling success. The work was reprinted three times in the space of just six months. Paris was split into two parties, the "baucherists" and the "daurists."[641] The dispute between the two factions culminated in a famous bet[642]. Lord Seymour, the first president of the Jockey Club of Paris, had a colt of three years, named Gericault, who had the reputation of being untamable. The owner declared that he would give him to the one who would be able to ride him along the Bois de Boulogne without being thrown. The first to take up the challenge was the Vicomte de Tournon, considered the most excellent among D'Aure's students, but he failed. The success smiled instead on Count Lancosme-Brèves, a Baucher student who, after collecting the stake, made a gift of the horse to his master. After less than a month of training, carried out in secrecy, Baucher presented Gericault in the Friday gala of the Champs Élysées *salon*. The exhibition attracted the Parisian intellectuals and fashionable society, from the Duke of Orleans to Dumas, from Gautier to Sue and Delacroix. Greeted on the circus ring by a tense silence, Baucher performed showing the perfect submission of his mount, finishing his exhibition with some masterful flying changes. It was a triumph.

Despite the success, Baucher was not able to get the official adoption of his method by the French cavalry, while his rival D'Aure was appointed director of the school of Saumur in 1847. In subsequent years, Baucher presented his horses and his method in various European cities, from Berlin to Vienna, achieving a great success, but also giving rise to the fierce aversion of many experts. In 1855, he was immobilized for several months because of wounds and fractures suffered from the fall of a large chandelier that illuminated the circus ring of the Champs Elysées, while he was working. His physical abilities were seriously compromised. This contributed to directing him to a thorough review of his method, which found expression in the twelfth edition of his book, which appeared in 1864. What is universally called Baucher's "second manner" so came to light. While holding fast to the basic principles that inspired him from the beginning, he significantly changed the procedures of the horse's training. He continued te-

---

640) BAUCHER, 1842.

641) In Flaubert's *Éducation sentimentale* (1869) we find a clear evidence of the popularity of this dispute and of the passions that ignited in the Paris of the mid-nineteenth century. In the fourth chapter of the Second Part, while they're having dinner at the restaurant after a day at the races, Frédéric and Cisy talk "about equitation and of the two rival systems. Cisy was for Baucher, Frédéric for the Count D'Aure" (Flaubert, 1980, p. 201). The discussion is abruptly interrupted by Rosanette's lapidary judgment, who in addressing Frédéric says, "Oh my God, stop it! He's a better judge than you, come on!." (Ibid.).

642) See Decarpentry, 1948, pp. 29–34.

aching and training horses until 1870. But his health, never fully recovered after the accident, constantly worsened. He died in February 1873.

The numerous works of Baucher's pupils contributed significantly to further disseminate his method. Among those we just mention that of General Faverot de Kerbrech (1837–1905), whose *Dressage méthodique du cheval de selle* (1891)[643] [*Methodical Dressage of the Riding Horse…*, Xenophon Press, 2010] is considered the most adherent transposition of the "second manner" of the master, and those of General L'Hotte who, despite being one of his most faithful disciples, did not adopt Baucher's method for military teaching when he became *écuyer en chef* of the school of Saumur[644]. As we have already seen, however, the new approach of Baucher also aroused strong criticism, not only at home, but especially in Germany. The most vehement German polemicist against the French was Louis Seeger (1798–1865), founder of the first private riding school in Berlin and student under Max von Weyrother (1783–1833) at the Spanish Riding School of Vienna. After exposing the principles of the classical doctrine of the German school (which, nevertheless, was deeply influenced by La Guérinière) in two previous treatises[645], he published in 1852 a pamphlet, entitled *Herr Baucher Künste und seine—Ein ernstes Wort an Deutschlands*[646] [summarized by General Decarpentry and contained in Appendix II of *Baucher and His School*, Xenophon Press 2011] in which Seeger warned the German riders against the dangers inherent in what he called "the high school at reduced prices" advocated by Baucher. Seeger, who did not hesitate to attack his opponent on a personal level, sharply criticized the standstill exercises provided by the new method to obtain the flexion of jaw and neck. According to Seeger this process frustrated the horse's natural impulse to move forward that, in his opinion, was the very "soul" of true equitation.

A similar aversion to the theories of Baucher is found in the fundamental work of Seeger's pupil Gustav Steinbrecht (1808–1885). A native of Saxony, he studied veterinary medicine in Berlin, where he also improved in the equestrian art. Afterwards he directed a private riding school in Magdeburg, before returning to Berlin, where he lived, except for a short period in Dessau, until his death. Over the years, he worked on the drafting of a summary of the principles of his art, but he couldn't finish it. The book was completed, on the basis of the author's notes, by his student Paul Plinzner[647] and published posthumously under the title *Das Gymnasium des Pferdes*[648] [*The Gymnasium of the Horse*, Xenophon Press,

---

643) See L'Hotte, 1905, L'HOTTE, 1906.

644) SEEGER, 1844 and SEEGER, 1850.

645) SEEGER, 1852.

646) In turn, the author of a short and controversial treatise: PLINZNER, 1887.

647) STEINBRECHT, 1886.

648) Carlo Emanuele III of Savoy (1701–1773), king of Sardinia, Duke of Savoy,

1994]. In it is exposed a detailed progression of the training of the horse, which is founded on the basic principles of straightness and forward impulsion. The first part is devoted to the description of the correct posture of the rider and of the aids through which he can direct his mount. Then is explained the purpose of the training, which consists of systematic gymnastics, intended to enable the horse's muscles to place its own mass in balance in the various contingencies of equitation, consequently being able to move with regularity and fluency. This gymnastics is based on a thorough analysis of the dynamics of the motion of the horse, but also on the respect of his nature and of his sensitivity. The horse is conceived as a harmonious whole, the parts of which lend themselves to a joint collaboration. For this reason, as his teacher, even Steinbrecht criticized the standstill exercises of the new French school, considering the motion, which starts from the impulse of the hind legs, the peculiar element of the horse.

For its accuracy and rationality, Steinbrecht's treatise is considered one of the most representative works of the German school and it is still considered one of the reference texts of modern dressage. In spite of too many clichés and of some real drift towards a physically coercive approach to the horse, it shows that the most authentic theoretical core of German equestrian is in fact based on a profound wisdom and on the full respect of the animal.

The long Italian transition

The history of Italian equitation in the nineteenth century is inextricably linked to the rise of the Savoia family. Since its origins, the Savoia held the equine production and the strategic role of cavalry in high regard. By the decree of Carlo Emanuele III[649], in 1769, a school of veterinary medicine was founded in Venaria Reale, modeled after the one in Lyon, France. The first director was Giovanni Brugnone (1741–1818), who was succeeded by Carlo Lessona (1784–1858). At the Venaria Reale, where ever since the second half of the eighteenth century a horse farm served the needs of the court, in 1823, a Military Riding School was established[650] (*Scuola Militare di Equitazione*), on the order of King Carlo Felice[651]. The epoch during which the Italian riders imparted their teachings to all of the courts of Europe, however, was by then, only a distant memory. The position of Chief Horseman was entrusted to the German, Otto Wagner[652], a native of Mecklenburg, who maintained it for twenty years. He based his teachings on the rules of German academic riding and high school, a trend which the school

---

Marquis of Monferrato and Saluzzo, Prince of Piemonte since 1730.

649) FAVEROT DE KERBRECH, 1891.

650) See AA.VV., 2009b.

651) Carlo Felice of Savoy (1765–1831) was king of Sardinia from 1830 to his death.

652) See Gennero, 2004.

retained even after his transfer to Pinerolo, in 1849. In the new location it changed its name to Military Cavalry School (*Scuola militare di cavalleria*) and was subsequently reorganized in 1862 under the name of Normal Cavalry School[653] (*Scuola Normale di Cavalleria*). A year earlier the standards of mounted training were fixed in the *Regulations for the exercise and evolutions of cavalry*[654] (*Regolamento per l'esercizio e le evoluzioni della cavalleria*).

We still have a testimony of extraordinary importance of Savoia's passion and concern for riding. Starting from 1770 until about the end of the nineteenth century, a large collection of books dedicated to the equestrian art and to the care and breeding of the horse was gradually gathered in the libraries of these three equestrian centers: the Royal Stables, the School of Veterinary Medicine and the Military Riding School. The entire collection of books is now kept in one of the three special collections of the Library of the Quirinale[655]. It is the richest and most important collection of equestrian books in Italy, with about five hundred volumes, from the first sixteenth century treatise up to specialized publications from the nineteenth century. A heritage that drew the attention of Luigi Einaudi[656], second President of the Italian Republic. In a documented study dedicated to the equestrian fund of the Library of the Quirinale, Raoul Antonelli shows a curious exchange of letters between the President-intellectual and Benedetto Croce[657], in which the first asked for news about the treatise of the Duke of Pescolanciano, which was offered to him to enrich the collection. Croce responded that he knew the work, which in his opinion had "no small curiosity value due to all its engravings"[658]

In the second half of the nineteenth century, in Italy, and particularly in Piedmonte, the need to update the training methods began to be felt by those in the high military ranks of the cavalry. Up until this point, the methodology had remained committed to the principles of classical equitation. The growing use and sheer power of firearms imposed mainly exploratory and disruptive tactics to the mounted detachments, to be taken in increasingly large battlefields ["theahers of war"], focusing the fights in sudden attacks.

---

653) See Morelli di Popolo, 1980.

654) MINISTERO DELLA GUERRA, 1861.

655) The Quirinale Palace, in Rome, was built in the sixteenth century as a new residence for the Pope. After the unification of Italy became the palace of the king. It is now the official residence of the President of the Italian Republic.

656) Luigi Einaudi (1874—1961), economist, politician and essayist, was the second President of the Italian Republic, 1948–1955.

657) Benedetto Croce (25th February 1866—20th November 1952) was an Italian philosopher, historian, politician, literary critic and writer, chief ideologue of the twentieth-century Italian liberalism.

658) «*non piccolo valore di curiosità per tutte le incisioni.*» See Antonelli, 1994, pp. 18–19.

Therefore a kind of equitation more geared to rapid deployments in the countryside became necessary. The need to give a new direction to military training was particularly felt by Colonel Luigi Lanzavecchia Buri, who was appointed commander of the School of Pinerolo in 1865. After visiting the schools of Vienna, Berlin, Hannover and Saumur, he chose to entrust the teaching to Cesare Paderni (1833–1923), former officer of the Austrian army, born in Cividale del Friuli. He studied at the Academy of Vienna and, in addition to a deep knowledge of classical horsemanship, he also had good experience in countryside equitation. He retained the post of horseback riding director for twenty-six years, until 1893.

While remaining tied to the traditional principles, Paderni was "the first to give practical demonstration that, in varied terrain, much could be achieved by the horse schooled and trained outdoors, and that in contrast with the theories of the time, based solely on the use of the school horse"[659]. In the countryside the horses had to be obedient and not only durable but also able to clear natural barriers, such as ditches, hedges and fences. This was the beginning of the training to what we now call cross-country and show-jumping. In fact, until then this aspect was not developed in classical riding and the jumps that were practiced in schools, a heritage of the Renaissance tradition, were demonstrations of skill and daring, but had no practical use, because they were performed on flat ground and almost on the spot. Even the first jumps over natural and artificial obstacles were performed with the academic seat, in a manner that now seems inconceivable. The rider remained firmly seated in the saddle, with long stirrups, and clinging to the reins he leaned his upper body back, in the unlikely intent to "help" the horse to lift the forehand. Needless to say, the poor beasts, being so burdened, could only clear low barriers. From this point of view, the teaching of Paderni was no exception, as demonstrated by his *Regole di equitazione sul modo di saltare e superare ostacoli*[660] (1883, Riding rules on the way to jump and go over obstacles), although having once led the horse over the obstacle, he at least recommended to "give immediately the hands, advancing almost imperceptibly the upper body."[661] However, a much more radical change was going to revolutionize the equestrian technique all over the world and just by the most brilliant student of the school of Pinerolo: Federico Caprilli.

---

659) Veneziani Santonio, 1996, p. 22.

660) PADERNI, 1883.

661) «*cedere prontamente le mani, avanzare l'appiombo, in modo appena percettibile.*» We quote from the new edition, Cesare Paderni, *Regole di equitazione sul modo di saltare e superare ostacoli*, Milano, LL Edizioni Equestri, 1981, p. 30–31.

Caprilli and the "natural system"

Federico was born in Livorno in 1868[662]. At the age of thirteen, he was admitted to the military college of Florence. In 1886 he entered the Military Academy of Modena, where he presented quite a bad school curriculum, mainly due to his intolerance for discipline and authority. His aspiration was to become a cavalry officer. Two years earlier, the first Italian show-jumping competition was held in Turin. Around the same time, the famous Italian writer Gabriele D'Annunzio wrote in "La tribuna," the chronicles of the new pastime of the aristocracy: fox hunting on horseback[663]. The career in the cavalry also meant, above all, the possibility of access to fashionable society. Paradoxically, when Federico underwent the first medical examination he was judged unfit for riding. He finally managed to get himself assigned to the cavalry after many difficulties. At the Academy, he befriended Count Emanuele Cacherano of Bricherasio and met Giovanni Agnelli, who in a few years (in 1899) left the cavalry to found the FIAT, the first and most important Italian car company. At the end of the two year course, another paradox: Caprilli was ranked among the mediocre riders.

He was assigned to the Piedmonte Reale Regiment, based in Saluzzo, and sent to the riding course in Pinerolo. His ability as a horseman rapidly improved, though he did not like the exercises in the arena, established by the regulations. Back in Saluzzo, however, he began to stand out for his skill and valor. In 1891, he attended the teaching course at the school of Pinerolo, to become an instructor, and in October of the same year he was sent to the first complementary course of specialization in country riding in Rome, at the new headquarters of Tor di Quinto. The opening of this new school—a sort of "branch" of that of Pinerolo, but with a much more pronounced orientation towards training outdoors—was commissioned by the Minister of War, Pelloux, after two military racing meetings, held in the Roman hippodrome of Tor di Quinto, in which horses and riders demonstrated an insufficient level of training. The facility (formerly a cowshed), was then purchased with the related land where the first course was directed by the Marquis Luciano of Roccagiovine, a Roman nobleman, who had already distinguished himself in steeple-chase[664] and fox hunts, frequently held in the capital and surroundings.

Caprilli was classed first in the course. Now, many admired the ability of this young officer, who had a run of successes in the training and competition fields, but who also began to become noticed as a champion of social life and as a seducer. However his brilliant lifestyle did not distract him from his

---

662) On the life and work of Federico Caprilli, see Giubbilei, 1911 but above all the charming biography by Lucio Lami: Lami, 2009.

663) The equestrian fervor of the *belle époque* is masterfully rendered in Lami, 1983.

664) Speed races that involve jumping large hedges along the course.

passion for horses nor from his intent to improve jumping technique, which in his eyes showed obvious limitations. He then studied the kinetics of the jumps of riderless horses, developing the belief that, in order to obtain a better result, it was necessary to follow the natural balance of the animal before, during and after the jump, rather than trying to impose on him an artificial balance, as was claimed by the then current dominant doctrine.

In 1894, he was detailed as an instructor in the school of Tor di Quinto, and the following year he was restationed at Pinerolo. But his stormy worldly life cost him his transfer to the Lancers of the Milan Regiment, in Nola. He continued to develop his new method and approach to the obstacles. Nevertheless, he continued unperturbed in his brilliant life, attending the Neapolitan fashionable society. His unit was later moved to Parma. Now his new system was "fixed on some innovative and essential rules: respect for the horse's mouth, freedom of the neck obtained yielding the reins by stretching the arms, without losing the contact, shorter stirrups and leg hinged by the knee, low heel. A few simple rules that can be considered a Copernican revolution with repects to the old school."[665] Despite the skepticism and outright hostility of the traditionalists, the results were plain for all to see. He could, in fact, jump large obstacles even with mediocre horses and he won many competitions and horse speed races. By now he was surrounded by a group of enthusiastic followers, but the general staff considered his successes and new methods with caution.

In 1900, his colleague, Lieutenant Count Gian Giacomo Trissino, suggested that he join the show-jumping competition of the second Olympiad, which was to be held in Paris in May of the same year. The Ministry of War initially granted the authorization, but then withdrew the permission. According to Lucio Lami, this did not prevent him from participating incognito, during an ordinary leave, and to rank second in the extension trial, jumping 5.70 meters in length. Trissino, instead, was first, equal with the French Gardère, in the elevation trial, overcoming a barrier of 1.85 meters. A height that at the time was considerable[666].

The following year Caprilli, who meanwhile was promoted captain, decided to draw up in writing the principles of his new system. He published, in two subsequent episodes, in the "Rivista di cavalleria" (Journal of chivalry) an essay titled *Per l'equitazione di campagna* (For country riding)[667]. The assumption on which he based his argument was very clear:

---

665) Lami, 2009, pp. 90–91.

666) Cfr. Lami, 2009, pp. 91–98.

667) CAPRILLI, 1901.

"I think we should aim to have the horse as he is in nature with natural balance, with natural head position, because if there is a need for some modification of balance, we will see how the horse can accomplish it by himself while working, when the appropriate freedom is left to him."[668]

The refusal of the high school tradition clearly appears: "The two ways of riding, in the school and in the countryside, are, in my opinion, opposite; they exclude and destroy one another. This happens all the more in the regiments, where the use of the closed arenas and of the many other dictates of an equitation that has too many connections and derivations with the high school give mediocre results, in fact, leaving aside everything else, they [the dictates of high school equitation] are too difficult to be well applied by soldiers"[669]. These concepts were further developed in a subsequent article, in response to the comments of Lieutenant Ettore Varini, entitled *Due altre parole sull'equitazione di campagna* (Two other words about country riding)[670]. A little later the provisional drafts of the first volume of the regulation for the cavalry were published, on an experimental basis. They were largely influenced by the new technique of Caprilli. But he wasn't completely satisfied by these new directives and wrote an article, *Sul nuovo regolamento di equitazione* (About the new riding regulation)[671], in which he pointed out some of their inconsistencies. This gave rise to a debate in which he participated with an additional article, simply entitled *Una replica* (A reply)[672], which earned him an increasingly broad support among his comrades-in-arms and even of the general staff.

After only a few months, in June 1902 Caprilli had the opportunity to give a sensational demonstration of the effectiveness of his system, in the international show-jumping competition in Turin. On that occasion he won the extension trial, jumping 6.50 meters in length but, after a disastrous fall in the test field, he was eliminated in the elevation trial. Disappointed with

---

668) «*credo che si debba tendere ad avere il cavallo quale è in natura con naturale equilibrio, con naturale posizione di testa, poiché se vi è bisogno di qualche modificazione di equilibrio, vedremo come il cavallo la possa compiere da sé durante il lavoro, quando gli sia lasciata l'opportuna libertà.*» We quote here from the new edition of the article in GIUBBILEI, 1911, pp. 70–71.

669) «*Le due equitazioni di cavallerizza e di campagna sono, a mio credere, opposte; si escludono e si distruggono l'una con l'altra. Ciò avviene tanto più nei reggimenti, ove l'uso delle cavallerizze e di tanti altri dettati di un'equitazione che ha troppe attinenze e derivazioni dall'alta scuola danno mediocri risultati; infatti, lasciando stare tutto il resto, sono d'una difficoltà troppo grande perché possano essere bene applicati dai soldati.*» GIUBBILEI, 1911, p. 71.

670) CAPRILLI, 1901b.

671) CAPRILLI, 1902.

672) CAPRILLI, 1902b.

the result, he then issued a challenge to get over two meters in height. On the first attempt he jumped a barrier placed at 2.08 meters, a measure hitherto unthinkable. The record, however, was not officially confirmed because it was not done in the official race. Despite this, the Italian press did not spare criticism to the new way of riding proposed by the Italian riders, who were beaten in the official competition by the French. Caprilli replied with indignation in his *Osservazioni sul Concorso Ippico Internazionale di Torino* (Observations on the International Horse Show in Turin), but the editing staff of the "Rivista di cavalleria" did not publish the article, considering it too polemical. It was then published posthumously by his pupil and first biographer, Carlo Giubbilei[673].

In 1904, at the behest of the new commander of the School, General Luigi Berta, finally Caprilli returned to Pinerolo. A few months later, with Berta and another officer, he went to visit the famous French school in Saumur, where, despite the aftermath of an accident, he gave proof of his own personal mastery, by leading on the obstacle a horse, that since day, was irreducibly reluctant to jump. Back in Italy, he was given the task of leading the international section of the apprentice instructors. Officers of different nationalities, eager to learn the new methods successfully tested in Italy, began to flock to Pinerolo. During this period, Caprilli devoted himself to the training of a chestnut mare named Itala, both to high school exercises, and to the principles of his natural system. This choice has very much intrigued Caprilli's interpreters and biographers, who alternatively consider it an expression of the desire to silence the critics who accused him of not fully mastering the classic technique, or of the opportunistic need to please the traditionalists at the top of the cavalry to finally obtain the desired promotion to major, or even as a second thought in view of the integration of his system with the techniques of the "flat work."

In 1905, he was appointed director of riding courses. He began to collect notes on scattered pages for the writing of a book. But he could not complete the project. Over the years, the incessant work and the many falls had undermined his physique. Despite this, he continued to ride and participate successfully in races. In the spring of 1907, he won the first Italian military championship in Rome. In December of the same year, however, he died after falling from a horse.

Bringing Italian equitation back onto the world scene, Caprilli's revolution accomplished the mission begun in the Renaissance. On the basis of the successes of the Italian riders on the racing fields, the adoption of the "jumping seat" developed by the "natural system" became generalized and still remains the foundation of the show-jumping technique. But the fact that Caprilli failed to fully systematize his method in an organic text covering all aspects of the use of the horse gave rise to a long controversy among

---

673) GIUBBILEI, 1911, pp. 167–187.

his pupils and followers, over which interpretation of his way to ride was the most orthodox and functional. Four years after his death, his pupil and friend Carlo Giubbilei collected and published the writings of his master. The dissemination of his teachings, however, was mainly orally transmitted, leading consequently to deviations and approximations. There were also some books that attempted to transmit the essence of Caprilli's doctrine. Among these we mention *Elementi di equitazione naturale*[674] (Elements of natural horsemanship) by Ruggero Ubertalli, one of his closest students, and *L'arte di equitare*[675] (1937, The art of riding) by Baldo Bacca, who wasn't a direct pupil of the master and who was accused by "purists" to have strayed from Caprilli's path. Of great historical, as well as technical, interest is the book written by the Russian officer Paul Rodzanko who, in 1907, stayed for eighteen months in Pinerolo and Tor di Quinto and, once returned home, published[676] his personal account on the life and teaching of the two schools at the time of Caprilli , entitled *La scuola di cavalleria italiana* (*The Italian school of cavalry*).

---

674) UBERTALLI, 1923.

675) BACCA, 1937.

676) RODZANKO, 1911.

Conclusion

"The rider who does not try to imitate his ancestors should not boast to be descended from them: because the greater the fame of the fathers, the more reprehensible is the negligence of the sons."[677]

These were Pasquale Caracciolo's words in the mid-sixteenth century, and his warning still applies today. Too often, the study of horseback riding's history has been colored by the chauvinism of authors who have openly distorted the data of their research, in the illusion that enhancing the prestige once enjoyed by their national traditions might also indirectly dignify themselves. Indeed, as Caracciolo correctly underlines, the effect obtained is often exactly the opposite. In most cases, in fact, the splendor of the past rather emphasizes the miseries of the present.

On the other hand, like any other cultural phenomenon the equestrian tradition of each country is the result of exchanges and reciprocal influences. If then, it is true that the Italian riding school enjoyed a special prestige in the Renaissance—and then again a return to the world stage at the beginning of the twentieth century—it is also true that this primacy stood in the context of an already extremely refined civilization of the horse, which embraced the culture of the entire European continent and of the same Muslim world. Therefore, if there was a supremacy, it was the result of the synthesis of shared techniques and knowledge, made possible by particular historical and cultural conditions. I emphasize this to clarify that the intent with which I studied the Italian tradition of equestrian art was not to magnify the reputation of my national riding tradition, but instead to deepen, through the process of rigorous and documented research, a significant chapter of Italian and European culture, which is still little-known but it is of great importance.

Unfortunately, today Italian equitation does not enjoy good health. The generations after that of Caprilli rested on the laurels of a handful of excellent riders who continued for several decades to take on the racing fields around the world. Meanwhile, the breeding of native breeds was destroyed by a senseless policy: the teaching of all equestrian professions (from blacksmithing to riding) was abandoned and the study of equestrian culture was completely neglected (apart from the meritorious efforts of a few). All of this happened while other countries, such as Germany, France, the Netherlands, even New

---

677) «*Il Cavaliere che non cerca d'imitare i suoi passati, non devria vantarsi d'esser disceso da quelli; perché quanto più grande è stata la fama de' padri, tanto più biasimevole la negligenza de figli.*» CARACCIOLO, 1566, p. 44.

Zealand, made horse breeding and equestrian sports into viable national industries, generating profits and employment.

The causes of this decline are different. In addition to those related to the mismanagement of sports and breeding policies by the institutions, there is probably also a motivation linked to the peculiarities of the "Italian School." Modern riding in Italy is, in fact, based on Federico Caprilli's teachings and on his "natural method," which the Master never formulated into a systematic and clear way as was done, by contrast, by other authors like La Guérinière and Baucher, whose works are still the foundation of French horsemanship. For this reason, Italian horsemanship lacked a coeherent trend, since the advocats of Caprilli's teachings have often interpreted them in diverging ways. And this vagueness was maintained by the inertia of our equestrian institutions, which never promoted a deepening and a systematization of the "Italian doctrine" by the experts. It is therefore not surprising that, paradoxically, just in Italy Caprilli's method has lost its force, and, with the passage of time, it has been contaminated by empirical practices of limited effectiveness.

I am also convinced that one of the factors that most negatively impacted horse riding in Italy (but we might say, all over the world) is the oblivion of the rich heritage of expertise, and therefore culture, developed in the equestrian field over the centuries. On the collective level, without culture there can be no progress, in the same way without reflection, analysis and study there can be no true fullness on the level of individual experience. While it is true that, as claimed by the authors of the first equestrian treatises, you can not think of learning through books such a complex and eminently practical activity like riding, it is equally true that the rider can tune his sensitivity and refine his technical skills only through a careful theoretical consideration of his relationship with the horse. In this sense, the experience gained over thousands of years of co-existence between man and this extraordinary animal, which had such a large part in the development of our civilization, represents an inexhaustible source of suggestions with which each of us can and must nourish his awareness.

Then the interest for the history of horsemanship has not an abstract "intellectual" value but, in my opinion, is the true fulfillment of the passion that animates every true horse lover. First of all, because it provides the rider the knowledge of a variety of techniques to solve different problems. To understand a horse one needs a lot of experience, because although it is a wonderfully expressive and sensitive animal, only a long familiarity with him allows us to interpret his behaviors, in order to aid him expressing at his best his potential. For this reason, only a very large fund of experience helps the rider to face the many challenges he encounters in the course of daily work. Every individual horse has different characteristics and reacts in a specific manner to the requests of the rider. This requires the rider to be both competent and sensitive, with

broadly studied and practiced. The lessons of the great masters of the past decisively augments the rider's personal experience..

Many think to solve this difficulty by resorting to methods that are claimed to be able to simplify the complexity of the relationship between man and animal through the application of universal patterns. Although in many cases the results may appear satisfactory, often in practice exceptions do occur, throwing the rigidity of a standardized routine into question. It is precisely at these times that the wealth of experience gained over the centuries proves to be even more useful to the modern rider. Rather than a dull fidelity to a method, I believe it is far more productive and pragmatic to combine the best experiences reached at international level in various equestrian disciplines with a deep knowledge of tradition. On the other hand, full knowledge of equestrian history allows us to easily recognize alleged "innovative techniques" fashionable today as mere revivals of widespread practices of the past, which the guru of the moment simply proceeds to repaint with the patina of marketing.

Cesare Fiaschi and the other Renaissance authors had already understood that the horse is an extraordinarily sensitive animal with whom the rider often tends to comunicate by too vehement means, which turn into useless and counterproductive violence. And for violence here I mean not only the use of beatings and other abuses, but also an inappropriate overuse of the aids. The most valuable lesson that comes from what we call "classical riding" is that we generally tend "to do too much," even when when we are motivated by the best intentions. The problem with these extraordinary animals is that unfortunately their impressive size, their strength and impulsiveness elicit an unconscious fear in most people who deal with them, including the most genuinely passionate and even many professionals. More than seven centuries ago, Dom Duarte had already understood this and exactly for this reason he devoted a large part of his treatise to the management of this particular emotional state, which can easily grasp the man in front of the horse's primordial energy. Fear leads inevitably to a lack of observation of the behavior of the animal and is generally exorcised by brutality, or at least by far more aggressive manners than necessary, which establish a vicious cycle of human actions and reactions of the animal that are the source of endless misunderstandings and repeated failures. The study of equestrian history teaches us that the stylization the of the "airs" in academic equitation, the theorization of the rider's "grace," the search for "natural" balance by Caprilli, are nothing more than a lesson in respect for this magnificent animal, who is able to impart to the rider the exiting sensation of his strength and elegance. This lesson that comes from our past is an essential encouragement to our present and future as riders.

Appendices:

Web resources on equestrian treatises

The Internet is a great tool also for anyone interested in the history of horseback riding and, in particular, to the tradition of equestrian treatises. Today all the major equestrian Italian and foreign treatises can be read and freely downloaded in PDF format from the web, complete with their beautiful illustrations. Although Italy had such an important part in the history of equestrian art is sad to note that most of the digital resources on this subject are available on the initiative of foreign institutions.

The Virtual Library of the National Veterinary School of Lyon

One of the richest and most accessible collections of equestrian treatises on the web is that of the *École nationale vétérinaire de Lyon*, in which are digitized about seventy French, Italian, German and English ancient books dedicated to horse riding and to the care of the horse:

http://www2.vetagro-sup.fr/bib/fondsancien/ouvonline/menuouv.php

Ancient books web portal of Saumur's National Riding School

The selection offered by Saumur's *École Nationale d'Equitation* is even wider. It's a real web portal dedicated to antique books about horses and riding. A site all the more useful because it not only makes available the books of the ancient collection of Saumur Library, but also about five hundred documents from other websites, such as Gallica (the digital collection of the National Library of France), Google Books, Archive.org , etc..:

http://fonds-ancien.equestre.info/index.php

Very rich in information and research tools is also the website of the ENE Documentation Centre:

http://documentation.equestre.info/

Maestrini collection of the University of Bologna's Digital Library

Books of particular interest, dedicated to the farriery and horse riding, are available on the website of the Maestrini Collection of the Central Library of Veterinary Medicine GB Ercolani of the University of Bologna:

http://amshistorica.unibo.it/fondomaestrini

EDIT 16 – National census of the Italian Sixteenth Century edition

As for the specific study of the Italian works published in the sixteenth century, you may find highly accurate bibliographic information in the website of the census conducted by the Central Institute for the Unified Catalogue of Italian Libraries and for Bibliographic Information:

http://edit16.iccu.sbn.it/web_iccu/ihome.htm

Google Books

For really insatiable researchers, much of what cannot be immediately traced on the aforementioned websites is directly available in the virtual library of Google Books that, among other things, also provides the possibility to search for text strings inside the majority of the works, facilitating the rapid identification of quotations:

http://books.google.it/bkshp?hl=it&tab=wp

The Works of Chivalry

Finally, the research work that led to the publication of this book continues and deepens in the author's blog, where you can find articles devoted to the history of horsemanship, to the equestrian myths and to the evolution of riding techniques, as well as a rich specific iconography, explanatory videos, bibliographies and links to other web resources:

http://worksofchivalry.com/en

Bibliography of the treatises on horsemanship

In this chapter you find the complete bibliography of the Italian treatises about horseback riding, from the Renaissance up to the beginning of the Twentieth Century, listed in chronological order. It is followed by the bibliography of the works by foreign authors directly quoted in the book.

Italian treatises on horsemanship Sixteenth Century

1550 GRISONE, Federico, *Gli ordini del cavalcare*, Napoli, stampato da Giovan Paolo Suganappo.
1556 FIASCHI, Cesare, *Trattato dell'imbrigliare, atteggiare e ferrare cavalli*, Bologna, Anselmo Giaccarelli.
1560 FERRARO, Giovanni Battista, *Razze, disciplina del cavalcare ed altre cose pertinenti ad esercitio così fatto* (del sig. GB Ferraro, cavallerizzo napoletano), Napoli, appresso Mattio Cancer.
1562 CORTE, Claudio, *Il Cavallarizzo*, Venezia, Giordano Zilletti.
1566 CARACCIOLO, Pasquale, *Gloria del cavallo*, Venezia, Gabriel Giolito de' Ferrari, (in 4°).
1581 DE PAVARI, Marco, *Escuirie de M. de Pavari venitien (en ital. et en franç.)* Jean de Tournes, Lyon, avec fig [we quote from the modern edition *Escuirie de M. de Pavari venitien*, edited by P. Arquint e M. Gennero, Collegno, Roberto Chiaramonte Editore, 2008].
1598 SILICEO, Ottaviano, *Scuola de' cavalieri di Ottaviano Siliceo gentiluomo Troiano, nella quale ... si discorre ... de' cavalli, in che mode si debbono disciplinare, & conservare*, Orvieto, Antonio Colaldi e Ventura Aquilini.
1599 MASSARI MALATESTA, Alessandro, *Compendio dell'eroica arte di cavalleria*, Venezia, a istanza di Francesco Bolzetta Libraro in Padova.

Manuscripts of the Sixteenth Century

XVI sec. CINQUINI, Lelio, *Il cavallo ammaestrato—Opera di Lelio Cinquini, nobile romano, Cameriero Secreto di Spada e Cappa della Santità di Nostro Signore Papa Paolo V*, diviso in Quattro Libri [the work comes to us from a manuscript of the early Seventeenth century].
XVI sec. CARACCIOLO, Pasquale, *Discorso de' freni, et de' maneggi*, Madrid, Biblioteca Nacional de España, BNE, mss. 7802.
XVI sec. FERRARO, Pirro Antonio, *Libro di Mariscalcheria* Madrid, Biblioteca Nacional de España di Madrid, BNM mss. Riservato 10116.
XVI sec. GRISONE, Federico, *Razze del Regno, raccolte in questo volume breve-

mente da federigo grisone gentilhuomo napoletano/ Dove appresso dona molti belli avisi convenienti alla cognitione de i polletri et al governo et reggere di ogni cavallo, Madrid, Biblioteca Nacional de España di Madrid, mss. 9246.

1598 *Bellissimi Secreti da Cavalli, di Pignatello. Diffinitione che vuol dir Arte veterali, o vero Marescalchena*, dated in-folio manuscript [it is listed as number 3785 in the catalogue of Biblioteca di J.B. Huzard's Library]. End of the Sixteenth-Beginning of the Sevententh century, RUGGIERI, Alfonso, *Ordine di cavalcare et amaistrare cavalli, dar loro lettione, secondo le qualità e dispositione di ciascheduno, cominciando da che son poledri*, Innsbruck, Universitäts-und Landesbibliothek für Tirol, cod. 782.

Seventeenth Century

1602 FERRARO, Pirro Antonio, *Cavallo frenato, diviso in quattro libri: Con discorsi notabili, sopra briglie, antiche, moderne, adornato di bellissime figure, & molte da lui inventate, insieme con alcune briglie, polache, e turchesche*, Napoli, Pace.

1606 DE GAMBOA, Don Giovanni, *Raggione dell'arte di cavalcare, nella quale si insegna quanto conviene di sapere ad un cavaliero a cavallo*, Per Gio. Antonio de Franceschi.

1607 MASSARI MALATESTA Alessandro, *Tractaus de modo equos fraenandi... cum diversorym fraenorum figuris*, Venetia.

1613 MASSARI MALATESTA, Alessandro, *Della ragione e modi d'imbrigliar Cavalli: con una copiosa raccolta di varie figure di Briglie, cioè, di Morsi, Guardie, Barbazzali, e Capezzoni*, Roma, Stef. Paolini [it is the Italian translation of the latin text published in 1607].

1621 MACETTI, Alfonso, *Regole de osservarsi nel cavalcare*, Augsburg, 1621.

1625 PALMIERI, Lorenzino, *Perfette regole et modi di cavalcare. Dove con chiarezza si mostra e con facilità s'insegna come si possi ridurre ogni cavallo all'intera perfettione: Et insieme si tratta della natura de' cavalli, si propongono le loro infermità e s'additano gli Rimedi per curarle*, Venetia, Paolo Frambotto.

1625 DE MONTE SIMONCELLI, Baldovino, *Cesarino ovvero dell'arte di cavalcare Dialogo*, Mantova, Aureli.

1630 D'AQUINO, Fra Giovanni Paolo, *Dell'uso del Piliere*, Vicenza, presso gli Heredi di Dominico Amodio [second edition *Disciplina del cavallo con l'uso del Piliere*, Udine, Schiratti, 1636].

1639 LIBERATI, Francesco, *La Perfettione del cavallo*, Roma, per Michele Hercole, (2 ed. Roma, 1669), in 4° [more than a treatise about horse riding this is a book dedicated to the care of the horse].

1650 GALIBERTO, Giovanni Battista, *Il cavallo da maneggio, ove si tratta della nobilissima virtù del..*, Vienna, Giacomo Kyrneri.

1685 ANONIMO, *Regole per ben cavalcare*, Venezia, (in 12°) [we know this work just through the mention of its bibliographic reference in Nicola Francesco Haym, *Biblioteca italiana, o sia Notizia, de' libri rari italiani divisa in quattro parti cioè istoria, poesia, prose, arti e scienze*, in Milano, appresso G. Galeazzi,

1773, Volume 2, p. 606].

1688 PERSA, Giovanni Battista, *Il cavallo ammaestrato*, Padova, nella Stamperia del Seminario, per Agostino Candiani.

1696 SANTAPAULINA, Nicola e Luigi, *L'arte del cavallo*, Padova, Stamperia del Seminario.

1699 TRUTTA, Gio. Battista, *Novello Giardino della prattica, ed esperienza*, Stamp.P.Sever.Boezio, Napoli,

Manuscripts of the Seventeenth Century

XVII secolo *Regola del cavalcare, da Papaleeni, cavallerizzo del gran duca di Toscana*, manoscritto in folio, 120 fogli, del XVII secolo (listed with the number 4693 in Huzard's Library catalogue).

Eighteenth Century

1711 D'ALESSANDRO, Giuseppe (Duca di Pescolanciano), *Pietra di Paragone dei Cavalieri, o Arte del cavalcare*, Napoli, D. A. Paolino (2 ed. *Opere di Giuseppe d'Alessandro duca di Pescolanciano*, Napoli, Antonio Muzio, 1723).

1723 ROSSELMINI, Niccolò, Il *cavallo perfetto: trattato in cui si descrive, quali esser debbano le qualità del cavallo perfetto, e con quai mezzi si arrivi a renderlo tale*, Venezia, Giuseppe Corona.

1730 ROSSELMINI, Niccolò, *Apologia del cavallo perfetto*, Siena, Francesco Quinza.

1733 MARINELLI, Giuseppe Antonio, *La Scuola moderna nel maneggio de' cavalli*, Bologna, Lelio Dalla Volpe.

1753 baron D'EISENBERG, *La perfezione e i difetti del cavallo, opera del barone d'Eisenberg, direttore e primo cavallerizzo dell'accademia di Pisa, dedicata alla Sacra Cesarea Real Maestà dell'Augustissimo Potentissimo Invittissimo Imperatore Francesco I Duca di Lorena e di Bar ec. Gran Duca di Toscana ec. ec. ec.*, Firenze, Giuseppe Allegrini [it is more a hippiatric treatise than a book about equitation. The author was German, but worked in Italy and the book was published in Italian].

1764 ROSSELMINI, Niccolò, *Dell'obbedienza del cavallo*, Livorno, Marco Coltellini.

1767 ROSSELMINI, Niccolò, *Lettera critica ed istruttiva di Niccolo Rosselmini*, Livorno, per Marco Coltellini in via grande.

1778 LOMBARDI, Vincenzo, *Modo facile, o sieno alcune brevi e principali regole per domare cavalli*, in Napoli, nella Stamperia Simoniana.

1785 INVERNIZZI, Filippo, *De Fraenis eorumque generibus et partibus apud veteres,* Roma, Monaldini.

1793 SAILER, Michele, *Del Cavalcare. Riflessioni critico-didascaliche,* Milano, Marelli.

1799 PASQUALI DI VENEZIA, Gio. Valerio, *Il perfetto cavallerizzo,* Ferrara.

Nineteenth Century

1802 MAZZUCCHELLI, Federigo, *Elementi di cavallerizza,* Milano, presso Pietro Agnelli librajo-stampatore in S. Margarita (new edition entitled *Scuola equestre,* Milano, presso Gio Pietro Giegler, Libraio sulla Corsia de' Servi, 1805).

1810 CAMPAGNOLA, Giovanni, *Sulla rigenerazione delle razze de'cavalli e sulla equitazione,* Mantova, Tip. Virgiliana.

1813 ARCELLAZZI, Stefano, *Lezioni di cavallerizza,* Modena, G. Vicenzi.

1823 CONTI, Enrico, *L'ipposiade o L'accademico equestre,* Stamperia Reale, Torino.

1825 LOCATELLI, Antonio, *Il perfetto cavaliere,* Milano, Fratelli Sonzogno Milano.

1843 LE MAIRE, Carlo, *Nuovo trattato d'equitazione,* Torino, Stamperia Sociale degli Artisti Tipografi.

1861 MINISTERO DELLA GUERRA, *Regolamento per l'esercizio e le evoluzioni della cavalleria,* Torino, Tip. dei Fratelli Fodratti.

1873 GLORIA, C.G., *Le resistenze e le difese del cavallo da sella, dal punto di vista dell'equitazione militare,* L, Torino, Beuf.

1878 CAGNI, Manfredo, *Nozioni elementari per la cavalleria,* Verona—Stab. tipo-litografico G. Vianini.

1881 ANGELINI, Achille, *Corso magistrale di equitazione saggio d'un maestro per l'istruzione degli allievi e delle maestre nelle ippiche discipline,* Firenze, Fratelli Bocca.

1883 PADERNI, Cesare, *Regole di equitazione sul modo di saltare e superare ostacoli,* Roma, A. Sommaruga.

1894 MARTINENGO CESARESCO, Eugenio (conte), *L'arte di cavalcare, con aggiunta, il cavallo attaccato alla carrozza,* Tip. G. Devoti.

Twentieth Century

1901 CAPRILLI, Federico, *Per l'equitazione di campagna* in "*Rivista di cavalleria,*" IV, nn. 1 e 2, gennaio e febbraio.

1901b CAPRILLI, Federico, *Due altre parole sull'equitazione di campagna* in "*Rivista di cavalleria,*" IV, n. 4, aprile.

1902 CAPRILLI, Federico, *Sul nuovo regolamento di equitazione* in "*Rivista di cavalleria,*" V, n. 2, febbraio.

1902b CAPRILLI, Federico, *Una replica,* in "*Rivista di cavalleria,*" IV, n.3, marzo.

1911 GIUBBILEI, Carlo, *Federico Caprilli, vita e scritti*, Roma, Casa Editrice Italiana.
1911 RODZANKO, Paolo, *La scuola di cavalleria italiana. Il nuovo metodo di equitazione di campagna e il suo insegnamento*, San Pietroburgo (ed. it. Milano, L. L. Edizioni Equestri, 1978).
1923 UBERTALLI, Ruggero, *Elementi di equitazione naturale*, Ferrara, Industrie Grafiche Italiane.
1937 BACCA, Baldo, *L'arte di Equitare*, Verona, Scuola tipografica Casa Buoni Fanciulli.

Treatises on horsemanship by foreign authors (quoted in this book)

1572 AGUILAR, Pedro de, *Tractado de la Cavalleria de la Gineta*, Hernando Dìaz, Sevilla.
1588 ANONYMOUS, *Gründlicher Bericht des Zäumens und ordentliche Austheilung der Mundstück und Stangen* (the work was published anonymously, but Georg Engelhard von Löhneysen, claims to be the author, commissioned by Augustus of Saxony).
1593 MARKHAM, Gervase, *A Discourse of Horsemanshippe*, London, Printed by I. C. for Richard Smith.
1607 MARKHAM, Gervase, *Cavelarice, Or The English Horseman: contayning all the Arte of Horsemanship*, London, Edward White.
1609 LÖHNEYSEN, Georg Engelhard von, *Cavalleria*, Rembling (printed by himself).
1610 LA BROUE, Salomon de, *Le Cavalerice François, composé par Salomon de La Broue,... Contenant les préceptes principaux qu'il faut observer exactement pour bien dresser les chevaux aux exercices de la carrière et de la campagne. Le tout divisé en trois livres. ... 3° édition, reveue et augmentée de beaucoup de leçons et figures par l'autheur*, Paris, A. l'Angelier (the frist edition was in 1593, but it is generally mentioned this second edition which was revised and enlarged by the author).
1620 LA NOUE, Pierre de, *La cavalerie françoise et italienne, ou L'art de bien dresser les chevaux, selon les preceptes des bonnes écoles des deux nations*, Strasbourg, chez Iac. de Heyden.
1625 PLUVINEL, Antoine de, *L'instruction du Roy en l'exercice de monter à cheval, par Messire Antoine de Pluvinel, son soubs gouverneur, conseiller en son Conseil d'Estat, Chambellan ordinaire, & son escuyer principal. Lequel respondant à sa Majesté luy faict remarquer l'excellence de sa méthode pour réduire les chevaux en peu de temps à l'obeyssance des justes proportions de tous les plus beaux airs & maneiges. Le tout enrichy de grandes figures en taille douce, représentent les vrayes & naisves actions des hommes & des chevaux en tous les airs, & maneiges, courses de Bague, rompre en lice, au Quintan, & combattre à l'espée, ensemble les figures ..., desseignées & gravées par Crispian de Pas le jeune*, Paris, M. Nivelle. [The Maneige Royal, Xenophon Press, 2010]

1650 MENOU DE CHARNIZAY, René de, *La Pratique du cavalier, ou L'Exercice de monter à cheval ....*, Paris: Guillaume & Jean Baptiste Loyson (la prima edizione è del 1612).

1657 CAVENDISH, William, (duke of Newcastle), *Methode et invention nouvelle de dresser les chevaux, par Guillaume Marquis et comte de Newcastle, etc.; oeuvre auquel on apprend a travailler les chevaux selon la nature, et parfaire la nature par la subtilité de l'art ; traduit de l'anglais de l'auteur*, Anvers, chez Jacques Van Mers.

1722 RIDINGER, Johann Elias, *L'Art de monter a cheval*, Augsbourg.

1727 EISENBERG, Baron d,› *Description du Manége Moderne dans sa perfection*, Paris (ristampato con il titolo *L'Art de monter a Cheval ou Description du Manege Moderne*, Le Haye, 1733 e successive).

1733 LA GUÉRINIÈRE, François Robichon de, *Ecole de Cavalerie, contenant la connoissance, l'instruction et la conservation du cheval*, Paris, Jacques Collombat. [Ecole de Cavalerie, Part II, Xenophon Press, 1992]

1733 OSSORIO Y VEGA, Manuel Alvares, *Manejo Real, en que se propone lo que deben saber los Cavalleros en esta facultad para llenar con la practica este gran nombre*, Madrid, Gabrièl Ramirez.

1734 SAUNIER, Gaspard de, *La parfaite connoissance des chevaux, leur anatomie, leurs bonnes et mauvaises qualitez, leurs maladies et les remedes qui y conviennent*, La Haye, chez Adrien Moetjens [written with his father Jean].

1734 RIDINGER, Johann Elias, *Le nouveau manège, représentant l'homme de cheval parfait dans tons ses exercices, invente et exposé en 26 planches. Expliquées en français, en allemand et en latin*, 2 Vol., Augsbourg.

1740 LA GUÉRINIÈRE, François Robichon de, *Éléments de cavalerie, contenant les principes propres à former un connaisseur & un homme de cheval*, Paris, J. Guérin.

1744 BOURGELAT, Claude, *Le nouveau Newcastle ou nouveau traité de cavalerie géométrique, théorique et pratique*, à Lausanne & à Geneve, chez Marc-Michel Bousquet et compagnie.

1749 SAUNIER, Gaspard de, *Les vrais principes de la cavalerie par Gaspard Saunier*, Amsterdam, chez Zacharie Châtelain.

1752 RIDINGER, Johann Elias, *Türkischer Pferdesaufputz sammt e. d. nöthigen Anmerkungen hierzu enthalten*, Augsbourg.

1756 SAUNIER, Gaspard de, *L'art De La Cavalerie Ou La Maniere De Devenier Bon Ecuyer.: Avec Une Idée Generale De Leurs Maladies*, Amsterdam and Berlin, Gaspard de Saunier chez Jean Neaulme.

1760 RIDINGER, Johann Elias, *Vorstellung und Beschreibung der Schul und Campagne Pferden nach ihren Lectionem, und in was für Gelegenheiten solche können gebraucht warden*, Augsbourg.

1761 RIDINGER, Johann Elias, *Description du Cheval selon ses poils principaux et leurs diverses divisions*, Augsbourg.

1761 RIDINGER, Johann Elias, *Remarques de Carousels*, Augsbourg.

1766 SIND, Johann. B. von, *Die Kunst Pferde zu zaumen und zu beschlagen*, Frankfurt, bei Heinrich Ludwig Brönner.

1766 SIND, Johann. B. von, *L'Art du Manège pris dans ses vrais principes*, Bonn.

1766a SIND, Johann. B. von, *Le Manuel du Cavalier qui renforme les connaissances nécessaires pour conserver le cheval en santé*, et., Paris, G. Desprez.

1766b SIND, Johann. B. von, *Sicher und geschwind heilender Pferde-Arzt*, Frankfurt.

1768 SIND, Johann. B. von, *Neue und sichere Lehrart, die Pferde in kurzer Zeit zu dressiren*, Frankfurt.

1768a SIND, Johann. B. von, *Völlstandige Abhandlung von der Rehkrankheit der Pferde, mit anatomischer Beschreibung des Vorderschenkels*, Frankfurt.

1769 DUPATY DE CLAM, Louis-Charles Mercier, *Pratique de l'équitation*, Paris, chez Lacombe.

1769 SIND, Johann. B. von, *Abhandlung der Pferdezucht und Anlegung der gestüte*, Frankfurt.

1770 SIND, Johann. B. von, *Churcollnischen Oberst an eines Cavallerie-regiments und ersten Stallmeisters Voltstandiger Unterricht in den Wissenschaften eines Stallmeisters*, Göttingen and Gotha.

1770a SIND, Johann. B. von, *Vollständiger Unterricht in den Wissenschaiten eines Stallmeisters*, Göttingen.

1771 DUPATY DE CLAM, Louis-Charles Mercier, *Traités sur l'équitation*, Paris, chez Lacombe.

1773 MOTTIN DE LA BALME, Augustin, *Essais sur l'équitation: ou principes raisonnés sur l'art de monter et de dresser les chevaux*, Amsterdam-Parigi, Jombert-Ruault.

1775 RIDINGER, Johann Elias, Anstellung der Pferde nach ihren Hauptfarben und verschiedene A*btheillungen*; Augsborug.

1776 DUPATY DE CLAM, Louis-Charles Mercier, *La Science et l'Art de l'Equitation*, Paris, Didot.

1766 MOTTIN DE LA BALME, Augustin, *Élémens de tactique pour la cavalerie*, Amsterdam-Parigi, Jombert-Ruault.

1778 MONTFAUCON DE ROGLES, Pierre-François, *Traité d'équitation*, Paris, Imprimerie Royale.

1790 ANDRADE, Manoel Carlos de, *Luz da liberal e nobre arte da cavallaria*, Lisboa, na Regia Officina Typografica.

1791 HÜNERSDORF, Ludwig, *Anleitung zu den natürlichsten und leichtesten*, Marburg, in der neuen akademischen Buchhandlung.

1833 BAUCHER, François, *Dictionnaire raisonné d'Équitation*, Rouen, Imprimé par D. Brière.

1834 D'AURE, Antoine Henri Philippe Léon Cartier, *Traité d'équitation*, Paris, Mme Leclère.

1842 BAUCHER, François, *Méthode d'équitation basée sur de nouveaux principes*, Paris, Impr. de Ve Dondey-Dupré.

1844 SEEGER, Louis, *System der Reitkunst*, Berlin, Herbig.

1850 SEEGER, Louis, *Züchtung, Erziehung, Ausbildung des Pferdes im systematischen Zusammenhange*, Berlin, Herbig.

1852 SEEGER, Louis, *Herr Baucher und seine Künste—Ein ernstes Wort an Deutschlands Reiter*, Berlin, Herbig.

1886 STEINBRECHT, Gustav, *Das Gymnasium des Pferdes*, Potsdam, Döring. [The Gymnasium of the Horse, Xenophon Press, 1994]
1887 PLINZNER, Paul, *System der Pferdegymnastik*, Potsdam.
1891 FAVEROT DE KERBRECH, François Nicolas Guy Napoléon, *Dressage méthodique du cheval de selle*, Paris, J. Rotschild Éditeur. [Methodical Dressage of the Riding Horse..., Xenophon Press, 2010]
1906 L'HOTTE, Alexis François *Questions équestres*, Paris, Librairie Plon.
1893 *Archivio storico per le province napoletane*, Deputazione napoletana di storia patria, Napoli, Detken & Rocholl e F. Giannini, Vol. 18, pp. 527–?
1990 *Stefano Guazzo e la Civil conversazione*, edited by G. Patrizi, Roma, Bulzoni.
2007 *À cheval! Ècuyers, amazones & cavaliers du XIVe au XXIe siècle*, edited by D. Roche e D. Reytier, Paris, Association pour l'académie équestre de Versailles.
2008 *Omaggio a Senofonte*, edited by M. Gennero, Atti del convegno tenutosi presso Il centro Internazionale del Cavallo alla Venaria Reale (15 novembre 2008), Collegno, Roberto Chiaramonte Editore.
2009 *Les Arts de l'équitation dans l'Europe de la Reinassance. VIIe colloque de l'Ecole nationale d'équitation au Chateau d'Oiron (4 et 5 octobre 2002)*, Arles, Actes Sud.
2009b *L'insegnamento dell'equitazione e della veterinaria alla Venaria Reale durante la Restaurazione*, Atti del convegno tenutosi presso Il centro Internazionale del Cavallo alla Venaria Reale (14 novembre 2009), edited by M. Gennero, Collegno, Roberto Chiaramonte.
2010 *Federico Grisone e l'arte equestre del Cinquecento*, edited by M. Gennero, Atti del convegno tenutosi presso Il centro Internazionale del Cavallo alla Venaria Reale, Collegno, Roberto Chiaramonte Editore.
2013 *Dal cavallo alle scuderie. Visioni iconografiche e rilevamenti architettonici*, atti del convegno internazionale (Frascati, 12 aprile 2013), edited by M. Fratarcangeli, Roma, Campisano Editore.

Bibliography

AGLIARDI, Danilo
    2008 La famiglia, in AA. VV., Villa Mazzucchelli. Arte e storia di una dimora del Settecento, Cinisello Balsamo, Silvana Editoriale, pp. 11–47.

ALBERTI, Leon Battista
    1991 *De equo animante—Il cavallo vivo*, edizione bilingue edited by A. Videtta, Napoli, Ce.S.M.E.T. Editrice.

ALDIMARI, Biagio
    1691 Historia genealogica della famiglia Carafa, Napoli, Giacomo Raillard.

ALFIERI, Francesco Ferdinando
    1640 *La scherma di Francesco Ferdinando Alfieri maestro d'arme dell'ill.ma Accademia Delia in Padova*, Padova, Sebastiano Sardi.

ALFIERI, Vittorio
    1967 *Vita*, edited by G. Dossena, Torino, Einaudi.

AMMIRATO, Scipione
    1580 *Delle famiglie nobili napoletane*, in Fiorenza, appresso Giorgio Marescotti.

ANDERSON, John Kinloch
    1961 *Ancient Greek Horsemanship*, Berkley & Los Angeles, University of California Press.

ANGIONI, Paolo
    2006 La letteratura equestre italiana del Cinquecento, testo della conferenza tenuta a Pinerolo nel Museo storico della Cavalleria il 17 giugno 2006 e pubblicato il 21 Nov. 2007, sul Forum Il Cavallo.
          (http://cavallo.forumer.it/).
    2009 Sintesi storica per trattare l'adattamento del Sistema natura
    le di equitazione alle attuali necessità dell'insegnamento
    dell'equitazione in Italia, in "Rivista di Cavalleria," n. 3, pp. 14–17.

ANHALT-KÖTHEN, Ludwig
    1859 *Descrizione di Firenze nell'anno 1598, di Lodovico principe di Anhalt*, compilata da Alfred von Reumont, di Aquisgrana in "Archivio storico italiano," nuova serie, tomo decimo, parte 1a, Firenze, G. P. Viesseux Editore.

ANONYMOUS
    1566 *Cavalerie della città di Ferrara. Che contengono il Castello di Gorgoferusa, il Monte di Feronia et il Tempio d'Amore*, Ferrara, F. Rossi.
    1805 *Necrologia: notizie di Federico Mazzucchelli*, in "Giornale dell'Italiana letteratura," Volume 10, pp. 281–282.
    1908 *Come lo imperatore Federico entrò in Napoli*, in Archivio storico per le province napoletane, Deputazione napoletana di storia patria, Napoli, Detken & Rocholl e F. Giannini, 1908, Vol. 33, pp. 481–?.
    1983 *Hippiatrìa. Due trattati emiliani di mascalcia del sec. XV*, edited by D. Trolli, Parma, Studio in Parmense.

ANTONELLI, Raoul
- 1992 Cavalieri dopo la Cavalleria. Indagine su autori e libri di equitazione tra '500 e '600, in AA. VV. Storici americani e Rinascimento italiano, Edizione 16 di Cheiron (Brescia Italy), edited by G. Chittolini, Mantova, Edizioni Centro Federico Odorici, pp. 177–195.
- 1994 Equitazione e veterinaria nelle antiche opere della Biblioteca del Quirinale, Segretariato generale della Presidenza della Repubblica, Servizio biblioteca e documentazione, Quaderni di documentazione, nuova serie, n. 7, Roma.
- 1997 Giostre, tornei, accademie: formazione e rappresentazione del valore cavalleresco, in AA. VV., I Farnese. Corti, guerra e nobiltà in antico regime, edited by P. Del Negro e C. Mozzarelli, Roma, Bulzoni, pp. 191–207.

ARQUINT, Patrizia,
- 2002 *"Gli ordini di cavalcare" di Federigo Grisone: nascita di un genere*, in "Milleottocentosessantanove. Bollettino a cura della Società per la Biblioteca Circolante di Sesto Fiorentino," n. 28, 2002, pp. 5–8.
(http://www.arquint.it/Home/articoli/grisone)
- 2004 *"Poi che ponesti mano alla predella." Studio sui freni per cavalli ai tempi di Dante*, "Studi di Filologia Italiana," LXII, pp. 5–90.
- 2010 *Federico Grisone: una prima biografia*, in AA. VV., 2010, pp.47–75.

BALDASSARRI, Guido
- 1985 *Cavalerie della città di Ferrara*, in "Schifanoia," 1, pp. 100–126

BALESTRACCI, Duccio
- 2001 *La festa in armi. Giostre, tornei e giochi nel Medioevo*, Roma-Bari, Laterza.

BANDELLO, Matteo
- 2011 *Novelle*, edited by E. Menetti, Milano, Garzanti.

BARRY, Jean-Claude
- *2005 Traité des Airs relevés*, Paris, Belin.

BARTABAS
- 2010 *La leçon de l'écuyer*, Avignon, Editions Universitaires d'Avignon.

BEDONNI, Tiziano
- *Il cavallo di razza lipizzana. Dati storici*, pubblicato sul sito dell'Associazione Italiana Allevatori (A.I.A.) all'indirizzo:
(http://www.aia.it/tecnico/equini/a_lipizzano.htm)

BELLONCI, Maria
- 1939 *Lucrezia Borgia*, Milano, Mondadori (si cita dall'edizione del 2011).

BELLUZZI, Amedeo
- 1998 *Palazzo Te a Mantova*, Modena, Franco Cosimo Panini.

BERNARDONI, Andrea
- 2007 *Leonardo e il monumento equestre a Francesco Sforza*, Firenze, Giunti Editore.

BIANCHI, Paola
- 2010 *Gentiluomo e cavaliere. Virtù e arti cavalleresche nel XVI secolo*, in AA. VV., 2010, pp. 33–45.

BLADO, Antonio
- 1565 *Descritione de la giostra fatta da l'ill.mo et ecc.mo Signor Conte Annibale Alta*

Temps et da altri Signori et Cavalieri In Roma Nel Teatro di Belvedere. Il Carnevale De l'Anno, MDLXV, In Roma, per Antonio Blado, impressor camerale.

BOCCACCIO, Giovanni,
1980 *Decameron*, edited by V. Branca, Torino, Einaudi.

BONIFACIO di Calabria
1988 *La Pratica di Maestro Bonifazio dei morbi naturali e accidentali dei cavalli*, trascrizione edited by P. Di Pietro, presentazione di L. Gianoli, Firenze, Nardini.

BRAGANCE, Diogo de
1976 *L'equitation de tradition française*, Paris, Odege (2ᵉ ed. Paris, Belin, 2005) [*Dressage in the French Tradition*, Xenophon Press 2011].

BRANTÔME, Pierre de Bourdeille
1981 *Dames galantes*, edited by P. Pia, Paris, Gallimard.

BRIDGES, Mike
2010 *The art of making a California-style vaquero bridle horse*, King City CA, Mike & Jill Briges.

CANDIDA GONZAGA, Berardo
1875 *Memorie delle famiglie nobili delle province meridionali d'Italia*, Napoli, Stab. tip. del cav. G. de Angelis e figlio.

CARDINI, Franco
1987 *Quell'antica festa crudele. Guerra e cultura della guerra dall'età feudale alla grande rivoluzione*, Milano, Il Saggiatore.

CASTIGLIONE, Baldassarre
1528 *Il libro del Cortegiano*, in Venezia, nelle Case d'Aldo Romano e Andra d'Asolo suo suocero (*Il Cortigiano*, edited by A. Quondam, Milano, Mondadori, 2002).

CHASTEL, André,
1995 *Luigi d'Aragona. Un cardinale del Rinascimento in viaggio per l'Europa*, Bari, Laterza.

CHATENET, Monique
2002 *Cheval et diplomatie a la cour de France sous François Iᵉʳ et Henry II: le témoignage des ambassadeurs de mantoue*, in AA. VV., 2009, pp. 48–67.

CHÉNIÈRE, Ernest
2002 *Étude des mors au XVIᵉ et XVIIᵉ siècles dans les traités de Pavari, Fiaschi, La Broue et La Noue*, in AA. VV., 2009, pp. 79–92.

CHRISTIAN, Arthur
1907 *L'art equestre à Paris; tournois, joutes et carrousels, académies, courses et cirques...*, Paris, G. Roustan, Champion.

CERVANTES, Miguel de
2002 *Novelle esemplari*, edited by P. L. Crovetto, tr. it di P. Gorla, Torino, Einaudi.

CIMMINO, Alessandro
2009 *I cavalli di Don Henricus,* in "Il Ponte," a. XXI, n. 3, marzo, pp. 42–43.

CIRNI, Anton Francesco
1565 *Narratione del meraviglioso Torneo rappresentato dall'eccellentissimo Sig. Conte*

Annibale Altaemps General Governatore di Santa Chiesa. Con molti illustrissimi Cavalieri e Gentil'huomini, in Roma nel nuovo Teatro di Belvedere a V di Marzo MDLXV, stampata in Roma.

COCO, Alessandra – GUALDO, Riccardo
    2008 *Cortesia e cavalleria, la tradizione ippiatrica in volgare nelle corti italiane tra Trecento e Quattrocento*, in I saperi *nelle corti. Knowledge at the courts*, Firenze, Sismel-Edizioni del Galluzzo, (Micrologus XVI), pp. 125–152.

CONTARINO, Luigi
    1569 *La Nobiltà di Napoli in dialogo, del... padre fra Luigi Contarino*, in Napoli, G. Cacchii.

CORTESI, Paolo (Paulus Cortesius)
    1510 De *cardinalatu*, in castro Cartesio, Symeon Nicolai Nardi imprimebat.

CROCE, Benedetto
    1922 *La Spagna nella vita italiana durante la Rinascenza*, 2ª ed. riveduta, Bari, Laterza.

D'AFFLITTO, Eustachio
    1782 *Memorie degli scrittori del regno di Napoli*, Napoli, Stamperia Simoniana.

D'ALEMBERT, Jean-Baptiste Le Rond
    1715–65 *Académie*, in *Encyclopédie, ou Dictionnaire raisonné des sciences, des arts et de métiers...*, Paris, Briasson, David, Le Breton, Durand, Tome I, p. 51–57.

D'ANDRADE, Fernando Sommer
    1991, *La tauromachie équestre au Portugal*, Paris, Michel Chandeigne.

D'ORGEIX, Jean
    2007 *Dresser c'est simple*, Paris, Belin.

DEBLAISE, Philippe
    2002 *Itinérarire du livre dans l'Europe de la Reinassance*, in AA. VV., pp. 253–265.
    2006 *Les chevaux de Venafro*, Monaco, Editions du Rocher.
    2009 *Le manuscrit de Pignatelli*, Editions du Rocher.

DECARPENTRY, Albert
    1948 *Baucher et son école*, Paris, Lamarre. [*Baucher and his school*, Xenophon Press, 2011]

DE CAVI, Sabina
    2013 *Emblematica cittadina: il cavallo e i Seggi di Napoli in epoca spagnuola (XVI–XVII sec.)*, in AA. VV. 2013.

DEL MONTE, Pietro
    1509 *Exercitiorum atque artis militaris collectanea*, Mediolani, per Ioannem Angelum Scinzenzeler.

DEL NEGRO, Piero
    2008 L'Accademia Delia e gli esercizi cavallereschi della nobiltà padovana nel Seicento e Settecento, in Il gioco e la guerra nel secondo millennio, edited by P. Del Negro e G. Ortalli, Treviso-Roma, Edizioni Fondazione Benetton Studi e Ricerche /Viella (Ludica: collana di storia del gioco, Vol. IX) pp. 35–67.

DOMENICHELLI, Mario
 2002 *Cavaliere e gentiluomo. Saggio sulla cultura aristocratica in Europa (1513–1915)*, Roma, Bulzoni.

DOUCET, Corinne
 2007 *Les académies d'art équestre dans la France d'Ancien régime*, Paris, Edilivre.

DUBOST, Jean-François
 1997 *La France italienne, 16e–17e siècle*, Paris, Aubier.

DUODO, Pietro,
 1598 *Relazione di Francia letta in Senato il 12 e 13 gennaio*, in AA.VV., *Le Relazioni degli ambasciatori veneti al Senato*, edited by. E. Albèri, Firenze, Società Editrice Fiorentina, 1863, vol. 15, pp. 73–236.

ERSPAMER, Francesco
 1988 *Il torneo nella trattatistica quattro-cinquecentesca*, in AA. VV., *Giostre e tornei nell'Italia di Antico regime: la società in costume* (Foligno, Palazzo Alleori Ubaldi, 27 sett.—29 nov. 1986), Foligno, Ed. dell'Arquata, 1988, pp. 27–36.

FERRARA, Daniele
 2013 *"Fè dipignere del vivo i più perfetti e più graditi cavalli":Enrico Pandone e il ciclo affrescato nel Castello di Venafro*, in AA.VV. 2013.

FLAUBERT, Gustave
 1980 *L'educazione sentimentale. Storia di un giovane*, tr. it. Vladimiro Cajoli, Torino, Einaudi.

FILIPPINI, Nadia Maria
 2006 *Donne sulla scena politica: dalle Municipalità del 1797 al Risorgimento*, in AA. VV., *Donne sulla scena pubblica: società e politica in Veneto tra Sette e Ottocento*, edited by N.M. Filippini, Milano, Franco Angeli, pp. 81–137.

FIZET, George
 2010 *Journal de dressage*, Paris, Belin.

FONTAINE, Marie Madeleine
 2002 *Le voltage à cheval chez Pietro Del Monte (1492–1509), Rabelais (1535), et Montaigne (1580–1592)*, in AA. VV. 2009, pp. 197–252.

FRADDOSIO, Giuseppe Maria
 2010 Sulle tracce del Corsiero Napolitano, in Eos Cavalli, n. 7
 (http://www.eosrivista.com/103.asp?id_articolo=44)
 2010 *Il Corsiero Napolitano*, testo pubblicato sul sito CavallodelleMurge.it
 (http://www.cavallodellemurge.it/Sulle%20tracce%20del%20Corsiero%20Napolitano.htm)

FRANCHET D'ESPÈREY, Patrice
 2002 *L'équitation italienne, sa trasmission et son évolution en France au temps de la Reinassance*, in AA.VV., 2009, pp. 158–182.
 2007 *La main du Maître. Réflexions sur l'héritage équestre*, Paris, Odile Jacob.

FRANCHINI, Maria—MARESCA Giuseppe
 2003 *La fabuleuse aventure du cheval napolitain*, Paris, Zulma.

FRATARCANGELI, Margherita
  2013 *«La perfettione del cavallo.» Manuali e trattati ad uso e consumo di uno status symbol*, in AA.VV. 2013.

GAREFFI, Andrea
  1982 *Cavallerie ferraresi*, in *La corte e lo spazio: Ferrara estense*, Roma, Bulzoni, pp. 467–487.

GENNERO, Mario
  2001 *Introduzione*, in Pignatelli, 2001, pp. XI–L.
  2002 *Jean Baptiste Pignatelli, maître de Pluvinel*, in AA.VV., 2009, pp. 151–157.
  2004 *Venaria Reale. Otto Wagner e la regia scuola militare di equitazione*, Collegno, Roberto Chiaramonte.

GRANGE, Yves
  2002 *La mise en cour des chevaliers*, in AA. VV. 2009, pp. 318–327.

GUALDO, Riccardo
  2005 *Ippiatria* in *Enciclopedia Federiciana*, Roma, Istituto dell'Enciclopedia Italiana, Vol. II, pp. 81–86.

HALE, John R.
  1985 *War and society In Reinassance Europe. 1450–1620*, Leicestr University Press and Fontana Paperbacks, Leicester, (tr. it. *Guerra e società nell'Europa del Rinascimento*, Bari, Laterza 1987).

HENRIQUET, Michelle – DURAND, Catherine
  1991, *Gymnase et dressage*, Paris, Vigot.

HERNANDO SÁNCHEZ, Carlos José
  1998 *La gloria del cavallo. Saber ecuestre y cultura caballeresca en el reino de Napóles durante el siglo XVI*, in AA. VV. *Actas del Congreso Internacional: Felipe II (1527–1598). Europa y la Monarquía Católica (UAM, 20–23 de abril de 1998)*, coord. J. Martínez Millán, Madrid, Parteluz, pp. 277–310.

HUTT, Frederick Henry
  1887 *Works on horses and equitation. A bibliographical record of hippology*, London, Bernard Quaritch.

HUYGHE, Edith et René
  1988 *Léonard de Vinci. Le cheval et la puissance*, Lausanne, Caracole.

ILARI, Virgilio,
  2011 *Scrittori militari del XV–XVIII secolo*, Roma, Litosroma.

LAMI, Lucio
  1983 *Quando l'Italia andava a cavallo*, Milano, Edizioni Equestri.
  2009 *Le passioni del dragone. Cavalli e donne: Caprilli campione della Belle Époque*, Milano, Mursia.

LAWE, Kari
  2005 L'alta *scuola equestre aragonese. I re aragonesi di Napoli e l'alta scuola equestre*, in "Eos," editore Fondazione Emilio Bernardelli, Anno 4, n. 10, pp. 9–18.

LEBALANC, P.
  1842 *Catalogue des livres, dessins et estampes de la bibliothèque de feu m. J.-B. Huzard*, Paris, Imprimerie et librairie de m.me Ve Bouchard Huzard, vol. I–III.

LEONARDO da VINCI
    1998 *Codice Arundel 263 nella British Library*, Edizione in facsimile edited by C. Pedretti, Giunti, Firenze.

LOCH, Sylvia
    1990 *Dressage. The art of classical riding*, London, Swann Hill Press.

L'HOTTE, Alexis François
    1905 *Un officier de cavalerie*, Paris, Librairie Plon.

LULLO, Raimondo
    1994 *Libro dell'Ordine della Cavalleria*. ediz.italiana con testo catalano a fronte di G.Allegra, Carmagnola, Arktos Edizioni.

MALACARNE, Giancarlo
    1995 *Il mito dei cavalli gonzagheschi. Alle origini del purosangue*, Verona, Editrice Promoprint.

MANZI, Pietro
    1973 *La tipografia napoletana nel '500: annali di Giovanni Paolo Suganappo, Raimondo Amato, Giovanni de Boy, Giovanni Maria Scotto e tipografi minori : (1533–1570)*, Firenze, Olschki.

MARESCA, Giuseppe e FRANCHINI, Maria
    2002 *La race napolitaine: origines historiques et réhabilitation*, in AA.VV., 2009, pp. 24–36.

MAYLANDER, Michele
    1926–30 *Storia delle Accademie d'Italia*, Bologna-Trieste, Cappelli, 5 vol. (rist. anastatica Bologna, Forni, 1976).

MAZZAROLLI ANCILLOTTO, M. T.,
    1931 *L'Accademia Delia. Storia delle Accademie d'Italia*, (1608–1931), Padova, Tipografia del Seminario, 1931.

MAZZATINTI, Giuseppe
    1897 *La biblioteca dei Re d'Aragona*, Rocca San Casciano, Licinio Cappelli.

MAZZELLA, Scipione
    1586 *Descrittione del Regno di Napoli*, Napoli, Gio. Battista Cappelli.

MAZZOLENI, Giancarlo
    2002 *Ogni cavallo dee hauere lo suo cavaliere: a chaque cheval son cavalier*, in AA.VV., 2009, pp. 37–43.

MENNESSIER DE LA LANCE, Gabriel-René
    1915–21 *Essai de Bibliographie Hippique donnant la description détaillée des ouvrages publiés ou traduits en latin et en français sur le Cheval et la Cavalerie avec de nombreuses biographies d'auteurs hippiques*, Paris: Lucien Dorbon.

MIOLA, Alfonso
    1878 *Le scritture in volgare dei primi tre secoli della lingua ricercate nei codici della Biblioteca Nazionale di Napoli*, in "Il Propugnatore," XI, pp. ??.

MONTAIGNE, Michel de
    1966 *Saggi*, edited by Fausta Garavini, Milano, Adelphi.
    2010 *Viaggio in Italia*, tr. di E. Camesasca, Milano, Rizzoli.

MONTEILHET, André
   1979 *Les Maîtres de l'oeuvre équestre*, Arles, Actes Sud (nuova ed. 2009).

MORELLI di POPOLO, Carlo Alberto
   1980 *La scuola di cavalleria di Pinerolo*, Milano, L.L. Edizioni Equestri.

MORI, Elisabetta
   2011 *L'onore perduto di Isabella de' Medici*, Milano, Garzanti.

MORRA, Gennaro
   1985 *Una dinastia feudale. I Pandone di Venafro*, Campobasso, Edizioni Enne.

MORRA, Gennaro—VALENTE, Franco
   1993 *Il Castello di Venafro. Storia, arte, architettura*, Campobasso, Edizioni Enne.

MOSCHINI, Giovanni Antonio
   1806 *Della letteratura veneziana del secolo XVIII fino a' nostri giorni...*, Venezia, dalla stamperia Palese.

MUTINI, Claudio
   1979 *Baldassarre Castiglione*, in AA.VV., *Dizionario Biografico degli Italiani*, Roma, Istituto dell'Enciclopedia Italiana, Vol. XXII, pp. 53–68.

NEYLAND, Ann
   2008 *The Kikkuli method of Horse training*, Mermaid Beach, Smith and Stirling.

OLIVEIRA, Nuno
   1991 *Principes classiques de l'art de dresser les chevaux*, in *L'art equestre*, Paris, Editions Crepin-Leblond.

OREFICE, Giorgio
   1966 *L'accademia Delia di Padova*, estratto delle *Memorie dell'Accademia Patavina di SS. LL. AA. Classe di scienze morali, lettere e arti*, Vol. LXXVIII (1965–1966), Padova, Società Cooperativa Tipografica, pp. 241–294.

PARKER, Geoffrey
   1988 *The military revolution. Military innovation and the rise of the West. 1500–1800*, Cambridge-New York, Cambridge University Press (tr. it. *La rivoluzione militare. Le innovazioni militari e il sorgere dell'Occidente*, Bogna, Il Mulino, 1990).

PASSARO, Giuliano
   1785 *Storie in forma di giornali*, editi da V. Altobelli, Napoli, Vincenzo Orofino.

PATRIZI, Giorgio
   1984 *Il libro del Corteggiano e la trattatistica sul comportamento*, in AA.VV., *Letteratura italiana*, edited by A. Asor Rosa, Torino, Einaudi, pp. 855–890.
   1993 *Galateo di Giovanni della Casa*, in AA.VV., *Letteratura Italiana*, edited by A. Asor Rosa, Torino, Einaudi, Vol. II (dal Cinquecento al Settecento) pp. 453–477.

PECO, Luigi
   1998 *I Bordiga: Benedetto e Gaudenzio Bordiga, incisori e incisori-cartografi*, Borgosesia, Valsesia Editrice.

PEREIRA, Carlos Henriques,
   2002 *Le traité du roi D. Duarte: l'équitation portugaise a l'aube de la Reinassance*, in

AA. VV. 2009, pp. 140 – 150.

2003 *Etude du premier traite d'equitation portugais. livro da ensinanca de bem cavalgar toda sela*, Paris, L'Harmattan.

PERINI, Leandro

1983 *Libri e lettori nella Toscana del Cinquecento*, in AA.VV., *Firenze e la Toscana dei Medici nell'Europa del 500*, Firenze, L. Olschki, 1983, pp. 109–131.

PIERI, Piero

1952 *Il Rinascimento e la crisi militare italiana*, Torino, Einaudi.

PIGNATELLI, Giovanni Battista

2001 *L'arte veterale. Sopra il medicare et altri secreti bellissimi de' cavalli*, edited by P. Arquint e M. Gennero, Bracciano, Equilibri.

PODHAJASKY, Alois

1965 *Die klassische reitkunst*, Mümchen, Nymphenburger Verlagshandlung GmbH (tr. ingl., *The complete training of Horse and Rider. In the principles of classical Horsemanship*, Chatsworth, Wilshire books Company, 1967).

PONTAYMERY, Alexandre de

1595 *L'Academie Ov Institvtion De la Noblesse Françoise, où toutes les vertues requises à vn Seigneur de Marque sont deduites, auec vne curieuse recerche [sic] des plus belles & riches matieres qui se puissent tirer des scices diuines & humaines*, Chez Iamet Mettayer & Pierre L'Huillier.

PORSIA, Franco

1986 *I cavalli del Re*, Fasano, Schena Editore.

PUDDU, Raffaele

1982 *Il soldato gentiluomo. Autoritratto di una società guerriera: la Spagna del Cinquecento*, Bologna, Il Mulino.

QUONDAM, Amedeo,

1982 *L'Accademia*, in *Letteratura italiana, vol. I Il letterato e le Istituzioni*, Torino, Einaudi, pp. 823–898.

2003 *Cavallo e cavaliere. L'armatura come seconda pelle del gentiluomo moderno*, Roma, Donzelli.

2010 *Forma del vivere. L'etica del gentiluomo e i moralisti italiani*, Bologna, Il Mulino.

RABER, Karen L. e TUCKER, Treva J.

2005 *The Culture of the Horse. Status, Discipline, and Identity in the Early Modern World*, New York, Palgrave MacMillan.

ROCHE, Daniel

1989 *La culture des apparences*, Paris, Fayard (*Il linguaggio della moda. Alle origini dell'industria dell'abbigliamento*, tr. it. di S. Luzzato, Torino, Einaudi, 1991).

2007 *Dei cavalli e degli uomini. Per una ricerca storica sulla cultura equestre*, in "Società & Storia," anno XXX, luglio settembre, 2007, pp. 453–468.

2007a *Le cheval et les loisirs (XIVe–XXIe siècle)*, in AA.VV., 2007, pp. 9–29.

2011 *La gloire et la puissance. Histoire de la culture équestre XVIe–XIXe siècle*, Paris, Fayard.

ROSSO, Gregorio
  1635 *Historia delle cose di Napoli sotto l'impero di Carlo V*, Napoli, Gio. Domenico Montanari.

RUFFO, Giordano
  1999 *Nelle scuderie di Federico II imperatore, ovvero L'arte di curare il cavallo*, edited by M.A. Causati Vanni, Editrice Vela, Velletri.
  2002 *Libro della mascalcia*, edited by P. Crupi, Soveria Mannelli, Rubettino Editore.

SAUREL, Etienne
  1971 *Histoire de l'équitation, des origines à nos jours*, Paris, Stock.

SCALI, Marion
  2009 *Ils ont inventé l'équitation. De Grisone à Ray Hunt*, Paris, Belin.

SCURATI, Antonio
  2006 *Il rumore sordo della battaglia*, Milano, Bompiani

SESTILI, Antonio
  2006 *L'equitazione nella Grecia antica. I trattati equestri di Senofonte e i frammenti di Simone*, Firenze, Atheneum.
  2012 *Cavalli e cavalieri nel mondo antico*, Roma, Società Editrice Dante Alighieri.

SENOFONTE
  2007 *L'arte della cavalleria. Il manuale del comandante della cavalleria*, edited by G. Cascarino, Rimini, Il Cerchio.

SHAKESPEARE, William
  1992 *Il mercante di Venezia*, tr. It. Agostino Lombardo, Milano, Feltrinelli.

SILVESTRI, Goffredo
  2006 *I bronzi del Giambologna*, in "la Repubblica," 26 aprile.

TAMALIO, Raffaele
  1994 *Federico Gonzaga alla corte di Francesco I: nel carteggio privato con Mantova (1515–1517)*, Paris, Champion,

TASSO, Torquato
1958   *Il Minturno overo della bellezza, in Dialoghi*, edited by E. Raimondi, Firenze, Sansoni, 1958, Vol. II.

TEBALDI, Dino – VINCENZI, Luigi – LOLLI, Stefano
  1992 *Ferrara e il Palio*, Ferrara, Vicentini ed.

TESIO, Federico
  1947 *Il purosangue: animale da esperimento*, Milano Editoriale Sportiva (rist. *Il purosangue: animale da esperimento. Tocchi in penna al galoppo* Milano, Ulrico Hoepli, 1984).

THOUROUDE, Nicolas
  2007 *Les prémices d'une equitation ludique à l'aube de l'epoque modern (XIVe–XVe siècle)*, in AA.VV., 2007, pp. 33–47.

TOSI, Mario
  1945 *Il torneo di Belvedere in Vaticano e i tornei in Italia nel Cinquecento*, Roma, Edizioni di Storia e Letteratura.

TUCKER, Treva J.
    2007 *From destrier to danseur: the role of the horse in early modern French noble identity*, a dissertation presented to the Faculty of the Graduate School University of Southern California.

VAN ORDEN, Kate
    2002 *Chorégraphies courtoises et militaires*, in AA. VV. 2009, pp. 388–405.

VASARI, Giorgio
    1857 *Le vite de' più eccellenti pittori. Scultori ed architetti*, Firenze, Le Monnier.

VENEZIANI SANTONIO, Giuseppe
    1996 *Storia dell'Equitazione Italiana. Volume I. 1862–1943*, Alessandria, Edizioni dell'Orso.

VIGILANTE, Magda
    1985 *Giuseppe d'Alessandro*, in AA.VV., *Dizionario Biografico degli Italiani*, Roma, Istituto dell'Enciclopedia Italiana, Vol. XXXI.

Table of Illustrations

Chapter I

page 37 *Brands of breed of the dukes of Mantua*, from Francesco Liberati, *La Perfettione del cavallo*, Roma, per Michele Hercole, 1639, p. 93.

page 46 *Master and disciple* in Pirro Antonio Ferraro, *Cavallo frenato*, Napoli, Pace, 1602, Libro II, p. 41.

Chapter II

page 53 Carlo Ruini, *Anatomia del cavallo infermita et suoi rimedii. Opera nuova, degna di qualsivoglia prencipe, & cavaliere, & molto necessaria à filosofi, medici, cavalerizzi, & mar escalchi, del signor Carlo Ruini, ... Adornata di bellissime figure, le quali dimostrano tutta l'anatomia di esso cavallo. Divisa in due volumi...*, Venetia, Appresso Fioravante Prati, 1618, p. 141.

Chapter III

page 69 Abraham van Diepenbeeck, *Neapolitan Courser, in* William Cavendish of Newcastle, *Méthode et invention nouvelle dans l'art de dresser les chevaux, par le très-noble, haut, et très-puissant Prince Guillaume Marquis et Comte de Newcastle*, 2e ed., Londres, J. Brindley, 1737, tav. 9.

page 76 *Neapolitan horse*, in Baron D'Eisenberg, *Description du Manege Moderne dans sa perfection*, Paris, 1727, tav. IV.

Chapter IV

page 81 *Coat of arms of the Grisone family*, in Scipione Mazzella Napolitano, *Descrittione del Regno di Napoli*, Napoli, Gio. Battista Cappelli,1586, p. 716.

page 83 Federigo Grisone, Ordini di cavalcare, Giovan Paolo Suganappo, 1550 Fronispiece

page 89 *"Cannon" bit*, in Federigo Grisone, *Ordini di cavalcare*, Giovan Paolo Suganappo,1550.

page 91 *Ditch for the training to the passade*, in Pierre de La Noue, *La cavalerie françoise et italienne, ou l'art de bien dresser les chevaux...*, Lyon, Claude Morillon/ Strasbourg: Jacob de Heyden, 1620. p. 37.

page 93 *First layout of the "torni,"* in Grisone, *Ordini di cavalcare*, Napoli, Giovan Paolo Suganappo, 1550, p. 55r.

page 100 "Chiappone" bit in Federigo Grisone, *Ordini di cavalcare Ordini di cavalcare*, Giovan Paolo Suganappo, 1550.

page 102 "Scaccia" bit, in Federico Grisone, *Ordini di cavalcare*, Giovan Paolo Suganappo, 1550.

Chapter V

page 107 Cesare Fiaschi, *Trattato dell'imbrigliare, atteggiare e ferrare cavalli*, Bologna, Anselmo Giaccarelli, 1556, frontispiece.

page 111 *Capriole*, in Cesare Fiaschi, *Trattato dell'imbrigliare, atteggiare e ferrare cavalli*, Bologna, Anselmo Giaccarelli, 1556, p. 126.

page 113 *One step and a jump*, in Cesare Fiaschi, *Trattato dell'imbrigliare, atteggiare e ferrare cavalli*, Bologna, Anselmo Giaccarelli, 1556, p. 119.

page 117 *The workshop of a bit maker* in Cesare Fiaschi, *Trattato dell'imbrigliare, atteggiare e ferrare cavalli*, Bologna, Anselmo Giaccarelli, 1556.

page 119 *"Fiasco" bit* in Cesare Fiaschi, *Trattato dell'imbrigliare, atteggiare e ferrare cavalli*, Bologna, Anselmo Giaccarelli, 1556, p. 51.

page 121 *Rider performing in front of a prince*, in Cesare Fiaschi, *Trattato dell'imbrigliare, atteggiare e ferrare cavalli*, Bologna, Anselmo Giaccarelli, 1556, p. 86.

page 127 *Blacksmith's forge*, in Cesare Fiaschi, *Trattato dell'imbrigliare, atteggiare e ferrare cavalli*, Bologna, Anselmo Giaccarelli, 1556, p. 123.

page 128 *Horseshoes*, in Cesare Fiaschi, *Trattato dell'imbrigliare, atteggiare e ferrare cavalli*, Bologna, Anselmo Giaccarelli, 1556, p. 164.

Large Images

p. 129 Giulio Romano e aiuti, View of the Horses' Hall, 1526-1528, Palazzo Te, Mantova (courtesy of the Municipality of Mantua)

p. 130 Paolo Uccello, Battle of San Romano, detail of Niccolo Mauruzi da Tolentino unseating Bernardino della Ciarda (1438-1440), Florence, Museo degli Uffizi (license of Ministero dei Beni e delle attività culturali e del turismo).

p. 131 Paolo Uccello, Battle of San Romano. Niccolo Mauruzi da Tolentino unseating Bernardino della Ciarda (1438-1440), Firenze, Museo degli Uffizi (license of Ministero dei Beni e delle attività culturali e del turismo).

p. 132 Anonymous, The bay Stella, fresco, Fifteenth cent., Castello Pandone, Venafro (Is) (license by Ministero dei beni e delle attività culturali e del turismo – Direzione per i beni culturali e paesaggistici del Molise - Soprintendenza per i beni storici, artistici ed etnoantropologici del Molise)

p. 133 Anonymous, The bay Stella, fresco, Fifteenth cent., Castello Pandone, Venafro (Is) (license by Ministero dei beni e delle attività culturali e del turismo – Direzione per i beni culturali e paesaggistici del Molise - Soprintendenza per i beni storici, artistici ed etnoantropologici del Molise)

p. 134 Anonymous, The gray Scorbone, fresco, Fifteenth cent., Castello Pandone, Venafro (Is) (license of Ministero dei beni e delle attività culturali e del turismo – Direzione per i beni culturali e paesaggistici del Molise - Soprintendenza per i beni storici, artistici ed etnoantropologici del Molise).

p. 135 Anonymous, The gray Scorbone (detail of the head and bit), fresco, Fifteenth cent., Castello Pandone, Venafro (Is) (license of Ministero dei beni e delle attività culturali e del turismo – Direzione per i beni culturali e paesaggistici del Molise - Soprintendenza per i beni storici, artistici ed etnoantropologici del Molise).

p. 136 Giulio Romano, The horse Dario(detail), 1528 ca., fresco, Palazzo Te, Mantova (courtesy of the Municipality of Mantua)

Chapter VI

page 139 Claudio Corte, *Il cavallarizzo*, Venezia, Giordano Ziletti, 1562, frontispiece.

page 147 *Layout of the "rote,"* in *Il cavallarizzo*, Venezia, Giordano Ziletti, 1562, p. 61v.

page 149 *Layaout of the "caragolo,"* in *Il cavallarizzo*, Venezia, Giordano Ziletti, 1562, p. 62v.

page 150 *Layout of the "esse serrato,"* in *Il cavallarizzo*, Venezia, Giordano Ziletti, 1562, p. 63r. and *Layout of the "serpeggiare,"* in *Il cavallarizzo*, Venezia, Giordano Ziletti, 1562, p. 64r.

page 151 Johann Jacobi von Wallhausen, *Ritterkunst: Darinnen begriffen, I. Ein trew-*

hertziges Warnung- schreiben wegen deß Betrübten Zustands jetziger Christenheit, Franckfurt am Main, printed by P. Jacobi for L. Iennis, 1616, cap. 2.

Chapter VII

page163 Colt taming, da Giovan Battista Ferraro, *Razze, disciplina del cavalcare ed altre cose pertinenti ad esercitio così fatto*, in Pirro A. Ferraro, *Cavallo frenato*, Napoli, Pace, 1602, Libro I, p. 19.

page 165 *Horse conducted by hand*, in Pirro Antonio Ferraro, *Cavallo frenato*, Napoli, Pace, 1602, Libro I, p. 1

page 167 *"Scaccia" bit with chiseled shanks*, in Pirro Antonio Ferraro, *Cavallo frenato*, Napoli, Pace, 1602, Libro I, p. 57.

page 169 *Hungarian and Polish bridles*, in Pirro Antonio Ferraro, *Cavallo frenato*, Napoli, Pace, 1602, Libro IV, p. 318.

page 171 *Neptune and the horse*, da Giovan Battista Ferraro, *Razze, disciplina del cavalcare ed altre cose pertinenti ad esercitio così fatto*, in Pirro Antonio Ferraro, *Cavallo frenato*, Napoli, Pace, 1602, Libro I, p. 1.

page 173 *Rider riding "a la gineta,"* in Pirro Antonio Ferraro, *Cavallo frenato*, Napoli, Pace, 1602, Libro III, p. 275.

page 177 *Armed knight*, in Pirro Antonio Ferraro, *Cavallo frenato*, Napoli, Pace, 1602, Libro II, p. 127.

page 181 *Riding harquebusier*, in Flaminio Della Croce, *L'essercitio della cavalleria*, Anversa, Haenrico Aertsio, 1625, fig. VII.

page 188 Johann Jacobi von Wallhausen, Ritterkunst : *Darinnen begriffen, I. Ein trewhertziges Warnungschreiben wegen deß Betrübten Zustands jetziger Christenheit*, Franckfurt am Main, printed by P. Jacobi for L. Iennis, 1616, fig. 6 chap. 6 and fig. 11 chap. 11.

Chapter VIII

page 192 Crispijn van de Passe, *Antoine de Pluvinel teaching Louis XIII*, in Antoine de Pluvinel, *L'instruction du Roy en l'exercice de monter à cheval*, Paris, M. Nivelle, 1625, tav. 28.

page 194 Etienne Dupérac, *Disegno del torneamento fatto il lune Carnovale in Roma nel Theatro Vaticano*, in *Speculum Romanae Magnificentiae*, Roma, Antonio Lafreri,1565.

page 197 Crispijn van de Passe, *Piliere unico*, in Antoine de Pluvinel, *L'instruction du Roy en l'exercice de monter à cheval*, Paris, M. Nivelle, 1625, tav. 5.

page 200 *"Pignatella" bit*, in Pirro Antonio Ferraro, *Cavallo frenato*, Napoli, Pace, 1602, Libro II, p. 155.

page 202 *"Pignatella" mouthpieces*, in Pirro Antonio Ferraro, *Cavallo frenato*, Napoli, Pace, 1602, Libro II, p. 157.

Chapter IX

page 220 Abraham van Diepenbeeck, *Use of the single pillar*, in William Cavendish of Newcastle, *Méthode et invention nouvelle dans l'art de dresser les chevaux, par le très-noble, haut, et très-puissant Prince Guillaume Marquis et Comte de Newcastle*, 2e ed., Londres, J. Brindley, 1737, tav. 23.

page 222 *Portrait of Nicola Santapaulina*, in Nicola e Luigi Santapaulina, *L'arte del cavallo*, Padova, Stamperia del Seminario, 1696, antiporta.

page 224 *Mid-air canter (Galoppo a mezz'aria)*, in Giovanni Battista Galiberto, *Il cavallo da maneggio,* Vienna, Giacomo Kyrneri, 1650.

page 230 Charles Parrocel, *Alures artificielles* in François Robichon de La Guérinière, *Ecole de cavalerie*, Paris, Jacques Collombat, 1733, p. 81.

page 231 *Le trot du manege a la muraille*, in Ridinger, Johann Elias, *Vorstellung und Beschreibung der Schul und Campagne Pferden nach ihren Lectionem*, Augsbourg, 1760, tav. 15.

page 234 *Portrait of Gennaro Cristallino*, in *Opere di Giuseppe d'Alessandro duca di Pescolanciano*, Napoli, Antonio Muzio, 1723, p. 313.

page 236 *Portrait of Carlo Miroballo*, in *Opere di Giuseppe d'Alessandro duca di Pescolanciano*, Napoli, Antonio Muzio, 1723, p. 297.

page 238 Niccolò Rosselmini., *Il cavallo perfetto: tratto in cui si descrive, quali esser debbano le qualità del cavallo perfetto, e con quai mezzi si arrivi a renderlo tale*, Venezia, Giuseppi Corona, 1723, p. 22.

page 242 Basilio Lasinio, *Portait of the with his horse, Stornello*, in Federico Mazzucchelli, *Scuola equestre*, Milano, presso Gio Pietro Giegler, Libraio sulla Corsia de' Servi, 1805, antiporta.

page 244 Basilio Lasinio, *Use of the long reins*, in Federico Mazzucchelli, *Scuola equestre*, Milano, presso Gio Pietro Giegler, Libraio sulla Corsia de' Servi, 1805, tav. 4.

www.ingramcontent.com/pod-product-compliance
Lightning Source LLC
Chambersburg PA
CBHW080119020526
44112CB00037B/2779